THE
DIVORCE
LAWYERS

THE DIVORCE LAWYERS

The People and Stories Behind

Ten Dramatic Cases

EMILY COURIC

St. Martin's Press   New York

THE DIVORCE LAWYERS. Copyright © 1992 by Emily Couric. All rights reserved.
Printed in the United States of America. No part of this book may be used or
reproduced in any manner whatsoever without written permission except in the
case of brief quotations embodied in critical articles or reviews. For information,
address St. Martin's Press, 175 Fifth Avenue, New York, N.Y. 10010.

Design by Judith Stagnitto

Library of Congress Cataloging-in-Publication Data

Couric, Emily.
    The divorce lawyers : the people and stories behind ten dramatic
cases / Emily Couric.
        p. cm.
    Includes index.
    ISBN 0-312-07083-7
    1. Divorce suits—United States. 2. Lawyers—United States.
I. Title.
KF535.C68 1992
346.7301'66—dc20
[347.306166]   91-35816
                                                                 CIP

First Edition: March 1992

10 9 8 7 6 5 4 3 2 1

To my family

NOTICE

Because state laws and precedents vary greatly and because they change over time, the reader should not use this book as a guide for specific legal advice. Every divorce case is unique, requiring the advice of those versed in the laws of the jurisdiction where the divorce will be granted. It is hoped, rather, that *The Divorce Lawyers* will provide readers with a general overview of the divorce process and divorce issues so that they can enter the legal arena better informed than they might otherwise have been.

CONTENTS

ACKNOWLEDGMENTS

Writing this book was a lengthy undertaking supported by the advice, assistance, and understanding of others. I am deeply indebted to the lawyers and their clients who opened their files and their lives to help others learn more about the legal process of divorce. Thanks also to my agent Sandra Choron for her ongoing advice and support; St. Martin's Press editor Michael Sagalyn for the detailed attention he provided my work; John Casey of the University of Virginia English Department faculty for his critique of early chapters; and University of Virginia sociology professor Steven Nock and demographer Daphne Spain for their review and commentary on the finished manuscript. And, finally, thanks to my husband George Beller and mother Elinor Couric for their commentary on each chapter, and to my father John Couric for his journalistic review.

THE
DIVORCE
LAWYERS

INTRODUCTION

Despite everything that has been written about divorce, and despite the widely cited estimate that at least half of all couples who marry today will divorce, few people really understand all that this agonizing process entails. Most media coverage is about high-profile divorces, for example, the breakups of movie star Jane Fonda and politician Tom Hayden, of former heavyweight champion Mike Tyson and actress Robin Givens, or of tycoon Donald Trump and his wife Ivana. But heartbreak is not the sole province of the rich and famous. At a rate of 50 percent, divorce plagues both the wealthy and the not-so-wealthy, the famous and the unknown.

This book is *not* about the divorces that fill the pages of supermarket tabloids. It is about the divorces of the kinds of people whom you, the reader, may know, people like those you see in your neighborhood, in your office, at the parent-teacher meeting at your child's school. In this book, ten true stories about individual cases dramatize ten couples' experiences. These cases are of the kind handled by divorce lawyers and divorce courts every day in cities across the United States. Taken together they form a mosaic depicting the issues husbands and wives face when the love that brought them together is replaced by anger, disappointment, bitterness—and reliance on the law. These real-life stories also portray the couples' relationships with their lawyers and the different ways in which spouses confront the legal system.

The world of divorce has changed drastically over the past two decades. With the advent of no-fault divorce, the profession of divorce lawyering has undergone a complete metamorphosis. No longer is it necessary to snoop around hotels or lurk in the bushes, gathering dirt on a client's spouse. No-fault divorce, now available in every state, has made such distasteful practices passé. Now no one need be proven guilty of adultery, abuse, desertion, or some other marital crime. Some practitioners may even suggest that no-fault has taken the fun out of divorce lawyering.

The best lawyers in the profession strongly disagree, however. Theirs is still a challenging business, albeit one of a different character. In addition to no-fault legislation, new rules for dividing marital assets have revamped the game from one of blame to a struggle over money and property. Today we witness a cerebral battleground fraught with skirmishes over property values, accounting techniques, and tax implications. Divorce practice has become more highbrow, especially if there is wealth at stake.

Large multicity corporate law firms are waking up to the fact that they can make money representing individual clients in divorce, particularly clients with sizeable assets. But the most famous of the divorce bar nationwide are still the superstar small-firm attorneys operating out of what some now call specialty "boutiques." At one time these lawyers were held in low esteem because their practices, with public disputes over clients' morality, seemed tawdry and unseemly. But given the new divorce laws, ever-changing rules for applying the laws, and a burgeoning clientele, these seasoned practitioners are more esteemed—and more popular than ever. They're smart, feisty, and tenacious.

Today's clients need good divorce lawyers. The issues are many, and every state has its requirements for resolving them. What's true in one jurisdiction may not be so in another. The disputes can become so complex and convoluted that unsuspecting spouses, already fragile and overwrought with emotion, enter the legal arena like soldiers on a mine field.

The big battle lies in the division of assets, following a format determined by the state in which the divorce takes place. But couples first have to confront other equally divisive debates, such as the separation of marital and nonmarital property and the need to decide on the marital property's value so that an exact accounting can be made for both sides. The concept of alimony—spousal support following divorce—still hasn't disappeared; rather, it exists in different forms. A young ex-wife may receive rehabilitative alimony to help her get back into the work force, a wealthy spouse may be awarded lump sum alimony in a division of assets, and an older wife may benefit from the more traditional permanent, periodic alimony. Occasionally, husbands get alimony, too. If the husband and wife signed a prenuptial agreement spelling out the division of assets in case of divorce—and these agreements are on the rise—one spouse may try to have it overturned in order to claim a greater share.

When children are involved, a different level of warfare ensues, one involving custody, visitation schedules, and support payments. Some parents accuse the soon-to-be ex-spouse of child abuse, usually sexual abuse, in an attempt to win the fight outright or to gain negotiating leverage in subsequent disputes over assets. In other cases parents simply try to move away with a child, sometimes hiding out and even changing the child's name. The battle can arise anew when a custodial parent decides to move out of town, or even out of the country, rendering the other parent's visitation difficult, if not almost impossible.

All of these divorce issues have been complicated by changing societal attitudes and mores. With more women in the work force, and particularly in higher-paying professions, women are less likely to win alimony unless they've made professional sacrifices for their husbands' careers. Divorced working women also are more likely to share in their children's financial support. If working women marry later in life, they may well demand a prenuptial agreement to protect their assets.

As increasing numbers of women work outside the home, men are asserting a stronger role in the home, and in cases of divorce they are demanding increased visitation, joint custody, or sole custody of the children they've helped rear. In another case of what's good for the goose is good for the gander, men also are staking their claims to their wives' earnings, including a share in the businesses and professional practices they built during the marriage.

Today men and women marry more often, so second and even third divorces are more common. With the rise in serial marriages, prenuptial agreements have become a way to protect the property interests of children from earlier marriages. And as more spouses become stepparents and then divorce again, some are demanding visitation and even custody rights with stepchildren. Courts today pay attention to unusual pleas, such as those of grandparents who, in an age of splintered, far-flung families, are asking judges to award them visitation rights, too.

Although every divorce involves multiple issues, each of the cases in this book has been chosen to represent one particular issue that divorcing couples may face today. Each issue is presented in the context of a divorce story to offer easier reading and provide a clearer understanding of how such a case might unfold. The introduction to every chapter briefly explains the issue confronted by the clients and their lawyers in the case that follows.

In capsule format, these are the issues and the cases illustrating them:

Chapter 1, Prenuptial Agreements. When Shirley Ann Rake married A. C. Warnack, a wealthy building contractor whose children she baby-sat, he convinced her to sign a prenuptial agreement that would give her nothing should they divorce. Shirley ended up leaving A.C., and she asked the California courts to overturn the agreement. Her Los Angeles lawyer, Stuart Walzer, argued that the worldly A.C. had taken advantage of the much younger and more naive Shirley and that she deserved to benefit from serving as his wife for fifteen years, regardless of any papers she had signed. This chapter explains how Walzer worked to convince the court that he was right and that A.C.'s prenuptial agreement was fatally flawed.

Chapter 2, Joint Custody. After George and Ingrid Nicholas separated, Ingrid didn't want George to spend too much time with their two-year-old son, Alexander. Ingrid believed she was the better caretaker and wanted sole responsibility for the child. But George was determined to have equal time with Alex; he wanted to pass his values on to his son as well. Faced with a court's overwhelming preference for giving custody to a homemaker mother, George pulled out all the stops, even altering his work schedule and moving closer to Ingrid's new home to win his case. His New Jersey lawyer, the famous Gary Skoloff, who handled the Baby M case for William and Elizabeth Stern, says he has never seen such a determined client take so much initiative on his own behalf.

Chapter 3, Equitable Distribution. Except for taking two weeks off from work after each of her three children was born, Felice Dubin worked alongside her husband Paul for eighteen years building a successful children's clothing manufacturing business in Miami. She also managed the Dubin household. But when the Dubins prepared to divorce, Paul claimed that the company was his alone because he was the president and general manager, and he demanded more than half of the marital assets. Felice's lawyer, Miami's Melvyn Frumkes, could not have disagreed more. On the contrary, he said, Felice was the one who deserved more than half because she had done more than half of the work in the marriage. This is a tale today's working woman can appreciate.

Chapter 4, Fighting Over the Business. Howard Wil catch, an established Chicago physician who specialize phisticated retina surgery. After marrying him, Gayle Wi pered life as a housewife in a fancy home in an elite suburb. When Howard left her, Gayle was furious. She as much as she could for her share of their marital assets—including half of Howard's medical practice, which Gayle argued was worth far more than Howard claimed. It took a lawyer like Chicago's Donald Schiller, a name partner in the country's largest firm devoted exclusively to divorce law, to devise the complicated legal strategy necessary for protecting Howard's interests.

Chapter 5, Child Snatching. When Claudine Bolling sent her two children to their school in Madrid every morning, she never dreamed that their father, San Franciscan Paul Bolling, could be waiting nearby to snatch them away from her. But one day he did, taking the older boy, Stephan, back to the United States and settling in a small Texas town, where he denied the child all contact with his mother. Claudine and her parents turned to San Francisco lawyer Lawrence Stotter and a team of international detectives to help find the boy. It took years of undercover work, pleas in the press, numerous court filings, and a high-speed police chase to get Stephan back. Stotter has become one of the nation's preeminent authorities on parental kidnappings, playing a leading role in the passage of federal legislation and an international treaty addressing the problem. According to a Justice Department survey about 350,000 children are abducted by family members every year.

Chapter 6, Tracing Assets. Sometimes when a couple marries, the husband or wife (or both) brings considerable wealth into the union. Yet if they don't keep their premarital assets separate from postmarriage income and they later divorce, everything that was once individual property is up for grabs in the legal battle that follows. When René Wright married her second husband, Danny Jack Nations, she was not aware of the extent of the stock holdings she had inherited, but apparently, Danny was. He quit his job shortly after their wedding to help René "manage" her money, which meant putting it in a brokerage account under both of their names. When René finally rebelled against Danny's controlling behavior, he claimed as his half of everything she had once owned. Dallas's Louise Raggio, a leader in the Texas bar and a pioneer for women's rights, came to René's rescue, with the assistance of her two sons and partners, Thomas and Kenneth Raggio.

Chapter 7, Relocation. Bob Jordan faithfully visited his sons from his first marriage every two weeks, either flying from his home in Darien, Connecticut, to visit them in Potomac, Maryland, or flying them up to see him. But when his former wife, Linda, announced that she was marrying an American engineer who worked in South Africa and was planning to take the boys there, Bob panicked and turned to the best Maryland lawyer he could find, Beverly Groner of Bethesda. She agreed to fight his uphill battle against an ex-wife who already had custody, in a court system that historically gave deference to mothers. While Bob did not want to keep Linda from going, if she did leave, he wanted the boys left behind with him. Relocation is a problem a growing number of divorced couples face today. Deciding whose interests prevail is one of our legal system's thorniest problems.

Chapter 8, Stepparents in Divorce. Dan Stockwell was with his girlfriend Patty when she gave birth to a daughter named Amber, who had been fathered by another man. When Dan and Patty married two months later, he treated the child as his own. Two years later Patty and Dan had a daughter together, whom they named Danielle. When they divorced and Patty tried to move away with the children, Dan sued for custody of both girls. The Idaho court said he could have Danielle, but because Amber was only his stepdaughter, she had to remain with her mother. Dan's lawyer, Paul Buser of Boise, broke new legal ground in asserting Dan's rights as a stepparent, and the case went all the way to the Idaho Supreme Court. But even though Dan won custody, Patty refused to acknowledge defeat, and their daughters suffered the consequences of this intense, drawn-out family feud.

Chapter 9, Violence in Divorce. It was a nightmare come true. When Diane Pikul finally mustered the courage to file for divorce from her hot-tempered, unpredictably violent husband, Joseph Pikul, he brutally strangled her. Amazingly, despite the murder charges filed against him, he was allowed to retain custody of their young daughter and son. Prior to her death, Diane had hired noted New York attorney Raoul Lionel Felder to file her divorce. He initiated a custody battle on behalf of Diane's cousins, Kathy and Mike O'Guin, hoping that they could wrest the children from the home of their murderous father. Yet a New York judge supported Pikul's parenting claim, ruling that his relationship with his children was still strong. Diane's friends and supporters were aghast by the decision, which had been made possible by a law that favors the natural parent over other people, even when that parent has killed his spouse.

Chapter 10, Divorce and the Elderly. While people generally think of divorce as a trauma facing younger couples, often it is a more severe problem for the elderly, who have less ability and time to change habits and attitudes necessary to adjust to unmarried life. When Ruth and Harry Lebeson divorced, she was seventy-eight years old and he was ninety. Although theirs was a second marriage, they had been together for thirty-six years. Harry thought it was a perfectly successful relationship, so when Ruth secretly filed for divorce and demanded a large share of his holdings, he was shocked. Most of his wealth derived from work he had done as a business executive before they married. Los Angeles attorney Ira Lurvey was most concerned about Harry and worked fervidly to resolve the divorce crisis quickly. On her side, Ruth hired Marvin Mitchelson, but then she fired him when a lawyer in Mitchelson's office tried to settle the case. While her second attorney was far more combative, perhaps to an extreme, Harry still would claim victory in the end.

Chapter 11, Hiring a Divorce Lawyer. Some divorce lawyers do a great job of helping clients argue for what is rightfully theirs and then negotiating with the spouse's lawyer to reach a satisfactory resolution for the case. When forced to trial these attorneys litigate masterfully, backed by thorough research and legal knowledge. But the divorce profession is not without its problems, such as exhorbitant fees, the need for an army of experts, and the complicated array of legal maneuverings that prove the bane of many a client, both in patience and in pocketbook. What's more, the profession has its share of rotten apples, incompetent, lazy, greedy practitioners who tend to spoil the reputations of their colleagues. Chapter 11 points out some of the common faults of divorce lawyers as seen through the eyes of their clients as well as the lawyers themselves.

The lawyers chosen to share their cases for this book are among the finest in the nation; they repeatedly are included on lists of the best divorce lawyers published in magazines and newspapers. Their professional credentials—memberships in the highest professional organizations, publications, speeches—serve to support their reputation for excellence. These attorneys represent a wide geographic distribution, ranging from California to Maryland and from Idaho to Florida.

This book also attempts to provide a variety of experiences and viewpoints as expressed by the clients whose stories are told, using real names in every case but one (chapter 5). Specifically, five of these clients are men, five are women. Although every fight, every divorce, every case has two sides, each chapter inevitably presents a more partisan perspective, favoring one spouse's point of view over the other, as presented by the lawyer who suggested the case for inclusion in this book. Yet where possible—through interviews, court filings, deposition transcripts, and trial testimony—the opposing spouse's viewpoint is expressed as well.

Where dialogue exists, it is a reconstruction of the conversations based on these same interviews, press clippings, and legal reports and on careful scrutiny of all of the legal documents in every case described here.

Finally, although this is a book about divorce, it should be noted that it deals with the divorce process rather than with the causes of divorce. Out of consideration for the individuals involved—and in recognition of the parameters set by libel law—the chapters that follow tread lightly over the purported reasons for each couple's marital failure.

1

PRENUPTIAL AGREEMENTS: PLANNING ON DIVORCE BEFORE MARRIAGE

Shirley Warnack v. A. C. Warnack

If you're at all a voyeur, then divorce is the place
for you.

—ATTORNEY STUART WALZER
LOS ANGELES

When 1990 headlines blared the news of Donald and Ivana Trump's impending divorce, gossipmongers fixated on Donald's curvaceous companion, Marla Maples. A less sexy topic also fueled speculation—four legal documents, each about thirty-five pages long and filled with fine print. One was a prenuptial agreement the Trumps signed before their 1977 wedding and three were postnuptial agreements signed during their marriage.

Just a few months after the Trumps' marital woes became public, John Kluge, called by *Forbes* magazine America's richest man, and his third wife, Patricia, announced that they were divorcing. Word soon followed that according to a prenuptial agreement, Patricia would be getting the couple's mansion in Albemarle, Virginia, and interest on $1 billion, calculated at a moderate 8 percent to be $80 million annually.

Prenuptial agreements are not only for the rich. A growing number of couples who are far less wealthy than the Trumps and the Kluges—even middle-income couples—are planning the financial ramifications of divorce *before* exchanging wedding vows.

Many, however, still shudder at the thought. Prenuptial agreements, they say, envision disaster; they rob commitment from a marriage. "Signing a prenuptial agreement is like putting ice water on romance," agrees Los Angeles attorney Stuart Walzer. But a few cold moments in the heat of passion can be a good idea. Even the starry-eyed couple that forecasts a happily-ever-after future may be deeply disappointed one day.

The purpose of prenuptial planning is to spell out exactly what will happen if a couple's romance does collapse. Typically couples talk about dividing money and property in the event of a divorce. Assets brought into the marriage by a spouse generally revert to that person, unless such assets have been irretrievably combined with earnings and property acquired after the marriage. Methods for divvying up income and property acquired *after* marriage vary from case to case.

Sometimes prenuptial agreements describe what will happen in case of death, particularly when one or both spouses have children from an earlier marriage for whom they want to guarantee an inheritance. If these children are older, they may more readily accept a stepparent knowing that he or she is not likely to deprive them of what is rightfully theirs.

To achieve these kinds of goals, a prenuptial agreement must, above all, be fair. Common criteria that courts use to assess the fairness of such contracts include evidence of separate, independent legal advice for both the man and the woman, full disclosure of all assets on both sides, and an absence of duress, that is, neither party was pressured to sign. However, because the growing use of prenuptial agreements is a relatively recent phenomenon, the rules in many places are still being written—and rewritten—by state legislatures and courts.

The following story describes one man's attempt to have his wife bound by a prenuptial agreement that clearly was unfair. Although they lived together and pretended to be married, Shirley Warnack waited years to wed her husband, building contractor A. C. Warnack. When he finally agreed, A.C. asked her to sign an agreement that said that should they divorce, Shirley would receive none of his extensive earnings or properties, including those acquired after the wedding. Essentially Shirley agreed, without realizing what she was doing, to a marriage that gave her no more than room and board—and that only for as long as she stayed married to A.C. In case of divorce she literally would be out on the street. Shirley foolishly signed A.C.'s prenuptial agreement without looking at it closely because she was in love, because she trusted him, and because she wanted to be with him for the rest of her life.

But one day she changed her mind, and then the prenuptial agreement came back to haunt her.

*   *   *

Shirley Warnack pressed the thick legal folder against her right side, shifted the plate full of homemade cookies from her right hand to her left, and gave the doorknob of Walzer and Gabrielson a forceful twist. As usual, the receptionist, Corinne, was sitting behind a desk, which faced into the small sitting room.

Corinne rose to accept Shirley Warnack's gift; the secretary chatted over her shoulder as Shirley followed down the hall. During recent months Shirley seemed to have spent as much time on the premises as the staff. Several times a week she visited the Century City high rise to confer with attorney Stuart Walzer about her case. The entire office had become accustomed to these gifts of baked goods and to Shirley's sincere inquiries about their families.

"Shirley," Walzer said after closing his office door, "I need to know more about your husband. He's being terribly difficult and unresponsive." Stuart Walzer settled into an easy chair next to the sofa where Shirley sat. "He won't give us the financial documents we need to handle your case—to work with your prenuptial agreement—and he won't give you nearly the financial support we think you deserve while the divorce is pending. He's very angry and bitter. But you already know that.

"What you need to do now," Walzer continued, "is to give me more background to all this so I can try to understand A.C. and your marriage. Tell me more about how you ended up with him. I know it was not a typical love affair."

Walzer could not help noticing how attractive his client was. Although she was forty-one years old, she retained much of her high school cheerleader perkiness and naïveté. He felt protective, even paternalistic. "Shirley," he prodded gently, "you've told me a great deal about you and A.C. But I still have some questions, so you *must* give me more details. It's the only way I can do my best."

The initials A.C. stood for Augustus Cleveland, but few people knew that. They simply called Shirley's husband A.C., a casual, backwoods-sounding nickname that belied his enormous wealth and tremendous business acumen. Shirley could barely think of him now without feeling waves of anger, disappointment, and pain. Lately such feelings had overwhelmed her, eroding her confidence and resolve.

Walzer already knew that Shirley and A.C. had first met in Lancaster, California, a small town northeast of Los Angeles, when she was fourteen years old. A.C., an electrician of modest income at the time, and his first wife, Betty, had asked her to baby-sit their children in their small tract home. Even as a teenager young Shirley Ann Rake appreciated A.C.'s charisma and enthusiasm. He exuded the Southern charm of a Georgian with a ready grin, fair, freckled face, and reddish hair. A large man, he dominated the household whenever he was around. Shirley was drawn to A.C. and the equally outgoing Betty, who had married him when she was seventeen. As Shirley spent time with the Warnacks she grew to care about that family as if it were her own.

But that was a long time ago, in 1956. This was 1984. Now, in the offices of Walzer and Gabrielson, Shirley studied her lawyer, observing his intense face and caring manner. She decided to tell him more about her life as a young woman, as painful as these memories were for her. This included the story of how she fell in love with *all* of the Warnacks, long before she herself became *Mrs. A. C. Warnack*.

"When I started baby-sitting for the Warnacks," she began, "Betty was pregnant with LuAnn. My sister and I both baby-sat Bobby and Susan, the two older children. But my sister, who was older than I, was more active in school and didn't have much time, so I started baby-sitting for A.C. and Betty all of the time.

"My parents moved from Lancaster to Rosamond, just a dozen miles north in a neighboring county, when I was a senior in high school. But I wanted to finish school in Lancaster, so my parents agreed to let me move in with A.C. and Betty. By then A.C. had started his own construction company, he was making more money, and they were living in a larger house. That year I took the kids to school, I picked the kids up, I did the grocery shopping, I took LuAnn to the baby-sitter, I did most of the housework.

"But they did a lot of nice things for me," Shirley quickly added, "things my family couldn't do." Essentially Shirley worked as a live-in nanny and the Warnacks paid her expenses. Her parents approved, for the arrangement served their financial needs, too. Shirley's father was a mail carrier with limited income.

A.C., whose business continued to prosper, paid Shirley's dental bills; he and Betty gave her spending money, sent her to modeling school, and, after high school graduation, paid her way through beautician school. Later Betty helped Shirley get a job in the salon where Betty had her hair styled. Over the years Betty became much like an older sister to Shirley, who in turn was like a big sister to Betty's children. Neither woman suspected that eventually they would become bitter enemies.

After Shirley started work when she was twenty years old, she met a college student named Tim Vezie. When they married six months later, A.C. and Betty traveled to Las Vegas for the courthouse wedding. Shirley wanted A.C. to give her away.

It seemed only natural that when Shirley and Tim had a son, Lance, A.C. and Betty would become his godparents. They regularly invited Shirley, Tim, and the baby to travel from their home near Lake Tahoe, California, to visit the Warnacks in Lancaster, about three hundred miles south. Tim even looked for a job in southern California so that his young family could be closer to Shirley's benefactors. When he couldn't join them for visits, the Warnacks paid Shirley and Lance's airfare. "They said they wanted to get to know Lance well," Shirley told Walzer, who nodded sympathetically.

"But when," Walzer prodded his client, "did you first have sexual relations with A.C.?"

"I never looked at A.C. in a romantic way while I was baby-sitting or first married," Shirley insisted, emotion rising in her voice. "He was almost like a big brother. He did a lot of nice things for me while I was growing up." Fists clenched in her lap, she was determined that no one blame her for the breakup of A.C. and Betty's home.

About the time Shirley and Tim got married, A.C. and Betty built and moved into an even larger house. By then A.C. owned several construction and building supply companies, and he and his partner were acquiring sizeable fortunes. With A.C.'s success, he and Betty could afford a glamorous, fast-paced life-style and their popularity in Lancaster grew. Everyone knew that the Warnacks had money and that A.C. had all of the business connections—and clout—he needed.

But the Warnacks' home life had long been troubled, a fact that Shirley recognized early on. Perhaps it was this realization that prevented her from feeling guilty later. Both A.C. and Betty were gregarious people, so when they weren't together, they went out separately. This independence led to harsh words and fighting, particularly when A.C. became jealous of Betty's socializing. But A.C. traveled on weeks-long business trips, leaving his wife alone. When he returned, heated arguments filled the house.

In September 1967, while Shirley and her son were visiting Lancaster, Betty and A.C. asked if she'd like to go to a cocktail party with them. Shirley agreed, and she and Betty found a sitter for Lance.

When they arrived at the gathering they stepped into a crowded room of loud conversation and swirling smoke. Shirley noticed that most of the people were older than she. In fact, she knew almost no one. "This is our friend Shirley Vezie," A.C. said as he introduced her to other guests. Most of them nodded and smiled; Betty quickly was caught up with her own friends.

Throughout the party Shirley stood beside A.C., engaging in small talk with those who approached him. He smiled at her several times and she smiled back.

"Hey, A.C., let's all go out for dinner," said one of the men, clapping him on the shoulder.

"Sure," A.C. responded. "All three of us will come."

"I don't feel well," Betty told her husband as they left for a nearby restaurant. "Why don't you go on without me?"

"Do you want me to stay with you?" Shirley asked her.

"That's OK, honey. You go ahead with A.C. It will be good for you to have a whole evening off from taking care of Lance."

It's unlikely that Betty ever worried about A.C. being alone with Shirley. Perhaps she should have been more cautious, for that evening she made a serious mistake, one that tipped the scales of her strained marriage.

In the restaurant the other couples, A.C., and Shirley crowded around a large table. Several rounds of drinks passed, and amid the jokes and laughter no one noticed A.C. putting his hand on Shirley's thigh. Her heart leapt at his touch. When A.C. reached over several more times throughout the evening, Shirley began to feel light-headed. Her own father had long thought she was secretly in love with A.C., as he would tell her much later, but she staunchly maintained that until that moment, she always believed that her feelings had been more those of an adopted daughter. She had cared for A.C., admired him, respected him. Still, in the restaurant that evening Shirley did nothing to stop his advances. In fact, she found herself magnetically responding to him, yearning for more of the same.

When they left and were in the parking lot, he kissed her. It never occurred to Shirley to stop him.

"Tomorrow I'm going to tell you the name of a hotel where we can meet," A.C. said.

"All right," she answered, flushed, her insides churning. They drove home silently. Shirley was twenty-five years old. A.C. was forty.

Shirley had had no idea sex could be so wonderful. She had been so inexperienced with her husband Tim that she had begun to wonder if she was frigid. Clearly now she knew that wasn't so. She began meeting A.C. secretly about every four to six weeks, either in Tahoe where she and Tim lived, or by traveling to see A.C. on his business trips. A.C. had bought property in Tahoe and planned to build a house there; it would become a secret hideaway.

"You know that I can never leave Betty and break up the family," A.C. told her, even as they professed their feelings and planned their next rendezvous. "No matter how miserable I am at home," he added for emphasis, referring to the marital discord.

"I know," responded Shirley, still dazed with the excitement of the affair. It didn't matter to her. She was more than willing to go on secretly, living only on the thrill of the present. She increased her visits to the Warnack household. By this time Betty, who did not have the same loving relationship with A.C. that Shirley enjoyed, had begun to grow suspicious.

"Bobby, do you know where Lance is?" Shirley called out to A.C.'s son on a Fourth of July visit the following summer, in 1968. She was in the kitchen fixing dinner when she noticed that her two year old was no longer nearby. A.C., Betty, and Tim, Shirley's husband, had gone to the hospital to see LuAnn, who was recovering from a high fever.

Bobby was in the family room with a teenage friend. "No, he must be with Susan," he responded, taking a shot at the pool table.

Shirley ran upstairs, but Susan hadn't seen the child, either. "Lance! Lance!" Shirley called out. Bobby joined her in looking for him. "Lance!" he shouted. They headed for the backyard.

Approaching the swimming pool they saw that the gate was ajar. "Oh, my God!" Shirley screamed as they spotted Lance in the pool. Reflexively Bobby dove in and pulled the child out. Shirley ran inside the house, shouting to Bobby's friend to call the fire department.

Just then, A.C., Betty, and Tim returned from their hospital visit. They heard Shirley screaming and ran in back to see Bobby giving Lance artificial respiration. Betty took over. Shirley, convinced that Lance had drowned, ran into the family room. Crying hysterically, she threw herself beneath the pool table. Bobby came and got her when the fire department's rescue squad arrived. "He's breathing, he's going to be OK," he tried to soothe Shirley.

The rescue workers had placed a mask over Lance's face to force air into his chest. A.C. held him in his arms, a tiny, limp body against his own large, muscular frame.

A.C. looked up and saw Shirley running toward them. "Get her out of here," he barked. *"Get her out of here!"*

As they put Lance into the ambulance, A.C. knew that Shirley's son was already dead.

Perhaps what happened next occurred because of her subsequent feelings of guilt, or perhaps it was due to her unfulfilling marriage with Tim, or her overwhelming adoration for A.C. Whatever the reason, she began to devote herself entirely to her clandestine love affair. By this time Betty most assuredly recognized the enemy in her own house.

*   *   *

Only months after Lance's death, in January 1969, Betty and A.C. fought what would be their final marital battle, and she moved out with the children. In March Shirley told Tim that she was leaving him, and she rented a room in Nevada to establish residency there. Nevada required only a six-week waiting period for a divorce.

The dissolution was not as easy as Shirley had hoped it would be. She and Tim fought bitterly over the sale of their little Tahoe house. Because Shirley had worked as a hairdresser, paid for Tim's schooling, and supported him when he was out of work, she thought the house should be hers. "Split it with him," A.C. told her. "You're not going to need the money anyway."

"You're never going to work again," he reassured her as they drove from Tahoe to Sherman Oaks. With money from A.C., Shirley had rented an apartment about sixty miles from Lancaster. She and A.C. were glad they would be close but still far enough apart to avoid the suspicious eyes of the Warnack children and the town's rumor mill.

Within six months, however, the logistics of maintaining residences in separate communities became too cumbersome, so A.C. rented another apartment for Shirley right in Lancaster, about a half mile from his own house. Most of the time the lovers simply stayed at A.C.'s. Shirley, who had grown up poor, was now living beyond her dreams. She had all she wanted and could dedicate her life to the man she loved.

When the Warnack children discovered that their father was sleeping with Shirley—their former baby-sitter, their "big sister," their surrogate mother—they were visibly upset. They learned the news from their mother, who, of course, reacted violently when her suspicions about Shirley finally were confirmed.

"How can you sleep in *my* house, in *my* bed, with *my* husband, when you killed *your* son in *my* swimming pool?" Betty screamed over the telephone to Shirley. "You broke up our marriage, you slut!" Betty's rage was matched only by her bitterness. She had been replaced as a wife and hostess, losing her stature and security. She would receive less than $22,000 a year in alimony and $150 a month in child support. Although her marriage had been marked by A.C.'s absences and their fighting, she mourned its passing.

Shirley and A.C. tried to ignore Betty and settle into their own routine. Shirley cooked, entertained A.C.'s business guests, kept house and washed their clothes, and even started a vegetable garden. The only times she retreated to her nearby apartment was when the Warnack children came to visit their father.

•   •   •

This arrangement worked for about a year, until 1971, when Betty decided that A.C.'s older daughter, sixteen-year-old Susan, should live with her father. "I can't handle her anymore," Betty announced. "You take her." Shirley panicked. They had never admitted to A.C.'s children that they lived together, even after Betty's verbal attack. How could they continue the charade with Susan in the house?

"I can't go and live in that little, dingy apartment and not be with you," Shirley cried to A.C. "We have to do something."

"OK, darlin'," he said soothingly. "But I'm not ready to get married. You know how nasty the divorce was. I just can't think about it yet. We'll work out something with the kids." A.C. told Shirley he would call a close friend who was a local judge.

"I want everyone to think we're married," A.C. confided to his friend.

"Well, that's easy to take care of," the judge responded. He was a man who often did favors for friends. "I'll just sign a marriage certificate and give it to you." But the judge also warned A.C. not to show the certificate to too many people, for he would be greatly embarrassed should anyone learn he had signed a fake document.

Shirley did not care about the deceit. She did not care that the marriage wouldn't be legal. She was delighted that at least she could live openly with A.C., as if they were married. To the world she would be Mrs. Warnack. From then on she and A.C. even filed joint income tax statements.

A.C. presented the fake marriage certificate with great fanfare, but at the same time he asked Shirley to sign another legal document, one he called an antenuptial, or prenuptial, agreement. It was important, he said, because everyone would think they were married.

The document, he told his bogus bride, would show what belonged to him and would show his business obligations and his obligations to Betty and the kids. A.C. knew that Shirley was really worried that people would think she had married him because he was wealthy. "Now no one can say you're with me for my money," he reminded her. A.C.'s argument was a clever one, designed to sway a poor girl who was beholden to her rich lover.

Shirley smiled at him. "I'll sign anything you want," she said. "Just tell me and I'll do it. You know I trust you about everything."

Prenuptial agreements first came into use in the 1920s among men of wealth who feared that young women might prey on their fortunes. A.C. must have regarded Shirley with the same apprehension. For a time, in the 1950s, courts frowned on the agreements as operating "against public policy"—that is, against society's view on the sanctity of marriage. However, today judges are increasingly open to prenuptial agreements if they are drafted according to certain guidelines.

These guidelines vary from state to state in both form and content. Some fifteen states, including California, have adopted some variant of the Uniform Premarital Agreement Act, which was passed in 1983 by the National Conference of Commissioners on Uniform State Laws. Other states, however, continue to rely on common ("case") law regarding the enforceability of prenuptial agreements.

Typically the agreements ensure that in case of divorce the spouses take from their marriage all assets they brought into it. But in Shirley's case the prenuptial agreement A.C. presented was more important to him than it was to her because he owned numerous companies and properties, while she had only a small savings account and her share from the Tahoe house she and Tim had owned. A.C.'s prenuptial agreement said that if he and Shirley were to marry and later divorce, property, possessions, and money he had at the time of marriage would belong solely to him. Furthermore, the agreement declared, any appreciation or earnings from those assets occurring *after* the marriage also would be his.

California law distinguishes between "passive" and "earned" income. Income that simply accumulates through growth of assets owned before a marriage is passive income and belongs to the spouse who owns the assets. But income actively earned through a job or other endeavor that takes place after the marriage is marital property and thus belongs to both spouses. There is, however, a gray area between passive and earned income. If an individual enters a marriage with his or her own assets and then, after marrying, reinvests those assets in new ventures rather than simply letting them grow, the new income from those reinvestments may be considered earned income. The person could be said to have earned this money by planning the new investments.

The prenuptial agreement Shirley signed said that no appreciation or income from A.C.'s premarital assets, whether passive or earned, would ever be hers to share.

The document did add, however, that should A.C. marry Shirley, all subsequent salaries and bonuses from his businesses would belong to them both. That is, were they to divorce, the salaries and bonuses earned during the marriage, and anything purchased with that income, would be considered marital property. This was fair: generally in a "community property" state like California, a husband and wife jointly own all income and property obtained during their marriage and these assets are divided equally during divorce. Other community property states are Arizona, Idaho, Louisiana, Nevada, New Mexico, Texas, Washington, and Wisconsin. The remaining forty-one states follow an "equitable distribution" philosophy, which considers numerous factors, including earning potential and need, when dividing marital property.

Although A.C. indicated to Shirley that the prenuptial agreement he gave her was important for both of them, he did not explain all of the details or their implications. He simply stressed that he would take care of her as long as she stayed with him, so she need not worry. And Shirley didn't worry. She knew that from then on they could be together, openly, so quickly picking up a pen, she scribbled "Shirley A. Vezie" at the end of the five-page document.

Some may say that in signing the prenuptial agreement Shirley simply was naive; others may call her stupid. Whether she was naive or stupid or only hopelessly, pathetically blinded by love, she did not have a chance against the older, more savvy A.C. He knew what he was doing—or at least he thought he did.

When Susan moved into the house, A.C. left the fake marriage certificate on a dresser where she would be sure to see it.

"Dad! You and Shirley got married," his daughter said, disgusted. A.C.'s plot was following its planned course.

"You saw the certificate!" he responded, ignoring her tone. "We were going to surprise you, but now that you know, Shirley and I want to take all three of you kids out to dinner to celebrate."

But Bobby, Susan, and LuAnn were not pleased. They were angry, convinced that without Shirley, their parents still would be together. That night Shirley recognized with sinking finality that she had A.C., but the family she loved, the one that had taken care of her through her teenage years and young adulthood, no longer existed for her. It was a trade Shirley had to make, but she was pained nonetheless.

The waitress at the restaurant asked Shirley for proof of her age after the five had been seated and she and A.C. ordered their cocktails. The unexpected emphasis on Shirley's youth hurt the Warnack kids all the more; for them the evening was nearly intolerable.

Later one of A.C.'s friends threw a party for the "newlyweds." Like the Warnack children, the entire community had been tricked into believing that they finally had married.

With Susan now living at home, the household was far from calm, but for awhile Shirley's "marital" bliss enabled her to ride through the storm of the teenager's adolescence. Eventually, the charade began to trouble her: she wanted to be the *real* Mrs. Warnack.

To make the situation even more painful Shirley had to forego some of her traveling with A.C. so she could make sure Susan attended school and did her homework. Before one of his trips Shirley packed A.C.'s suitcase as usual, placing coordinated outfits in layers—the matched shirt, tie, and socks carefully selected for each day. Lastly, underneath all of A.C.'s clothes, she slipped in a greeting card designed for lovers. Inside she wrote:

> Hi Sweetbaby, I can hardly wait for tonight—my Baby will be home. I love you so much I can't stand it without you. I love it when you just touch me. I still get goose bumps and my stomach still does flip-flops.
>
> I'm sorry if I have been short with you lately but it takes me so long to get over hurts. But I will try to be better from now on. You'll never know how much it bothers me and eats at my insides that we aren't married. I have begged and begged for it to be changed and it doesn't seem to do any good. I keep telling myself to accept the fact that it won't ever change so I might as well try not to think about it. But I can't. It isn't right no matter what lies we've made up about it. I always ask you when or why not and you never give me an answer. You finally said there was no reason why not but never "we'll try soon" or anything.
>
> I guess I have not proven myself yet. I'll keep trying. Just remember that I think of it every day. I love you so much there isn't anything I wouldn't do for you. I need your love so badly, Sweetheart. Please always love me and be with me. I'll love you forever.

When Susan graduated from high school the teenager moved back into her mother's house. Shirley was relieved, and she and A.C. went to San Francisco for a weekend celebration. "Boy, what a lover my Baby is," Shirley wrote in a card a few days later. "He is too much for me. I loved every minute of it."

Once again they traveled full time, and Shirley even helped with A.C.'s work. She accompanied him on building site inspections, and when he and his partner bid on large government jobs, she took down subcontractors' estimates over the telephone and fed them to the men as they calculated a final offer. Shirley felt she was becoming part of a team, even though she wasn't paid. Eventually she became the one to carry final bids to the government contracting officers, often stopping at a telephone just minutes before the bid package was due to obtain A.C.'s final calculation.

Even in Lancaster A.C. kept Shirley by his side, refusing lunch or drinks with male friends. Instead he brought his friends home and Shirley cooked for them all.

One day in September 1975, more than four years after A.C. had obtained their fake marriage certificate, he announced to Shirley that finally he was ready to get married—legally married. They were preparing to go on a business trip to Oklahoma, where A.C. was bidding on a job.

"Wonderful!" exclaimed Shirley, hugging him.

He walked over to his briefcase, snapped it open, and pulled out some papers. "Shirley," he said in his most casual and loving voice, "I'm so happy, darlin', but you know it's important that we protect our future. I don't think the old prenuptial agreement will be any good, so let's sign another. And this way, no one can say you married me for my money. I know you don't want that."

Shirley was sensitive about what other people thought, but she wasn't sure what A.C. was talking about. She remembered the document she had signed when they supposedly married the first time and decided it was probably more of the same.

"What does it say?" she asked.

A.C. started to read parts of the agreement aloud. "'Whereas, the parties hereto anticipate entering into marriage each with the other,'" he began, "'and whereas, A. C. Warnack hereto has been previously married, and whereas, husband has certain definite obligations arising from his previous marriage'—Shirley, you know, this part just says I've had to take care of my obligations to Betty and the kids—'all of which are set forth specifically in that certain property settlement agreement executed by and between husband and his former wife, said agreement being a part of. . . .'"

Shirley stopped listening. She was just too excited. Her soft, dark curls framed her face as she gazed at A.C., hardly believing that her wish was finally true. They really were going to be married.

"Do you want to read it?" A.C. asked her, thrusting the document in her direction. It was still in a rough form because he had cut and pasted together paragraphs from the prenuptial agreement his business partner used.

Shirley laughed. "You know it would take me all day," she said. "And I'd have no idea what it said when I finished." She reached for a pen on a nearby desk. "Where do I sign?" There would be no questions about A.C.'s love now, she decided.

But how much could he have loved her? She did not know that the document he held out protected him even more than the first one. In case of divorce, it would deprive Shirley of *any* property or possessions or investments, even those acquired after they married. The second agreement clearly dictated that both the assets A.C. brought into the marriage *and* salary and bonuses he earned during the marriage would remain his alone. What the agreement did give Shirley was room and board—so long as she stayed married. But should they divorce, she would be on her own, with nothing to show for her years as A.C.'s wife. It was an outrageously one-sided agreement, drafted only for A.C.'s benefit.

Nor did Shirley realize that while A.C. bestowed on her her greatest wish, the legality of marriage, he still would treat her as he always had. At his side she forever would feel as if she were his pretty prize, a fun-loving playmate and constant companion.

They married in Chickasha, Oklahoma, far from Lancaster so that no one could possibly learn that they had not already been married. It was September 9, 1975, exactly eight years to the day since they had first made love.

A.C.'s youngest daughter LuAnn moved into their house in Lancaster, just as Susan had done, through high school. Both girls were rebellious, and few signs existed of the love for Shirley that had formed while she was their baby-sitter.

"A.C. gave you a rich life," observed Stuart Walzer, bringing his client back to the present, "and I'm not surprised that the girls were jealous or at least resentful."

"I loved him so much that I wanted to do everything for him," Shirley explained. "I was just fortunate that I got so many nice things. I didn't do things for him because I was going to get something in return. I did them because I wanted to and I loved him. I was happy to be there and to get to live the life I lived."

She did get a lot in return. The life she talked about included buying anything she desired. Whenever mail-order catalogs arrived, Shirley routinely marked what she wanted and simply phoned in her requests. When out shopping with A.C., her purchasing power was unlimited. The couple would buy large quantities of antiques at one time. They never gave a second thought to spending thousands of dollars during a single shopping excursion.

In return, Shirley told her attorney, "I packed for him; I also cut his hair, did his manicures and his pedicures. I polished his shoes and had his clothes tailored. I laid them out for him every morning, from the socks and shoes to the belt. I even put his contact lenses in for him.

I gave him foot rubs and back rubs every night. I gave to him far more than any other woman could. I can *really* give to a man I love," she said forcefully, with a pride that showed she had done just that. "And I wanted him to think that I deserved to be there." He would appreciate her, she had decided, if she filled three roles, those of wife, lover, and servant.

Even her love of gardening and canning contributed to helping A.C. "Why are you making so much?" he asked her one day as she pickled and canned jar after jar. In one year she made twenty-eight quarts of strawberry jam and thirty-two quarts of peach jam, along with spiced peaches, zucchini bread, and other goods.

"Because we can give it away at Christmas to all your business friends and contacts," she responded enthusiastically.

She convinced A.C. to join in her kitchen hobby, and the pickles and jams did ultimately become his holiday offerings to friends and business colleagues, people to whom he previously had given more ordinary, store-bought gifts, such as cases of liquor.

"The response," Shirley told her attorney, "was overwhelming. And the garden became a huge part of our lives." Shirley and A.C. planted fruit trees together and worked for hours in the vegetable garden, often retiring at the end of the day with a bottle of Dom Pérignon.

One day, five years after they had been legally married, A.C. announced over drinks that he had torn up their prenuptial agreements. He didn't say why, but Shirley presumed it was because he didn't think they were important anymore. So many women in Shirley's position hope that their husbands will do the same. Sometimes it happens, but often the offer is never made. It never occurred to Shirley that A.C. was lying. (Later A.C. would say she had misunderstood.)

He also told her that he had created a trust to provide for his heirs, a common legal tactic for minimizing estate and inheritance taxes. He would place in the trust his business assets and real estate holdings, and when he died, Shirley would inherit two-thirds of everything. A.C.'s children would receive the rest.

She should have been happy for the rest of her life. But somehow, over the next few years, the idyllic existence began to lose its appeal and an unfamiliar malaise crept in.

"I don't know what's wrong," Shirley told her husband as the Christmas holidays approached in 1983, "but I don't feel independent or separate enough. I don't have any identity of my own; I'm just an extension of you. And I'm always relying on you to do and buy for me. I don't think you even trust me to make my own decisions or to manage money myself." Shirley was becoming more mature and sophisticated, primarily because A.C. had taught her so much. But the change in her attitude still caught him off guard.

"Don't you have everything you want?" he asked in disbelief. "We have this house, a place in Palm Springs, and all kinds of property. You're active in lots of groups and organizations. We travel a lot. You get along with the kids again. What else could there be, Shirley?"

She agreed that they had grown as close as a husband and wife could be. He was sharing with her all of his feelings, feelings about his children, work, investments, and estate planning goals, and she offered her advice and support. But she'd begun to feel that she was only a puppet at A.C.'s side when it came to making decisions. He was always in charge; he was the powerful one pulling her strings.

"I don't know," she responded, looking down, away from her husband. "These should be the best years of my life."

What troubled Shirley was that she exerted no control over her life, even in the smallest ways. She had no money of her own, only checkbooks with small balances, and she regularly asked A.C. to replenish them. She even had to ask for grocery money. While she had been allowed to help A.C.'s bookkeeper manage some of the household bills and she had started monitoring investments he made for the children, she still had to give his bookkeeper a monthly report of everything she spent. It was important for tax purposes, A.C. had said. But Shirley felt she was being treated as a child.

A.C. realized that he had to do something to appease his wife. "I'm going to give you your own company," he announced several days later, a generous and perhaps extreme response to Shirley's desire for some personal autonomy. "We'll call it SAW Company, Inc. to stand for Shirley Ann Warnack. You can manage it."

"Sweetheart!" Shirley shrieked in delight.

A.C. explained that he would fund the new company with the $9 million he was expecting from the pending sale of his construction firm. A.C. and his partner had just recently decided to concentrate their efforts on their other businesses and on their real estate holdings, so the construction company was on the block. "This will prove to you once and for all that you are a part of everything," he said as he kissed her. "Please don't doubt me again." He set up SAW Inc. as a Virgin Islands corporation, for tax purposes. It was to be used as an investment vehicle for business profits.

The idea of managing SAW kept Shirley happy for a time. But soon she came to realize that while she was allowed to call the bank to suggest how the money in SAW be reinvested, only the bank could move the funds. Nor could Shirley take money out of the company without A.C.'s written approval. She was not a signatory on the account. Her much-heralded management authority was hollow, and she was in the same position of helplessness as before.

I don't want the money, she thought to herself, plagued by her powerlessness in the marriage. But I want the right to reinvest it wherever I think best. Otherwise it shows that he still distrusts me. She still remembered that friends had once warned A.C. that she was only after his riches. Surely a new request would raise his sensitivity to that attack. Shirley's need for some control over her life—any control—continued to build. She didn't want to find a job, and she didn't think A.C. wanted her to do so either, so she had to seek her own power through her husband, who perhaps was understandably hesitant to share business activities with his young and comparatively inexperienced wife. Little did A.C. realize that Shirley might have been happy with a modest gesture—perhaps a larger bank account would have sufficed.

"We went to see a counselor," she told her attorney, "which was A.C.'s idea. And the counselor said I was unhappy because I had become more mature, I had grown in our relationship and A.C. hadn't. I couldn't make A.C. understand that I just needed some flexibility and freedom. He bought me everything, but in terms of having my own money, he kept me on a very short leash."

Shirley's reactions were not at all surprising. Granted, she was uneducated and inexperienced when she married A.C., but the very nature of their life-style together changed her. Unfortunately A.C. could not learn to accept her maturation, her growing independence, confidence, or ambition. He refused to recognize that Shirley would not always be the cute young baby-sitter who had come into his home so long ago.

Even with professional counseling Shirley and A.C. could not resolve their predicament. She thought he treated her as he always had, staying close, watching, monitoring her activities and spending, just as he had done from the beginning of their romance. He needed to be in control.

In frustration that spring, in 1984, she suggested that she and A.C. try a trial separation. She wanted to see what it was like to be on her own, in charge of her time and activities for days on end without having to answer to anyone. He agreed reluctantly but was confident that she quickly would discover how much she missed him and needed him. Shirley moved out of the Lancaster house and into their Palm Springs condominium.

Shirley was lonely by herself in the condo, so she spent hours on the tennis courts at the adjacent country club and quickly became friendly with a man she met there. Their affection blossomed, and before long they became lovers. When A.C. found out about the affair—Shirley never revealed how—he flew into a rage. He thought Shirley had left him for this new beau, although she tried to explain that she simply had left him—period.

"If you think you're going to take me for everything, you're crazy," he shouted during one of their heated telephone calls.

"I don't want that," she replied coolly, even though her heart was beating furiously and her hands were shaking. "I just don't ever want to have to work again. I deserve that after all the time I've spent with you. I *worked* for that!"

Shirley visited a lawyer in Palm Springs, and he referred her to Stuart Walzer in Los Angeles. "Most of the property is in L.A., and A.C.'s business is in L.A.," the Palm Springs lawyer explained to her, "and I guarantee if you file here, he'll have the case transferred there. Now, I can represent you. I can drive to L.A., and I'm willing to do that. But judges tend to like their own attorneys rather than an outsider coming in."

Stuart Walzer was recognized throughout California and nationally for the big-money divorces he handled. In addition he had top credentials as a state-certified family law specialist and a fellow of the American Academy of Matrimonial Lawyers. At age sixty, he was a dean of the divorce bar, one who had made the specialty his long before many recognized that family law was a fast-growing and highly lucrative field. His fee: three hundred dollars an hour.

As soon as Shirley retained Walzer he began plotting strategy for her case, gathering data on A.C.'s wealth and calculating how he could get the best possible settlement for his client. Based on what he learned, Walzer figured that A.C. could be worth more than forty million dollars. But it was going to be hard tracking down those dollars because A.C.'s money was scattered over a multitude of corporations and holdings. Like many very wealthy entrepreneurs, he probably did not even know exactly how much he was worth.

Walzer filed for Shirley's divorce on August 1, 1984, in Los Angeles. "While Shirley Warnack has asked us to hold off for about three weeks before commencing serious discovery," he wrote in an inner-office memorandum that circulated among the firm's lawyers, "I think it important that we immediately start working on the case." Walzer's partner, Jan Gabrielson, was going to help.

"You know that this is psychological warfare," Walzer announced to his colleagues. "With a client such as Shirley, with any client for that matter, we should try to bring her along with us every step of the way. We should tell her regularly exactly what our next steps will be and then follow through on them promptly and let her know what happened. Unless Shirley knows that she is fully armed and has the upper hand at all stages, she is likely to make concessions to A.C. that are unnecessary and not in her best interests."

Shirley's case was not the first Walzer had encountered in which a baby-sitter had married the father in a family. In such situations, as in more common cases involving executives who marry their secretaries or receptionists, the wives tended to be subservient.

Shirley and Walzer soon learned that A.C. had not destroyed the prenuptial agreements. These documents would be a powerful weapon on his side. "The first thing we have to do," Walzer stressed to his colleagues in the office, "is to start planning how we are going to set aside those prenuptials. By the time we finish, we're going to be the world's leading experts on the subject."

Having heard the full story of Shirley's early relationship with the Warnack family and with A.C. in particular, Walzer felt more confident that under California law he could convince a court that her agreements were blatantly improper—and illegal.

When lawyers research the facts in a case prior to trial, in a process called discovery, they can question under oath ("depose") the opposing party in the case (the husband or wife) as well as the other side's lay and expert witnesses. Depositions often last for days and can be just as upsetting and frightening as testifying on the stand during the trial itself. Walzer and Gabrielson took A.C.'s deposition in early April 1985; one of A.C.'s lawyers, Jerald Gale of Anderson, Ablon, Maseda & Lewis, was with him. Neither Gale nor the firm's senior partner, Charles Anderson, who oversaw A.C.'s case, were divorce lawyers per se. Theirs was a small general business firm that had drawn up the trust for A.C. while helping with his estate planning. Neither Walzer nor Shirley knew why A.C. had hired generalists rather than a matrimonial lawyer to handle his divorce.

A judge named Harry Shafer oversaw the deposition (although judges do not always sit in on these proceedings); the meeting was held in Shafer's office, where everyone but the judge seemed anxious and tense. A.C. obviously was suffering from a head cold. He did not appear well.

"Mr. Warnack, have you ever had your deposition taken before?" Walzer asked after A.C. had been sworn in.

"Yes."

"Just for the record and so that we may be on the same wave length,

I will be asking you questions. My questions and your answers will be taken down by the court reporter," explained Walzer, nodding in the reporter's direction. "Despite the informality of these proceedings and [our] just sitting around the table, the booklet that will be printed up will be part of the court record and may be read into the record during the course of the trial."

A.C. did not respond.

"You will have an opportunity to read the deposition transcript and to change your answers if necessary," continued Walzer formally. "If you change them in any significant way, I will have the right to comment on that at the time of trial and to point out that you have made drastic changes.

"For that reason it is very important that you understand my questions the first time and that if I don't ask sensible questions or a question that you understand, then ask me to restate it or to do it over because you don't want to have to go back through the booklet and start correcting all of your answers. Is that clear?"

"Yes," replied an expressionless A.C.

"Are you under any kind of a disability today?" Walzer asked, noting A.C.'s cold. "I mean, do you feel all right? Is your health good?"

"Do I look that bad?" shot back A.C. Warnack.

Walzer suppressed a groan. It was going to be a long day.

"You look fine," Jerald Gale interceded.

"The judge says I look like Clint Eastwood and you ask me if I'm dead," sniped A.C., referring to the predeposition banter while ignoring his own lawyer and glaring at Walzer.

"He only asked you the question," said Judge Shafer patiently, "because if you are taking any drug or any medication or anything like that, he wants to know you are in a good condition to answer the questions."

"I feel great," said A.C. He scanned the room as if he thought everyone there was a fool, everyone except himself.

Walzer then began, through a series of questions, to walk A.C. verbally through his early relationship with Shirley, his acquisition of the first prenuptial agreement in 1971, and his phony marriage.

He read from the first prenuptial: "'Whereas, the parties hereto anticipate entering into marriage each with the other. . . .' Did you marry Shirley Warnack at that time?"

"No," replied A.C.

"Why not?"

"I guess we just didn't want to or we didn't do it for whatever reason."

"When you say, 'We just didn't want to,' does that mean that you and she decided not to get married together?"

"We didn't get married, so I guess we did." A.C. was surly.

"I am not asking you to infer anything," continued Walzer. "Do you remember any conversations that you had with Shirley Warnack about getting married at that time? I am speaking of March 1971."

"We did not get married nor did we ever plan a wedding during March."

"You did have a wedding reception during April, did you not?"

"No," countered A.C. adamantly.

"Did you have a group of people over to the house in Lancaster and entertain them?"

"Not that I remember," said A.C.

"Did you and Shirley Warnack have any conversations with regard to getting married or not getting married during the month of March 1971?"

"No."

"Then, *what did you mean* when you said that 'the parties hereto anticipate entering into a marriage each with the other after the date of execution of this agreement'?" demanded Walzer.

"We entered into a—I guess it would be called a hoax, mistruth, or whatever," admitted A.C. as if discussing a bad business decision, "in that we told people we were married. I even had a judge friend of mine give me a marriage license, but there was never a ceremony."

"You have answered the question," said Gale, shooting a look of warning toward his client.

As the questioning continued, A.C. grew increasingly impatient, then angry. In the recesses of Walzer's mind he worried that A.C. might become violent toward him. This is not an unreasonable concern for lawyers caught in the cross fire of heated divorce battles, particularly when a domineering husband is rejected by a formerly submissive wife.

At one point Walzer showed A.C. an album containing photographs taken at the party A.C.'s friends had thrown after they thought A.C. and Shirley had married.

"Do you recognize these pictures?" asked Walzer.

"Yes."

"Do you see a wedding—"

"No, wait," interrupted A.C. "I don't recognize the pictures. I don't remember seeing them, but I remember the people in them."

"Do you remember the occasion?" asked Walzer.

"No, I don't," replied A.C.

"Do you remember a reception given for you?"

"No."

Walzer turned to a page he had marked in the album and put it close where A.C. could see it. "Take the picture at the top of the page on the left-hand side," he instructed. "Does that appear to be you in the left-hand picture?"

"It's me or Clint Eastwood," said A.C. dryly.

Preparation for the trial itself was long and arduous. The lawyers fought at every bend in the road, throwing up roadblocks, each blaming the other for prolonging the process. But as in all big-money divorces, the lawyers' time was for the asking and the parties were more than willing to pay. Shirley was determined to fight until she thought A.C. had given her enough to live on. And she demanded that he pay her legal bills, too.

On September 6, 1985, the judge split the case and ordered two hearings, one to determine the validity of the two prenuptial agreements and the other to determine how A.C. and Shirley's wealth should be divided between them.

In drafting his trial brief for the first hearing Walzer argued that the 1971 prenuptial agreement was unenforceable because Shirley and A.C. did not then marry—nor did they have any plans to marry. Therefore, as a contract the agreement had no purpose and was void. If Walzer's argument worked, it would wipe the first agreement off the books without further debate.

But to be on the safe side he continued, a prenuptial agreement is also invalid if it involves "undue influence"—that is, if either the husband or the wife takes advantage of the other's weaker frame of mind, greater needs, or distress. Undue influence also exists when two people have an intimate, trusting relationship, what lawyers call a "confidential relationship." In these cases one person easily can take advantage of the other.

"This is a blatant example of undue influence," Walzer told his partner Jan Gabrielson as they discussed the trial brief in their offices. "It ought to be in the textbooks."

"I think you're right," Gabrielson replied. "Shirley's relationship with A.C. over time—her initial contact as a family baby-sitter and her subsequent financial dependency on him, even after they married—show how little bargaining power she had with him. He had been controlling her life for so many years, telling her everything she should do; he even got her to sign a fake marriage certificate."

They didn't talk about the judge who had written the bogus license. He was a man who had abused his office on numerous occasions, and when confronted with his indiscretions, he was eventually forced into retirement. He died in the late 1970s.

Drafting his trial brief, Walzer turned back to his yellow pad and the time of Shirley's first prenuptial agreement. "In March 1971, there was a distinct inequality in the bargaining powers of A.C. and Shirley. A.C. was the sole source of financial support for Shirley. A.C. was already worth millions and Shirley had nothing. Due to her lack of financial and emotional independence, Shirley was vulnerable to the demands of A.C. Further, A.C. was sixteen years older than Shirley and was quite sophisticated in the ways of the world. A.C., being a self-made millionaire, was quite knowledgeable about business. Shirley had no business experience at all. Finally, Shirley had no independent representation [that is, her own attorney] at any time during the drafting or executing of the prenuptial agreement. Thus, not just one of the above factors apply in this case but all of them. Clearly, A.C. used his position of power to unduly influence Shirley into signing away her rights."

The same charge of undue influence, Walzer continued in his legal brief, held for the second, 1975 agreement. Even though Shirley and A.C. did marry then and the contract was valid in that sense, they had been living together for an even longer period and their "confidential relationship" was all the stronger. "A.C.'s wealth had grown, and Shirley had become even more dependent upon him for financial assistance," Walzer wrote. And here again, he added, she had had no independent legal advice.

Pausing for a moment, he looked up and then rose from his desk to pace the floor. He had more strong points to make.

A.C. did not keep accurate records separating his individual premarital assets from his and Shirley's marital assets, Walzer reasoned. Wording in both the 1971 and 1975 prenuptial agreements required this. They had said that should there be any ambiguity in the separation of A.C.'s individual property and income from the marital property and income, the ambiguities would work in Shirley's favor. "There are no records concerning the separation of income and property as required by both prenuptial agreements, nor are there any records distinguishing separate property from community property," Walzer scrawled on his pad. How could one be any more ambiguous than not having any records at all?

Last, he decided to argue that A.C.'s actions over the past several years showed that he considered his property to be his *and* Shirley's. A.C.'s financial statements in the late 1970s were entitled "A.C. and Shirley Warnack Statement of Personal Net Worth." Shirley also believed that A.C. had torn up the prenuptial agreements in 1980 (even though he had not), and he announced that same year that he had set up the joint trust as part of his will. Over a period of time A.C. placed in the trust, among other items, deeds to his Palm Springs condominium; twenty acres of property in Kern County, California; his Lancaster home; four parcels of land in Los Angeles; a Montana ranch; and a tract of land in Palmdale, California. By putting all of this property and other assets into a joint trust, Walzer claimed, A.C. was in fact transforming it into community property.

Like many lawyers preparing for trial, Walzer had marshaled every argument possible to support his client's case. He felt he was convincing, but of course he had no way of knowing how the judge would react.

And at the same time he knew that A.C.'s lawyers would labor equally long over their trial brief, taking issue with every point he had raised. Shirley, A.C.'s attorneys would argue, "knowingly, voluntarily and freely executed the agreements, and understood the nature and effect of them prior to the marriage." A.C. did keep separate books and records in order to manage separately his premarital property, they would insist, and he lived up to his obligation to support his wife. Furthermore, the trust A.C. created did not negate the prenuptial agreements because the trust clearly indicated that all property transferred to it would "retain the same character it had prior to conveyance or transfer to the trust." Thus, A.C.'s property and earnings were still his alone.

The first hearing, or trial, began on February 25, 1986, and ran four days. Judge Richard P. Byrne of the California Superior Court reminded the lawyers for both sides that he first wanted to hear testimony on the charge that Shirley had been subjected to undue influence. If he found that she had not, Judge Byrne said he would consider the other two related issues—whether A.C. had kept proper records as required by the agreements, and whether the formation of the joint trust had changed the ownership of the property. "If the court finds that the agreements are invalid [because of undue influence], it does not appear that it will be necessary to address the [other two] issues," he explained.

Walzer presented his case first. Rather than calling A.C. to the stand, he chose to read to the judge portions of his deposition, a tactic lawyers can follow if the deposition is that of one of the parties to the case—that is, of the husband or the wife, not of a witness. For the entire first day Walzer read aloud his questions and A.C.'s answers; the process was long and fraught with arguments as A.C.'s chief lawyer, the somber Charles Anderson, regularly objected to the passages' relevancy. Sometimes the judge ruled in Anderson's favor, other times in Walzer's.

The second day Walzer called Shirley to the stand. She was impeccably groomed in a conservative, tailored dress, her hair pulled back. "I want you to stay calm and answer my questions as we discussed them in the office," Walzer told his client before the judge called the court to order. "And then when Anderson cross-examines, just keep cool and simply respond to what he asks. I'll be watching out for you."

"I can't help it . . . I'm nervous," she replied.

A.C.'s attorney was determined to prove on cross-examination that Shirley had known exactly what she was doing when she signed the prenuptial agreements.

"Mrs. Warnack, did you ever, prior to March 8, 1971 [the date of the first prenuptial agreement], had you discussed with Mr. Warnack the fact that you, you being collectively the two of you, needed some form of property agreement before you got married?

"I don't remember if we discussed it or not," replied Shirley.

"Did you ever discuss your concerns that you didn't want his family or your family or friends to feel that you were marrying him for his money?" The gray-haired Anderson was leaning over the table where he had assembled his notes. With both hands spread before him, he peered at Shirley over the tops of his glasses.

"Yes," she replied.

"And that was discussed on a number of occasions, was it not?"

"Yes."

"And that was, in fact, your feeling at that time, was it not?"

"Yes."

"And your desire?"

"Yes." Shirley glanced over at Walzer. He was looking straight back at her, without expression, silently willing her to have the strength to proceed.

"Did that change between 1971 and 1975?" continued Anderson.

"No."

"So you have always been concerned, prior to the time that you married Mr. Warnack, in fact, in 1975, about that issue, haven't you?"

Shirley was starting to hate Anderson. She didn't want people to think she had married A.C. for his money, but then she didn't feel he should throw her out into the cold in a divorce. "Yes," she said quietly in response to the lawyer's question.

"And you," he seemed to announce, "wanted it settled once and for all, didn't you?"

The next day, the third day of the trial, Anderson put A.C. on the stand. A.C. made it clear that he thought Shirley had been well aware that a prenuptial agreement was intended to protect an individual's property when getting married. "Shirley told me, during the first agreement, the interim period in between, and at the time this [second] agreement was prepared," A.C. testified with the full force of his self-confidence, "that she was in full agreement for me to retain ownership of all the property that I had—and all the other conditions that were in the agreement if something happened to us. That was always her understanding. She told me that; she told other people that. There is no doubt about that."

Walzer cross-examined A.C. for the rest of that day and into the next, clarifying for the judge that, in fact, Shirley had not really understood the full impact of either agreement.

"And what did you tell her would happen if you ever got divorced?" Walzer asked A.C.

"I don't remember discussing divorce that night," he responded.

"Did you ever discuss—before September 7, 1975 . . . did you ever discuss divorce with Shirley Warnack?"

"Do you mean divorce in a general sense?" interjected Anderson. "I object to the question as being ambiguous." A.C.'s lawyer appeared frustrated by so much legal wrangling.

"You could be a little more specific," the judge agreed, nodding toward Walzer.

Walzer began again. "Did you ever discuss what would happen if you and Shirley Warnack got divorced? Before you entered into this 1975 prenuptial agreement, did you ever say to her, tell her what her rights would be under this agreement if you and she got divorced?"

"No," answered A.C.

At the end of the fourth day of the trial, the judge decided that the Warnacks' relationship clearly had been one in which A.C. had the upper hand. Shirley, indeed, had put too much stock in him; she simply had been willing to do anything that A.C. asked of her. "With respect to that, the court finds that there was a confidential relationship that existed between Mr. and Mrs. Warnack at the time that the two agreements were executed," Judge Byrne announced from the bench. He looked up from his notes and scanned the faces before him.

"The court, in arriving at this conclusion, considered the nature of the relationship," he explained. "The age differential was only a fact in that connection." A.C. was a sophisticated businessman and Shirley had accepted the agreements on faith, the judge continued. Yet both agreements adversely affected her rights. "She signed the agreements," concluded Judge Byrne, "and, I believe, did so as a result of her trust and confidence and love for Mr. Warnack."

For once in his life, A.C. Warnack had exerted too much power. His attempts to control his marriage, as he did his many businesses, had backfired. A.C.'s prenuptial agreements were wiped off the books.

The second trial, to determine the division of the Warnacks' assets, was set for the following November. While Shirley was gaining confidence, Walzer and Gabrielson saw another long battle ahead, and they agreed to alternate responsibility for arguing this part of the case. Their goal was to convince the court that everything A.C. owned was community property because he had no accurate measure of the value of his individual assets before he married Shirley. Therefore, it was impossible to separate premarital assets from marital assets, reasoned the lawyers, and everything would have to be divided.

"Just how are we going to convince the judge that our theory is the right one?" Walzer asked his partner.

"I don't know," he responded honestly. "It's reaching a bit. Given A.C.'s vast holdings, which are spread out all over the place, and the accounting nightmare over their past and present value, we may have a pretty hard time of it."

Nor were Walzer and Gabrielson certain that their second theory would work, either, the theory that the transfer of A.C.'s assets to a trust for estate planning automatically turned those assets into community property. So much of the lawyers' success with either argument would depend on the judge they drew for this second trial, and they wouldn't know who that was until it began. "Another crap shoot," Walzer muttered under his breath.

When the new trial started, lawyers for both sides entered the courtroom. Papers were soon piled high on the desks before them. As usual, Shirley and A.C. sat on their respective sides. The testimony, focusing on A.C.'s assets, when he acquired them, and how much they were worth, wore on day after day. A.C. grew impatient; Shirley was anxious.

"We want to make a suggestion for settlement," a weary Walzer finally told A.C.'s lawyers, Gale and Anderson, after two weeks of testimony and argument. Gabrielson had typed a draft proposal on the portable computer he carried into the courtroom daily, and he printed it out on the printer right then and there.

"We think we've got a settlement going," Gabrielson told the judge as lawyers for both sides sweated over sentences and paragraphs, molding words and massaging phrases to better suit their respective aims.

"I like the second draft better than this third one," Walzer told his opponents. "Let's look back at it." More drafts rolled off Gabrielson's printer. A.C. and Shirley ignored each other while they waited to see the final product their lawyers would present for their approval. Shirley tried to stay composed; Walzer and Gabrielson had taught her to suppress all facial expressions and any display of emotion in the courtroom. But she was tired, too; neither she nor A.C. had missed one minute of the trial.

When they finally concurred on a settlement, both A.C. and Shirley announced that they were satisfied. A.C. agreed to pay Shirley $2.7 million in cash. Three hundred and fifty thousand dollars of that money was to be paid to Walzer and Gabrielson. The settlement also provided that Shirley would own furniture, clothing, artwork, antiques, and jewelry that were already in her possession and the bank accounts, stocks, and bonds in her name alone. A.C. agreed to give Shirley three of their automobiles, including a Mercedes-Benz and a Cadillac, and the Palm Springs condominium, which had been paid for in full, and all of its contents. Given A.C.'s vast holdings, a judgment from the court could have been much worse for him.

As for Shirley, she was happy, too. While the marriage had begun under less than admirable circumstances, she had held up her end of the bargain, caring for A.C. and waiting on him for years. She certainly deserved a share of his earnings from that time.

Perhaps A.C. could have avoided the messy divorce altogether if he had only allowed Shirley—for whom the issue of control had taken on immense importance—some personal independence, or at least had given her some area of autonomy during their marriage. She might have stayed with him forever.

In August 1989 Shirley again visited Walzer's office, this time simply to say hello—bringing with her, of course, her hallmark plate of homemade cookies—and to share with the lawyer news of her current activities. Her relationship with A.C. continued to be awkward, she said, but she occasionally saw him at their Palm Springs tennis club. Shirley told Walzer about her new two-acre home in Carmel, which she maintained along with the Palm Springs condo. She also talked about a successful businessman she'd gotten to know, someone about whom she cared deeply, but her tone was cautious when she considered a possible new commitment. "I was always a firm believer that when you said 'I do' and 'for better or for worse, till death do us part' that that was really it," she told Walzer that day. "I've been through two divorces and I'm a little bit leery of saying those words, knowing that I might change later and not want to be in that situation.

And then basically I'd be saying a lie starting out." It was clear that lying about commitments, about the meaning of marriage, was still a strong issue for her.

"People think so differently about divorce now," Shirley continued, pondering out loud, "and it's sad, real sad." But already she was planning that should she marry a third time, this time she would have to have a prenuptial agreement. Everyone—her accountant, her financial adviser, Walzer, and Gabrielson—had told her that this time *she* had something to protect.

Shirley later told her new boyfriend, "I'm not with you for any reason except to be with you. If we get married, it won't be because I want your money, or because you want mine. When the time is right, I'll be happy to sign a prenuptial agreement with you."

"I know," he responded, "and if it will make you feel better, I'll write one up and you can sign it next week."

Shirley smiled, knowing that this time it wouldn't be so easy. She would be involved in the drafting of the document. Walzer would have to see it. And she would have to think long and hard about exactly what she was signing. Even more important, she would have to force herself to think about divorce again. She was barely able to contemplate getting married; pushing her mind further ahead to the possibility of divorce left her shaken.

But Shirley was no longer the unsophisticated, naive daughter of a small town mail carrier. She was a wealthy woman with two homes and steady investment income, and she clearly had figured out how to take care of herself. Like many other modern couples, she and any new husband would need to protect their individual assets.

A few months after Shirley's last meeting with Walzer, A.C. married his secretary, a woman thirty years younger than he—the age of his youngest child—someone he clearly could dominate. When Shirley learned about the wedding, she wondered if A.C. had asked his third wife to sign a prenuptial agreement, too. He should have, given his wealth, and he probably did, but this time he probably was a lot more careful. If he divorced again, he would have to argue that this new prenuptial agreement had been fairly written and executed. Given the even greater age differential in this marriage, he would have to be particularly wary of charges of undue influence, insisting on independent legal counsel for both sides when the agreement was drawn up.

And what happened to A.C.'s first wife, Betty? Divorced a second time after a ten-year marriage that she had hoped would fend off loneliness, she moved in with her daughter Susan in Lancaster and, at age fifty-six, enrolled in real estate school. She was distraught that Shirley's settlement with A.C. was so much larger than her own—that she had to work for a living while Shirley did not. Even sharing her grandchildren with Shirley, who kept up relations with the family, became a source of rancor.

2

JOINT CUSTODY:
A QUEST FOR
SHARED PARENTING

Ingrid M. Nicholas v. George Nicholas

*Most clients at the end of their matrimonial cases
don't like their lawyers. It's like going to the
dentist. What's to like?*

—ATTORNEY GARY SKOLOFF
LIVINGSTON, NEW JERSEY

After a divorce, mothers and fathers supposedly have equal rights to custody of their children. But in truth the winner of this often brutal legal battle is more often the mother, with the father receiving only a visitation schedule for his time alone with the kids.

Over the last fifteen years a new push toward joint or shared custody has gained momentum, with experts in divorce and family matters advocating that children need more time with both parents. Fathers also have lobbied for nonsexist, egalitarian postdivorce parenting arrangements. Thus a steady stream of new state laws has begun to embrace the philosophy of shared parenting. The first such law was in Oregon in 1977, and today thirty-eight states have joint custody statutes. Some locales merely authorize joint custody; later statutes strongly encourage or show a preference for it and even offer guidelines. Only a few states require that both parents agree to joint custody before a judge can order its implementation.

Many joint custody laws differentiate between joint "legal" custody and joint "physical" custody. In the first the parents share in decisions regarding the child's well-being, even though the child may live primarily with one parent or the other. In the second both parents also share in the child's physical care.

Under these laws courts around the country have accepted or ordered a growing number of joint custody arrangements. Specifics, for example, how the children's time is split, can vary considerably.

As joint custody proliferated, however, its flaws also surfaced. Couples on whom it was imposed by courts continued to fight, to the detriment of their children. In one study of divorced families in the San Francisco area in which 35 percent of the children observed were in joint physical custody arrangements, researchers Judith Wallerstein and Susan Steinman of the Center for the Family in Transition found that these children were plagued by developmental problems, parental physical aggression, and a high incidence of emotional and behavioral problems. For reasons like these the California legislature in 1988 changed the language in its joint custody statute to remove any possible interpretation of a presumption in favor of joint custody over sole custody.

Even in more harmonious joint custody arrangements, changing needs and circumstances may alter the desirability of earlier schedules. Ironically, says New Jersey matrimonial lawyer Gary Skoloff, fathers who fight so hard for greater visitation or shared custody may within a short time stop taking advantage of the rights they have won. "I probably bring as many motions against husbands [where I insist that] they spend *more time* with their children than the reverse," he says.

"A lot of guys make this whole big war that they want these extraordinary visitation and custody rights and the women go nuts fighting it. And then one year later—between the husband's work and his new girlfriend—I get a phone call and he says, 'You know what . . . it may be a little too much time.'"

This chapter tells how Skoloff helped one father who never would turn down time with his child. George Nicholas wanted to share equally with his ex-wife the parenting of their young son Alexander. After a long, hard battle against great odds, George won his case, and he has continued to live up to the job until this day. Here's how he did it—and his advice to others.

"I don't believe in it," announced attorney Gary Skoloff after listening to the new client in his office.

The man sitting on the other side of Skoloff's desk, a casually dressed tall, athletic-looking man with an urgency in his voice, clearly was not deterred by the attorney's pronouncement. George Nicholas wanted joint custody of his three-year-old son Alexander, and he was determined to get it no matter what his wife Ingrid demanded—full custody with limited visitation for George—and regardless of his lawyer's advice to the contrary.

George, forty-two, looked back at Skoloff (the attorney later made famous by the Baby M case, in which William and Elizabeth Stern sued surrogate mother Mary Beth Whitehead). George acknowledged that Skoloff undoubtedly thought him crazy; he felt as if he were standing outside a labyrinth, staring at the entryway, preparing to embark on a long, confusing journey through a maze—the legal system. In the very center of this maze, this tangle of legal, emotional, and psychological factors he must sort through, resided the prize: the right to help raise his own son. Why he would have to exert himself like this confounded him deeply. After all, he was Alex's father.

George wanted what he described as "true joint custody," not just "legal joint custody." Sometimes a court grants both parents in a divorce shared custody of a child—but then places the child's primary residence with one parent or the other. This resolution, what some call "legal" or "paper" joint custody, mandates that both parents share in major decision making for the child, such as schooling and health care, but does not require that both parents be intimately involved in day-to-day child rearing. George considered child rearing to be the true province of parenthood and he was fearful that if Alex's mother had sole custody, allowing him only visitation, or if they had only a legal joint custody, she would not support him as a full-fledged father. Based on his reading—George had been educating himself on the topic—he knew that custody arrangements could vary in a multitude of ways. "Look," he explained to Skoloff. "I know the system works against real—physical—joint custody. Most fathers work nine to five, five days a week. They don't have time to parent. I own a restaurant, a pub, in New York with two other people. We cover for each other. My partners have agreed to let me double the number of hours I work every other week so during the weeks in-between I have no business commitments at all. I would like Alex to live with me during those weeks off. And when I am working, he can live with Ingrid. It will be an every-other-week deal."

Despite his own beliefs about the problems of joint parenting after divorce, Skoloff tried to open his mind to George. He contrasted his new client to other fathers who request joint custody of their children in divorce hearings. Typically many of these fathers want their children for different, less admirable reasons.

First, some fathers demand joint custody simply for leverage in negotiating financial settlements. Later, by agreeing to forego custody completely, they may get the wife to take less money in return. Second, because their marriages are ending, in order for them to hold on to something, some want to have the children part of the time, even though it may not be in the children's best interest. These fathers need their children psychologically because the walls of their home life are crumbling around them. Third, among a variety of still more reasons, some fathers seek joint custody simply to punish their ex-wives.

Skoloff believed that George was different from these men—he did want joint custody for the right reasons—but the lawyer wanted to set the record straight on his chances of winning. "Judges in New Jersey," Skoloff began, emphasizing his words for impact, "have the authority to order joint custody even if one parent objects, but they *hesitatingly* do it for a variety of reasons." They question, the attorney explained, whether true physical joint custody can work if one of the parents does not enter into the arrangement willingly. The logistical problems are sizeable and the dissenting parent has ample opportunities to throw up barriers. It can be a recipe for long-term warfare.

Furthermore, Skoloff added, George was fighting what is known as the "tender years doctrine," an overriding (although now outmoded) preference for giving sole custody of young children (generally under the age of ten) to the mother, in the belief that that would be in the children's best interests. (Although the tender years doctrine has been replaced in most states by sex-neutral custody laws, some judges still adhere to its premise.)

"I believe myself that a child under five is better off with his mother," Skoloff asserted as he talked with George.

"How do you know?" the client shot back defiantly. "Have you ever tried raising a child under five? You don't know." George was never willing to accept automatically the law's "current wisdom."

"That's right, I don't," admitted the attorney with a shrug. "But that's the way the courts tend to feel. Anyway," he continued, "if this case goes slowly, it won't hurt you because the child is getting older. That means you have a better chance. But it's going to be hard. Look at the facts: a mother at home, a very young child, and a father who works. On the face, it doesn't look good for you."

George and Ingrid met in February 1977 in upstate New York at a ski resort called Hunter Mountain. George, then thirty-seven, owned and managed two small winter resort hotels there, Hunter Village Inn and Hunter House; Ingrid, thirty-one, held assorted jobs as a waitress, receptionist, and salesperson for a local real estate agent. Within a year she had moved into George's apartment in one of his hotels and began working—as a bookkeeper, as a dining room hostess, and in various other capacities—to help him with his businesses. Their child, Alexander Nicholas, was born on March 24, 1979. George and Ingrid married just over a year later, on April 26, 1980.

Even before their wedding day, however, George sensed that their love relationship was suffering. George and Ingrid's life philosophies seemed compatible in the idyllic, romantic Hunter Mountain retreat where they first fell in love. But their differences became pronounced with the added responsibility of a new baby. Ingrid directed all of her energies and attention to Alex, and her concerns for his well-being controlled what had been their former routine as a couple. "All she lives for is Alex," George would complain to friends. Ingrid also worried constantly about their son's health and insisted that no child-care arrangement, even George's mother's care, was adequate. Alex's schedule locked their days in its rigid grip, despite George's pleas for some flexibility.

At the same time Ingrid complained that George was away too much taking care of hotel business, leaving her feeling lonely and isolated. In response her obsession with Alex grew stronger and she focused even more on her mothering.

George had believed Ingrid when she said she would feel more secure and less anxious if only they were married. But first he wanted to draft a prenuptial agreement. George had been married once before (he also had a son from that marriage with whom he maintained a close relationship), and he worried about how his finances would fare should a second marriage fail. Ingrid agreed that should they divorce, she would waive alimony and accept instead a flat payment pegged to the number of years she and George were married at the time of divorce: $25,000 after one year, $27,500 after two years, and so on, up to $47,500 after ten years' marriage. The agreement, they concurred, would be void after ten years. Both Ingrid and George hired independent attorneys to help draft their prenuptial agreement.

Perhaps George was clairvoyant. Or perhaps the earlier signs of trouble were too strong for him to deny the possibility of divorce. The conflict he and Ingrid had begun to experience over Alex's care and their own time schedules escalated. To make matters worse, Ingrid soon grew restless in Hunter and decided she no longer could live in the country. George would explain later that his wife had hoped to work as a model and actress and wanted to live closer to New York City. If true, this request would not have been far fetched, for Ingrid was a beautiful woman whose striking blond, blue-eyed, and high-cheekboned Germanic features lent credence to that big-city ambition. However, she later maintained that she wanted to move because the Hunter

Mountain environment in which they lived was unsuitable for raising a child. Whatever her reason, George agreed to the change and sold his businesses.

In April 1981 they moved to the town of Mahwah in suburban Bergen County, New Jersey. George bought a new restaurant business in nearby Manhattan, a pub called Keats at Second Avenue and Forty-fifth Street, a block from the United Nations. He loved to work at his new place, an establishment similar to the setting of the television sit-com "Cheers." His partners, two men in their mid-thirties, were good friends, understanding and supportive. George spent a lot of time with them setting up the new business, time away that made Ingrid more resentful.

Ingrid's obsession with Alex intensified further, to the point where she no longer trusted George with the child. In late 1981, the day after Thanksgiving and six months after Keats opened, Ingrid told George she was divorcing him; she had contacted a lawyer. George set out to do the same.

Along with his business partners, George had another friend who proved most important of all. He had met Virginia Gray in 1967 when both were vacationing in the Hamptons. They had dated and later broke off the romantic relationship, but they had kept up a friendship off and on over the years. After separating from Ingrid, George began spending time again with Ginny, a New York City high school teacher. Seven years George's junior, she was as relaxed and steady as Ingrid had been intense and unpredictable. Over the months and years ahead, Ginny would become George's partner in the fight for joint custody of Alex, helping plan strategy and assisting when the little boy was in George's care, especially after she and George started living together. Later both George and Ginny would maintain that he could have handled his case alone, but Ginny's friendship, companionship, and emotional support contributed to his ability to endure the long custody battle.

"You could not get two people who are more different than Ingrid and I," George told Ginny when she first learned about the impending divorce. "I graduated from high school and then went out in the world and made my fortune. She keeps wanting to go to school again; she thinks she's more intelligent than I am." George, the street savvy son of a city florist, grew up in New York with limited concern about advanced, formal education. Ingrid, the daughter of first-generation German immigrants, lived a strict, sheltered childhood in suburban New Jersey and graduated with honors from New York University, majoring in English literature.

Their contrasting upbringings produced contrasting life philosophies, brought out most dramatically by Alex's birth. Ingrid wanted to protect, shelter, and nurture the child in ways reminiscent of her own childhood; George was far less concerned about strict child-rearing rules. George told Ginny that his and Ingrid's parenting differences could doom his future as an active father, especially if Ingrid won custody of Alex. He worried—because his relationship with Ingrid was so stormy, because she fretted so about Alex's well-being, and because she considered him an inept father—that Ingrid would never let him spend much time with the boy, especially not in the ways he wanted.

As he explained to Ginny, "One of the biggest problems with a mother having custody is that she uses the child as psychological leverage: 'If you don't get him home on time, you're not going to see him next week,' she says, even if she has no legal right to do that. When the mother has full custody, the child lives with her, and for all practical purposes, the mother can call the shots. But with true joint custody—joint physical custody—there is no leverage. She can't say, 'If you don't get him home on time, you can't have him next week.' It just can't happen, because neither parent has that kind of control over the other." In other words, the mother and father are equals in a shared parenting arrangement.

For George, another issue played in his mind as well—he did not consider Ingrid the ideal parent, and for this reason, too, he did not want her alone dictating how Alex would be raised. While she was devoted and loving and good for Alex in that regard, he questioned her style of mothering. Ingrid's overinvolvement, as he saw it, was smothering and detrimental to Alex's development. If George could have his son half of the time, he reasoned, Alex would be better off. George wanted to offset some of Ingrid's behavior and values with his own.

Generally, says Skoloff, fathers who think their wives are excellent mothers are far less likely to demand extended visitation, joint custody, or full custody during a divorce. Of course, when the animosity level is high, neither is likely to recognize or acknowledge the other's parenting skills, even if they exist. Instead they point fingers: the spouse is too liberal or too conservative; too easygoing and short on discipline or too rigid and iron-fisted.

George had some savings, but not enough for a high-powered lawyer. But a friend, a guitar player who had worked for him at the Hunter Village Inn, was the nephew of a senior divorce attorney named Philip Solomon, a leader in the American Academy of Matrimonial Lawyers and one of the first big names in the field. The guitar player asked his uncle to talk with George.

They hit it off immediately, and Solomon filed for divorce on George's behalf in the state of New York, listing his Manhattan business and a residence in Hunter as the basis for jurisdiction. But Ingrid filed her suit in New Jersey, where the court ruled that it had jurisdiction because that was where the Nicholases, as a couple, lived. So Solomon, conceding to the ruling, decided to send George to his Newark friend and colleague, Gary Skoloff, to whom he regularly referred big cases for New Jersey clients. Skoloff agreed that his firm would take George's divorce as a favor. (The exchange of favors among lawyers who serve as steady referral sources is commonplace in the profession.) He gave the case to one of his younger associates, that is, one with a billing rate significantly lower than Skoloff's 1983 hourly fee of $150.

"Gary, I want *you* to handle this case," George announced after meeting the younger lawyer. George certainly did not lack chutzpah. It didn't matter to him that he was far less wealthy than Skoloff's average clientele. Skoloff finally conceded, charging an initial retainer of about $2,500, half the amount he asked from other clients at the time. George agreed, however, to pay Skoloff's full hourly rate as his time in the case built up.

Even though George finally had the lawyer he wanted, he found it impossible to meet with Skoloff because the attorney was so inundated with calls and demands from other clients. Then George discovered that Skoloff began work at 6:00 A.M., so he started meeting him at his office door, bagels and coffee in hand. The initial sessions were rough because each man suspected the other. George thought Skoloff did not care about his case and was not working hard enough on it; like many overwrought clients in a high-emotion divorce, he wanted his lawyer to be immediately available and working for him all the time—an impractical request, particularly when the client chooses a highly successful attorney. For his part, Skoloff, a nationally respected authority on divorce who juggled a plateful of the toughest cases in New Jersey, questioned George's confidence and self-proclaimed knowledge about the law and legal strategy. George even would try to quiz Skoloff, asking him questions for which he thought he knew the answers, just to see what the lawyer would say. Each time, George was satisfied. Slowly but surely, meeting after meeting, the two men—the expert senior lawyer and the anxious, determined father—began to form a team.

"I think we're going to get along," George told Ginny one day after an early session. Skoloff had in fact started to like George, too. Even if he was a crazy kind of guy. Crazy but charming.

*   *   *

Gary Skoloff has had ample opportunity to develop his expertise in child custody disputes. Although generally he does not believe in joint custody because, he says, parents continue to fight through the children, he does believe that children need frequent, positive contact with both the mother and the father. What Skoloff cares about more than anything among his clients are their children. All of the pamphlets and literature placed around his waiting room for clients to read deliver one simple message: You can hate your spouse, but remember, you love your kids.

"It is what makes me the craziest," says Skoloff of custody and visitation fights, "because when I see [suffering in the kids], it's where I attack my own clients the most. They may honestly believe they're not hurting their children to get back at their spouse, and they can pass a lie detector test on the subject, but they *are* [hurting them]. They just hate their spouse so much and they're so shattered by all that happened, there's nothing but trouble for the children."

He gives an example: "Sometimes a woman will say, 'I want him to have visitation two hours a month—on a Sunday, supervised.' And I say, 'Tell me about it.'

"And they start talking. And I say, 'Go on.' And when they're done I say, 'Wait a minute. Isn't there anything else you have to tell me [about the father]? Drugs? Alcohol? Tremendous violence?'

"'No, no, no,' they say.

"'What do you mean *two hours?* He *is* the biological father, right?'

"'Right.'

"'*What do you mean two hours a month?*'" His strong New Jersey accent rising to a new crescendo, Skoloff gestures with sweeping arms, his eyes wide open with horror.

The recounted dialogue may be exaggerated, but Skoloff clearly makes his point. In every such case he explains to his client how unreasonable her view is. It usually takes awhile for her to understand.

Sometimes, Skoloff adds, his clients are fathers who in essence want to be as unreasonable as some of the wives who come to him. And some of these fathers are airline pilots or executives who travel heavily and are hardly ever home.

While he has handled scores of custody cases in his matrimonial practice, Skoloff is best known today for the case of William and Elizabeth Stern, the couple who paid surrogate mother Mary Beth Whitehead to bear them a child through artificial insemination. The Sterns sued Whitehead when she decided to keep the child, in what became a test case regarding the enforceability of surrogate mother contracts. Even though the court declared the contract invalid, Skoloff feels that he won the highly publicized and dramatic Baby M trial when he convinced the judge to give Stern custody of the child and Whitehead visitation.

George Nicholas would assert later that the only reason he had a chance in the courts was because he had hired Gary Skoloff. "The judges listen to him," he says.

"It's important that we not take out after the mother," Skoloff warned George when they began discussing strategy for his case. "You don't want to knock her out." George nodded his head. "You're going to argue that Alex will only come out OK between you if you have him *half* the time."

George's girlfriend Ginny listened to the lawyer's directions carefully, too. As the case progressed, she increasingly would accompany George on his visits to Skoloff's office.

Skoloff emphasized to them both that the best way to win a custody suit was to argue that the result desired was in the best interests of the child. This was what the judges considered of foremost importance, not simply what each parent wanted. "It boils down to two things," the attorney said, "your fathering capabilities and your time availability. Are you a good parent and do you have the time to put into it? We have to develop a record of your parenting strengths, not merely as a game plan to win joint custody but as a plan for the remainder of your life."

George looked back at his lawyer in disbelief. If I weren't a good parent, I wouldn't be here, he was thinking. But the issue was not whether George *thought* he could do the job. The challenge was to convince the judge that this was indeed true.

Still, George had as much in favor of his case as any father could have. He had a good, steady job that was totally flexible and under his control. He did not want to cut Ingrid out of Alex's life; he only wanted to be equally involved. He wished to guarantee that Alex's childhood would have the love and companionship of both of his parents, a situation he truly believed would be best for Alex.

"If you don't get joint custody," concluded Skoloff after learning of George's devotion, "I don't know why they have it on the books."

In the meantime, while awaiting his day in court, George was having trouble when he did see his son. He complained in one of the pleadings he filed with the court that even though he and Ingrid had agreed on a temporary joint custody arrangement—with George voluntarily moving out of the house in return for seeing Alex there every other day—Ingrid made his visits difficult. According to their agreement, George was to be with Alex from 2:00 to 6:00 P.M. every other day, except that two nights of the week he could stay in the house from 2:00 P.M. until 9:00 A.M. the next morning. Sometimes he brought along his other son from his previous marriage, eleven-year-old Steven.

"I did move out of the house and I saw Alex on a regular basis," George wrote in his pleading, a document filed with the court to state his case, "although there were problems where she would do a variety of things to interfere with my visitation, including alleging that Alex was ill when he wasn't, and [her] not leaving the house on those nights that I had overnight visitation. . . . allegedly to protect the child and make sure that the child was well taken care of."

George protested that Ingrid was unduly concerned about his parenting style. "She actually called the police and asked them to watch the house to make sure that the child would be safe. Even more horrendous was the fact that she went around and told everyone in the neighborhood terrible things about me and everybody was watching the house to protect Alex against the 'ogre.'"

Clearly, Ingrid and George had different standards for judging their son's health and well-being. Ingrid said George was too lax a caretaker, while George charged Ingrid with being overprotective. George also complained about Ingrid's rigid adherence to the visitation schedule. "If I came ten minutes early then she would complain about that, and the next time I came she would not arrive back home until exactly on the minute so that I didn't get the 'extra ten minutes' with Alex. If I came five minutes late she complained that I didn't love the child or want to see the child or I wouldn't have been late. On a few occasions when I actually didn't leave until 9:15 or 9:20 A.M., she would call her lawyer and complain. So then what she would do is that at 9 o'clock in the morning on the button, if I was still in the house she would take Alex and leave and go somewhere."

Ingrid would deny the harshness of George's charges. She had only called the police, she said, because one day she didn't know where George and Alex had gone. And she had not, she added, said terrible things about George to the neighbors. Rather, she'd told them, "about the nature of the legal battle." For every criticism George leveled at Ingrid's child-rearing philosophy and behavior, she adamantly defended her own choices for the three year old.

And she was filled with contradictions. "The only way joint custody can be initiated in toddlerhood is when both parents have participated in daily parenting," Ingrid insisted. George had not helped with raising

Alex so far, she continued, so he did not deserve equal involvement in the child's future. Ingrid wanted sole custody in order to guarantee that Alex would be cared for as she thought best. The child's primary bonding was with her, she argued. Of course, George felt he had never had a chance with Alex because Ingrid was so particular and insistent about the kind of care he received. If George wasn't allowed equal time as the child's caretaker, how could he possibly bond with his son?

Yet, despite the turmoil and complications of their temporary shared custody arrangement, George felt that his relationship with his son was starting to blossom. "This schedule that was set by [the judge] for the joint custody between Ingrid and myself," he wrote the court, "allowed me to develop and foster a relationship with my son that I had never even had while I was married, simply because I was for the first time being allowed to have my own free time with Alex." Ingrid had other ideas in mind.

While George wanted to care for Alex on a daily basis, he still would have been a progressive father if he simply had settled for joint legal custody, the general term that describes shared parental decision making and responsibility, regardless of how the child's time is divided between parents. (Joint physical custody, by way of contrast, mandates sharing the child's time *living* in the two parents' homes.) "Joint legal custody symbolizes *both* parents' formal commitment to their children," writes University of Wisconsin sociologist Judith Seltzer in the June 1990 *Social Science Quarterly*. "It also implies a more egalitarian division of child-rearing responsibilities than does sole custody by the mother" when the father has only visitation rights. Joint legal custody is generally preferred over sole custody by more educated couples, says Seltzer, because "education is associated with egalitarian gender-role attitudes." Also, joint legal custody occurs more frequently among high-income families because high support payments may motivate fathers to seek a more active role in child-rearing decisions as justification for their financial contributions to the child's upbringing.

In contrast, Seltzer continues, shared "physical custody—children's living arrangements—depends largely on the parents' actual rather than symbolic division of labor before divorce. Children typically remain with their primary caretaker when parents separate. In the vast majority of cases, mothers provide most child care." Thus, although the parents may have a joint legal custody arrangement, the child may well spend more or most of the time living in the mother's home following a divorce.

George wanted both the right to help make decisions about his child's welfare, as provided in joint legal custody, and the less commonly shared right to be an equal participant in Alex's physical care, as expressed through the broader joint physical custody. Although Ingrid was Alex's primary caretaker before the Nicholases separated—indicating that the most likely outcome in their divorce would be sole custody for her with only visitation and no decision-making responsibility for George, or at best, joint legal custody—George clearly wanted to increase his own level of participation and responsibility in Alex's child-rearing activities.

Joint custody of any kind would have been to Alex's advantage. In a paper published in the January 1991 *American Journal of Sociology* Seltzer contrasts joint legal custody with sole-mother custody and argues that "joint legal custody encourages similarities between the way divorced fathers and fathers in two-parent households invest in their children." Acknowledging fathers' rights may help them become more involved in child rearing, she explains, and it gives them more opportunity to share financially with their children beyond mere child-support requirements.

Furthermore, the Los Angeles–based Joint Custody Association reports that based on one study, fathers in joint custody arrangements are only 6 percent to 7 percent delinquent in their support payments (which was equal to the national unemployment rate at the time). This is compared with a 50 to 72 percent default pattern for fathers with visitation only.

Joint custody fathers, adds the advocacy group, have an overall record that is far superior to that of fathers whose ex-wives have sole custody. For example, other studies show that joint custody fathers voluntarily contribute extras, such as camps and music lessons, to their children's support (60 percent versus 20 percent) and return to court less frequently (16 percent versus 31 percent).

In his case, George Nicholas wanted to meet all of the measures for successful joint custody. He was determined to be the ideal divorced father.

What George liked most about having Skoloff as his lawyer was that he was open to suggestions—and George had a lot of ideas about how he was going to win his case. Many of his ideas were ones he could carry out himself.

"I want to find out more about Danzig," he announced to Skoloff one day. Howard Danzig, a divorce lawyer with offices in Short Hill, New Jersey, was Ingrid's attorney. George started frequenting courthouses to watch him work. "Some day I may have to sit in front of this guy," he reasoned to Skoloff, "and I'm going to see how he operates."

Eventually, after seeing George in court, Danzig realized that his client's spouse was attending his other cases. "It annoys the hell out of him," George told Ginny with a smile after one of the courtroom visits.

In truth, Danzig did not know what to make of George's attentions. He called Skoloff, demanding to know why Skoloff's client was watching him. "Well, he wants to learn more about you, Howard," was Skoloff's reply. Inwardly, he felt disbelief—he had never had a client who would give so much time to this kind of endeavor.

Nor could Skoloff ignore another factor that could influence Danzig's performance in the case—his own experience with divorce. Danzig had lost a custody fight several years earlier. While he had fought valiantly to protect his rights as a father, a court permitted his ex-wife to move away to Chicago with their daughter. And who was the attorney who had represented Danzig's ex-wife in the case? None other than Gary Skoloff. Skoloff believed that his professional relationship with Danzig remained solid; nonetheless, he offered to find George another lawyer. George refused. He did not want his divorce to become a revenge case for Danzig, but more important, he did not want to lose perhaps the best lawyer in New Jersey.

George knew he had the best representation because at the same time he was checking out Danzig, he also was checking out Skoloff. While working on case strategy with his own attorney, George was simultaneously meeting with another prominent New York divorce lawyer, Harriet Cohen, who had been recommended by still another friend. Some days George would stop by Cohen's office to explain Skoloff's strategy and ask if she concurred. He considered her to be fair, a straightshooter who often spoke out on behalf of women in divorce. From this vantage point, certainly she would say if she thought George was being unreasonable or if Skoloff was not presenting his case appropriately.

"Look, I know Gary Skoloff," Cohen would say reassuringly in a soft, calming tone. "He's the best you can get in New Jersey. Don't worry. When he gets to the judge, you're a good candidate for joint custody." George always felt better when he left Cohen's office.

When Danzig took George's deposition he focused on his finances. Ingrid believed that George could afford more support and a larger financial settlement than the one laid out in the prenuptial agreement. George was fighting her on this, but he cared most of all about custody.

Skoloff, on the other hand, recommended against taking Ingrid's deposition. "What do we have to learn?" he asked George. There was nothing new on the financial issue. "If the deposition can't address custody, there's no sense in taking one from her." The point was that he did not want to attack Ingrid's ability to parent Alex. He did not want to take custody away from her, he only wanted her to share. "It will just be another expense, anyway," Skoloff added. George went along with his advice.

Nor did Skoloff depose any of Ingrid's witnesses, another decision that saved George money. "They're going to have to present their case first," he explained, "so we can learn then what they're going to say and respond later." As the plaintiff—that is, the spouse who had filed for the divorce—Ingrid had to argue her side first. George already had made lists of the people he thought she might call to testify in her favor, and he prepared notes for Skoloff on what these witnesses might say and how he might cross-examine them to show George in a more positive way.

Thus, instead of scurrying for information against Ingrid, George and Ginny collected evidence to support George's goals. As Skoloff had suggested, it was a positive approach, one that tried to build up George rather than to diminish his wife.

As for his own lay witnesses, George drew up a list of those who were well aware of his involvement with Alex on a day-to-day basis, people who knew him from Hunter Mountain and locally in New Jersey. He and Ginny typed each name on a separate piece of paper, with identifying characteristics, such as age and profession, followed by information each could offer as a witness in a trial.

So they would know what to expect, George briefed his witnesses on Danzig's courtroom manner as he had observed it. "He will throw out questions just to find out what kind of answer he will get," George would say. "He can phrase a question to sound like he knows the answer, just to get your reaction." George felt that his research paid off because when he took the stand himself, he would know exactly what kind of opponent he faced.

George and Ginny collected photographs, mounted in a simple scrapbook, to show the homes in which George and Alex lived, both in New Jersey and at Hunter Mountain, where George continued to vacation with his son. (By then he was allowed more flexibility during his time with Alex.) The lists of his witnesses and Ingrid's possible witnesses, along with all of the information about Ingrid he could gather—her employment record, previous domiciles, the baby-sitters she had hired—were placed in another book, a three-ring binder, with copies of everything made for Skoloff.

Under Skoloff's direction, George put together a second notebook as

well, complete with dividers and tabs, providing all of the information
he could about himself—a full description of his employment; a chro-
nological description of how he and Ingrid had cared for Alex while
he lived with them and how he cared for the child from then on; a
description of his home, the neighborhood, the schools, and nearby
recreation facilities; a list of neighboring children, complete with names
and ages; a description of Alex's relationship with his half-brother Steven and their activities together; George's views on problems related
to visitation; the schedule of his own activities with Alex on a daily
basis; a list and description of all of his relatives; pointers on why he
would be a good custodial parent for Alex; and even a list of Alex's
likes and dislikes. It would be hard to imagine any parent, anywhere,
compiling such a thorough assortment of information concerning his
child. Many nights George and Ginny (whose continued presence in
the home angered Ingrid) sat at their kitchen table for hours, trying to
think of more information they could gather, data they could collect
in order to help Skoloff win the joint custody case. Each page was
going to help George find his way.

In one section entitled "Good Relationships" he wrote down questions and then answered them:

> Would you encourage a good relationship with his mother?
> How?
>   Definitely. A child needs to interact with BOTH parents.
> I believe the relationship Alex has with his mother can com-
> plement and enhance the relationship he has with me and
> vice versa. What would I do to encourage this relationship?
> • Show enthusiasm for experiences he shares with her.
> • Allow him to have her picture in his room if he wishes.
> • Allow him to call her if he asks.
> • Buy cards and presents he can give her for special occa-
>   sions.
> • Work on my own relationship with her as Alex's
>   mother. Open the lines of communication so that my
>   approach with Alex does not undermine hers (particu-
>   larly in regard to discipline).
> • Make Alex aware that BOTH of us love him very much
>   and that his love for one of us does not detract from his
>   love for the other.
> • Go for family counseling.
> • I would not try to "top" Ingrid in the things we do with
>   Alex.
> • Make a special effort to inform Ingrid about Alex's life/
>   problems/behavior when he is with me.

Later George and Ginny would neatly type all his answers on a clean sheet for his notebook. For the moment, however, George couldn't think of any more ways to convince a court that he simply wanted to share his son. But if there were more, he would find them.

Ingrid objected to sharing her parenting with Ginny, and she expressed those objections in one of her pleadings filed in late 1982. "George told me," Ingrid wrote, "at the beginning of May, he had 'hired' a woman named Virginia to 'help' him care for Alex, i.e., do the cooking, cleaning, laundry, etc." Ingrid suspected this was "the same Virginia who had cared for Steven at the time of his separation from Barbara [George's first wife], and who is the only woman George's mother ever wanted George to marry."

> I have since learned through friends in Hunter, where they have been seen many times together *and with Alex,* that it is, in fact, the same woman. While I am totally aware of both George's and my right to a private life, at this time, I do *seriously* question the appropriateness of Virginia's essentially living with George during the time Alex is with him, and traveling with them to Hunter and Florida. It was, and is, my belief that at least in the beginning of a separation both parties have a moral obligation to their child to not upset or confuse the child more by allowing another "mate" to be present.

Skoloff acknowledged that George's relationship with Ginny could prove sticky should the case ever go to trial. Judges are supposed to make decisions about living arrangements and other moral issues based on how these behaviors actually affect the child, not on allegations about their effect or on whether the judge thinks such behaviors are morally correct. Still, many judges are prejudiced by their own upbringing and personal standards. If necessary, Skoloff was prepared to argue in court that in many respects Ginny was very good for Alex. She was an old friend of George, a friend of his family, and a teacher to boot. She had worked consistently since college and offered a role model few could reject. When George first separated from Ingrid, his mother was in the house a lot with George, Alex, and Ginny. But as the months passed on, it was Ginny who took over the mothering role.

Early in the case the court appointed a psychiatrist to interview both George and Ingrid to help determine their abilities to parent Alex. Each of them visited Dr. Allwyn Levine three times.

In his January 1982 report, Levine pointed out parental weaknesses on both sides: George had not been available consistently to his child; Ingrid needed to be more flexible. In fact, the psychiatrist wrote that George's and Ingrid's parenting styles stood in sharp contrast to each other, and Ingrid's extreme mothering even served to hamper the development of a close relationship between George and his son. Nonetheless, perhaps because Levine viewed Alex as more emotionally tied to Ingrid than to George, the doctor concluded by recommending that she be granted sole custody and that George be allowed visitation every other weekend—from Friday night through Sunday evening—and two weekdays a week, for four hours each day. Levine refused to support Ingrid's concern that she needed to be a chaperone whenever George was with Alex to prevent any negative impact from George's parenting.

After receiving this report, the judge wrote Skoloff a letter asking if he wanted to continue the case. To him it seemed all but over.

George was distraught. Even though Levine reportedly had told George that he did not believe in joint custody, he had hoped to convince him otherwise. Now it seemed as though George had failed his test. Recognizing the importance of such an opinion but unwilling to give up, he tried to think of another way to win the battle over expert advice. "I'm never giving in that easy," George told Skoloff. Many fathers would have been discouraged enough to turn away from a custody suit.

Eventually Skoloff petitioned the court for more opinions from different psychiatrists. But Danzig refused, suggesting instead that Ingrid and George go back to Dr. Levine for what would be a final edict. He probably counted on Levine being true to his earlier opinion.

But George saw this as a new passageway of hope. "I know a little bit about this now," he told Skoloff. "I'm going to hire another psychiatrist to teach me how to prepare myself for Levine."

And he did just that, making an appointment with a female doctor who spent hours talking with him about the case and how he could help himself. Together they practiced how George should answer Levine's questions and how he should discuss his hopes for joint custody. The second psychiatrist pointed out the subjects George discussed best, those he handled less adeptly, and those he should stay away from for fear of making a bad impression. "Talk a lot about Alex," the new psychiatrist suggested. "You make a good impression when you're talking about your son."

She gave George some firm rules: Don't contradict Dr. Levine. Don't battle with him on any subject. Don't attack Ingrid. And don't second-guess what Dr. Levine might say. George made some notes on scrap paper in his pocket. He had been guilty of some of these errors in earlier interviews with the court's psychiatrist.

The second doctor also warned him to watch his tone of voice so that he would not appear hostile. "It might even be a good idea to admit that you are nervous about the interview," she added. A little humility would serve George well when confronting a specialist who clearly was used to being in control.

"Above all," she told George, "try to relax." George smiled. He realized that before he had come off as an angry, anxious man. This time would be different.

George's final visit with Dr. Levine took place more than a year after their initial encounter, allowing ample time for George to prepare and to solidify his parenting skills with Alex. His efforts paid off. Levine wrote Danzig a letter that had to have shocked him. Skoloff, who received a copy of the letter, could hardly believe it himself.

The letter began with an explanation that Levine had interviewed George again on April 4, 1983. As a result of that meeting, the doctor explained, he wanted to amend his initial report. The letter was two pages, single-spaced.

George, wrote Levine, was far more relaxed and comfortable in the most recent meeting. It obviously had helped George make a better impression, for Levine said that George's arguments for joint custody now seemed sensible and he had faith both in George's ability to make the appropriate arrangements as well as in his sincerity for wanting to do so.

The psychiatrist went on in his letter to point out why he thought a joint custody arrangement for Alex could work after all. First, he said, George had a flexible work schedule, and it appeared that he would be in control of his workdays and hours for an indefinite period of time. Second, Levine was impressed with George's commitment to Alex, as evidenced through his willingness to move closer to Ingrid's new home. And finally, Levine noted that George was most interested in doing what was best for his son.

Skoloff reached for the phone to call George. He had to hand it to his client. George was a very dedicated man. "I don't know how you pulled this off," Skoloff joked when George answered the phone.

"Get a check out this morning to that psychiatrist before he changes his mind!" George laughed.

Levine was not George's only challenge. Some three months after beginning his campaign for joint custody, he faced a completely different kind of problem.

From December 1981, when he and Ingrid separated, until the following April, George had missed only one of the visitations allotted him. He had kept a diary of his activities and Ingrid's reactions to every visit, and a calendar with a record of the number of hours he and Alex had spent together. Even though the visitation routine was unpleasant because of Ingrid, George was determined to live up to his commitment.

But in April 1982, the shared parenting became even more stressful for George. Ingrid moved. She left Bergen County for Morris County, about fifty miles away because she wanted to be nearer her mother, who worked as a companion to a wealthy elderly woman and lived in the woman's house.

George asked the court to stop the move because the added distance would make his visitations with Alex so much more difficult, but the judge ruled that he had no legal right to prevent Ingrid from relocating anywhere in the state. George grew increasingly frustrated—he had rearranged his working hours at the restaurant to fit the visitation schedule. The extra time would make his days all the more difficult.

Eventually he decided to follow Ingrid, but the opportunity to do so did not arise for nearly a year. One night when George and Ginny were at a party at an old friend's house in Staten Island, George bumped into his friend's brother, who, it turned out, also was going through a divorce.

"I'm just trying to sell my house," the friend explained over their drinks. The proceeds from the sale were going to be split.

"Where is your house?" inquired George.

"It's in Gladstone," the man replied. Gladstone was in the county adjoining Morris County, where Ingrid had moved. The house was even on the same road as Ingrid's, less than two miles away.

"The house is empty?" George inquired excitedly.

"Yea," he replied.

"Can I rent it until you sell it?" George asked on the spot. Soon he and Ginny moved in, and eventually they would buy the house.

But by then one of the Bergen County judges had ended George's every-other-day sharing arrangement for Alex's custody, giving Ingrid full custody pending a final resolution of their case. George was left with visitation rights three weekends a month.

He pleaded with the court: "The most important thing of all is for the court to understand that my rapport and relationship with Alex is one hundred percent. We are very close friends, we are good companions, we have a terrific time engaging in both play and the beginning of sports; we go together hiking, boating, trips to Hunter Mountain, swimming . . . I am perfectly capable of feeding Alex, clothing Alex, taking care of his medical needs. He looks

forward to being with me, playing with me, doing things with me."
Alex was a rugged kid, big for his age, a boy who could enjoy a
good time outdoors with his dad.

"I believe that the combination of alternating weeks between his
mother and myself will give him the best shot at developing into a
well-rounded healthy and happy child. I don't want to be a baby-sitter,
visiting father or counselor. I want to be the real father that Alex deserves and I can put real input into his daily life for our mutual better-
ment and satisfaction."

How could the court doubt George's sincerity? "I carried out the
joint custody [every-other-day] arrangement for the period of time while
my wife lived in Bergen County, and I actually carried it out for six
months when she threw the most horrendous of all barriers at me, an
extra hundred mile round-trip."

While pleading his case, George continued his research into the
court system, focusing on the judge in Bergen County he believed
would preside over his future. He studied the files of other custody cases
Superior Court Judge Harvey Sorkow had heard and tracked down the
fathers to see how they felt they had been treated. He was able to
locate a few. "I feel a little more confident now in this judge," George
told Skoloff later.

Of course, Skoloff already knew all of the judges in Bergen County,
and he agreed with George's conclusions. "I am very confident that
this is a guy who will really consider a real joint custody once he knows
that you are serious," said the attorney.

"But Ingrid has temporary custody," countered George as he started
pacing the room, staring out the window of Skoloff's Newark office
building. "And I know as well as you know that judges hate to change
kids around, so he'll say, Leave Alex where he is."

The temporary custody trap is one with which many fathers are familiar, a step in the divorce process and custody determination that
can, in advance, sound a death knell.

Little did George know that Ingrid's temporary custody of Alex
actually would help him argue his side of the case. What happened
was that it made him so angry to think that he had lost Alex even
before beginning to plead his cause that he fought for him harder
than ever before. I'm going to fight like a bull to turn this around,
George told himself as he left his lawyer's office. I hope they don't
do a lick of work because they're so damned confident now that
they'll win.

•   •   •

"Gary," said George during one of their morning consultations, "suggest to the judge that during the first months of joint custody Ingrid and I meet weekly with a psychologist to discuss our situation."

Skoloff willingly agreed. "Let's see what happens," he said about the idea. "I'll write the judge a letter."

"It's one more log we can throw on the fire," added George. "Maybe one of these ideas will hit." He was still trying to find ways to convince the court of his sincerity about parenting Alex.

A few days later Skoloff announced that the judge loved the idea.

An imminent trial, says Skoloff, "brings everybody as close to reasonableness as they ever get. If your case doesn't settle then, everybody has to accept the fact that it can never be."

He, like many divorce lawyers, much prefers settlement over trial because the final outcome is one that the two parties have worked out and agreed to accept. Their chances of abiding by it, and of resolving subsequent difficulties, are much greater than if a resolution is imposed on them. Few people can turn off the hostility that builds so strongly during the days of preparation for trial and then simply accept a judge's pronouncement with total equanimity, says Skoloff. So when a settlement offer is reasonable, he tries to talk clients into accepting it. In the Nicholases' divorce George had hoped to settle by convincing Ingrid that they could work together on Alex's behalf; like his lawyer, George also wanted to avoid the hate-filled courtroom trial.

But without any settlement, the big day suddenly arrives—a judge says, "You're up next. We're going to start the trial. You've been talking settlement for two years. Now you've got sixty minutes before I begin, and if you don't make it now, we're ready to go."

"This is when everybody gets to the final moment," Skoloff warns, "when they're going to put their case in the hands of a judge who can *never* know what the two people and their lawyers know, simply because the judge can never have the time" to listen and learn all the facts.

On April 26, 1983, George Nicholas sensed that for him, the moment had arrived. This was it. He was going to trial. He knew that a judge would decide his fate shortly, and that of four-year-old Alex, and the judge might decide it in a way George didn't want. After all of his detective work, his planning, his preparation, and his more than two dozen meetings with Skoloff, George's goal still was beyond his reach and his success uncertain.

He knew that he was well prepared. He knew that Skoloff was enormously respected in the courtroom. "Some lawyers, the judges could care less if they ever show up in their courtroom," George had told Ginny a few days earlier, "and they don't believe a word they say. Some lawyers, they believe everything they say because they have a record of being legitimate. And Gary has a heck of a record in the courts. Judges will take notice of what he says."

Even at this eleventh hour, Skoloff still held out hope that George and Ingrid would negotiate the economic aspects of their case—alimony, child support, equitable distribution of their assets—and he counseled George to offer Ingrid more money. "What you don't give her, you're going to give me if you go to trial," he explained. But Skoloff had absolutely no hope that they could settle on the custody issue. "After two years, I'm convinced she'll never agree to real joint custody," the attorney adamantly insisted. George and Ingrid were headed for trial, he knew, at least on the issue about which George cared the very most—*true* joint custody, joint *physical* custody of Alex. Skoloff estimated that they would need five days. Their witness list—expert and lay witnesses who would testify on George's behalf—was lengthy.

But by then they were ready. Lawyer and client were working like a team, a smooth machine, moving forward in exact synchronization. Skoloff would ask for information; George would supply it. And then George would try to quiz Skoloff, as only he would dare, to make sure the lawyer actually read what he had given him. He always had. The time had come.

When they arrived at the courthouse, Judge Robert Hamer, who was to hear the case, was not ready for them. Because New Jersey followed a system providing that any available judge could hear a motion or preside at a trial, four judges in all, including Judge Sorkow, whom George had thought would be deciding his case, had issued rulings or been involved in the Nicholases' case in some way by the time it reached trial. Hamer was the fourth. When he finally was ready and was told that George and Ingrid could not agree, he dove directly into the heart of the matter.

"Why shouldn't Mr. Nicholas have joint custody?" the judge asked.

"Because the mother and father do not agree on how the child should be raised," replied Danzig, Ingrid's attorney.

"Well, my wife and I don't agree on how our children should be raised," the judge announced. "That's not enough reason."

With Hamer's reply, Skoloff hoped that Danzig might sense that the custody fight was not going in his direction. Raising children is an issue parents never agree on, Skoloff would say later, recalling the judge's comment in George's case. "One parent is always stricter than the other. What happens if a couple is in court and the wife says the child got a B [on his report card], so he can't have a bike, and the husband says a B is a good grade, and he can have the bike. And they want the judge to decide this? These are the kinds of things that parents never agree on!" Still, Danzig gave no clue that he was starting to cave.

What happened next could not have shocked Skoloff more: Ingrid announced, before testimony could even begin, that she was willing to share custody of Alex with George. In return, she wanted more money. "OK," said George grudgingly.

Ingrid agreed to the joint custody because she realized she had no other choice. Danzig, she says, convinced her that George had taken so many steps to make joint custody work, including moving and re-arranging his work schedule, that "no judge in the country would deny him joint custody." If George had been a more typical father with a more typical life-style and work schedule, the case might have gone differently, the lawyer explained.

In the end, under his settlement with Ingrid, George would have 50 percent joint legal and joint physical custody of Alex. The physical sharing would occur through a phase-in process, but it would not take long—George would keep Alex two weekends in a row, and then on alternating weeks he would increase his time with Alex from four to five to six days. After that he and Ingrid would each have Alex on a seven-day rotating basis.

At the same time they agreed to another step that would help guarantee their joint custody success: together they would select a psychologist to help monitor their arrangement for the first six months. George would pay 75 percent of the cost not covered by insurance and Ingrid would pay the remaining 25 percent. If the psychologist decided that the shared custody arrangement was not working out, the court would be contacted immediately.

George was convinced that that never would be necessary. His years of hard work had paid off and he wasn't going to let any future disagreements or arguments endanger his relationship with Alex now. He was determined to make the joint custody work. He would pay three hundred dollars a month in child support, provide Alex's Blue Cross and Blue Shield health insurance coverage, pay all other medical, dental, and drug expenses, buy Alex's clothing, pay nursery school costs, and maintain a twenty-five-thousand-dollar life insurance policy with Alex as beneficiary. George also agreed that should he die before Alex turned eighteen, Alex would receive 25 percent of his father's estate. Over the years, George consistently would comply with all of his financial obligations and more. In this regard Alex was a fortunate child. Roughly half of all fathers ordered to pay child support under any visitation or custody arrangement do not pay at all, and of the half who do, 50 percent do not pay the full amount.

Finally, George and Ingrid agreed to live in the same or neighboring counties (specifically, Morris or Somerset counties in New Jersey), close enough to each other to guarantee that the arrangement for sharing Alex could be carried out easily. Neither could move without the permission of the other or, in its place, a court order.

George remained convinced it was the original prediction of his slim chances for winning true joint custody that had led him to the victory he wanted so badly. "I don't think Danzig did as much work on custody as he might have because he thought they were going to win," he told Ginny, a wide grin covering his face.

George paid a price, however. In lieu of his prenuptial agreement, he agreed to give Ingrid a total of $32,500—alimony of $10,000 for one year in equal monthly installments followed by $5,000 for a second year, plus another lump sum of $7,500; and as equitable distribution, $10,000, $5,000 immediately and $5,000, with 10 percent interest, one year later.

"Congratulations," said Skoloff as he shook George and Ginny's hands in the courthouse hallway. He, too, was pleased because he had thought that joint custody would never be successful for George—or, especially, Alex—if Ingrid did not willingly agree to the arrangement. But already the attorney was looking ahead. While his client was ecstatic with the custody settlement, he could see that George also was nervous about putting the plan into action. Ingrid still wasn't George's favorite person to be with or talk to, but he would have to make her part of his life routine.

Skoloff sensed his apprehension. "In twenty years," he warned, "you and Ingrid are going to be at Alex's wedding. So you'd better start getting along."

He knew that in too many cases the tension from a divorce carries over to all of the major events of a child's life. He tries to head this off, attempting instead to set a different tone for future parental dealings. Otherwise, he says sadly, "it destroys a kid."

While Alex was young, Ingrid and George used a shared driving plan: on a given Friday, Ingrid would drive the child to George's house, and on the following Friday, George would drive him back to his

mother's. In this way Alex could never sense that one parent had come
to take him away from the other; rather, the parent with whom he
resided during one week would willingly drive him *to* the other parent
for the following week.

When Alex reached school age he simply took the school bus home
to his mother's house or his father's, according to the schedule. George
and Ingrid continued to live in the same school district, a requirement
for implementing the joint custody arrangement they finally had negotiated.

As George had suggested, he and Ingrid met weekly with the psychologist they had selected during the first few months of their joint
custody arrangement. The sessions were so successful that George cred-
its them today with making the shared parenting arrangement work.

"He took the sting out of it," says George. "I would go to a session
and say, She did this, or she did that, and Ingrid would say something
just as idiotic, like 'He did this, or he did that,' and the psychologist
would say, 'Don't you two hear each other?'"

The psychologist, who was also an Irish Catholic priest, made simple
suggestions to help George and Ingrid resolve their sticky points, and
both tended to go along with him. "He has the right—it's in the court
order—to change the custody if he doesn't think either of us is trying,"
George told Ginny. "That scares the hell out of me." The priest regularly criticized both parents when he thought they weren't trying hard
enough for Alex's sake.

After several months George and Ingrid found that they could talk
with each other about Alex, and they even decided that they could
work out their parenting problems by themselves. The counseling sessions stopped. They had come a long way since the hostile days of the
custody fight. They weren't friends—for instance, they had bickered
some after the settlement about Ingrid's remaining bills and the return
of individual property—but they were coparents. Slowly but surely they
began to prove that at this task they could be successful.

Today Alex is twelve years old and he has been living under the
original every-other-week arrangement for more than eight years.
George and Ginny continue to live together (they've never married)
and Ginny continues to help with Alex. George's older son, Steven,
is a student at Cornell, which, George jokes, "is more expensive than
Gary Skoloff."

On holidays George, Ginny, Ingrid, and Alex may share a meal at
one house or the other, and they have all attended Alex's celebrations
and special childhood events together. Ingrid has never remarried.

"It can get sticky sometimes," says Ginny of their joint activities,
"but we do it."

George nods in agreement. "I have to accept that because of Alex, Ingrid is going to be in my life forever."

While Ingrid readily acknowledges that she doesn't think she and George "have ever gotten along better than right now," her acceptance of their shared parenting is still rife with reservations. She is, she says, concerned about "the long run."

"What are the long-range ramifications of this type of arrangement?" Ingrid asks. "Is Alex going to be all right? Or is this schizophrenic lifestyle going to have long-range repercussions no one knows about yet?" She claims that her son is still "torn over the back and forth."

And to this day Ingrid, who recently completed a master's degree and plans to become certified in elementary education, questions George's parenting skills. "On a day-to-day basis, even when two parents live in the same town, even when the child goes to the same school, the [consistency] of the input, the time spent on studies and academic skills, depends on the educational match of the two parents," she says, clearly implying that she and George are poorly matched.

But George is satisfied that Alex is doing well. Based on the boy's report card, at least, it appears that his mother's fears are unjustified. It's covered with A's and B's, and even an A-plus or two.

The question remains, however, as to whether Alex himself can continue comfortably in this split arrangement through adolescence. The National Council for Children's Rights reported from a survey of twelve hundred children whose parents were divorcing that 90 percent under the age of eight had a strong desire to live with both parents, while "76 percent between the ages of 8 and 10, 44 percent between the ages of 10 and 12, and only 20 percent between the ages of 13 and 16 wished to live with both parents." Adds the council: "Most studies which show joint custody children to have better adjustment than their sole custody counterparts . . . focus on younger children." Still, few if any studies reveal how children who began living in a joint custody situation while quite young respond after reaching their teenage years.

After he won his case, George tried to help other fathers in similar circumstances. "I'm not the only one hanging out in corridors of courthouses," he told Ginny one day. Other fathers, too, needed to know how to apply pressure through the legal system to protect their rights. George had long believed that mothers seeking custody had a leg up on fathers, but if the mothers' lawyers were overconfident and didn't work very hard as a result, and the fathers committed themselves, then maybe they, like him, could break through to victory, whether that meant a good visitation schedule or joint custody.

"Visitation. I hate that word," says George today. "Why should a father have to 'visit' his own child? But I'm not against the idea behind it, because I tell fathers that they can make a good part-time father arrangement into a pretty good deal.

"I tell them, 'You can be a hero every weekend. You don't have to discipline, tell them to do this or that. The kids can't wait for that time when you're coming—that's good time. What's Mom doing? She's stuffing spinach down their throats and making them go to school.'" Some, like him, however, still prefer to share all aspects of parenting, although George knows of no other father who has joint custody of his child a full 50 percent of the time.

Yet he thinks that today, arguments for joint custody are stronger than ever. "A lot of the wives work full time, too," he reasons. "They can work it out. There are arrangements."

"I've helped dozens of fathers since I got involved in my case," he notes when describing his recent activities in fathers' rights support groups, helping other men try to protect their relationships with their children, either through a custodial arrangement or an enforced visitation schedule.

But he is not always successful. "I can't get them to do what I did," he explains. "They say, 'My lawyer didn't do anything,' and I say, 'But what did *you* do?'" It seems that although divorce is one of the most important events in a person's life, many are too paralyzed to take any steps to help themselves.

"They don't do anything that really helps the lawyer," agrees Skoloff. "They just talk about it all the time, but they don't take any action. They just ramble and mumble, but they don't get into whatever has to be done to get it put together." Other lawyers—and therapists—have noticed the same response, he adds. "It's got to be a psychological impediment. It's like a contradiction within themselves" when a client has a major battle going on in his life but won't fight for himself. Skoloff speculates that the pain of the divorce may cause client paralysis. But he doesn't really know.

George and Ginny found that George's intense involvement in the preparation of his own case was therapeutic. "It helps to be doing something," George advises other fathers, rather than just waiting for some greater power to make decisions that affect the rest of their lives.

But George thinks that Skoloff is unusual in his willingness to form a team with his clients. "Gary really works well with his client," says George. "Most of the lawyers I've found are very pushy and bossy. In some instances I've tried to go with a father I'm helping to visit his lawyer to kick ideas around like I did with Gary. But you can't do that with ninety-five percent of the lawyers. They want it done their way."

It was clear that the lawyers George met through his fathers' rights activities resented outside interference. But then, most lawyers are not used to being told by an outsider what they might do to win a case.

Through the fathers' rights group George and Ginny befriended a number of men, inviting them to their home for dinner and offering moral support. But George's volunteer activities have lessened recently, partly out of frustration over fathers' unwillingness to help themselves. "I think I burned myself out," he says.

Skoloff still expresses amazement over George's case. "The bottom line on this, which is beyond my comprehension, that I would have bet everything I had [would not have happened], is that *we have never gone back to court once.* He has never needed me as a lawyer since we finished the case. In the friendliest situations, at least once a couple of years later we go back to court," the attorney explains, shaking his head in disbelief.

He notes that George has not had to pay him a cent since the case was over, unlike most of Skoloff's other custody clients, who fight recurring battles. In all, George paid him $19,550, which, says Skoloff, was "a steal," considering the result. But the reason George's case cost less than most hotly contested custody suits was because he had done so much of the work—information gathering, preparation of witness lists, planning of strategy, preparation of testimony. "George was a guy who always took the next step," reiterates Skoloff. "Whatever it was, we'd talk about it and he'd work it up. I was never so well prepared to try a custody case."

"I had a gun," Skoloff likes to say, "and George kept filling it with bullets. He was a client who did his share of the work and more. There are many clients who call all the time, bitching, but never do step one." Other clients—in divorces everywhere—would do well to note Skoloff's observations.

Despite his enthusiasm for George as a client, Skoloff remains convinced that his reservations about joint custody are well founded. In fact, shortly after George and Ingrid settled, Skoloff published an article in *Trial* magazine arguing against imposed joint custody. Both parents must be in favor of the shared route, he insisted. "What they can do to their kids, in the continuous shuffling back and forth, when [the parents] hate it, and they want to jab [at each other], after a while the kids are totally wrecked. [The children are] forever delivering bad messages, they carry soiled clothes back and forth, and the parents are forever back in court." Because communication between the parents is sanctioned by the joint custody, and because angry parents, who are only human, cannot easily suspend their animosity, the battles may never end. A sizeable group of experts now agree with this assessment of joint custody ordered by a court without the parents' full agreement.

In fact, joint custody, and the imposition of this arrangement on divorcing couples, is less in vogue among legislators and judges than it was just a few years ago. Australia, which became the first country to allow judicial imposition of joint custody, later became the first to forbid it unless the two parties agreed.

Of course, both parents' full support for joint custody still creates the ideal situation. "A divorce does not [in itself] harm children," says Skoloff. "It's a trauma, but there's no permanent harm from it. It's when two spouses hate each other more than they love their kids, that's where the child gets destroyed. If they work together—the kids know both parents love them, they know that both parents will take care of them, and the parents handle themselves in a civilized manner—those kids come out OK."

Granted, Skoloff's prescription for taking children through divorce unscarred is a tough one to follow given the emotions and hostilities that plague the process. But whether a couple provides for their children through joint custody, visitation, or any other plan for postdivorce parenting, keeping the welfare of the children in mind is vital.

3

EQUITABLE DISTRIBUTION: WHO OWNS WHAT?

Felice Dubin v. Paul Dubin

A key player in divorce is the accountant.

—ATTORNEY MELVYN FRUMKES

MIAMI

Once upon a time when a couple divorced, the man routinely provided for his former wife with monthly payments called "alimony." He remained the breadwinner even after the marriage dissolved, and, to whatever extent possible, the woman kept her standard of living. This arrangement was rooted in legal doctrines born centuries ago, when a woman lost her financial identity and the right to manage her own affairs upon marrying. She became the legal dependent of her husband, who kept all marital assets in his name alone. If the marriage ended in divorce, alimony was considered fair compensation for her loss and her need for support.

Alimony also was necessary because until recently most women did not enjoy equal access to the workplace, nor did they have the skills needed to support themselves. Moreover, in the traditional family, women devoted their days to child rearing.

Partly in response to the women's movement of the 1970s, state legislatures have revamped the rules of divorce, property ownership, and financial support after divorce. We entered the era of no-fault reform, in which the requirement that a couple have grounds for divorce, such as adultery or cruelty, was removed. The states also began to dictate that all assets acquired during a marriage belonged to the couple jointly, even if the woman was a homemaker and even if the man held the property in his name alone. In such cases, the wife's efforts were said to have supported her husband in acquiring those assets. State legislatures further decided that all marital assets should be divided "equally" (in community property states) or "equitably" (in equitable distribution states, which, unlike community property states, consider factors such as need). In either kind of jurisdiction both spouses would leave the marriage with assets of their own.

While the states were rewriting their divorce laws, women also began to acquire work skills and job experience, enabling them to provide for their own long-term financial support. As a result of both trends, the first in state government and the second in the workplace, more women today have both property and earned income following divorce. Thus, the requirement for alimony—now called "maintenance"—has lessened considerably. Of course, there are still cases in which the wife, often an older woman, is not employable or does not have sufficient assets to guarantee a secure life-style following the divorce.

Whether women now feel that they are treated fairly during divorce remains a source of controversy nationwide. Miami attorney Melvyn Frumkes says that despite the law's new attempt to be just, women in Florida generally have received less than half of the marital assets in their divorces. But Frumkes has developed into a science the ability to win an equitable distribution of assets for his clients. Many of the women he represents do win their fair share.

When Felice Dubin walked into Frumkes' office in December 1988 and told the attorney her story, he concluded that she was a client who deserved *more* than half. Felice not only filled the traditional role of housewife and mother, but she also worked full time with her husband Paul to found a highly successful children's clothing manufacturing business. And when Paul became ill for several months, she ran the company.

But Paul Dubin was a traditional man who would argue that Felice only assisted him in the business and that without him, she would have little to show for herself. Paul had indeed introduced Felice to the garment industry. She admitted this. But in her discussions with Frumkes it became clear that Paul was the one who might not have been successful without *Felice's* help. Frumkes became determined to win for his client at least the fair half of her marriage's rewards.

Felice agreed with her lawyer's goal, but at the same time she refused to destroy the amicable relationship she maintained with Paul, especially when it came to parenting their three children. The legal fight over ownership of their business and personal assets would be a tough one, but despite the divorce, the personal ties the Dubins had built would stay strong. In this regard they were an unusual couple, one that confined divorce warfare to lawyers' offices and the court without contaminating their children and their home.

As one of the leading divorce lawyers in the country, Miami's sixty-two-year-old Melvyn Frumkes is no stranger to acrimony. In thirty-seven years of practice he has almost gotten used to the tears, the bitterness, the name-calling, the angry attacks that mark the dissolution of many marriages. The nation's moviegoers might have been surprised by the ferocious divorce battling between Oliver and Barbara Rose (Michael Douglas and Kathleen Turner) in the hit movie *The War of the Roses*, but lawyers like Frumkes know that such hostilities and destructive antics are not all that far from reality. So Frumkes was pleasantly surprised and pleased when he met Felice Dubin. She wanted a divorce, but she displayed none of the rancor that added a wrenching dimension to so many of his cases.

Felice, thirty-nine, sought out Frumkes after she and her husband Paul had been separated for a year. Her hesitation in taking the final step of visiting a lawyer was not atypical. Breaking up any relationship is a disappointment, even if it does not involve a marriage, and Felice simply felt that she was "in no rush" to end the long-term marriage that had provided structure for her life. For awhile she was content simply to live apart, taking time to analyze her feelings.

Eventually, when she did decide to forge ahead, she began to check out lawyers' reputations. "I want the very best," she flatly told Frumkes during her first meeting in his office. Her friends had warned that he was expensive, but she didn't care. You get what you pay for, she felt.

Frumkes knows divorce firsthand. A veteran of two broken marriages, he became a single parent after the first divorce, raising three children, then ages twelve, six, and three. Frumkes understands the stresses and hardships that clients face every day. "I've had aggravation and heartache and I know some of the problems people go through," he says. It makes him a better divorce lawyer, and his years as a single parent have given him greater sensitivity when it comes to custody and visitation issues. Frumkes has written and lectured widely on his area of expertise. Today he is married to a divorce attorney, his third wife, forty-seven-year-old Marsha Elser, the first woman president of the prestigious American Academy of Matrimonial Lawyers.

Melvyn Frumkes' reputation extends well beyond his home state of Florida. Like all of the best-known divorce attorneys, his high profile and high fees were earned through years of hard work. He has represented such clients as Roxanne Pulitzer, former wife of the newspaper magnate, and the former wife of Freddie Laker, the British airline entrepreneur. The lawyer also represented Saudi Sheika Dena al-Fassi when her husband took their four children to the Bahamas; the Bahamian courts awarded him custody, but Frumkes had the decision ruled invalid in the Florida District Court of Appeals.

Felice had gone right to the top for her divorce, and she was prepared to pay. Frumkes asked for a fifteen-thousand-dollar retainer, half of it an "engagement fee"—payment made simply for taking the case—and the other half to fund a trust account that would be Frumkes' protection against unpaid bills along the way. Once all bills were paid at the end of the case, he said, he would refund the second seventy-five hundred dollars. His hourly rate: $260. Later it would go up to $300. Frumkes also told Felice that sometimes when he gets a "good result," he asks a client for a bonus, a kicker payment, at the end of the case.

"You have to be sure you want to get a divorce," he announced after explaining his fee structure, "and I don't think you're sure." Felice listened intently.

"I know I'm ready," she responded.

She may have seemed unsure to Frumkes because she still loved Paul—and she would keep loving him for a long time—but she finally had accepted that their future as a couple was over. It was time to move ahead on her own.

Frumkes handed her a thick questionnaire to complete before their next meeting. It was an imposing document typed on twenty-five legal pages with one hundred questions in all, ranging from basic inquiries about marital history to questions about homes, cars, bank accounts, and credit cards and requests for detailed descriptions about health, habits, and hobbies. The questionnaire would help Frumkes learn about the Dubins' life-style, both individually and as a couple, and about their income, assets, and expenses.

The financial scrutiny Frumkes undertakes is particularly intense. He also provides clients with a hefty, thirty-four-page Financial Information Worksheet. The opening paragraph says,

> The purpose of this worksheet is to enable you to provide to us sufficient information to prepare required financial affidavits for the Court. Please fill out the form below in as much detail as possible. . . . We must know more than what you are spending at this moment. We want to be able to reflect what it will cost as if you are spending to maintain yourself as you did when your marriage was intact, whether or not you can presently afford it.

To Felice, the assignment seemed overwhelming. Frumkes' worksheet asked for information ranging from the cost of her children's birthday parties to installment payments for home improvements, from the value of loans against insurance policies to documentation on the Dubins' retirement plans and savings. "Remember this is a worksheet and the information you give to us will be kept confidential," the document announced in boldface italics. The information was so confidential that even after the divorce, Felice agreed to be interviewed about her case only if dollar amounts associated with it would not be published along with her story. Suffice it to say, however, that her assets were substantial. She had good reason to seek the best lawyer she could find.

Frumkes believes that some of the most important papers in his cases are the financial affidavits, detailed declarations he provides the court on a client's behalf. "We must work on these very carefully," he told Felice when giving her the financial worksheet in preparation for the affidavits. "We have to set up your needs and recommend an asset distribution." Invariably, says Frumkes, clients have trouble providing all of the information the forms require, so either he or an accountant helping with the case will work through the process with them.

After six months of gathering data and calculating the value of the Dubins' assets and Felice's living costs, Frumkes filed her divorce petition on June 19, 1989.

> The wife has made a substantial contribution to the marriage inasmuch as she helped start the various business enterprises in which the parties are involved and has worked side by side with the husband in order to develop the businesses into the successful operations that they are today. In addition, she has also provided for the care and raising of the minor children of the parties and maintained the former marital residence. Furthermore, after the Husband was taken ill, the Wife, in addition to caring for the children and the household, assumed full responsibility for operating and managing the family business. The contributions of the Wife are those of a truly equal marital partner and entitle the Wife to an equitable distribution of the marital assets.

To clarify his view of an "equitable" distribution, Frumkes also would file a pretrial memorandum setting out all of the facts in Felice's case, and he would introduce into the court record an extensive, exhaustive financial affidavit detailing her monetary needs. They were notable. Felice and Paul Dubin had led a good life, with a fancy home, expensive cars, and deluxe vacations. They had worked together to afford that life together, and now Felice wanted the same chance as Paul to continue living in the style they both enjoyed.

They met through a mutual friend in 1971, when Felice was a clerical worker at a Miami investment firm. One day Felice was visiting her friend, who lived in the apartment next to Paul's, and Paul stopped by to say hello. He was struck by the freckled, brown-eyed blond dancing to lively music in the living room, and he asked Felice for a date. Felice was shy, though, and for the first few weeks during the courtship, she asked the friend to go along, too.

"Why do you want me?" the friend would inquire, both amused and annoyed.

"I've lived in Colombia," Felice replied, referring to childhood years in South America, where she and her parents had made their home. "You just don't go out alone in the beginning."

Her self-protective posture soon gave way, however. Felice, twenty-three, and Paul, thirty-five, were married in Miami only months later, on March 31, 1972. Later Felice would recall that it was she who had proposed marriage. "Someone had to do it," she would laugh, her shyness disappearing as she talks. Paul, a tall man whose dark looks contrasted with Felice's blondness, had been married and divorced before, and he had a son, eleven, and a daughter, thirteen, from that earlier marriage. With Felice he would be starting a family all over again. Their age difference was never a problem, for Felice liked mature men.

Even before the marriage she melded her life into Paul's, quitting her clerical job and helping him open a small garment contracting plant called P & F (the couple's first initials), in which articles of clothing were sewn for other manufacturers. Paul's father had always worked in the garment industry, as had Paul for eight years, and he wanted to be a clothing manufacturer himself. And because Felice had worked in her parents' jewelry factory and their jewelry stores in Colombia, the notion of establishing a business seemed natural to her.

Initially, to maintain a steady income, Paul continued working for his father's firm while Felice managed their new company, P & F. Paul hired a woman who knew the industry to handle quality control; she watched over the P & F workers seated at the row of nine sewing machines that the Dubins had set up in a rented loft, and eventually the woman taught Felice to supervise the workers herself. Paul handled sales. It was a modest beginning.

While the heart of the garment industry traditionally is considered to be New York City, Miami hosts its own share of manufacturers, those like the Dubins, who set up shop in an environment that may be less cutthroat than that of the garment trade on Manhattan's Seventh Avenue. Paul and Felice started small by contracting with larger manufacturers to make clothing orders they already had received. These firms would bring or ship the cutwork (the cut-out pieces of clothing before they're sewn together) to P & F, the Dubins' employees would sew the pieces, and then the Dubins would return the finished clothing to the original manufacturer. The manufacturer would then ship the clothing to the various stores that had placed orders. Essentially Paul and Felice sold labor as part of the manufacturing process.

Though the garment industry was foreign to Felice, she worked hard alongside her husband to learn the ropes of her new occupation. "I don't know how to sew a button, let alone tell the difference between a sleeve and a leg," she told Paul when they first began. "To me, the pieces all look the same." But she was a very fast learner. Within months she was doing everything on site—keeping the books, handling the payroll, paying the taxes, signing checks, sorting, shipping. She even sewed buttons and buttonholes—although she didn't do any major sewing jobs. She and Paul sometimes fought, but Felice shrugged off the arguments, attributing them to the stress and strain involved in running a new business.

Despite this early history together, Felice would recall later that Paul did not want his wife to work permanently. He was a traditional man who believed that a husband and father should provide for his family, the old-fashioned way. But because Felice had grown up with two working parents, she thought that the best marriage would be one like her parents', in which both husband and wife dedicated themselves to a common interest. What's more, Felice loved to work. Paul tried to accept her enthusiasm. Or so Felice thought at the time.

Slowly but surely they developed their clothing contracting business with dreams of one day manufacturing and marketing their own design labels. In 1975 they changed the P & F name to M & J, Inc., this time standing for the Dubins' two daughters, Michelle, born in August 1973, and Jennifer, born in February 1975. At the same time, the company also moved to a better location.

In 1976 Paul, Felice, and a friend fulfilled their goal of manufacturing their own line of children's clothing, called Sunshine Girls of Florida. But the friend left about a year later, leaving the Dubins to complete unfilled orders by themselves. They succeeded and continued to grow. Paul bought out his father's business and formed Jennelle, Inc., to serve as the corporate umbrella for their own garment businesses, including the Sunshine Girls line of children's apparel and the contracting firm M & J. The Dubins also purchased two buildings in Hialeah, a manufacturing district in sprawling Dade County where they previously had leased space. They formed another entity—Dubin Rentals—to own the property. Dubin Rentals met its mortgage payments with rents paid by Jennelle and other outside tenants.

During the time of this latest success, however, something began to change in the way Paul and Felice worked together and in Paul's attitude toward Felice. Throughout their past business expansion they had done everything in tandem. Felice had taken only two weeks' leave when each of their daughters was born, and she frequently brought them in with her to work on the weekends. She also ran the household and took care of Paul's personal needs, operating somewhat like the classic "supermom," although she did have a live-in maid. Felice bought Paul's clothes and coordinated his outfits, offering him advice on the latest men's fashions. When she gave birth to their third child, Jason, in August 1980, she again returned to work after two weeks' time. Yet despite this history, Paul abruptly insisted on top billing as Jennelle's president and general manager. While Felice had shared equally in P & F, and then M & J, Paul made sure that the Jennelle stock was in his name alone. An alarm sounded in Felice's head, but she tried to ignore it.

The Dubin companies continued to prosper, eventually employing about a hundred people, and stores around the country sold their moderately priced children's clothes. Paul and Felice reaped the rewards of years of hard work, enjoying the high standard of living they could now afford—fancy cars, elaborate trips, and private schools and summer camps for the children.

The family business did have problems at times. In the mid-1970s, when the partner who had helped them establish Sunshine Girls suddenly left for another job, he took the designer with him; the Dubins had no one on the remaining staff who could do design work. Paul became terribly upset, convinced that they would fall into ruin. An industry show for children's clothing manufacturers was only months away. If they failed to make the deadline, Sunshine Girls' orders for the coming season would drop precipitously.

"We're going to go broke," he told his wife. "We should just close up."

"Why don't we wait until the show, and if we don't do well, then we'll close," Felice responded.

She began to pick up the work of the departed designer, learning the skills of the trade, hit or miss, on the job. Felice hired a woman to make patterns based on Felice's ideas, and they worked together to fine tune the new designs. When time for the show rolled around, Felice and her pattern maker were ready. They took in their samples and, to their delight, drew orders for the new products. Obviously Felice had a knack for designing girls' clothes. Paul's despair lifted.

They had another tumble in the mid-1980s, when Felice took a few months off from work, in part to relieve the tension they were beginning to experience in their marriage. However, she grew bored, the market turned sour, and she returned to work. Paul became depressed again, this time for ten or twelve weeks, from August through October 1987, and Felice actually had to take the reins at Jennelle while he recovered. Later he would attribute his "mental breakdown" to their marital problems.

Felice was beginning to realize that through much of their married life, she never had felt that she and Paul were pulling together like a team. Instead they fought each other constantly.

"It's like I'm in competition with you," she would complain to her husband. "You can't accept that anything is my idea. If you like my idea, you wait three days and then come up with the same idea and say it's yours!" It was a scenario that drove her crazy. Furthermore, because Paul adamantly, steadfastly refused to put Jennelle in both of their names, she found that she resented him terribly.

"What's the difference?" he would ask. "When I die it's going to be yours anyway."

Of course, Felice could have argued back, asking, What's the difference? Why don't we go ahead and put my name on it now? But Paul was a strict disciple of the old-fashioned view that the man has to be in control.

"This is a major problem for me," Felice told him repeatedly. "You are a very capable man, but you could not have built up the business without me, just like I couldn't have built it up without you. Paul, I feel like I'm going against a current," she practically shouted in frustration. "This is a joint venture. It's something we're building together. *I'm not competing with you!*"

"I'm never going to change," Paul replied, disregarding Felice's logic. "This is the way I am, and that's it."

Every woman—every human being—needs to be praised, Felice reasoned to herself. She tried to identify her problem: Everyone needs a pat on the back, to be encouraged, not discouraged—and recognized. There comes a point where you just rebel. The urgency for change grew stronger.

Confronted with this adversity in her professional life, and knowing that her professional life was also her personal life, Felice started to shift her attitude toward working with Paul. She was reaching the point where it was intolerable for her to continue as his underling. She would have to do without him.

"We can't live together anymore," she announced finally. "It will be better for all of us." Paul, who also had become angry over the sustained battling, agreed that the marriage was not working. In December 1987 he moved out, leaving the house to Felice and the children. After renting a room in a hotel for a few weeks he moved on to Coconut Grove, where he later bought a condominium. Yet despite the separation, Paul visited the house regularly, nurturing his close ties with the children, and he and Felice continued to work together at Jennelle. Felice even thought they still loved each other. They just could not get along.

In early 1988, after the separation but while Paul and Felice were still working together, one of their salesmen told them that a Miami children's dress company called Sweet and Pretty wanted to sell out. He asked the Dubins if they would like to be partners with him in buying the company.

"It would be a great opportunity for Andrew to start from the bottom," Felice told Paul, referring to his son from his first marriage. Andrew was old enough to move into his own career.

"It takes a lot of years to know a business. We can't hand everything to him on a silver platter and expect him to have any feeling for it. Why don't we arrange for him to start with this?" Paul agreed, deciding to hold stock in the fledgling company for his son, to whom he eventually would give his share.

Paul would be a one-third partner, as would Felice and their salesman. Jennelle, Inc. lent money to buy the girls' clothing company, which was renamed Felicia, Inc. and operated out of a corner of Jennelle. The plan was for Paul's third of the stock to revert to his son Andrew after a year if he proved that he could manage the young firm. Because Felice was going to serve primarily as a consultant, eventually Andrew would have a dominant role in running the new business.

The plan went awry, however, when Paul later decided that he wanted his son working with him at the much larger, established company, Jennelle, instead of beginning at the bottom of the trade with a start-up business. In August 1988 Paul signed his one-third share of the Felicia company's stock over to Felice, giving her two-thirds' ownership, and she was left to make a go of it with the remaining partner, the salesman. For several months Felice continued to work for both Jennelle, Inc. and Felicia, Inc. Then she began devoting all of her time to the new company.

But the strain of the dying marriage was proving too great for such close working quarters. When tenants moved out of the smaller ten-thousand-square-foot building next door to Jennelle in April 1989, Felice and her partner moved there. They were free to do so because the Dubins owned both buildings as part of Dubin Rentals.

Working independent of her husband for the first time Felice began developing more new lines of clothing under the Felicia label. Paul took away from her all of the books, bank accounts, and liquid assets belonging to Jennelle and began running that company by himself. The personal split became a professional split as well.

Felice began worrying about her own financial security and future now that Paul essentially had pushed her out of Jennelle. But by then Frumkes had been working on Felice's case for several months and was almost ready to file for the divorce. He wanted to assert Felice's claim to Jennelle as quickly as possible.

To represent him in the divorce, Paul hired a respected Miami litigator, Richard Lapidus, a lawyer experienced primarily in general civil matters. Frumkes knew him; they had handled opposing sides in cases before. The tie was personal, too—at one time, Frumkes' daughter baby-sat the Lapidus children. Lawyers are used to being on opposite sides of a case without taking their courtroom advocacy as a personal affront.

Lapidus began his attack against Felice by arguing that all of the Jennelle company should belong to Paul because he was the company president and manager and because all of the stock was in his name. The attorney also pointed to the financial risk of running a garment manufacturing company, and in doing so he argued that, to balance any potential losses he could incur, Paul should be awarded *more* than 50 percent of the marital assets.

Felice was very upset by this logic. After all, *she* was willing to accept Jennelle—and its risks—as part of her share in the divorce, so long as the company was part of an even split of the couple's assets. On the other hand, if she had Jennelle, Paul could have Felicia, Inc., and she wouldn't ask for alimony or child support because she would earn enough for herself and the children. Wouldn't that be fair? Why did Paul want Jennelle *and* more than his half of everything? But the battle lines had been drawn.

Paul was feisty when the day came on January 17, 1990, for Frumkes to take his deposition. Felice came to listen, as spouses often do in divorce depositions. Frumkes and Paul began sparring immediately.

"You are married to Felice," began the attorney after confirming Paul's name and address for the record.

"I am," he replied.

"Is the marriage between you and Felice irretrievably broken?"

"I believe so," said Paul.

"Why?" the attorney inquired.

"Because I would not want to live with the woman any more."

"Why?"

"She does not make me happy any more," Paul snapped.

"Do we really have to get into that?" broke in Lapidus.

Frumkes agreed to back off, at least from that topic. But he and Paul were quickly at each other again while discussing the guidelines for the day of questioning.

"If I am asking a question too fast tell me to slow down," said Frumkes.

"Okay," Paul replied.

"If you don't tell me and you answer the question I will assume your answer is responsive to the question. Take all the time you need and let me know if anything bothers you."

"Fine."

Paul was being curt, but Lapidus elaborated for him. "Other than the vultures flying," he added sarcastically.

Frumkes smiled. "That," he noted for the record, "is professional courtesy giving a salute."

Frumkes proceeded to grill Paul about the money he used to buy his new condominium; Felice was claiming the residence as marital property because Paul had made the down payment with their savings. Frumkes also asked about Felice's role in their various businesses. According to Paul, he was the brains behind their companies and she was merely an employee.

"Did Felice ever take part in the operation of Jennelle?" Frumkes asked.

"She worked as an employee, salaried employee, while she was there."

"What period of time was she there?"

"She was on the premises through January of 1988," Paul answered.

"She was there through '88?" Frumkes repeated. Felice had told him that she had continued to work alongside Paul even after their separation and that the company Felicia had not moved into the neighboring building until more than a year later.

"Through January of '88," Paul insisted.

"From 1977 to January of 1988?"

"That is correct."

"What did she do as a salaried employee?"

"She was the supervisor running different departments," Paul replied.

"What departments?"

"Office, design, production."

"Did she ever have any experience with sales?"

"She did not like sales and stayed out of it."

While Felice listened, she became increasingly distraught as Paul downplayed her involvement in their business. At one point she even left Frumkes' conference room, where the deposition was being held, to cry privately down the hall.

"Paul, why are you doing this?" she asked when it was over. Based on his testimony, it was almost as if she was hearing about a different marriage and a different business than Jennelle.

But he refused to acknowledge what she claimed was her true role.

Felice begged Paul to settle. "Just give me fifty percent," she asked him repeatedly. But Paul wanted to go to court. He was certain that he would win more than half because that was what he thought he deserved.

"Honey, you're wrong," Felice confronted him, mustering her courage to remain strong. "I'm going to get at least half. And maybe more."

In the pretrial brief he filed shortly before their court date, Frumkes pointed to Florida's 1989 equitable distribution statute, which was written to clarify already existing case law. In doing so he stood on good authority because he had chaired the Florida Supreme Court Commission on Matrimonial Law committee that drafted the statute. It says that when dividing marital assets, a court must consider the following variables:

- Each spouse's contribution to the marriage, including homemaking and childrearing
- The economic circumstances of the parties
- The duration of the marriage
- Any interruption of a career or education
- The contribution to the other spouse's career or education
- The desirability of retaining any asset solely in the hands of one spouse
- The contribution of each spouse to producing income or incurring liabilities

But first, said Frumkes, the basic starting point is a fifty-fifty split. Under the new law the percentages can shift only if "there exists justification for disparity." It was that justification for disparity that Frumkes was going to emphasize.

He started by noting that clearly, the Dubins' business, although titled only in Paul's name, was marital property, for the Dubins had acquired Jennelle after they married. Felice was entitled to her share. Then Frumkes hit the court with his zinger: "It is equally clear," he wrote, "that the roles of the parties in the present case were not the typical partnership found in a marriage where the Wife stayed at home taking care of the house and the children while the Husband worked to acquire the family wealth and income. Felice's extraordinary contributions to the development of the family business while also managing the children and the household provides the 'special justification' necessary for an award of more than a fifty percent interest in the marital assets to the Wife." However, he added, Felice would, nonetheless, be satisfied with 50 percent.

Then Frumkes moved on to the subject of alimony. In 1980, when Florida's supreme court first established through its rulings the concept of equitable distribution, it included forms of alimony that could be awarded at the same time. As Frumkes explained in his pretrial memorandum,

> Equitable distribution was developed to recognize the role of a wife in developing marital assets accumulated during the marriage which exist as of the time of divorce. Such awards compensate a wife for that contribution because she earned them. Alimony, on the other hand, addresses a different, less tangible, concern, the need of a spouse for continued support after dissolution of marriage (a future need).

Equitable distribution and alimony, Frumkes argued, may be interrelated and may affect each other, but "they are not mutually exclusive remedies" under either Florida case law or its new equitable distribution statute.

Nationwide, not just in Florida, where Frumkes practices, alimony can take several forms—lump sum alimony, a one-time payment; permanent periodic alimony, the traditional notion of postdivorce monthly support payments; and rehabilitative alimony, which provides for short-term support while an ex-spouse seeks training or education to further employability.

As an illustration Frumkes offers a hypothetical case in which he would request that the husband provide permanent periodic alimony as well as an equitable distribution of assets. The numbers are larger than in most divorces and they are grossly simplified to make the example more clear. Consider that the couple's total assets equal $2 million. The court awards to the husband the couple's $1 million business, from which he receives an annual salary of $200,000. The court awards to the wife the $300,000 home, $100,000 worth of jewelry, and $600,000 in securities. Invested at 7.5 percent the wife would receive $45,000 a year in income from those securities.

However, according to the wife's financial affidavits in this hypothetical situation, she needs $90,000 a year to maintain her current lifestyle. Furthermore, imagine that she had married right out of high school and never worked during the twenty-five-year marriage. In such a case Frumkes would request alimony of $45,000 annually for the wife's support, leaving the husband with $155,000 a year in income. The wife, says Frumkes, should not be required to work, especially since any job she could get would be demeaning. However, a younger woman divorcing after a shorter marriage may decide to accept rehabilitative alimony until she can obtain further education and training to help her find suitable employment. Child support obligations are shared, based on each parent's income.

After divorce, taxes must be paid on any alimony payments. (Income in the form of child support is not taxed, however.) In the Dubins' case, because Paul voluntarily was paying Felice temporary support pending their divorce, this payment was not considered alimony in a formal sense (because it was not court-ordered), so it was tax-free to her. Although Felice did not think Paul's support was sufficient, she hesitated taking him to court for a larger temporary support award while the divorce was in process, since any amount formally ordered by a judge would then be taxable. In the end Felice could lose more than she stood to gain.

As for long-term alimony Frumkes emphasized in his pretrial brief that should the court award Felice the financially lucrative Jennelle, Inc., then she most likely would not need any additional support (alimony or child support), because she would be drawing a good salary from the business. But, should the court choose to give Paul the company and require that he buy out Felice's share of its ownership, she no longer would have a steady income. Felicia, Inc. was too new to provide sufficient earnings. If his client was awarded only Felicia, Inc., said Frumkes, she would demand both permanent monthly alimony payments and child support to maintain her standard of living.

A key player in Felice's case was the accountant. "You cannot try a case like this without an accountant," Frumkes told Felice early on, "and the accountant I most frequently use is a brilliant, capable man named Martin Sobel. I started working with him about thirteen years ago, and he is in *great* demand in divorce circles. You're going to like him."

Frumkes is careful when hiring accountants. "The tax implications and the valuation problems are so complicated that it really takes a sophisticated expert," asserts Frumkes. He demands that the accountants he retains be accessible, knowledgeable, convincing, and consistent. "I cannot have an accountant testifying for the wife's position one day and testify to a completely different position [in another case] another day," he says when lecturing on the use of experts in divorce cases. A lawyer can do that because that's an attorney's job, to be a hired *advocate* for any client, but an accountant is an *expert* who, if he or she is to remain credible, cannot embrace different accounting principles in different cases. To assist in preparing Felice's financial affidavit, Frumkes wanted Sobel to examine the financial records from the Dubins' personal purchases and investments and from their businesses. The affidavit would tell the court the value of the Dubins' assets—their companies, properties, and investments—the exact manner in which they should be divided, how much money Felice needed to live on a daily basis, and, if necessary, how much alimony and child support Paul should pay.

Martin Sobel, who for the previous ten years had devoted half to two-thirds of his practice to divorce litigation, lived up to Frumkes' expectations. Felice found the accountant perfect for her needs. While he tried to explain the intricacies of her financial position and claims in layperson's terms, Felice felt that she did not have to worry about understanding every detail. "I make children's clothing," she told him one day. "If I want somebody to do something for me, I go to the best. Melvyn's philosophy in hiring you is the same. What you say is fine with me."

Felice would have the same feelings about the business valuation expert Frumkes hired, a Pennsylvanian named Jay Fishman who was flown in for the case. One of the major problems in the Dubin divorce case would be the valuation of Jennelle. Paul valued it at a much lower rate than Frumkes thought it was worth, obviously because Paul wanted to pay as little as possible to buy out Felice's share. "It's an outrage," Frumkes told her when he saw Paul's figures. It was on this point that Felice and Paul would have one of their greatest battles.

Frumkes and Felice would need still one more expert, someone to help them value Felice's jewelry. She had quite a collection, given that her parents had been in the business all her life, and Felice maintained that most of the jewelry she owned was either hers before the marriage or given to her later by her parents, making it nonmarital property not to be taken into consideration when dividing assets for the divorce. Yet Paul wanted to claim the jewelry as marital property, arguing that Felice had acquired much of it after marrying him, which would entitle him to half of its monetary worth. To help resolve this dispute Frumkes first would have to value the jewelry, so he hired an appraiser who had worked against him in another case; the man had been so impressive that Frumkes wanted him on his side of the courtroom. Maurice Rittner went out to the Dubins' house to appraise Felice's jewelry there—an important service, says Frumkes, because no woman would want to remove all of her jewelry from her home at one time.

Frumkes never confronts an opposing expert when taking a deposition; he only wants to find out what the expert knows. Once challenged, Frumkes figures, the expert will race to source materials and reference books to better clarify a position before trial. "I just want to nail down his theories," Felice's attorney explained. Investigate, don't educate the expert—that was Frumkes' philosophy.

A few days before he deposed Paul, Frumkes also deposed Paul's valuation expert, Lawrence Mizrach, asking him about his experience brokering businesses and the technique he had used to value Jennelle, Inc. Mizrach, a real estate broker and previous owner of a comparable children's manufacturing company, was one of Paul's friends. He offered as credentials his enrollment in two courses, one a two-day business brokerage class at the University of Miami. At his deposition Mizrach explained that he had worked with an accountant to reach his dollar value for Jennelle. Frumkes also deposed the accountant about his approach in helping with the task. Neither of these men, according to Frumkes, had done a suitable job. "We'll tear them up in court," he told Felice after learning what he needed to know from the two depositions.

The experts for the two sides also disagreed about the value of Felicia, Inc. Frumkes argued that the company was worth nothing because it was so new; Paul's expert claimed that Felicia would bring several hundred thousand dollars on the market. Of course, if Felice was going to end up with Felicia, Inc. on her side of the postdivorce ledger, Paul wanted that company to be highly valued by the court in order to help balance out his ownership of Jennelle, Inc.

After the experts' depositions Frumkes went back to Sobel, his accountant, and Fishman, his business evaluator, to review their findings and recommendations in light of his new information. The attorney also reviewed with Felice how she would testify given what he then knew about Paul's case. "Always tell the truth," he instructed. "But there are *ways* of telling the truth, things to emphasize."

Throughout the months when Frumkes and Sobel prepared for the Dubin trial, they considered Felice an ideal client. "Clients need to be able to reach out and contact their attorneys," explains Frumkes, "but they have to have a little perspective and know every problem can't be solved by the attorney." Clearly he is one who is used to being asked too often to settle arguments in matters that fall outside the legal arena. Too often clients think of their lawyers as therapists, father (or mother) confessors, or even good friends. On the contrary, they are paid professionals trying to do a specific job.

"Felice let us do what she knew we had to do without interfering," says Frumkes. "She had confidence in me and in the accountant and that made it easier for us to do the job."

He finally decided to offer the court two alternatives for resolving the Dubins' divorce. In one, Felice would get Jennelle, Inc. and Paul would have Felicia, Inc.; in the other the result would be reversed. Whoever ended up with Jennelle, however, would owe the other a considerable payout to equalize the asset distribution. Frumkes offered both suggestions because he feared that the court would award Jennelle to Paul simply because he was on site at the business and operating it daily. Courts tend to want to preserve the status quo.

Later, only weeks before the trial was to start, Paul's lawyer, Lapidus, hired another valuation expert, perhaps because he sensed that he would need a second business opinion to support his client's claims. Ironically, Leon Korros assigned a value to Jennelle that was almost identical to the much higher value that Frumkes' valuation expert had offered. "This is the most amazing thing I've ever seen," Frumkes announced. His opponent's expert was agreeing with the numbers on Felice's side of the case!

The trial lasted two days, May 23 and 24, 1990. The two lawyers and their clients gathered in the judge's office (most divorce trials in Florida are not held in courtrooms), where they sat at a long table perpendicular to the judge's desk. Frumkes and Felice were on one side, with Lapidus and Paul facing them. A court reporter and a clerk positioned themselves at the top of the T-shaped arrangement, one on either side of the judge. The various experts and witnesses called to testify would sit at the far end of the long table, facing the judge.

On the first day, testimony was heard from Frumkes' two experts, Martin Sobel and Jay Fishman. Two of Frumkes' lay witnesses, people who had worked with Felice at the garment manufacturing business, spoke as well. But first Frumkes presented his opening statement.

"Judge, this is a culmination of an 18-year-old marriage. Throughout the marriage, the parties worked very hard in the industry. This is not the traditional marriage. This was a marriage where the wife managed the home, raised the kids, and worked just as hard or perhaps harder in the business than the husband. . . . [T]he wife worked very hard because she wanted to live a good life, and so did the husband. So they both expended a great effort along the line."

Paul, Frumkes said, suffered from depression on separate occasions along the way, "so much so that he could not make decisions. He did not work during those episodes and the wife ran the business.

"What does the wife want out of this? She wants to operate Jennelle, Inc. She did operate it and it will provide her the security and the income that she needs. If she gets the income-producing assets of the parties, she does not need alimony, she does not need child support."

But if the court decided to award Jennelle, Inc. to Paul, Frumkes added, Felice would need a payout in compensation. The end result either way, he insisted, should be a fifty-fifty division of the marital assets. That would be only fair.

Before Frumkes called his witnesses, Lapidus delivered his opening statement on Paul's behalf. "Jennelle has always been run by Mr. Dubin," Lapidus asserted as he introduced his side of the case. "Mrs. Dubin worked in the business, and you will hear testimony [to that effect] from the employees of the business as well as from the lendors. . . . The company is Mr. Dubin's. Mrs. Dubin took a salary over the years. Whatever she wanted, she was put on as a salary [that is, she was paid for her work]. She helped.

"She has certainly run the company when [Paul] was out with a bout of depression. No one is degrading her efforts in this company but the company was run by Mr. Dubin and has always been run by Mr. Dubin."

Of course, if Paul got Jennelle, as he wished, Lapidus wanted to make sure that the payout to Felice was as small as possible. Despite his expert's valuation agreeing with that of Frumkes' expert, Lapidus argued that the garment industry had fallen on hard times recently, so Jennelle should not be considered as valuable as either expert had determined. "We have *The Wall Street Journal* articles telling what has happened to the garment industry with the leveraged buyout hangover of the eighties and the fact that one after another, the major retailers are going into Chapter 11 [bankruptcy].

"The credit line of the ones that are out of bankruptcy court is dropping precipitously. The customers of Jennelle, as well as the customers of a lot of garment industries in the United States are going." If Paul had to pay Felice what she and Frumkes suggested, claimed Lapidus, Jennelle would be financially ruined.

When Lapidus sat down, Frumkes began calling the witnesses to support his version of the case, presenting it with all the detail he could muster. First, he walked Sobel through the steps he followed to determine Felice's needs and her share of the Dubins' marital assets. As he questioned the CPA, Frumkes presented exhibit upon exhibit of financial data and calculations.

The judge, Ursula Ungaro, who had been on the bench only a short time, listened intently. In a learning mode, she showed her determination to understand the intricacies of the case. "I have to ask a real stupid question," she broke in at one point while Sobel was testifying about a certain point. "There is something that I don't understand here." Frumkes, who watches judges closely in a trial to help him refine his own tactics, was impressed by her open-minded approach and by how much she really did understand.

"That judge is so goddamn bright," he whispered to Felice later. "It's hard to believe she's new. She cuts right through and gets right to the heart of things. She's making it easy for all of us." Felice nodded in agreement. Lapidus, too, thought that Ungaro had grasped the financial issues of the case quickly.

After Sobel testified at length, Frumkes called his next witness, a Hispanic woman named Dulce Pena, who had worked for the Dubins' garment businesses for sixteen years. She testified that during the early days of P & F, Felice had run the clothing factory.

"Were there times that you were around that you would hear Mr. Dubin speaking to Mrs. Dubin?" Frumkes asked Pena.

"Yes, always," she replied, trying to speak carefully because she had more trouble with her English when she was nervous. And nervous she was, looking tentatively at both Felice and Paul, who stared back at her in turn.

"How did he treat her in and about the business?" Frumkes asked.

"Well, sometimes just fine." Pena hesitated. Then she spoke again. "Sometimes they argue," she admitted.

"Did he ever degrade her?" asked Frumkes.

"Well, this is to . . . I have to say that through . . ." Pena was tripping over her words. She clearly did not want to answer. Paul waited for what would assuredly be a response that was unflattering to him; everyone in the room was growing tense.

"What do you have to say?" Frumkes prodded the witness patiently. "Can you explain how he treated her?"

"They used to have fights and they . . . if they had a problem, they had an argument. They had a fight and he would tell her, 'Get out of here.'"

"What else?" asked the lawyer. He knew what Pena would say.

"He . . ." Pena looked down in embarrassment.

"Yes, what else? I take it you do not want to say those words in front of the judge?"

Lapidus was getting annoyed. "That is their problem," he announced, referring to Pena and Frumkes.

"They had strong arguments," Pena spoke up.

"Be honest, tell the truth," Paul directed her from his side of the table. He was trying to be civil.

"Go fuck yourself," Pena replied. The judge looked incredulous.

"Is that what you are telling him now?" Frumkes asked for clarification, motioning toward Paul.

Pena shook her head no. "That is what he used to say, that. The truth," she insisted. "I came here to say the truth."

"It was the garment industry," interjected Lapidus.

Frumkes was not going to buy that excuse. "My father was in the garment industry," he countered. "He never treated my mother that way."

"It happens, because couples do have fights, you know," Pena, the factory worker, spoke out again. "I am telling the truth. I am saying the truth, Paul," she said, looking directly at him.

"We had arguments, and we fought," Paul shrugged, leaning over to confer with Lapidus. Felice began talking as well.

"That is really . . ." the judge broke in. Despite her keen attention, she sensed that she was losing control. "You know, this is an emotionally charged . . . wait!" she instructed as she tried to regain command of the noisy courtroom. "Excuse me. Let me say this now." The others finally stopped their conversations.

"It is very important that Mr. Dubin and Mrs. Dubin both refrain from interjecting during the course of the proceedings, and if they wish to say something, they should communicate it with their lawyers," Judge Ungaro announced firmly. "They should not speak out of turn. Okay?" The room was silent. Some nodded in assent.

Frumkes had seen far worse, when the clients on both sides stood up and started screaming at each other, or both broke out in tears. Despite the sporadic confusion, the Dubin trial was actually one of the calmer ones in his career.

After the lunch break Sobel came back on the stand for cross-examination. Lapidus grilled the accountant mercilessly about Felice's household and general expenses, about Sobel's opinion that Felicia, Inc. had no monetary value, and about Jennelle, Inc.'s financial health. Their exchange was detailed and intense.

When Felicia, Inc.'s bookkeeper, Ordean Ardoin, took the stand following the accountant Sobel, Frumkes first made an announcement. "I am going to be gentle with this witness," he said, "because she has

M.S. [multiple sclerosis]. She is a great bookkeeper but she has a physical problem. I trust my colleague will abide by the same rules." Lapidus nodded. Ardoin testified that Felice had run many aspects of Jennelle. She had run it when Paul was sick and could do so again without him at her side.

Jay Fishman, the Pennsylvania valuation expert, followed, testifying about Jennelle's worth; Lapidus cross-examined him late in the afternoon. The next morning, May 24, Frumkes' last witnesses came to the stand—Felice herself and a bank officer who had lent money to both Jennelle, Inc. and Felicia, Inc.

Shortly before the lunch break that second day—and before Lapidus would begin presenting his experts and witnesses for his side of the divorce proceeding—he plunged into a lengthy cross-examination of Felice's testimony.

"Ma'am, you are here today for a divorce from your husband?"

"Yes," Felice replied softly. She was understandably nervous.

"And you testified that the marriage has been irretrievably broken?"

"Yes."

"You testified quite emotionally that you still love Mr. Dubin?" asked Lapidus, referring to Felice's earlier direct examination.

"Yes," she acknowledged.

"And do you?"

"Yes," she reiterated.

"On the same examination, you accused him of being . . . a perjurer and, I kept a running account, nine times in your testimony you referred to one incident where he suffered from a depression.

"Now," continued Lapidus, "let's go over exactly what you could accuse him of.

"First of all, you testified that he lied on his deposition, that he perjured himself on his deposition, and he admitted to you that he did so. Do you recall that testimony?"

"That is not exactly what I said," Felice objected.

"Well, I think I took notes," Lapidus insisted. "You said that after the deposition, you accused him of lying and he said, 'I did because I had to—'"

"Well, it was more like a comment, an accusation, 'Why did you lie, Paul?'" Felice interrupted.

"Ma'am, lying on a deposition is perjury, did you know that?"

"No, I did not."

"You did not?" Lapidus acted surprised. "Well, let's go to Mr. Dubin's deposition and I would appreciate it if you would point out for us where he lied. What did he lie about in your mind?"

"I'd have to read the whole deposition to be able to tell you that," said Felice.

"Well, ma'am," Lapidus pushed harder, "you come into court and you testified against a man that you claim that you love, emotionally crying, all that stuff, and you said he's a liar, he lied on his deposition and he admitted lying to you. One instance, give me one instance, where he said . . . where you think he lied."

"I answered the question that my attorney asked me," she explained, growing increasingly uncomfortable. "And if you would like me to during lunch, I will go over the whole deposition and highlight where he lied."

"Do you recall at—"

Felice cut him off. "Not at this moment," she said. Lapidus was missing the point. It was the tone of Paul's testimony that bothered her so much, the emphasis he placed on his role over hers.

"Well, that's the deposition which was taken on January 17, 1990. You were present, Mr. Sobel, your accountant, was present, and your lawyer was present, right?

"We had frequent breaks during the deposition," the attorney continued as he bore down hard, "[and] you had ample opportunity to tell Mr. Frumkes, your lawyer, able lawyer that he is, 'My husband is lying. Get him on this one.' Correct? You had an opportunity, you were present at the deposition with your lawyer and your accountant, Mr. Sobel."

Frumkes was getting increasingly annoyed with Lapidus's badgering. He couldn't hold off any longer. "I must respectfully now say that you are arguing with the witness," he objected.

"I am not," Lapidus shot back.

"Ask questions," Frumkes insisted. "You are not entitled to argue with her."

The judge agreed.

During the rest of his cross-examination Lapidus challenged Felice's early business experience, her memory about the details of her marriage and business operations, and her financial affidavits listing her needs and those of the children. It was a grueling, at times almost harassing, experience. Halfway through Felice became so upset that Judge Ungaro called a recess.

When time came to call his own witnesses, Lapidus brought to the stand Clara Valdez, a production manager at Jennelle, who testified very briefly that Paul had run Jennelle and Felice had only helped. Lapidus also called Lawrence Kabat, the CPA who had worked for both Paul and Felice for several years. Kabat, too, testified that he had dealt with Paul as the person who ran Jennelle.

"Has Jennelle been a well-run company?" Lapidus asked the accountant.

"Yes," he replied.

"And you have worked there for many years with Mr. Dubin?"

"Yes."

"Is he experienced?"

"Yes."

"And knowledgeable?"

"Yes."

"A good manufacturer?"

"Yes."

Frumkes took over for his cross-examination. "Did Mrs. Dubin ever run the business?" he demanded of the accountant. "In the sense of managing, taking care of employees, taking care of buying, selling, working with the accountant for a period of five months?"

"Yes," answered Kabat. "There was a period there that I was working closer with Felice than with Paul. A short period of time."

"Five, six months, yes?" Frumkes reminded him.

"That would be about right."

"Was she doing a great job? You saw the books and records."

"I had no problems during that period of time," said Kabat.

"No large problems in sales?"

"No."

"Or in inventory?"

"No."

"Was there a great increase in expenses?"

"No."

"Things were going along pretty well, they kept rising?" asked Frumkes. "Isn't that correct?"

"I think there was a rising period during the time," Kabat admitted.

Lapidus finally called Paul, who described his employment history with the garment industry and his view of how he had run the companies—with Felice's help. Paul was angry and impatient with the attack on his primary role in their work efforts. He staunchly defended his claim to Jennelle, Inc. and his view that business was declining. Should the court allow him to keep Jennelle, he definitely wanted his payments to Felice limited.

Finally, after Frumkes called as his rebuttal witnesses Jay Fishman, who had valued Jennelle on Felice's behalf, and, once again, Martin Sobel, his accountant, the Dubins' divorce trial ended. It was a quarter after seven in the evening.

* * *

But the arguing continued on paper. In a post-trial memorandum Lapidus attacked Felice's claim that Paul could not run the company:

> Her sole argument for taking the company seems to be the fact that Mr. Dubin has suffered from depression in the past. For one five-month period he was incapacitated. She asks the Court solely based upon that fact to take the company from Mr. Dubin and award it to her. She offered no medical evidence that Mr. Dubin was unable to run his company. No doctors testified that Mr. Dubin would again suffer from depression. While her argument might have been devastatingly effective in a Florida Court in 1890, in 1990 it is somewhat specious. Persons who have in the past suffered from depression or any other mental problem are no longer branded for life or committed to state institutions.

Even though the two sides' valuation experts had agreed on Jennelle's monetary worth, Lapidus continued to refute their combined view. He sought to lower the figure to protect Paul's pockets. "That value cannot be taken in a vacuum," Lapidus wrote about Jennelle. "In dividing the assets of the parties, it ought [to] be understood that that value was based upon earnings which the company no longer enjoys, sales that the company no longer books and a market place for its products that no longer exists."

Frumkes would continue his quest on paper as well, hoping, like his opponent, to influence the judge as she made up her mind about the Dubins' fate. In his post-trial memorandum he argued strongly that based on her contributions to the Dubins' garment business and to their home, Felice deserved half, or likely more than half, of the marital assets. To prove his point, he paraphrased an ancient Hebraic prayer. This is what Frumkes wrote about Felice:

> Had she been a wife, maintaining the household, and not also mainly in charge of raising the three children, it would have been enough.
>
> Had she been mainly in charge of raising the three children and not given her husband encouragement and wise counsel in business, it would have been enough.
>
> Had she given her husband encouragement and wise counsel in business, and not taken over and [run] the business when he was sick, it would have been enough.

Had she run the business when her husband was sick and not worked for 17 years right beside her husband, as hard as he did and as long hours as he put in, it would have been enough.

This woman did it all: She maintained the household, she raised three children, she gave encouragement to her husband and wise counsel in business affairs, she took over and ran the business when he was sick and she worked for 17 years right beside him as hard as he did and as long hours as he did.

Frumkes' description of the marriage made a convincing—and catchy—summary.

To reach a decision about the Dubins' divorce, Judge Ungaro needed to address three issues. First, she had to classify their various assets as either marital or nonmarital; the former would go into a kitty for division between Felice and Paul and the latter would continue to belong to the spouse who was the individual owner. Second, the judge had to decide how much the various marital assets were worth so that she could divide them equitably between the two Dubins. And third, she needed to determine how she would do the actual dividing—that is, she would need to assign a percentage ownership of all of the assets to Paul and a percentage ownership to Felice, these being a reflection of what was equitable in view of their marriage history, individual needs, and all of the other pertinent factors.

After the judge made all of these assessments, Felice ended up in a position rare among divorced women. In a decree dated August 23, 1990, two and a half years after the Dubins first separated, the court awarded her 60 percent of their marital property and Paul 40 percent. The judge agreed with Frumkes that Felice had worked not only in the home but also alongside Paul from the beginning and that the two of them had contributed equally to making the business successful. There was, she said, justification to stray from any general rule that marital assets be divided equally, for Felice's contributions to the home and the business, contributions that were in total greater than Paul's, justified awarding her more than half of all marital assets. It was a victory all hardworking women could celebrate.

Still, when the assets were parceled out, Paul was the one who got Jennelle, Inc. as part of his share of the deal. In return the court scheduled a five-year payout for the money he owed Felice for her share.

"I knew he would get it," Felice now says of the company, although she would have liked to have retained Jennelle herself. But, she shrugs, "it doesn't matter. I'll make it on my own." Paul also was going to have to pay back singlehandedly the seed money borrowed from Jennelle and from the bank to get Felicia, Inc. started.

The court's logic in parceling out the two firms, Jennelle and Felicia, was actually a tribute to Felice. As stated in the final judgment,

> The parties, becoming divorced in their personal life, should also be divorced in their commercial lives and therefore this Court has to decide which spouse should own the shares of stock of Jennelle, Inc.

The fact that the company stock was all in Paul's name made no difference, because title alone did not determine the distribution of marital assets, the judge emphasized. The final opinion continued,

> While the Court finds that both parties are capable of running the operation of Jennelle, Inc., what tips the scales in favor of the distribution of this asset to the Husband is that he is ten years older than the Wife; in comparing Jennelle, Inc. with Felicia, Inc., Jennelle, Inc. is the safe business venture; the Wife is more innovative and industrious and the Court does not think that the Husband can, if he is awarded the interest of Felicia, Inc., start over again nor can he do so as well as can she; Felicia, Inc. is new and relatively untested and is therefore tantamount to starting anew; the Wife is more capable of handling such a "fresh start" than is the Husband and therefore the Husband should be awarded the 100 percent interest in the outstanding capital shares of stock of Jennelle, Inc., with the Wife being awarded the two-thirds interest [Felice's partner still owned one third] in Felicia, Inc.

As a result of the judge's decree, Felice would place in Felicia, Inc. all of her hope for future professional success. No one involved in the case doubted that she could make it.

Because the experts from both sides were so close in their valuation of Jennelle, Judge Ungaro accepted their dollar figure, refusing to lower it, as Lapidus had suggested. She also rejected Paul's claim that Felicia, Inc. had any monetary value. That, said the judge, was just wishful thinking. Thus, after awarding the much larger and far-better-established company Jennelle, Inc. to Paul and the much smaller company Felicia, Inc.—which had no value because it was so new—to Felice, the judge had to turn to the task of balancing out the assets on both sides of the ledger to end up with the sixty-forty split overall. Along with ordering a five-year payout to Felice to compensate her for the loss of Jennelle, the judge also awarded her 75 percent of Dubin Rentals, with Paul receiving only 25 percent. Their marital home, certificates of deposit, pension funds, and the cash value of life insurance policies also fell on Felice's side of the ledger.

To secure Paul's payment to Felice, the court ordered Paul to give her a lien on all of the shares of stock in Jennelle, Inc. and on his interest in Dubin Rentals. Should Paul default on his payments, these companies would belong to Felice.

She would not receive any alimony, however, although the court's judgment included a provision allowing her to request it at a future time should she ever be without a salary from Felicia. Had some kind of provision like this not been included in the judgment, Felice would have foregone any future opportunity to request monthly support, because once alimony is denied, it cannot be awarded later on. The court also supported Felice on the jewelry debate, ruling that all of the jewelry she had acquired before the marriage or received as a gift from her parents was nonmarital property and would not be subject to equitable distribution.

Although he had won Jennelle, Inc., Paul was very unhappy with the judgment. He was unhappy that Felice got 60 percent of their assets while he got only 40 percent, a net win for her.

Ironically, Frumkes says today that Felice would have settled if Paul had offered her only 40 percent, but he never did. Frumkes says that Paul wanted Felice to have less and did not believe that she possibly could win more.

Felice laughs over this. "I think in the long run, I got screwed," she says, because her payout for Jennelle, Inc. is premised on Paul's business success. If Paul were ever in a position where he could not manage Jennelle and make a continued go of the company, Felice's future payments would disappear before her eyes—unless, that is, she once again took over Jennelle herself.

"She's not the kind of person who would go in and cut his heart out," says Frumkes about the lien on the company the court provided in case Paul defaulted. "She'd go in and save the business [for him]. But she's got the protection" in case there is a problem.

Such concern is not without foundation. According to *The Wall Street Journal*, "many bedroom/boardroom partnerships flourished in the [eighties] decade's flush years, but are now dissolving under financial and other strains," including divorce. With more women in the work force the number of husband-wife proprietorships grew significantly, yet today they are increasingly threatened by personal rifts, which are further exacerbated by economic difficulties plaguing the beginning of this decade.

As for the Dubin children, the judge congratulated Paul and Felice for their handling of custody and visitation and ruled that they were both responsible for the children's support. Paul agreed, to his credit, to pay for college for all three. While a court in Florida has no power to order either spouse to pay for education beyond the age of eighteen, the court could enforce an agreement to do so as long as the parent had volunteered in the original divorce settlement to make these payments.

The *Florida Law Weekly* wrote up the Dubin divorce opinion, undoubtedly because Felice, the wife, had won more than half of the marital assets under what the court determined were extraordinary circumstances in a marriage. Frumkes, who argues for a fifty-fifty split wherever possible, says that only extraordinary circumstances would produce this kind of result in any case. Today, "under the new[est] pronouncements of the courts, it's usually fifty-fifty," he says.

Despite the judge's clear explanation of her decision and logic, Paul appealed. By then the divorce had already cost Felice about seventy-five thousand dollars in legal fees, and Frumkes encouraged her to reach a settlement to end the battle. While she would refuse to give up the percentage of assets the court had awarded her, she said she would agree to spreading Paul's payout over a longer period of time.

Not all women are as pleased as Felice Dubin with current-day divorce rulings. In fact, the new philosophy of dividing marital property and requiring the husband and wife to support themselves after divorce has engendered cries of protest. Unlike Felice, many women find that equitable distribution, despite its more egalitarian approach, which was brought on by the women's liberation movement, often works against them. They say that even if courts treat them as equals when dividing property, they lose in the end, because unlike their husbands (and, in this case, Felice Dubin), they typically have trouble maintaining their customary life-style with their generally smaller incomes. As a group women remain less equipped than men to enter and succeed in the work force, especially if they retain custody of the children. It follows, some advocates argue, that many women still need alimony, or maintenance.

Lenore Weitzman forcefully criticizes the new divorce and property rules in her controversial book *The Divorce Revolution* (The Free Press,

1985) which documents the effect of community property on California divorces. The long-term result, Weitzman maintains, is "a systematic impoverishment of women and children." In a recent column, the *Boston Globe*'s Ellen Goodman notes that "nationally, five years after divorce, a woman's income is still 30 percent of what it was during the marriage. A man's income is 14 percent more." Although the exact percentages may be disputed, a man's steady career advancement and increasing income generally enable him to better his situation during the years after divorce, while the woman more often has limited earning potential because her career or job skills development took a backseat to marriage and because women, on average, earn less than men. Equitable distribution and community property will work only once women have equal opportunity and experience in the workplace with accommodations for child care that do not jeopardize their career development.

Yet while women protest, men like Paul Dubin also object to equitable distribution and community property divorces. These men say that if they earn most or all of the money in a marriage, it is unfair to make them hand over so many of the assets to the women who brought in little or nothing. This traditional position dies hard.

Felice has every confidence that she has the skills to make her children's fashion firm, Felicia, Inc., a success. While she never learned to sew herself, "I can *tell you* how to sew," she asserts today, referring to her supervisory skills and ability to inspect for quality production.

"I *can* put in buttonholes," she is quick to add. "I know how to run the machines. An operator can't tell me, 'Oh, no, you can't do this,' because I know better. And I can sit down and say, 'Yes, you can,' and show her how."

Recently she designed a new denim line for little girls, sporty outfits with an American flag motif, and another line of party dresses, which she's preparing to show to buyers. Her factory and warehouse, a ten-thousand-square-foot cavern of a room, now house about a dozen sewing machines at which workers sew up samples of the fashions that Felice designs. She contracts out the actual production of her clothes to companies much like the one she and Paul started early in their marriage. Near the work area the pattern maker has a separate room to herself, as does the bookkeeper.

Felice is perhaps most proud of her own office, a cozy, sun-filled peach-colored retreat not far from the warehouse's front door. It's filled with fashion magazines, bric-a-brac, and photographs of her children. She is there at her desk almost every weekday and at least part of the day on weekends, checking on patterns, orders, and inventory logged into her computer. It's a life she loves. "Paul would never let me have my own office" at Jennelle, Felice says. Now she is independent and can make her own decisions about the fruits of her success. The self-satisfaction with this budding new business is well deserved.

For the moment she says she is not ready for another romantic involvement. "It takes a lot out of you, a divorce," Felice says with some understatement. And she has her hands full with three children, who at the time of the divorce were ages seventeen, fifteen, and ten.

Most important, despite Paul's legal appeal, he and Felice have remained friends. Amazingly, Felice forgives him for trying to take away her rightful share of their success. "He believes everything he says," she explains with some pathos in her voice. "He really thinks that I wouldn't be where I am without him."

Her philosophy is an anomaly that those in the legal profession don't see too often. For some outsiders it can be very hard to understand. How can a couple be married for eighteen years, as the Dubins were, have three children, build a prospering business together, argue mightily over who would own what after they break up, and then remain friends? "It's very important to get along," says Felice now, only one month after the divorce became final. "The children—even though they're confused—are better off." While no longer a family, Paul still comes to the house for dinner on Friday nights and he, Felice, and the three kids go to the movies together.

"We get along much better now," Felice attests. "I think we'll always remain friends. We'll always be there for each other."

Felice's subsequent behavior would help make that prediction more likely. In May 1991, she not only agreed to spread out Paul's payments to her over a longer period of time, but she also consented to a 55-percent share of the marital assets, rather than the 60 percent the judge had originally awarded her. In return, Paul dropped his appeal.

4

FIGHTING OVER THE BUSINESS: HOW MUCH IS IT WORTH?

Gayle L. Wilder v. Howard L. Wilder

What really impresses a judge are the more mechanical, professional arguments rather than the emotional ones.

—ATTORNEY DONALD SCHILLER
CHICAGO

What happens after a divorce to the business a spouse successfully built, the law practice nurtured over time, or the store founded years ago? Today a marriage partner's claim to part ownership is made possible by new community property and equitable distribution doctrines that dictate how a couple's assets must be divided. Under these rules, a medical or law practice, for example, or a company developed during a marriage may be deemed marital property, even if one spouse alone did all of the work. And marital property is property to be shared.

This logic makes sense particularly when one member of a couple is the homemaker, usually the wife, and the other the family's wage earner. The homemaker does, in fact, support the establishment and growth of such professional practices and business enterprises through her activities in the home. She should, therefore, in case of divorce, receive her share of the financial rewards. Of course, as more women become entrepreneurs and professionals they will find their livelihoods considered marital property, too.

However, as with any critical issue in a marital dissolution, the process of identifying and assessing marital property is fraught with hazards.

A question first arises as to whether the practice or business truly developed during the marriage or whether it was established beforehand. If it was already established, was the business's subsequent growth and prosperity due in part to the role of a supportive spouse? And if the spouse does have a claim, how much is it worth?

The value of a practice or business includes, of course, its hard assets—buildings, furnishings, inventory, accounts receivable, and the like. Their monetary worth may be fairly easy to calculate. But the overall value of a practice or business also can include a sizeable intangible factor called "goodwill"—the value of a professional practice or business above its hard assets. In other words, how much more, once on the block, could a company or practice bring on the market? A firm well known for quality products, for example, surely will draw a higher bidder than will an unknown enterprise, simply because the reputation of the first company's name will attract future customers.

This added value, or goodwill, represents the future of a professional practice or business enterprise in terms of earnings potential. Goodwill is assigned a dollar value above and beyond the value of existing tangible assets, but because goodwill is so hard to measure, valuation debates become extraordinarily heated. For both sides in a divorce, many dollars are at stake.

This chapter explains how a Chicago homemaker, in her divorce from her ophthalmologist husband, argued that his medical practice was hers as well. She further maintained that because of the practice's alleged goodwill value, it was worth far more than her husband claimed. Gayle Wilder would make the case that her husband Howard was an acknowledged success story, a surgeon to whom many others turned for assistance with delicate and complicated retina problems. His name was so great, she said, that his practice was worth far more than the face value of its hard assets—precisely because of the goodwill the doctor had established and built up.

But Dr. Wilder strongly differed with his wife, whom he had married when he was well into his forties. He was a success before Gayle came along, he said, so the medical practice was all his. And the value of his share—he was in practice with a partner—was already predetermined at a relatively low figure by a buy-sell agreement the two doctors had devised should one decide to buy out the other, an agreement that did not take into account any value for goodwill.

What's more, argued the doctor, his practice was not worth any more out in the marketplace simply because of his own particular surgical skills, for in this instance a surgeon's reputation without the surgeon meant nothing. Goodwill? There was, he said, none there.

It took him more than four years and a precedent-setting legal victory to prove that he was right. In the Wilder case an Illinois appellate court handed down a landmark decision that established a new way to approach the difficult question of deciding how to calculate what a spouse deserves when divorcing from a practicing professional, such as a doctor, whose income depends in large part on his own unique abilities.

Dr. Howard Wilder loved nothing more than practicing medicine. He began specializing in retinal eye surgery in the mid-1950s, about ten years after earning his M.D. from the University of Illinois, and from 1957 on he limited his practice completely to that field. A pioneer, he was widely recognized as the first retinologist in Chicago. Other ophthalmologists with more general practices referred patients to him from far-flung areas including Canada and many parts of the United States.

Much of Dr. Wilder's work involved the repair of detached retinas—that is, reattaching the delicate light-sensitive membrane that lines the back wall of the eye. The retina is connected by the optic nerve to the brain and cannot function if it becomes separated from the back wall. In the mid-1960s *Newsweek* magazine, in an article about advances in medicine, ran a photograph of Dr. Wilder with a laser used to repair retinas.

Retinal surgery is a highly demanding specialty. It requires intellectual acuity, manual dexterity, and regular training in the newest scientific research and treatment methods. The job also requires not just highly developed levels of expertise in dealing with a very sensitive part of the body, but also a keen sense of empathy when treating diseases that, while they may not be life-threatening, can drastically alter a patient's life-style. Dr. Wilder recognized the psychological devastation that occurs with loss of sight. "I've never refused to continue seeing a patient," he once said, "even if there was nothing left for me to do to cure a disease or condition. If regular visits gave them hope and a reason to keep going, who was I to say 'Stop hoping?'"

He decided in 1968, after maintaining a solo practice for fifteen years, to employ another physician, Dr. Charles Vygantas, to help out. The two doctors incorporated their practice two years later to form Drs. Wilder & Vygantas, Ltd. At first Dr. Wilder owned all of the stock in the professional corporation in exchange for contributing to it his medical library, medical and surgical equipment, and office furniture and artwork. According to their agreement, Dr. Vygantas would receive his shares in the corporation over a ten-year period, at the end of which the men would be equal partners. Several years later they expanded further, asking a third younger doctor to join the growing practice.

*   *   *

Throughout these early years, while Howard Wilder was fortunate in his widely acknowledged professional success, he was, one might say, unlucky in love. He was divorced twice, and in his mid-forties, quite alone.

In 1967, shortly before he started working with Dr. Vygantas, Howard met a pretty younger woman who lived down the street, a medical technician named Gayle, who was divorced and had a six-year-old daughter named Kelly. Howard and Gayle married on May 17, 1968, when Howard was forty-four years old and Gayle was twenty-eight. About six months later he adopted Kelly.

Gayle quit her job as a specialist in electronmicroscopy, and they purchased a large home in Northfield, Illinois, one of the elite North Shore suburbs of Chicago. When they moved in, Gayle was eight months pregnant with their first daughter, Leslie. Fifteen months later a second daughter, Amy, was born.

Howard's practice continued to prosper. He and Gayle purchased a vacation condominium in Palm Springs, California, and invested in apartment buildings and other real estate. Over the years they filled their lives with numerous pursuits and expensive hobbies, most of them—like their investments—under Howard's direction. They accumulated an exquisitely maintained classic car collection (including three Mercedes-Benzes, a Rolls-Royce Cornice convertible, and a BMW), partially housed in the Wilders' five-car garage. They added extensively to Howard's Indian and Oriental art collections and purchased numerous other pieces to decorate their showcase home. Howard's favorite pastime, tennis, also played a tremendous part in their marriage. A superb player, he taught Gayle the game, and together they built a court on their two-acre lot. Howard even put down the filling and laid the tapes himself.

As with most marriages that fail, the stresses and cracks in the Wilders' marriage were hardly visible at first, niggling little details that one or the other would shrug off in the course of daily living. But the signs of strain grew nonetheless, and eventually a chasm opened that neither Howard nor Gayle could deny, even if their individual accusations differed. One day Howard simply left.

Gayle desperately wanted him to come home. The rejection hurt her so badly and seared so deeply that without any recourse for repair, her pain was transformed into anger. To Gayle, a woman scorned, everything bad in their lives became Howard's fault. "You are a deserter and abandoner!" she would scream at him whenever he came back to the house. Howard was certain Leslie and Amy could hear the yelling. Nonetheless, he and Gayle fought often and vehemently—over their houses, the cars, the artwork, money Gayle needed, their children's medical care, their schedules, and their religions, for Howard was Jewish and Gayle was not.

She was determined not only to safeguard her style of living after he left but to make him pay for his hurtful behavior, too. Gayle claimed as her own the homes, the cars, the furniture, the artwork, the real estate investments, a healthy portion of Howard's income, and a share of his medical practice. It had thrived, she said, because in her role as a homemaker she had supported Howard, and, therefore, she deserved to be compensated for its value.

Gayle had a valid basis for her argument. Among the assets that divorcing couples can divide under community property or equitable distribution laws is ownership (or part ownership) in a business or professional practice. If, for example, a couple has been married for a number of years while either the husband or the wife built up a business or a practice, such as a medical or legal practice, the value of the business or practice must be shared between the husband and wife.

The big question, of course, is determining how much that business or practice is worth. While the book value of Howard's ownership in his medical practice was only about $157,000, which included the hard assets (for example, the office furniture, equipment, and accounts receivable), Gail argued that the actual value was at least two times higher because Howard's professional reputation enhanced the practice substantially. His personal involvement added to its market price through that intangible factor called goodwill. For prospective buyers, it would represent the probability that patients would continue to use the services offered by the practice even after the founding doctor had left.

But Howard bristled at the very thought that Gayle could claim that she had contributed to his professional success. Hadn't he already been well established before they even met? Gayle had not done a thing to make him a highly respected doctor. Clearly this is a point of view with which many men would agree.

Donald Schiller came to Howard's attention through another Chicago lawyer who handled some divorces but maintained a more general civil practice overall. This lawyer had thought that Howard's situation merited the attention of a more specialized practitioner, one like Schiller, who was familiar with complex, large-asset divorces. Schiller, who gets up at 5:00 A.M. to catch a train from his suburban home to the Loop, where he works, approaches these divorces with the dedication and ambition of a man who will be second to none.

He arrives at work fashionably dressed. His refined demeanor is consonant with the sophisticated, big-money divorce cases he handles. Schiller represents the new breed of divorce lawyers, those who subscribe to standards of professional excellence that in prior decades would not have been associated with matrimonial practice—a specialty that became prestigious only in recent years.

"Howard is not only a very good client for me," the referring attorney told Schiller when passing the Wilder case on to him, "but he's also a close friend of our family. He's a great guy and very important to us, so I'd be very grateful if you would spare nothing to help him." Schiller, then thirty-seven, readily agreed. He enjoyed the intellectual challenge of a tough, large-money divorce, and Howard's case sounded like it met all of his criteria.

Schiller is also a lawyer who enjoys demonstrating his finely honed skills before the judges who hear such complicated cases. "In Illinois, divorce trials are bench trials," he says, rather than jury trials, as they are in some other states. "My approach sells judges. What really impresses a judge," continues Schiller, "are the more mechanical, professional arguments rather than the emotional ones."

Jury trials tend to be far more emotional because the lawyers argue to an audience. They are too focused on who is wearing the "black hat" and who is wearing the "white hat," which leads to finger pointing and hysteria. In those cases, because the litigants work so hard to dirty each other up, most judges end up thinking that neither party is any good.

His practice philosophy makes Schiller a favorite among Cook County (Illinois) Circuit Court judges. "In a field long distinguished by flamboyant shouters and screamers," says a *Crain's Chicago Business* article, "Don Schiller—master researcher, tax specialist, mediator and arbitrator—is an anachronism." In fact, in May 1981, while Schiller was handling Howard's case, the magazine named him Chicago's outstanding divorce lawyer.

When Schiller first met Howard Wilder, he recognized him as an intelligent, capable, and exacting client. The fifty-eight-year-old doctor was meticulous in appearance, and everything he touched was handled thoughtfully, thoroughly, and with great personal care, whether he was refurbishing a prized car, repairing a patient's damaged retina, or overseeing his own divorce. Despite his short stature, Howard's guardedly intense demeanor and taut, athletic build gave him an aura of self-confidence and command. Schiller found his new client a fascinating and charming conversationalist, one who could hold his own on almost any topic. And for Howard, no topic could be treated superficially; his need to understand was too keen, and it drove him to great depths. Being his lawyer would not be easy.

Schiller quickly saw that Gayle Wilder was out for all she could get because, the lawyer told Howard, "she thinks you're the cause of the marriage breaking up." Yet in Illinois the division of assets during divorce has nothing to do with blame; even in 1980, when the Wilders separated, before Illinois became a no-fault state, division of property already relied on solely objective, no-fault-like criteria. Everything earned or purchased by either spouse during the marriage was marital property, and during a divorce either it had to be split or the ownership had to be resolved through negotiation. (Illinois, one of the last two states to allow no-fault divorce, began doing so on July 1, 1984.)

Schiller was convinced that because Gayle had no outlet for expressing her anger, she would try to hurt Howard financially during the division of their property and possessions. She could do this by trying to prove that his car and art collections, for example, and more important, his medical practice, were part hers and that they were worth a lot of money, with the result that Howard would have to pay her more.

Howard quickly rose to the challenge. He told Schiller that his medical practice had been established and successful long before he married Gayle, so she had no right to claim a share, regardless of its worth. It was *his*. Schiller nodded in agreement. Nor did the mere fact that it was worth more at the time of the divorce than it had been when they were married automatically prove that Gayle had contributed to Howard's current success.

But regardless of what Howard thought, his lawyer realized that the fight against Gayle would be tough. Howard had been divorced before he married Gayle, and at that point he had little more than his professional reputation. Then he married Gayle, and for almost twelve years, with her support in the home, he built his practice to its current level of success. Most important, after he married Gayle, Howard went into partnership with another doctor and then incorporated the practice, receiving at that time stock in the medical corporation. A judge could decide that the practice was transformed into marital property when Howard acquired the stock, making it part Gayle's. Gayle could argue further that the partnership and subsequent incorporation added to the value of the practice's goodwill, because it could conceivably continue without Howard. The burden would be on Schiller to prove all of these arguments wrong.

"The state of the law in Illinois is such that it is likely that a single practitioner would *not* be found to have goodwill," explained Schiller. "The smaller the [professional] group, the less the valuation of the goodwill would be." Schiller's job would be tougher because of Howard's decision to take in other doctors and incorporate.

Some other states, such as California, say that goodwill exists even in cases of a sole practioner. Suppose that a husband and wife are married for twenty years, and during that time, the wife helps the husband build a highly successful law practice. He is a sole practitioner who earns $2 million a year. Then they divorce. On paper the value of the practice is the desk and other furniture, a bank account, accounts receivable, unbilled work in process, and, basically, any other hard assets.

Yet it may be that the husband cannot sell the law practice because only he can attract the clientele it serves. It takes his personal efforts to make the $2 million a year. After a divorce, the wife would walk away with no compensation for nurturing her spouse's career, while the husband would continue to make $2 million annually. In such a case, a California court might say that the husband had built up his reputation and developed his skills during the marriage, and the court might seek a way to apportion some of the income to the wife for her role.

To do so a judge could begin by noting the annual earnings of the average "very successful" California lawyer with experience comparable to the husband's in this case. Assume here for purposes of illustration that the average annual earnings figure is $1.2 million. According to California judicial thinking, the earnings of a specific lawyer that were in excess of the average would represent a basis for determining the goodwill value of his practice. If the hypothetical attorney earned $2 million annually, then his "excess" earnings would amount to $800,000 a year. That goodwill amount could be shared with the wife along with any hard assets acquired by the law practice. Business valuation experts might further magnify, by some additional multiple, the dollar value calculated for goodwill to take into account the lawyer's total future excess earnings, not just those that accrue in one year.

But Howard Wilder was divorcing in Illinois, not California, so he and his lawyer had to pay strict attention to the laws in his own state.

"What will happen if a judge decides my practice is marital property?" the doctor inquired as they discussed his case. "And what if a court decides that the value of the practice includes goodwill—and part of that value is Gayle's?"

"Well, then you might have to make a lump sum payment for her share of the practice, in addition to any alimony and other payments you might be ordered to make. And if you can't make the entire payment at once, you will have to spread it out over time, with interest." Or, Schiller added, the court could award Gayle more of the other marital assets to make up the difference.

Sometimes in business valuation circumstances, a spouse ends up owning a business after a divorce—with the "privilege" of work-ing—and literally nothing else. The rest of the marital assets may go to the other spouse if the value of the business or professional practice, including its goodwill, is so large that everything else must be put on the opposite side of the dividing line to make the division equitable. Sometimes, if the business is not saleable at that time, the owning spouse is stuck with it. In such cases, the potential exists to make a lot of money—probably far more than his or her spouse—but the busi-ness owner is also a prisoner of the job.

The concept of valuing a business or profession as part of the distri-bution of assets during divorce first came about in California and the other community property states. It is a relatively new phenomenon in equitable distribution states, such as Illinois, home of Howard and Gayle Wilder. Traditionally in these states, a business or professional practice belonged to the individual in whose name ownership resided. But today, in equitable distribution as well as community property states, a spouse, typically the wife, receives a right to share in every-thing obtained during the marriage, including any occupational asset. Thus, the national trend is to value any business, enterprise, or profes-sional practice that came about during the marriage in order to divide it along with the more traditional marital assets—or, as usually hap-pens, to split the entire pool of assets so that the value of the total share for each spouse is fair.

Since spouses started fighting over their businesses and professional practices, the actual nature of these battles has, in some cases, taken on peculiar twists.

In mid-1989 United Press International distributed a story relating how the divorcing wife of the chief executive of Dunkin' Donuts had cited that company's rejection of a forty-three-dollar-a-share tender of-fer as a reason for claiming a higher value for her husband's stock. The husband, who owned 200,000 shares of Dunkin' Donuts, testified in his divorce proceedings that it was worth thirty-two dollars a share, the current trading price, yet later he rejected as "inadequate" a takeover offer from a Canadian group wanting to pay forty-three dollars a share. "Lawyers for the wife said that her husband cannot use one stock value for the corporate world and another value for his wife," says the UPI report.

And consider the historic 1985 case of Loretta O'Brien, a school-teacher who helped finance her husband's medical education only to be divorced by him two months after he received his diploma. A New York State court decided that Dr. O'Brien's medical license was marital property that had to be divided equitably with Loretta. Treating the license as if it were a business or investment, the court appraised its value at $472,000 and gave Loretta 40 percent. New York, however, is in the minority in its stance on this issue. Most states have ruled that a medical or law license is not divisible property.

Yet it still holds that a professional practice or business—as opposed to the license itself—may be considered marital property in a divorce and can be valued when dividing the entire pool of marital assets.

There is, however, a caveat when determining a price tag, including any dollar figure for goodwill if it exists. Attorneys and their clients must be cautious in dealing with alleged monetary values that are insep-arable from the individual. For example, if a well-known woman's clothing store is sold, the seller may maintain that the name of the store connotes for the buying population a certain standard or level of merchandise and that the right to continue using that store's name is, in itself, as a goodwill factor, worth some additional price.

But in the case of an individual who provides a very specialized pro-fessional service, such as a doctor in an esoteric medical specialty—and Howard Wilder's practice was a good example—the reputation built as a result of that doctor's superior care could be viewed as no longer viable without his working on the premises. Thus, the practice would be said to be without goodwill. This would be one of attorney Schiller's arguments against Gayle Wilder's claims.

As Schiller worked his way through the necessary preparation and paperwork, readying himself for what would assuredly be a hard-fought trial on the valuation issue, and on every dispute in the Wilders' di-vorce, he was at times frustrated with Howard's involvement in the case. Schiller never doubted that his client wanted to be fair to Gayle—he was not the kind of man who would want to get away with giving his wife as little as possible—but Howard did not seem to under-stand exactly what "fair" would mean, so he repeatedly questioned Schiller's decision making. When Schiller thought the case was going well, Howard might not necessarily agree. The physician wanted to measure developments by his own scientific standards, which meant seeking exact, predictable reactions to given actions or events.

"In science or mathematics you're dealing with clinical settings," ob-serves Schiller today in recalling the Wilder case. "In courts of law it's much less precise. You are not in a clinical setting. Nothing is controlled. There are variations all over the place, depending on the judge, the lawyers, even who woke up in the morning not feeling well." Decisions are made taking into account all of these variables. Thus, the environment in which Howard's divorce unfolded was the antithesis of the carefully controlled scientific setting in which he was so comfortable, a setting in which only one variable can change at a time. It's not surprising that the legal process was so disconcerting to him.

One development early in the divorce clearly highlighted the differences between the two men's approaches. In June 1980, six months after the Wilders' separation, Schiller negotiated with Gayle's attorney a temporary monthly support arrangement pending the outcome of a trial. He was pleased with the result, thinking that it was very favorable for Howard. While most clients would have been delighted, accepting their lawyer's professional determination that the overall arrangement was a good one, Howard demanded a detailed explanation as to exactly why and how each and every sentence and provision had come about. He was driven to understand, and no nuance was too small for his attention. Schiller had to replay for him every discussion that had unfolded in the negotiation process and explain how he had reached a decision on each point. In the end he practically had to force Howard to sign the agreement. For an attorney of Schiller's stature, the questioning and probing were both frustrating and draining. A less confident lawyer might have been insulted.

Within a week it did, however, become clear to Howard that he had made an excellent deal. Gayle fired her lawyer.

Fireworks between the Wilders exploded regularly, and the sparks fueled their personal battle as well as the legal one. One major source of contention was their extensive car collection, a source of pride and prestige for both Wilders. Gayle argued that it was partially hers, much to Howard's horror. He considered the cars to be his sole preserve.

In the September following their separation, Howard discovered that Gayle had driven off in the Rolls-Royce, a car which had cost eighty-five thousand dollars. He had thought that she never drove it. As Howard would explain in his deposition a few months later,

> Mrs. Wilder "hid" [the Rolls-Royce] in the city someplace so that I did not know where the car was or could not find it. And then she apparently took the car out of hiding and started driving it around as her personal car. Plus she let *some male* drive the car.
>
> And this was told to me by a friend of mine who saw *that person* driving *my car* in downtown Chicago.

When Howard discovered one day that Gayle had taken the car to their daughters' school, he followed her. While she was inside the school, he hopped inside the Rolls-Royce and drove away, leaving behind the Chrysler station wagon he'd driven there. When Gayle came back outside and realized what had happened, she was furious, the loser in a spiteful game. At times like this, a degrading pettiness seemed to rule their days.

Howard kept close tabs on the discovery, or fact-finding, part of his case. "The importance of effective discovery can't be overstated," Schiller told him time and time again. "All a trial does is play out what we're able to come up with during discovery."

The lawyer developed his theories for Howard's case by talking them through with various experts and witnesses. To begin with, Schiller needed to identify marital versus nonmarital property. Like Howard, he, too, questioned whether the ophthalmology practice was marital property at all; even if it were, Schiller would maintain that it essentially had no goodwill value. Ultimately he also would argue that allotting the wife a portion of her husband's business, including goodwill, would allow her to benefit twice. "If goodwill is the ability [of a business] to earn future income," Schiller would write in his trial brief, "then if Gayle gets a portion of that goodwill now and also receives maintenance from Howard's future income, she shall be obtaining a double payment from the same asset." Schiller's reasoning presented a novel argument.

Of course, he also would have to decide how to value what he and Howard did agree was marital property. This included the Chicago home and Palm Springs condominium and their furnishings, the car collection, the art pieces throughout the house, and much more.

Gathering all of the facts he could, Schiller's goal was to develop, through direct examination of experts and witnesses and through cross-examination, a credible position for Howard that would hold up at trial and that, ultimately, a judge would buy. Sometimes Howard was more of a hindrance in this effort than he was a help.

"I need a list of all your cars and the value of each one," Schiller instructed him one day. "And can you give me the names of some people who really know these cars, people I can put on the stand to attest to their value?"

"That's not necessary," Howard replied. "They're mine, so it doesn't matter how much they're worth. Anyway, if you have to know, I can tell you."

"Well, Doctor, just because you know the value doesn't mean the judge is going to accept your opinion."

"But I *know* the value," Howard insisted, as if dealing with an obvious line of reasoning. It was hard for him to understand that his lawyer would have to hire people to testify about something about which he already knew the truth.

"Well, Gayle is going to hire an expert who will say these cars are worth much more than they are," replied Schiller patiently. "So if you want to keep them, you would have to pay her that much more money to balance it out."

"That's not true," cried out the doctor. "Then he's a liar!"

"Doctor, if it's going to be between the opinion of a classic car expert and the opinion of an eye surgeon, I have to tell you that the judge is going to lean toward the opinion of the car expert. And you have a *bias.* So we have to have experts if she's going to have experts."

Ultimately Howard would get his way. When it came time for the trial, the only valuation experts Schiller would call to the stand were those Howard himself had chosen. For the business valuation he used Howard's own accountant; for the cars he called a man with whom Howard had dealt; and as an art expert Schiller used a gallery owner from whom Howard had purchased a painting.

At the same time he was planning Howard's case, Schiller also was thinking about what Gayle's lawyers might be using as their strategy. Schiller carefully analyzed their expert lists and himself deposed the experts so he would know before the trial began just what each might say. One of their major arguments in the case would be that Howard's entire medical practice should be considered marital property because he had incorporated it after his marriage to Gayle and because many of his patients had been acquired during the marriage. Schiller would counter that although Howard had incorporated his practice after the marriage, he had received his stock in the corporation *in exchange for* the proprietorship, that is, his individual, personal ownership of the practice that he had before the marriage. Still, he admitted to himself, it would be close. The judge could go either way.

As the days wore on it also became increasingly clear to Howard that his case was not just a question of trying to decide what was fair. With the legal war Gayle was waging, hoping to claim as much money and as many of their assets as possible, Howard would soon feel that he was fighting for his life.

In late 1981 Gayle fired her second lawyer, perhaps because he recommended that she sign a settlement agreement, and hired instead a general practitioner named James Hardy, a neighbor who had known both Wilders for a long time. "You shouldn't sign this," he told Gayle when she asked his advice about the proposed settlement the other lawyer had negotiated. "Let me handle the case for you." Gayle felt relieved and immediately switched her trust to Hardy, a Mormon and father of nine who was admired universally throughout their neighborhood.

Because Hardy was new to the case, effectively entering at the eleventh hour, he asked that the trial date be postponed to give him enough time to prepare. But because the entire matter already had taken almost two years to resolve itself, and the settlement Schiller had sought was no longer in sight, he asked that the case be bifurcated, or split in two, separating the actual divorce proceeding from a decision about the division of marital property. The judge agreed, and Gayle and Howard were officially divorced November 5, 1981, on grounds of desertion, grounds uncontested by Howard.

On January 19, 1982, Hardy asked Judge John Reynolds to review a disagreement over Howard's support payments. At the time a second support order, which was different from the first one and had been entered after a hearing, was in effect. Both Schiller and his associate, David Yavitz, who had been working on the case with him, spoke up on Howard's behalf at the hearing.

"Your Honor," said Schiller, "we take the position on behalf of Dr. Wilder that this matter should not be before the Court . . . what Mrs. Wilder is attempting to do is to modify a temporary support order . . . within weeks of a final trial date where the Court will hear all the evidence with respect to needs and ability—"

"The previous order entered with respect to maintenance," broke in Judge Reynolds, "that was based upon a certain salary [of Howard's], was it not?"

"Your Honor," replied Hardy, "it was a percentage order. There was originally, as I set forth in my petition, there was an order entered which required the respondent [Howard] to pay $3,500 per month. That was on June 27 of 1980."

"That was vacated," broke in Schiller.

"On August 20, 1980," continued Hardy, still pleading his case, "a percentage order was entered, and the respondent was ordered to pay 40 percent of his net income from his medical practice to the petitioner [Gayle] for unallocated support. Your Honor," he emphasized, "we are not attempting to modify any orders that have previously been entered in this Court. We are attempting to enforce orders which have been entered because there has been obviously, as you will see as we review the figures and take testimony as is necessary, a concerted effort to deny the wife the support which he should be paying.

"He is far in arrears," Hardy stressed to the judge. "My calculations put the arrearage at approximately $61,000. My client cannot afford to pay the bills and take care of the family and take care of a large home in Northfield."

"He is not in arrears," insisted Yavitz. Because Schiller's firm involves at least two attorneys in a team approach for every case, the younger lawyer knew Howard's position intimately and he disagreed with Hardy's calculations. "He has paid more than [required]," said Yavitz. "In order for Your Honor to understand, it will take just as long on his motion, on his petition, as it will take on the trial." Yavitz wanted to avoid the mathematical wrangling.

"When is the trial set?" asked the judge.

"February 16," said Yavitz. "[This] is totally duplicative to what we will have to do with the trial of this case."

Hardy, ever the zealous advocate, simply would not give up. He wanted that extra money for Gayle and he wanted it now. "It will take us ten minutes to put before the Court the facts of this matter," he insisted. "It is very obvious on the basis, the tax returns, which the doctor has filed—"

"We are going to try the matter in two weeks' time," Judge Reynolds interrupted.

"Yes," nodded Schiller.

"Let's do it all at once," said the judge.

"We are talking about a month's period of time," Hardy corrected him.

"All right. Four weeks," said the judge.

"We are talking about a situation—" Hardy could not get out a full sentence without Judge Reynolds interrupting.

"Is she destitute?" he demanded.

"She is destitute," Gayle's attorney insisted. "She cannot make the mortgage payment."

"How much is she getting a month?" the judge wanted to know.

"She is now getting $2,500. These were people that were accustomed to living—"

"Don't tell me she is destitute on $2,500," snapped the judge. "She is *not* destitute with $2,500 a month. We will continue all matters until the trial of the case. We will dispose of it all on February 16."

"Your Honor," Hardy pleaded, "we have an order of Court [regarding support payments] which we should be permitted to enforce—"

"*Counsel,*" Judge Reynolds warned, "everything has been continued to the trial date, and that will be . . . February what?"

"Sixteenth," Yavitz quickly responded.

"That's the date, February 16."

Gayle would have to wait.

*   *   *

The trial began on schedule. Hardy first called Gayle, forty, to the stand. Both she and Howard, fifty-eight, would appear in court throughout the entire eight-day trial. Gayle's voice was controlled, soft, and gentle, and her lawyer had to ask her to speak up.

As time wore on during the questioning and Schiller's objections started mounting, Gayle's anger and determination began to surface. One of her primary arguments for not being able to work herself, and therefore needing more support, centered on the Wilders' daughter Leslie. The child had had diabetes for four years and, Gayle maintained, needed constant monitoring that only a mother could provide.

But Schiller was convinced that Gayle was magnifying the child's needs and that Gayle could in fact work. Howard had told him that Leslie knew how to give herself her own shots and that she was not as sickly as Gayle had portrayed her.

In his cross-examination Schiller first emphasized that Gayle had no intention of working or even looking into the possibility, regardless of the family's needs at home. He would not accept her argument that she had completely lost touch with the field of electronmicroscopy.

"What does a technician in electronmicroscopy do?" Schiller asked Gayle when it was his turn to question her.

"Processes biopsy tissue and takes pictures of cell structure with an electronmicroscope," she responded.

"And did you use an electronmicroscope?" he asked, referring to her earlier employment.

"Yes."

"And did you make up biopsy slides?"

"Yes."

"What has changed in making up biopsy slides since the last time you did this?"

"Technique."

"There is a better way of doing it," Schiller suggested.

"Equipment," Gayle added. ". . . I have been out of it for fourteen years."

"There could be clinics doing it the same way," Schiller suggested.

"No, they are not," Gayle insisted. "I am in touch with a person in New York that is still doing it."

"Who is that?"

"It is the woman who trained me originally," she replied.

"So all you know, you talked to some woman in New York and from this you draw a conclusion that you are obsolete?"

"Yes."

"What other study or investigation did you make to see if you were obsolete?" he asked.

"I didn't study anything."

"Did you look at any trade journals?"

"No."

"Did you go to any laboratories or hospitals to ask them about their new techniques?"

"Yes," Gayle replied. She had been to Mount Sinai in New York five or six years earlier.

"Were they using electronmicroscopes for this technique there?"

"Yes," she admitted.

"Now, did you make any inquiry as to a retraining program in this field?"

"No," said Gayle.

On the second day of the trial, February 17, 1982, Schiller challenged Gayle's claim that Howard had not shared the income from rentals of their Palm Springs condominium, and he produced Howard's cancelled checks to Gayle proving her wrong. Schiller also asked Gayle about the Wilders' various collections, Howard's support payments, and her ability to keep up with her bills. Gayle argued that she could not even pay the mortgage on the house.

"Now, when you weren't paying the mortgage or income taxes on the money you were receiving," Schiller asked, "you went in December of 1980 to California for three weeks, did you not?"

"Yes," Gayle answered. She also had taken the three children.

"How much was the airfare that you paid?" demanded the lawyer.

"I don't know," she replied.

"You paid that rather than pay the mortgage, is that correct?"

"My children are *used to* being there every Christmas!" shot back Gayle.

"Now in November of 1981," continued Schiller, "you flew to Palm Springs, did you not?"

"Yes," Gayle answered again.

"Who did you go with?"

She was getting annoyed. "I don't believe that has anything to do with his case," she announced. "I was divorced on November fifth." She clearly did not want to continue with this line of questioning.

"Who paid your airfare?" demanded the attorney. Gayle was caught in a bind. Either she would have to say that she had paid it or she would have to reveal a romantic relationship.

Hardy broke in and objected on his client's behalf. "I have a right to inquire," Schiller argued to the judge. "She is pleading poverty."

Judge Reynolds agreed, indicating that Gayle should answer.

She said that her traveling companion paid all of their travel expenses, including a baby-sitter for Leslie and Amy.

"Did you purchase at the Northshore Racquet Club a man's Prince Pro tennis racquet?" demanded Schiller. He had done his research.

"Yes," said Gayle.

"Do you play with a man's Prince Pro tennis racquet?" he taunted her, a woman who said she did not have enough money to live on.

No, it was a gift for someone else, she said, and so were the pair of men's tennis shorts she had bought.

Schiller had made his point.

Judge Reynolds postponed the trial's continuation for several weeks. On March 8 the lawyers again reconvened and immediately began arguing over a deposition Schiller had requested. He said he wanted to gather information from the trustees and attorney for Gayle's father's estate. He reasoned that since equitable distribution can be based in part on the parties' financial needs, evidence that Schiller obtained through the deposition about Gayle's independent wealth could affect Judge Reynolds' decision in dividing the Wilders' marital assets. Gayle had said earlier, while on the stand, that she did not know the amount of her inheritance.

Schiller reported the results of his efforts to find out.

"If the Court please," he began, "Your Honor, the deposition, it is an evidence deposition of the trustees and attorney for the estate. We learned from Gayle Wilder at trial from her testimony that she had no knowledge about her father's estate.

"Mr. Hardy and my firm agreed [that] the attorney for the estate would furnish us with the information. Despite that, the attorney for the estate wrote us a letter on March first telling us that Mrs. Wilder forbade him to give us any information."

Hardy wanted to block the deposition, arguing that it was too far into the trial to be permitted.

"Well," responded Judge Reynolds, "what she inherited from her father's estate is important, and they are entitled to know."

"She telephones her lawyer not to give any information?" the judge incredulously asked the lawyers.

"No," responded Hardy, "I think [it was] a trust officer."

"No, [it was] her lawyer," Schiller insisted. "He is a trust officer, too."

"She is acting erratically," the judge said, looking straight at Hardy.

"Your Honor, she did that without consulting me," he protested.

"You know," lectured Judge Reynolds, "I have heard a lot of things she had done erratically and she is only putting herself in a spot. If I see a letter like that, where she is obstructing, trying to hide something, that is not the way we are doing things here.

"I want to find out *all* the assets, and after a determination of assets it will be divided up," he said. "She doesn't seem to want to let us do that."

"Your Honor," Hardy began to plead, "she is not certain—"

"She is not certain?" broke in the judge. "She testified under oath she didn't know."

"That is true."

"And they wanted to find out. They are entitled to find out. She says, don't let them know. . . . Counsel, your client needs a little talking to. If that conduct persists, she is just going to prejudice me." Schiller could take the deposition, Judge Reynolds announced.

"Do you have a witness?" he asked, turning to Hardy as the new day of trial began.

Hardy called two experts that day to testify on the goodwill value of Howard's medical practice. Schiller was ready, because he already had taken the experts' depositions. "You always worry that a judge will be impressed by somebody who gets up there and calls himself an expert and throws figures around," Schiller says today, "but to me it was so clear that it was a lot of guesswork and they weren't even good at their guessing. Their history and experience, once we got into it and analyzed it, was much less than they wanted us to believe." None of the experts, says Schiller, had the necessary experience in valuing surgical ophthalmology practices.

John Wright, a broker who specialized in the appraisal and sale of professional practices, took the stand as Hardy's first expert. He explained that he had reviewed the financial statements and the assets and liabilities of Howard's practice but had focused in particular on its goodwill. In valuing the goodwill he used a "market" approach, that is, a determination based on what he thought the market would pay for the practice.

"What documents did you rely upon in appraising Dr. Wilder's corporation with respect to goodwill?" Hardy asked Wright.

"Well, I was primarily interested in the corporate tax return of the last two years," responded Wright. "I looked at the individual, personal tax returns and then I reviewed the pension fund, and the profit sharing returns that were submitted to me."

"Did you then, based upon your review of the documents which were provided to you, make an appraisal as to the goodwill, the value of the goodwill in the corporation insofar as Dr. Wilder's share is concerned?"

"That is correct."

"What is, in your opinion, the value of Dr. Wilder's goodwill in the professional corporation?"

"My opinion on the value of the goodwill of Dr. Wilder's practice is that it could be sold on the marketplace for $139,000," testified Wright. Of course, it was understood that the practice's hard assets would need to be factored in to reach a total value, which ultimately would equal $296,533.

Hardy asked Wright to explain how he had arrived at his $139,000 figure.

"Specifically," he replied, "we reviewed other similar types of practices that we have sold and calculated that this practice would sell on the marketplace at a multiplier of approximately sixty percent of his adjusted net earnings."

That is, Wright had estimated the goodwill value to be approximately 60 percent of Howard's annual income from the corporation, including contributions to his pension and profit-sharing plan.

Schiller did not buy this line of reasoning. He questioned whether Wright had enough experience valuing eye practices to appraise the goodwill value of Dr. Wilder's and whether he had done the prerequisite research for this particular appraisal. The cross-examination was lengthy and brutal in its attack on Wright's qualifications:

"Isn't it true that only about ten to twenty per cent of your business is appraising?" Schiller asked sharply.

"I am not sure that's true."

"Well, isn't eighty percent of your business brokering *sale* of businesses? . . ."

"That, I suppose, is approximately correct, yes."

"So it is correct to say maybe ten to twenty percent of . . . your business is in the appraisal field?"

"Yes."

"Now, the brokering, or the appraisal and brokering, of dental practices makes up the greatest percentage of your appraisals, does it not?"

"Yes."

"Would you say that three quarters of your appraisal work is in the dental field?"

"Somewhere in that area. A half to three quarters. . . ."

"Well, of your business ten to twenty percent is doing appraisals. Then of that ten to twenty percent of doing appraisals less than half of that, is it not true, are medical practices?"

"Well, I can't give you exact percentages. We do a lot more dental than we do medical, I can tell you that. . . ."

Wright also admitted that when he prepared the appraisal of Howard's practice, he did not know that Howard was a retinologist.

"And you didn't inquire anywhere in the medical community about what Dr. Wilder's expertise or specialty was, did you?" asked Schiller.

"No, I didn't," the expert replied.

Nor had he understood the extent to which the practice was surgical rather than medical, or that it was a practice based almost entirely on doctor referrals rather than on patient referrals. In the case of surgery patients are more likely to select a surgical practice based on the person performing the surgery rather than on the general reputation of the practice. If a famous surgeon heads a highly successful practice and then leaves, that particular practice would be less likely to attract the same patients. Similarly, if the surgeon leaves and a large proportion or all of the practice is based on referrals from other doctors, the referring physicians are less likely to continue sending their patients there.

Both factors would decrease the value of any practice's goodwill, according to Schiller, who was careful to point out those facts to the judge. If the judge agreed, then the intangible value of Howard Wilder's practice would be diminished and Gayle's share of this intangible asset, or goodwill, would decrease correspondingly. And that was Schiller's goal.

"Now, you have no comparison upon which to base this percentage for selling a retina practice, have you?" Schiller continued with his questioning.

"I don't have an ophthalmology practice of this size with this same circumstance, no," admitted Wright.

In fact, to determine the value of the goodwill in Howard's practice, he had compared it to two very different types of practices—one an orthodontic practice and the other an industrial medical practice.

By the end of Schiller's questioning, Wright admitted that he had never appraised and sold a surgical practice of any kind.

The second expert, John Jansen, was more threatening because he testified that Howard's share of the medical practice was worth a far higher figure—$413,000. Jansen derived his figure from a combination of three approaches, "comparable sales," "price/book value," and "price/earnings."

Under the first, comparable sales, he testified that in his experience with sales of ophthalmology practices, they sold for 80 percent to 105 percent of the most recent year's gross income, with the average percentage being 88 percent of gross income. Wilder & Vygantas's most recent gross income was just over $1 million, producing a fair market value of roughly $890,000. Howard's 50 percent share, then, would be $445,000.

Using the second approach, price/book value, Jansen explained that comparable companies historically sell at their book value multiplied by a certain number. Because Howard's company was a medical practice he applied a multiplier of two to the book value calculated for Drs. Wilder & Vygantas, Ltd. (including, for example, adjustments for accounts receivable and accounts payable). The resulting sum equaled $920,000, Howard's share equaling $460,000.

Finally, under the third approach, price/earnings, Jansen said that ophthalmologists should expect to receive an annual salary of only $120,000. Howard and his partner, however, each earned $180,000. Thus, according to Jansen, the doctors together were "overpaid" $120,000 relative to other eye doctors. At the same time, the corporation as an entity earned a net $180,000 a year. If its $180,000 was added to the doctors' $120,000 in collective excess earnings, the corporation could be said to have earned $300,000 in one year. (That is, this is what the corporation would have earned if it had not "overpaid" its two employees, the two doctors, $60,000 each.) Jensen then multiplied the $300,000 earnings by 2.5 because he, as a valuation expert, said he believed that a medical practice should sell at two and one half times its value. The net result for the value of the medical practice using this technique came to $750,000, half of it, $375,000, Howard's.

Jansen weighted and combined the three values he had reached (based on which approaches he thought had the greatest validity) to determine a final medical practice valuation of $826,000. Howard's share, then, would be $413,000. The final sum included the corporation's assets, accounts receivable, and goodwill, minus its accounts payable and any other liabilities.

Schiller was quick to recognize that every valuation approach chosen by both of Gayle's experts relied on gross generalizations. Methods such as these "make valuing businesses so treacherous," he says today. "All of these are just abstractions" that may or may not apply in a particular case. "In fact," he adds, "experts rarely value something that is like anything they've valued before. Businesses are not similar and many sales are confidential and private so the data [for making comparisons] are not available."

He got an opportunity to make his point the next day, March 9, 1982, the fourth day of trial. First he attacked Jansen's credentials, and again he was brutal. Schiller once said in a press interview that he did not take his young sons to court to see him work because he could be so hard on the witnesses he cross-examined. "Divorce court is . . . such an unpleasant place," Schiller told the interviewer back in 1981. "Sometimes I have to inflict pain on people—and I don't want to expose [my sons] to that."

Surely John Jansen felt pained under Schiller's cross-examination that day in early March. All the law requires in accepting expert testimony is that the expert know more than the average person—he or she need not be a genius—but the weight the judge gives that expert's opinion depends on how impressive he or she may be both in credentials and in the nature of the testimony. Schiller set out to destroy any credibility Jansen might have with Judge Reynolds.

He began by asking Gayle's expert to produce material from his postcollege courses on business valuations. Schiller wanted to show that Jansen did not even have enough training to be considered an expert in valuing professional practices.

"Now, did those courses deal with valuation of professional corporations?" Schiller asked Jansen.

"They dealt with valuations of all types of businesses including professional corporations," the expert replied.

"And what you have in front of you . . . are those not the text materials that you had in those programs?" Schiller continued.

"That is the outline material, yes."

"Now, could you show me in that material any reference to valuing professional corporations?"

Jansen could not answer.

"Show me the chapter on professional corporations in any of those volumes," Schiller demanded.

Jansen pointed to the first chapter in one of the books.

"And this Chapter One, aside from the cover page, consists of three pages, right, or I'm sorry, consists of six pages if you count both sides of the sheet, is that right?" the attorney asked.

"It looks that way," Gayle's witness was forced to admit.

"And most of—in fact, all of these pages have blank lines," Schiller continued ruthlessly. "Three—four out of these pages have blank lines to be filled in, right?"

"Yes," said Jansen.

"For notes?"

"Yes."

"You didn't fill in [the blank lines] with any of these notes, did you?"

"No," said the expert, "I did not, and I don't believe I did in any of the books."

"Right. And could you show me the words of this chapter that explain to you how to value a professional corporation?"

"This is strictly a course outline as I explained to you in the deposition." Jansen was exasperated.

"And where in this outline does it make reference to valuing a professional corporation or a medical corporation?" Schiller again demanded. ". . . This doesn't deal with professional corporations, does it?"

"It did, yes," Jansen insisted.

"Could you show me the words in this chapter that use the reference of a professional corporation?"

"As I said to you, this book is strictly an outline."

"The book is an outline of what the instructor covers, isn't it?"

"Partially," replied Jansen.

"Are you saying that the lecture varied from the outline?"

"Oh, they always do."

"And you didn't think it was significant enough to put in one note, did you?" Schiller was unrelentless. "Now, aside from [this] course, you haven't taken any courses that in any way deal with valuing a professional [practice], have you?"

"That is correct," said Jansen.

But the coup de grace came only when Schiller asked Gayle's expert if he had ever brokered a retinology practice.

"Would you spell that for me, please?" asked Jansen.

Howard Wilder, who had been sitting in the courtroom during the entire cross-examination, could not contain himself. "R-e-t-i-n-o-l-o-g-y," he spoke out.

"Have I ever brokered a retinology practice?" Jansen repeated, hedging for time. "Would you tell me what a retinology practice is?"

"Just answer the question," Gayle's lawyer, Hardy, directed him. It was an awkward moment to say the least.

"You don't know what a retinology practice is?" chided Schiller, enjoying every moment of the man's discomfort.

"I could guess what the word is," began Jansen. "The word is not in any dictionary. I found 'retinol.' 'Retinol is one of a group of hydrocarbons obtained in the rectification of the products of the dry distillation of turpentine resins,'" he read from the notes he carried with him. "My opinion is that the doctor is an ophthalmologist, and I don't know if he is practicing the study of turpentine."

Perhaps Judge Reynolds couldn't believe his ears—expert witnesses usually don't admit that they don't know what they're talking about—but regardless, he surely discounted Jansen's testimony. Schiller had made the expert look like a fool and implicitly may have cast doubts on Hardy as well, because it appeared that Gayle's lawyer had not even told his own expert witness about the highly specialized practice he was evaluating.

Schiller's turn came to present his case when the trial resumed in mid-March. He first called witnesses who would testify that Howard could not possibly sell his practice to another physician and then expect that physician to receive the same referrals. Logic would then follow that the practice had no goodwill value.

Ophthalmologist William Hughes, former chairman of the Department of Ophthalmology at Rush Presbyterian St. Luke's Hospital, testified that in 1968 (the year the Wilders had married) Howard had been specializing in retinal surgery as a consultation (doctor-referred) practice for many years.

"Now," Schiller asked Dr. Hughes, "if Dr. Wilder were to sell his interest in the practice to a third person, a different person, and he recommended to you to have that person take over your referrals, would you automatically follow that recommendation?"

"No," replied the ophthalmologist. "I think all referrals are made to individual doctors, not to a clinic or to an office in a specialty."

Schiller also asked Dr. James McDonald, chairman of the Department of Ophthalmology at Loyola University's School of Medicine, a comparable question, and he replied in much the same way. "I think referrals for ophthalmologists—to send patients to a specialist—is a very personal thing," replied McDonald. "You want to do best by [your] patients and it would depend entirely on the qualifications of the fellow who bought the practice. You can't transfer the authority or the respect that was built up over the years for the previous doctor."

On the sixth day of trial Schiller called Howard's certified public accountant to the stand, a man named Sam Olefsky. When offering his own expert the attorney would highlight a fact those experienced with valuations already knew: in a trial, experts can suggest unlimited ways to value disputed property or assets. Some ways are more reliable than others and very capable valuation experts can have honest differences of opinion, but some experts are more reliable than others. The attorney's job is to prove to the judge that the expert called is the best available and is one who uses the most plausible valuation techniques.

Olefsky, who had been working as an accountant for Howard for more than fifteen years, based his valuation of Howard's practice on the corporation's buy-sell agreement. The agreement set out a formula for determining how much either doctor would receive for his share of stock if he terminated his employment with Wilder & Vygantas, Ltd.

The agreement took into account the impact of three factors on stockholder equity: (1) the cash surrender value of the stockholder's life insurance; (2) the corporation's accounts receivable minus back debts and the income taxes applicable to the tax on those receivables; and (3) the fair market value of the furniture, equipment, and leasehold improvements.

Olefsky had prepared a financial statement for the corporation as of the end of its previous fiscal year, May 31, 1981, and had adjusted it by those three factors to reach a total practice value of Howard's shares equal to $157,553. Nowhere in his calculations did Olefsky include a value for goodwill.

In his testimony Howard's accountant also addressed the value of his pension and profit-sharing plan. Even though all savings during a marriage are considered marital property, Schiller did argue that part of Howard's pension fund should not be shared with Gayle. After the separation and before the trial, he said, Howard had put money into his pension and profit-sharing plans at the same time he was paying Gayle's support. Therefore, continued Schiller, Gayle should not receive any portion of that additional savings, even though, technically, she and Howard were married at the time. Although the pension fund's value did not add to the value of Howard's ophthalmology practice because it was considered separately, Schiller hoped that his reasoning would influence the judge's thinking when he made his ultimate decision on the division of all of the Wilders' assets.

Finally, Howard, then fifty-eight years old, took the stand. Schiller asked about his practice, its incorporation, its hard assets and liquid cash, real estate investments, his support of his family, including his adopted daughter Kelly, the car collection, art collection, and furnishings in the Wilders' home. He inquired about Leslie's health problems, arguments with Gayle over the girls' religion, and his goals for visitation with his daughters.

"I would like to have it somewhat loose," replied Howard, "because I realize that children age twelve and thirteen have other priorities that possibly come before a father. . . . I think one of the most important things I would like is that they didn't feel bound to a certain exact time, that they could come to me and say that they have this or that and can we make it the next night.

"I am," concluded Howard, trying to show signs of flexibility and understanding, "totally open to anything that would be compatible with the children." Howard did not add that what he wanted most was to break his ties with their mother.

．　　　．　　　．

The Wilders' trial lasted eight days spread over six weeks, from February 16 until April 1, 1982. Along with the valuation experts who testified about Howard's medical practice, Hardy and Schiller called on different experts to offer their opinions about the value of the Wilders' other assets. Of course, their conclusions differed drastically. Gayle's goal was to prove that everything Howard wanted to keep after the divorce—the cars, the art, and any other possessions he held dear—were valued as high as possible so that if Howard did in fact keep them, he would have to pay her even more money to balance out her share of the assets. In all, she insisted that the marital property in her case was worth more than $2 million, mandating that she herself received from her husband assets and cash totaling more than $1 million. On top of that she wanted more than seven thousand dollars a month in maintenance.

Schiller was incensed. In the counterarguments he filed in response to Hardy's closing trial memorandum, he wrote, "It is a wonder that counsel can sleep at night making absurd claims such as this. . . . Maintenance should not be used to give an otherwise employable healthy adult, such as Gayle, a free meal ticket for the rest of her life."

The judge must have been thinking the same thing.

In his May 26 ruling, which he read from the bench, Judge Reynolds held that the Wilders' marital property was worth not $2 million but well under $1 million. He divided the assets roughly in half.

To begin with, the judge awarded Gayle the Northfield house, which had a net value of $328,000, and Howard the Highland Park home he had bought while he and Gayle were separated, which had a net value of $35,000. Each of them were to make their own mortgage payments.

Judge Reynolds also awarded Gayle the Chrysler and Lincoln cars the couple owned, $20,000 in cash, and $50,000 in personal property, such as furnishings and jewelry. He ordered Howard to give her $2,400 in maintenance per month for five years only and $500 in child support per child per month until they reached age eighteen, plus all of the children's medical and college expenses. The judge noted as well that Gayle was the beneficiary of a $125,000 trust her father had established before his recent death. What's more, he added, "despite [Gayle's] claims to the contrary, there is nothing preventing her from becoming employed or contributing to her own support, considering her age, education, and past experience."

For his part, Howard held on to the car collection, which the judge valued at $147,000; the Palm Springs condo, with a net worth of $70,000; the Indian art collection, valued at $25,000; and his pension and profit-sharing plans, totaling about $160,000. The Oriental art was considered Howard's as well, as he had acquired the bulk of it before his marriage to Gayle.

Judge Reynolds further held that Howard and Gayle each had to pay their own divorce lawyers, explaining that Gayle had taken it upon herself to reject the settlement agreement her earlier attorney had offered and push the case to trial. Hardy had urged unsuccessfully that Howard be forced to pay his ex-wife's legal bill of more than $31,000. Schiller's bill would already total about $75,000.

Most important, perhaps, Judge Reynolds said that he was holding Howard's medical practice to be nonmarital property, and worth very little at that, exactly the $157,553 figure cited by Howard's accountant, Sam Olefsky. *The practice was deemed to have absolutely no goodwill value.* And even if he had determined that the practice was marital, said the judge, it would not have changed how he chose to divide the Wilders' assets, because he was dividing everything as fairly as he could based on each spouse's individual needs and circumstances.

Gayle appealed the ruling, arguing that the awards of property, maintenance, and child support were inadequate. The first two issues raised in her appellate brief asked whether the trial judge erred in classifying Howard's stock in his medical corporation as nonmarital property and whether he should not have considered the factor of goodwill in valuing that stock.

Schiller met the appellate challenge head-on. "Illinois law does not require that there must be a goodwill supplement to value found in a professional medical corporation," he wrote in his brief. The one and only Illinois case Gayle cited to support this belief involved a dentist whose patients returned regularly and to whom they referred friends, family members, and neighbors. But, wrote Schiller,

> It was not an exclusively doctor referral type of practice as is Drs. Wilder & Vygantas, Ltd. It is also not a surgical practice to which a patient never expects to return, as is Drs. Wilder & Vygantas, Ltd. Therefore, as discussed above, while there may be a valuable ongoing clientele attached to an ordinary dental practice, this is not the case with a surgical practice such as Howard's.

Yet as even Gayle acknowledges, the "expectation of continued patronage" is precisely what goodwill is comprised of.

The appellate court reached its decision on April 6, 1984, almost two years after Judge Reynolds had first ruled in the case. Among the many issues the higher court addressed, it ruled that the classification of Howard's stock in his professional corporation as nonmarital property was harmless in light of the trial court's explanation that even if the property were marital, the overall division would have been unaffected.

Most important—for its precedential value—the higher court also upheld the decision not to attach a goodwill value to the medical practice. If goodwill reflects an ability to generate income, the appellate court held, following Schiller's own line of reasoning, that ability is taken into account already in the division of property and maintenance award. That is, under Illinois law, the courts already consider the earning power of the husband and wife when awarding maintenance and determining property division in order to help out the spouse with the lower income. To value a professional husband's earning power or reputation in the form of goodwill and then divide the value of that goodwill between the husband and wife would in effect allow the wife to claim twice the money she deserved, or, in effect, to "double dip."

The court's explanation made the Wilder case a landmark in Illinois law regarding the treatment of goodwill in a professional practice. The opinion has been cited repeatedly by other Illinois lawyers handling comparable divorce scenarios for their clients. "This case has made it very difficult for people to get awards for goodwill," says Schiller. What's more, the rationale behind the double dipping argument has attracted the attention of attorneys around the country trying to fight against awards for goodwill. "I got a lot of calls about the Wilder case," Schiller says proudly.

Eventually Howard split his practice off from that of Dr. Vygantas and then sold it to a medical retina specialist. Although he still works there under the new ownership two days a week, at age sixty-eight he no longer operates on patients. He continues to live in the Highland Park house he bought shortly after he and Gayle separated, a house complete with his all-important tennis court. (Ironically, this is the house in which Howard lived with his second wife, who preceded Gayle. Mary Wilder had received this house after her divorce from Howard. She sold it, and when that owner put it on the market again, Howard, who was by then separated from Gayle, snapped it up.) After his divorce from Gayle, Howard married a fourth time in the mid-1980s to a woman who had been his patient. They divorced in May 1990, but Howard seems philosophical about that ending, without bitterness or rancor toward his last wife. His dislike for Gayle, however, remains strong.

Today he splits his time between Chicago and Palm Springs, where he still maintains his condominium. Wherever he is, Howard continues to play tennis about four or five days a week.

He has no ties to Kelly, Gayle's daughter from her first marriage. Kelly completely turned against him during the divorce, in large part, Howard thinks, due to Gayle's influence. Of the two children from Howard and Gayle's marriage, the older, Leslie, attended the University of Arizona for awhile and the younger, Amy, enrolled at James Madison University in Virginia, where, to Howard's delight, she joined the tennis team. Both girls, now young women, see their father regularly.

Gayle, who continues to live in the Northfield house, never went back to work or remarried. She still despises Howard, refusing to let him call the house even to speak with Leslie, who now lives there. Angry and bitter about the legal system, she remains convinced that she was treated unfairly—"railroaded," as she puts it. "I feel [that] financially I was really done in by the system," she explains today, "by Dr. Wilder and Don Schiller and lack of good representation." Subsequent events did give her cause to question the caliber of her legal counsel and of the judge who heard her case. Gayle never specifically criticized James Hardy's handling of her divorce, but he was indicted and pleaded guilty in 1986 to defrauding other clients of hundreds of thousands of dollars. Despite his outwardly religious posture and his church's prohibition of alcohol, Hardy turned out to be a closet alcoholic who accepted settlements on behalf of his personal injury clients, deposited the money into his own accounts, and then kept the clients on the hook for years by telling them that their lawsuits were still pending. He voluntarily surrendered his law license in a plea bargain arrangement.

Judge Reynolds later ran into trouble as well. His problems also stemmed from developments unrelated to the Wilder case. As part of the federal government's far-reaching Operation Greylord investigation into corruption in the Cook County court system, he was convicted in 1986 of accepting kickbacks from three attorneys to whom he referred lucrative cases and of fixing drunken driving cases for a fourth attorney in return for bribes. Reynolds was sentenced to ten years in prison.

The only major player in the Wilders' case who remains unscathed is Donald Schiller. He had transformed the hatred and bitterness a man and woman felt for each other into a precedent-setting legal victory with the court's ruling on goodwill. In fact, Schiller's reputation as a winner has not stopped growing. He became chairman of the American Bar Association's Family Law Section in 1985 and president of the Illinois State Bar Association in 1987; some predict that he one day will be president of the American Bar Association. While his position in professional associations was reaching new heights throughout the 1980s, Schiller's practice assumed even greater stature, both locally and nationally, assisted by the ongoing metamorphosis of divorce proceedings into complex business negotiations. Today his eighteen-lawyer firm, Schiller, DuCanto and Fleck, is the largest law firm in the country devoted solely to matrimonial law. To hire him personally a client first has to put up $10,000 to $20,000 as a retainer and agree to a *minimum* hourly rate of $250 for noncourt time and $300 for court time. For a good result he tacks on an additional charge. In general, Schiller, Du-Canto and Fleck won't take a case in which a couple's assets are less than $1 million.

Even Gayle Wilder praises her former courtroom adversary. "He has a lot of clout," she says with grudging admiration. "You don't go with the local yokel and try to win against Donald Schiller." So far she's referred four clients to him and probably will send more. "He did such a number on me," says Gayle, her voice laced with irony, "and I'd like him to do a number for my friends." It never occurs to her that she contributed to her own loss in the divorce, that her angry legal battling only deepened her wounds. A sound settlement negotiated with the help of good counsel and a decision to move on in her life and put the marriage behind her would have been a far better salve.

Along with the friends Gayle has referred to him, Schiller's client roster includes astronauts, movie stars, sports personalities, and the scions of business and industry. Names bandied about by the Chicago press include Indianapolis Colts owner Robert Irsay, former Chicago Bears player Gale Sayers, and Doris Corboy, ex-wife of famed personal injury attorney Philip Corboy. While Schiller's clientele generally is split between men and women, he says that more men come to him for cases involving business and practice valuation, specifically because of the reputation he earned representing Dr. Howard Wilder.

Summary of Facts and Decision

WIFE
Gayle Wilder
41 years old
Occupation: housewife
Unemployed

HUSBAND
Howard Wilder, M.D.
58 years old
Ophthalmologist
1981 gross income: $182,250

Date of Marriage: May 17, 1968
Date of Separation: January 1980
Children: Custody awarded to Gayle by agreement.
  Kelly (Gayle's daughter, adopted by Howard), born October 28, 1961
  Leslie, born March 7, 1969
  Amy, born March 28, 1970

Court's Findings as to Classification and Values of Property and Division of Property

PROPERTY AWARDED TO GAYLE		PROPERTY AWARDED TO HOWARD	
Nonmarital		*Nonmarital*	
Trust	$125,000	Medical practice stock	$157,553
Art objects	4,140	Furniture	5,425
TOTAL	$129,140	Other personalty	unknown
Marital		TOTAL	$261,249
Marital home	$328,000	*Marital*	
Chrysler auto	3,825	Highland Park home	$ 35,000
Lincoln auto	2,500	Car collection	144,500
Cash	20,000	Park Springs condo	70,000
Personalty	50,000	Tax shelters (50%)	unknown
Tax shelter property		Indian art	25,000
(50%)	unknown	Personalty	unknown
TOTAL	$384,325	Money market fund	5,000
		Pension and profit-sharing plans (as per Pretrial Order)	158,675
		TOTAL	$438,175

Maintenance Awarded to Gayle: $2,400 per month for 5 years
Child Support: $500 per month
Gayle's Petition for Attorney's Fees ($31,077): Denied without hearing
Kelly's College Expenses: Howard 60 percent, Gayle 40 percent (final year)
Gayle's Petition for Arrearages: Denied

5

CHILD SNATCHING: RUNNING
FROM THE LAW

A Story of International Abduction

You can win just by hanging on.

—ATTORNEY LAWRENCE STOTTER
SAN FRANCISCO

Many parents worry about children disappearing, stolen away from neighborhood streets and playgrounds or local shopping malls. School-teachers recognize this danger and regularly teach young pupils not to talk to strangers. But the villains in child snatchings are not always the sinister deviants who haunt adults' imaginings. Abductors are often much more familiar: they are members of the children's own families, families already torn apart by separation and divorce.

According to the 1990 Justice Department survey "Missing, Abducted, Runaway, and Thrownaway Children in America," more than 350,000 children were abducted by family members during 1988. While the study's original purpose was to determine generally how many children are abducted in the United States, abductions by strangers proved to be a much smaller problem than family abductions. During 1988 between thirty-two hundred and forty-six hundred children were abducted by strangers for brief periods, typically involving sexual assaults; two hundred to three hundred children were kidnapped by strangers for longer periods.

Family kidnappings occur most often when divorced parents embroiled in custody disputes feel that they can or should take the law into their own hands. When releasing their findings, the Justice Department study's authors expressed shock at the count of children abducted by family members. Earlier estimates had placed the annual number much lower, between 25,000 and 100,000. The number of these abductions probably will continue to rise, according to the study's authors, because of the growing number of custody battles, a cumbersome legal process that moves at a snail's pace, and the calloused, desperate nature of some parents who will do anything to strike back at an ex-spouse—or reclaim a child.

"The legal system for adjudicating custody is not very flexible, and it doesn't respond to emergency situations and the kinds of fears and needs that arise in a bitter divorce case," one of the study authors, Professor David Finkelhor of the Family Research Laboratory at the University of New Hampshire, told *The New York Times*. "For many people, going into court for custody is too risky, too expensive and too time-consuming, so they grab the child."

Of the estimated 354,100 family abductions each year, 81 percent were abductions by parents, 12 percent by other relatives, and the remainder by a companion of a parent. Sometimes grandparents are the perpetrators of the crime, as in the case of Hillary Morgan Foretich, whose mother Elizabeth Morgan went to jail rather than reveal where her parents had taken the child. Eventually Hillary and the grandparents were found in New Zealand.

The Justice Department study, commissioned by the department's Office of Juvenile Justice and Delinquency Prevention, did find that most family-abducted children were back home in two to seven days. Only 10 percent were held more than a month. But that does not mean that parents whose children are taken for only a short time are any less distressed by the event. Not knowing for certain who took the child, where the child is, or how long the child will be gone—or even if he or she will ever be back—strikes terror in any parent's heart. What's more, these kidnappings usually follow heated divorce and custody battles.

However great the pain that an intrafamily kidnapping may cause the bereft parent, often this anguish is slight compared to the potential repercussions for the children, who are uprooted from their homes, deprived of their other parent, and perhaps forced to live on the run. Of the parents who were questioned during the Justice Department study, about one third said that their children had suffered emotional harm. Clinical research cited by the National Center for Missing and Exploited Children also indicates that parental kidnapping victims suffer one or more kinds of trauma.

Claudine Michaux Bolling, whose story is told in the following pages, had no doubts about who had stolen her son Stephan* from his school building. The teachers and the schoolchildren had seen Stephan's father forcibly whisk the boy away. His disappearance would generate an international manhunt that led from Claudine's home in Spain through Europe and to the United States, where Stephan's father had moved and was hiding. There Claudine sought the assistance of a San Francisco lawyer named Lawrence Stotter.

Yet, despite the numerous detectives hired, despite the assistance of European lawyers and of her American attorney, Claudine Bolling would not see her son again for four and a half years.

At about ten minutes before nine in the morning, forty-year-old Paul Bolling drove up in front of the schoolhouse door. He had been to his son's school before, so he had no trouble finding it this day. The school building, which had been converted from an imposing private home, looked different from the schools he had known while growing up in the United States. Now that Paul was finally at his destination, he stared at the building one last time, gathering strength. He was nervous and frightened, worried whether his plan, admittedly a drastic one, would proceed as anticipated.

It's so unfair, Paul muttered to himself, trying to bolster his courage to go inside. Why should Claudine always have the children and make it so hard for him to see them? Didn't he have as much right to be a parent as she did? Was it fair for her to take them to Spain? They had lived together for seven years in Geneva, Switzerland, where he had worked. Switzerland was her home country, too; it was where her parents still lived. Was it fair for Claudine to make his visitations after the divorce so complicated?

I have my rights as a father, Paul said to himself. The Bollings' divorce had been fairly easy, and Paul had not fought Claudine over the boys' custody. She was the mother, he had reasoned, and she was doing a good job of raising them. But he wanted to have time with his sons, too. Anger welled up in Paul's chest, as it had so many times during the five years since the divorce, whenever he and Claudine fought

---

*In every other chapter in this book, real names have been used, but in this case, Stephan, who was a minor at the time of his abduction and who suffered considerable trauma, has asked for pseudonymity. Therefore, his name and those of family members have been changed. All other facts—times, places, events, and the names of others who were involved—remain as they were.

about their sons. He loved Stephan and Jean Paul, and he was particularly angry that Claudine's move limited his relationship with them. He felt she was making visitation too difficult.

"They're boys. They need me," he would often say to his mistress. Stephan was almost eleven, and he would be approaching puberty soon. The time had come for his older son to have a man around to guide him to adulthood.

Like so many fathers who feel isolated from their children after a divorce, Paul was driven by a mosaic of intense emotions—loneliness, fear of alienation, and frustration were among the strongest. He worried that as time went on, he would become even more of a stranger to his son, and he was convinced that that was what Claudine wanted.

Like many parents who steal a child away, he insisted that his ex-spouse had forced him into this desperate act. "If I had been able to see the children on a regular basis, this never would have happened," he would explain of the kidnapping long after that fateful day. He petitioned the Swiss and the Spanish courts, claiming his visitation rights had been denied, but they had not responded to his pleas. Claudine steadfastly denied hindering Paul's visitation.

Marie, his lover, would be joining him once this was over. He had sold his apartment in France, where they had been living together since 1974, to get ready for the trip to Spain and their move to the United States. Together they could form a *new* family with Stephan and Marie's daughter Mariette, and Paul could forget about Claudine and all of the problems she had created. The boy would, too, for that matter. It would just take a little time once they settled down together.

Parked outside the school, Paul decided he had better go find Stephan before he lost his nerve. He got out of the car and without looking back, walked in through the front door as if he were any other father on his way to visit his child's teacher. But he paused a little longer before each open classroom door than most visitors might, and each time, his eyes hungrily scanned the faces of the students behind the rows of desks. Stopping before a bulletin board, he pretended to read announcements posted there as a cluster of students walked by.

Suddenly he saw his son. Stephan was chatting with a friend as they entered the school building, his dark hair falling forward over his dark-complexioned face. Paul's heart lurched. Stephan had grown recently, but he still had the baby fat that clings to some children longer than others.

"*¿Puedo ayudarle, Señor?*" "Can I help you?" A teacher smiled as she approached Paul. He was tall and thin with dark hair, a handsome man to any passerby. A bespectacled research scientist who had worked both in the United States and abroad, Paul had the air of an educated, sophisticated professional. There was no reason for the young woman to suspect that he was a desperate, driven man.

But Paul didn't hear her, because he was already in full stride toward Stephan. Looking up toward the two adults, the boy suddenly recognized his father; his expression was one of surprise, but he remained silent.

"Stephan, we need to talk," Paul quietly said to his son in English, firmly taking him by the arm of his brown school jacket and guiding him down toward the door. "Come outside with me a minute."

"Papa, what's wrong?" Stephan asked anxiously. The boy was stunned. He didn't know why his father had come to Spain, why he was suddenly there in the middle of his school. It was clear that something was amiss, and a panicky feeling welled up in Stephan's chest.

"I'm sorry, but you must tell me where you are taking Stephan," said the now-alarmed teacher rushing toward the two of them. She wondered why the boy's mother hadn't said anything about his father coming today. "Please," she said again. "I do not have the authority to let you take him from the building."

Paul did not even turn to look at her. Sensing his own helplessness, Stephan started to whimper. "Papa, what are you doing?" he pleaded, struggling to maintain his footing. "No, I don't want to . . ." he cried out when he realized that his father was forcing him outside. He suddenly had remembered that during an earlier visit, his father had said that he would like Stephan and his younger brother Jean Paul to stay with him forever. Is this what was happening now?

The other children, rushing forward to investigate the commotion, began to protest as well, a clan of little people realizing that one of their own was in danger. In their push toward Stephan, some dropped their books to the floor. "¡Basta!" "Stop!" the children cried out. Most of them had no idea who the strange man was. He did not seem to treat Stephan kindly. "Stop!" called out a twelve-year-old girl with pigtails.

"¡Señor! ¡Señor!" The teacher hurried after Paul and Stephan down the hallway, shaking her hands. "¡Ay, Ay, Ay, Dios mío! ¡Dios mío!" she wailed. Paul's heart was pounding; he could feel it against his chest. But all he could think about was getting out of the building. The brave little girl ran after Paul as he and Stephan raced from the building, chasing them across the street toward the blue Renault. After Paul had shoved Stephan inside, she grabbed the car door handle, hoping that the strange man could not take her classmate away if she held tightly to the car. But with the sweep of his arm, Paul simply pushed the child away. He ducked inside the car. "We're going on a vacation," he lied to Stephan as they drove away.

Paul's eight-year-old son Jean Paul, whose classroom was in a neighboring building, had no idea that his father was there or that his brother had left. Paul had not even looked for Jean Paul. He didn't want to take the younger boy, whom he still considered a baby, a child too young for the father to handle, given the demands of his own life. Jean Paul was more attached to his mother. Paul believed that Stephan, on the other hand, favored him, and he was at a perfect age—he could care for himself and he obeyed. In the end Paul hoped that Claudine might be forced into a joint custody arrangement for both children. Even if they lived in different countries, even if Paul moved back to his native United States, he thought, *something* could be worked out.

If Stephan had been a teenager already, just a few years older, he might have called his mother after the kidnapping, asking her to rescue him. But he was a passive child by nature, and Paul's stern and forceful demeanor made him all the more hesitant to act. Perhaps like many young victims of divorce, Stephan also knew that both parents loved him deeply, and he was afraid, even paralyzed, in the face of his father's decisiveness.

The day was June 14, 1977, just twenty-four hours before Spain's first free elections since 1936, and Barcelona was buzzing with the excitement of the event. But for Claudine Michaux Bolling, thirty-six, the historic moment had lost all import, for all she could think about was finding her child. "He has taken him away forever," she insisted hysterically when she contacted the police. As proof she told them that Paul had taken both boys two years earlier, in 1975, for a summer visit in northern California, where his parents lived, and then had petitioned a court there to award him custody.

In response, Claudine had hired an American lawyer, Lawrence Stotter, who convinced the court to honor the original Swiss judgment awarding custody to Claudine. When Claudine later complained to the Geneva court about Paul's California petition, the Swiss magistrate said that from then on Paul would have to leave his passport with Claudine every time he visited Stephan and Jean Paul. She was to return it to him when he brought the children back.

"The last time we did this," she told the police officer who met her at the school building after the kidnapping, "was when he took the boys ten days ago. I gave him his passport when he came back and he left the boys at home and from that day on, he started to threaten by phone to take the boys away with him if I continued to humiliate him by holding his passport." Claudine, of course, viewed keeping Paul's passport not as a humiliation but rather as a guarantee that her sons would be returned.

In spite of the speed with which she reported Stephan's kidnapping from the school, the confusion and activity of the national election prevented the police from finding him; Stephan and his father left Spain. The boy had no passport with him, but Paul had been ready for that; he had, by some unknown means, acquired an American passport for his son. Soon Claudine would learn that her former husband had quit his job in France, sold his apartment, and shipped his furniture by steamer to San Francisco, California, where he went underground. Claudine's child was gone—and would remain missing for four and one half years.

The local Barcelona newspapers picked up the story. ELEVEN-YEAR-OLD BOY ABDUCTED BY HIS FATHER, read one headline. "The children did not want to be with him," Claudine had told the reporter who wrote the piece. "He attacked the eldest because he is very docile. The youngest would not have been easily taken."

After days of waiting with no word, she again telephoned American attorney Lawrence Stotter, the same lawyer who had helped her in 1975 when Paul tried to keep the boys in the United States. Stotter, who worked in San Francisco, had an international reputation for his family law expertise, and he expressed a special interest in child stealing.

Stotter knew that many of the reports of missing children flashing through law enforcement networks were not the crimes of strangers but the work of the children's own parents, divorced mothers and fathers who fought to keep their offspring and who, after losing custody, ran away with them in defiance of court orders. Sometimes these parents went into hiding, even changing their names and identities. Other times they simply looked for courts in different jurisdictions where they might get a more favorable verdict from a more sympathetic judge. At the time Stephan was kidnapped, many judges still believed that they had an obligation to investigate fully all aspects of any matter concerning a child's welfare, and they felt compelled to hold a full trial on custody, even though another state might have already completed the same process. Their willingness to reconsider every case encouraged widespread "judge shopping."

Stotter had helped block judge shopping by working to make laws governing custody more uniform. In 1972, as chairman of the California State Bar Association's Family Law Section, he successfully urged that state to become one of the first to adopt the Uniform Child Custody Jurisdiction Act (UCCJA), drafted by the National Conference of Commissioners on Uniform State Laws, to eliminate nationwide the legal incentives for child snatching and judge shopping. Generally the UCCJA requires courts to defer to standing custody orders in a child's home state. Thus, if a divorced noncustodial parent kidnaps a child and moves to another state, the courts there would defer to the order of the state that had original jurisdiction. Today all fifty states adhere to this law.

Despite Stotter's activities to prevent child snatching and to strengthen the laws governing such cases, he knew full well that the judicial system and the courts could do little to help find Stephan. Worse, he had learned that psychological scars plague kidnapped children long after they are found. For some, the wounds never heal. One ten-year-old New York boy, retrieved after three months' road travel from coast to coast with his father, was so terrified that he refused to leave the house and often cried out during the night, "Don't take me!" Another six-year-old Illinois girl was whisked away by her father to a bus terminal during the middle of the night, and they fled to a different state. Years later, as a teenager, she still responded to crises in her life—such as flunking an exam or having a fight with a boyfriend—by returning to the same bus station, picking up an older man, and going off with him for two or three days. Some children, Stotter recognized, even develop a hostage mentality, shifting their affection to the kidnapping parent and illogically venting their anger on the custodial parent who let them be taken away. The attorney would not tell Claudine about any of these cases—her pain was overwhelming already. He hoped instead that Stephan would react like still other children, who viewed a kidnapping only as a puzzling adventure, a time of excitement and new experiences, although perhaps worrisome.

With the sense of emergency that arises from an international crisis, Stotter began to take charge of Claudine's plight. "Can you fly over here immediately?" he asked his client when she called with the news.

"Of course," she replied, already planning her departure.

The boys' Swiss nanny would be with Jean Paul, but Claudine also would ask her parents to move in while she was gone. She was grateful for Stotter's assured approach. The Spanish police had seemed so inept, seemingly unconcerned about her tragedy.

Claudine put her work as a translator on hold while she made the trip to California only a couple of weeks after Stephan's disappearance. Before heading to the United States she gathered together as much information as she could about Paul and his current living situation with Marie. She also collected information about police efforts and investigative activities in Europe since Stephan had disappeared.

Although she was very upset and tearful throughout her visit to Stotter's office, Claudine maintained her composure sufficiently to tell him about the criminal charges that had been brought against Paul and about the search into France by Interpol, the 120-country international police network. Despite the horror of the situation, Claudine's refined high-society upbringing and reserved demeanor would help her preserve her concentration and dignity throughout the long search for her son.

"I think Paul is coming back here, if he hasn't already," Claudine told Stotter in impeccable English once seated in the picturesque Victorian building that housed his law firm. "You may remember—from when I was here in 1975—that his mother lives in this area. She has a lot of money to help him."

"We'll send out word to the police in the area to be on the lookout," Stotter reassured her.

"It's important that you stay in touch not only with me but also with my father and my lawyer in Geneva," Claudine explained. "Everyone needs to coordinate their activities so we can be checking both in the U.S. and in Europe."

Although Claudine was typically an introverted and soft-spoken woman, she knew she had to exercise some control, some semblance of authority, to help assure Stephan's return.

Stotter pulled out the folder from his work two years earlier, when Paul had filed his custody suit in California. Paul had claimed that Jean Paul needed emergency surgery on a clubfootlike condition he had had since birth, surgery that he said could not be performed adequately in Spain. But Stotter had been able to block the suit under the UCCJA, proving that the surgery was not needed on an emergency basis and that Claudine was caring for the child's needs appropriately through the Barcelona hospitals. Instead of granting Paul's wish, the court had ordered Stephan and Jean Paul back to Spain with their mother.

"I'll contact some private investigators here—my recommendation is Harold Lipset—to start working on this right away," said Stotter of the new crisis. "They'll put a man on Paul's mother and check out the Bay Area as a beginning."

At the time Claudine had no way of knowing that her search was only beginning. Before it was finished she would engage, through her parents' financial support, the assistance of private detectives and law enforcement agencies in Switzerland, France, Spain, Great Britain, Canada, and the United States. In all they would spend more than $160,000 trying to locate Stephan.

*   *   *

After leaving the Barcelona school Paul and Stephan drove into France and then flew to Montreal, Canada. When they reached Toronto they headed for the U.S. border and a stop in Detroit. Paul had told his son that they were taking a vacation to see his grandmother, Paul's mother, in San Francisco.

"I'm going to phone her," Paul told Stephan when they got to the United States. "She'll send us the tickets to fly to San Francisco and meet us at the airport." He headed for a phone booth to place the collect call.

After they arrived in San Francisco, Martha Bolling took her son and grandson home for the night to her house. Paul welcomed the sheltered respite following his tense, long journey. The next day he and Stephan would travel to a small, neighboring town to see other relatives and ask for help.

With his family's assistance, Paul and Stephan—and eventually Marie and her daughter Mariette—settled in Texas, south of Houston, where Paul got a job as an engineer for a private company. They would stay there until 1981, evading any attempts by Claudine and the investigators to track him down, leading what Paul described as "an utterly prosaic, ordinary, common, bourgeois life." He coached Stephan's soccer team and Marie taught ballet lessons, and together they tried to forget their past. It seemed to them that Stephan was adjusting to the new living arrangement. His scores in school were high and he regularly received praise from his teachers. Whether he truly was happy remains unknown, of course. Surely he missed his mother and his younger brother.

Back in San Francisco, Stotter and Lipset continued their search, never suspecting that Paul had left their territory. They were stumped. Lipset was particularly puzzled—the case was one of the more challenging ones he had handled—because Paul was satisfied to have only one of his children. Normally, the private detective told Claudine, the abducting parent takes all of the children from the marriage, or if he takes only one, he does so as a bargaining chip for gaining greater access to the others. This is what Paul appears to have wanted originally, but perhaps he grew frightened, because he completely let go of his younger son Jean Paul, dropping all contact with him. He would say later that through his California lawyer he continued to "put out feelers" for joint custody but that Claudine and her family "wouldn't hear of it." Stotter denies any such overtures. At the same time, given that Paul was in hiding, he completely ignored any support obligations for Jean Paul.

In fact, he was glad not to have to think about child support payments anymore. Originally Paul had agreed to pay one thousand Swiss francs a month child support plus another thousand francs in alimony, but a few years after the divorce he had stopped paying Claudine anything. He was out of work, he said.

When she complained to the Swiss courts, Paul was ordered to start payments again, although the court significantly reduced the required child support and eliminated the alimony, supposedly to compensate him for the additional expense of visiting the boys after they and Claudine moved to Spain. Yet, soon after this battle Paul refused to make even the reduced payments.

Claudine and Paul's arguments over support payments and visitation arrangements—and the linking of the two subjects in their own minds and conversations—were typical of battles waged in postdivorce debates involving children. The linkage of these two supposedly unrelated issues is what often triggers child snatchings. What generally happens is that the custodial parent, angry about late or nonexistent support payments, retaliates by denying visitation. The frustrated noncustodial parent, in return, becomes angry and snatches the child. Or sometimes the custodial parent first denies visitation and the noncustodial parent retaliates by withholding support and, eventually, stealing the child away. In other situations a mother may run with the children to keep them from their father.

Support payments and visitation schedules have no legal relationship; the violation of one does not excuse the violation of the other. Parents must treat each as a separate issue. A custodial parent, for example, must seek child support through the courts while continuing to allow visitation, and a noncustodial parent must continue making child support payments while seeking help from the courts to enforce visitation rights.

But Paul claimed that Claudine often had not been at home when he traveled to Barcelona and the Swiss courts had refused to enforce his visitation rights; that was why he had tried to get a new custody ruling from a California judge, to no avail, several years earlier. At the same time, however, Claudine maintained that she had never denied Paul visitation, although she did insist that he leave his passport with her when he was there. Whatever the truth about the visitation dispute, in the end Claudine's anxiety proved valid. Her attempts to protect her custody were fruitless and what she had always feared actually happened.

• • •

After Stephan was taken, Claudine certainly stopped worrying about Paul's support. All she wanted was to find her child. Although she did not know for certain, she suspected that Paul's mother, Martha Bolling, had helped him escape. Yet when Claudine or her lawyers called the mother, she refused to talk about Paul and where he might be. No criminal charges had been brought against Paul in the United States; no one could even prove he was there.

In an emotional appeal Claudine mailed to Martha Bolling and nineteen other Bolling relatives copies of a color snapshot showing Stephan and Jean Paul arm in arm. In the message that accompanied each one, she begged for assistance. But not one Bolling relative answered her plea.

As the weeks turned into months, Claudine began worrying that Paul might try to come back and take Jean Paul, too. Every time she sent the younger boy to school or out to play she wondered if she would see him again. She firmly believed that Paul was fearless enough to try a second kidnapping, despite the even greater risk it would bring.

On August 12, 1977, Stotter filed a petition with the superior court asking for warrants directed to "all available law enforcement agencies of the State of California," including the police departments in neighboring cities and the sheriff's departments for surrounding counties, commanding them to apprehend and take into custody both Stephan and his father. The court complied with Stotter's request on August 23 by issuing an order for the warrants.

Stotter also filed a $500,000 lawsuit against Paul, Martha Bolling, and his brother Dennis Bolling, alleging a conspiracy to kidnap Stephan.

But when it actually came to finding Stephan there was little the attorney could do other than wait for the investigators to turn up some clues. Six months passed, and still Stotter heard nothing. Paul's furniture had arrived at a San Francisco warehouse in early August, addressed to Paul's mother, and the warehouse supervisor said that a man matching Paul's description had picked it up. But he had no idea where Paul had been headed. With their lack of information, Stotter, Claudine, and private investigator Harold Lipset continued to believe, erroneously it turned out, that Stephan was living somewhere in the Bay Area. It was Paul's home turf, they reasoned, and he had attended Stanford University nearby.

They decided that it might help to offer a reward for any information leading to Stephan's recovery. Why not hold a press conference and explain to the entire community what had happened? As much media attention as they could get would be helpful. Claudine's father, who had a prominent job with the Swiss government, was paying her legal and investigative costs, and he also offered to provide a ten-thousand-dollar payment for anyone who came forward with a lead.

They retained a room for a press conference at the St. Francis Hotel on a Monday in mid-December 1977. It was centrally located, an easy walk for reporters working at the newspapers downtown. Claudine was nervous. She worried that her European accent might put off the reporters, but she knew that by standing in front of the press she could tell a story that would make a compelling human interest article for any publication. A small, slim, striking woman of thirty-six, Claudine pushed her dark, medium-length hair back behind her ears and straightened her tailored suit as she began to make her presentation. She only hoped that the publicity attempt would lead to a clue—*any* clue.

The press conference had been set for 10:00, and by 9:55 a half dozen reporters had wandered in. A television crew snaked cables across the floor and set up their tall, stemmed lights. Claudine worried whether the reporters would be interested in her plea, but some were women, who she felt might be able to identify with her. Perhaps their empathy for her pain would provoke curiosity.

"Ladies and gentlemen," began Stotter before the assembled group. "I have passed out to each of you—and I have additional copies for latecomers as well—a paper describing the story we are about to share with you here. It involves the case of a kidnapped child, who was snatched from his school and his home in Barcelona, Spain, by the divorced husband of the boy's mother—the boy's very own father—to be taken into hiding in the United States, never, *never*, we are led to believe, to see his mother again.

"The father, Paul Bolling," continued the attorney in a strong, authoritative voice that projected forcefully across the room, "has done this in violation of the custody order of the Geneva court, where he and my client, Claudine Bolling, were divorced. From that time, last summer, when her child was snatched suddenly from her, Claudine Bolling has fought indefatigably to locate her son, using my assistance and that of detectives and the police with the aid of Interpol. We all have worked hard to obtain a lead to the location of this man who kidnapped his own son."

As Stotter began to introduce Claudine, a young woman from the *San Francisco Chronicle* carefully scrutinized the distraught mother. Julie Smith, the reporter assigned by the city editor to cover the kidnapping-and-reward story, wondered if a private interview with the mother would be possible. Of course, Claudine agreed.

"What message would you send to Stephan if you knew he could receive one?" Julie asked Claudine when they were alone together after the emotional press briefing, the announcement of the $10,000 reward, and the barrage of questions that followed.

Tears welled up in Claudine's eyes as she looked off into the distance and thought about what she might say. "Jean Paul, his brother, misses him very much," she began, crying, "and he said the best Christmas present I could give him is the return of Stephan."

Claudine continued, her voice laden with sadness yet filled with anticipation at the thought that her son actually might read her words. "Please tell him that I wanted to give him for his birthday a Scrabble game, a stuffed bear, a transistor radio, a magic set, some blue and red pajamas . . . and a lot of other presents.

"But Stephan's birthday was November 19," Claudine explained to Julie as she scribbled furiously in her reporter's note pad. "And I just didn't know where to find him."

For Christmas Claudine sent Paul's mother a box of gifts for Stephan, hoping that she would forward them. The senior Mrs. Bolling simply returned the package unopened.

Increasingly despondent, Claudine decided several months later to try an appeal to President Jimmy Carter. The detectives had led her to believe that Paul was indeed in the United States. "Dear Mr. President," Claudine's letter began. "It is in desperation, because I have used all the legal means at my disposal without result, that I am taking the liberty of appealing to you."

She continued, after explaining the history of the case,

> My parents, Mr. and Mrs. Gerard Michaux, of Geneva, Switzerland, and I have done all we can to locate Stephan. All the searches that we have undertaken both through the Spanish police and through Interpol, private detectives in Europe and in the United States and the California police have not produced any result up to date.
>
> On two occasions I have traveled to San Francisco to direct these searches and to comply with certain official formalities. All without success.
>
> My family has offered and I myself have announced over Channel 7 of the American TV a reward of $10,000 to anyone giving us information allowing us to locate Stephan and his father. There has been no result [there] either.

Claudine was trying not to cry; she did not want tears to smear the page.

> Under this condition of impotence, I am writing to you, Mr. President, as my last hope, so that justice may be done to me, that I may recover my son and that both brothers who are suffering a painful separation may be reunited. I beg you, Mr. President, as a father who believes in moral values, to take close heed of my petition. The happiness or unhappiness of my sons and myself depend on you.

But even the White House could not help.

Stephan's school tried to assist Claudine. The parents and faculty felt terrified because someone had stolen one of their own students right from the schoolhouse itself. In July 1979 the director personally delivered to the United Nations in New York a letter signed by the students' parents asking for help. In a united plea, the school wrote to the UN office overseeing the "International Year of the Child," asking for that organization's help in finding Stephan. Please reunite this family and these pupils from our school, the letter said.

Two years passed, and neither Lipset nor any of the European investigators hired by Claudine's family could find Stephan. They had checked with the U.S. immigration authorities, the Social Security Administration, the Internal Revenue Service, the FBI, and every other possible governmental resource, but to no avail. They had no leads. Either Paul and Stephan were using fictitious names or the government's computer systems had not caught up with them. In October 1979 Claudine retained a new international private investigator, Ian Withers of Intercity Investigations, who was based in Brighton, England. Claudine and Withers met in Geneva, where they agreed, because she was running short of funds, that he would handle the case on a contingency basis. Working through an international cooperative of detective agencies, Withers asked Jack Webb & Associates, a San Francisco–based private investigation agency, to cover the California area. His West Coast firm would stay on the case for another eighteen months.

Stotter encouraged Claudine to use any detectives she selected herself as well as those he knew and recommended. The decision to use private investigators, Stotter says, is a highly emotional one made in a time of desperation. Because so many firms compete for business—and the private detective trade is *big business*—the attorney prefers to leave the choice up to the families involved. "You can go crazy with costs," says Stotter, "with all these people vying for the job saying *they* can locate the kid." And at times, he adds, some of the firms engage in activities that are legally questionable. He tries to keep his distance for that reason as well.

Despite all of the money Claudine and her parents continued spending to find Stephan, none of the detectives were able to produce her child. As the months grew into years, Stotter grew increasingly concerned that when they finally did locate Stephan, and he believed that eventually they would, he would have been brainwashed by his father—and completely alienated from his mother.

While working on the Bolling case, Stotter continued his more general activities to stop parental kidnappings both in the United States and abroad. As the hunt for Stephan covered several countries and two continents, the attorney also was lobbying for federal legislation supporting the individual states' adoption of the Uniform Child Custody Jurisdiction Act. He felt that the country needed a nationwide law to guarantee uniformity of enforcement. While Stotter was chairman of the American Bar Association's Family Law Section from 1977 to 1978, he led a task force to convince the ABA's House of Delegates that such a law was critical, and he asked the ABA to give the proposal its endorsement.

A large number of the delegates, however, opposed the idea; they said that the abductions were a family matter, not a criminal matter, and that the children were taken because the parents loved them. The House of Delegates voted down an ABA endorsement. Refusing to give up, during the following year Stotter wrote letters to all six hundred delegates referring to all of the research and evidence gathered and explaining in more detail how parental abductions are very negative, scarring experiences for the children. Stotter's exhaustive effort proved successful. At the ABA's next annual convention in August 1979, the House of Delegates reversed its position and endorsed a resolution supporting federal antikidnapping legislation.

When the Parental Kidnapping Prevention Act (PKPA) finally was introduced to the U.S. Congress, Stotter testified on behalf of the ABA in support of the bill. It passed on December 5, 1980. Keeping with the spirit of the state legislation on child custody jurisdiction, the PKPA requires every state to enforce custody and visitation orders made by the courts with original jurisdiction over a case. The federal law thus prevents courts in two states from accepting jurisdiction over the same custody suit.

While Stotter and other family law experts around the country lobbied for this national legislation, it also was becoming increasingly clear
that child snatching was an international problem, too. The case of
Claudine Bolling was only one of many examples rising from the growing number of divorces and facilitated by the greater ease of international airplane travel.

To address the growing global concern over kidnapping, the president of the ABA appointed Stotter to join the U.S. State Department
delegation to the Netherlands for the 1979–1980 Hague Conference on
Private International Law. There, as a U.S. representative, Stotter
helped draft the 1980 Hague Convention on International Child Abduction. This treaty set up a system of administrative and legal proce-
dures to be followed by the signatory countries to guarantee the prompt
return of abducted children retained in those countries.

The legal framework first initiated by the UCCJA, later incorporated
into the Parental Kidnapping Prevention Act of 1980, and then endorsed by the Hague Convention, was one that avoided subjective issues, such as what resolution of a case would be in the best interests
of the child and which parent should have custody. The laws focused
instead on identifying which legal forum has the most information and
the greatest contacts with the child's family background. Such a jurisdiction can make a custody decision based on a full, panoramic view
of the child's life. In effect the new philosophy on child abduction
eliminated the need to deal with the merits of the custody problem in
each and every courtroom in which one of the parents appeared. The
international legal system shifted instead to a consistent approach to
identify the single court that should deal with a case—that is, the court
of the child's home state. Such a philosophy effectively eliminated the
benefits of child snatching and running away, because no matter where
the abducting parent ran, the courts there would send the child back
to the original home jurisdiction.

Unfortunately, despite these new laws, and despite the increasing
attention focused on parental kidnappings, the problem continued to
grow.

While Stotter was laboring to stem all international child kidnappings, the investigators in the Bolling case continued their hunt for
Stephan. Claudine's lawyer kept in contact with them as well as with
the attorney who had represented Paul in the earlier, 1975, proceeding,
when he tried to get custody of both children during a vacation visit
there. He also was in touch with Paul's subsequent attorney, Robert
Moran, a divorce and criminal defense lawyer who took over the case

later. Even if these lawyers knew where Paul and Stephan were, they would not talk about it with Stotter. Nor would they share any information about Stephan's schooling, his physical condition, or his emotional state.

Finally, in November 1981, more than four years after Stephan's kidnapping, Jack Webb & Associates learned that Paul was in the San Francisco area. They had found his trail at last. That very year, Paul had moved from Texas back to California, right where the detectives had concentrated their search. Jack Webb's men called Ian Withers of Intercity Investigations to come over from England.

As they tracked Paul down, they periodically reported in to Stotter, informing him by mid-December that the net was tightening and they expected to nail Paul at any time. They had learned that he was employed by a high-tech firm outside the city. By January the detectives had figured out that Paul and Stephan were living in a house in the suburbs just south of San Francisco. Stephan was attending a school nearby. Stotter and his associate Rick Chamberlin, who also had been following the case over the last three years, prepared their strategy.

Claudine's Swiss attorney, Luc Hafner, "suggests the following as alternate scenarios," Chamberlin wrote Stotter in an inner-office memo.

> Michaux [Claudine—by then had returned to her maiden name] comes to the San Francisco area. Stephan is located by Withers with her help (Withers needs a positive visual identification which we feel only she [Claudine] can accomplish). Stephan is picked up by his mother. Stephan and his mother meet with one of us in court, where we ask the court for an order directing that they spend one week together in an undisclosed location in San Francisco, with the goal of permitting them to become re-acquainted and at the same time of permitting Stephan to develop an independent determination as to whether he wants to stay or go with Michaux. At the end of the week, everyone returns to court and the kid speaks his mind. Michaux will be bound by his determination.

Worried that Paul would not allow such a peaceful resolution of Stephan's kidnapping, Chamberlin noted in the same memo that the Swiss attorney also had suggested a second, more radical approach.

> If past experience is any indicator, Paul may be prepared to split at the drop of a hat [taking Stephan with him]. Ian and Hafner feel this may happen again, and therefore they

feel that a second option should be available to us. That option is to pick Paul up, place him in custody and hold him until Michaux is able to get the kid.

This is at the bottom of their list: Neither the client nor anyone else wants to pursue this option unless it is absolutely necessary. The two obvious reasons are that arresting dad will irrevocably alienate son from mother, and that if dad doesn't show up at home on schedule, the new wife [Marie] may have a system for running with the kid.

Let me know what else I can do.

Stotter could feel the tension, the uncertainty as to what would happen, as he read through the possible scenarios for recovering Stephan. Claudine's case had turned into cloak-and-dagger intrigue. When the time came to move in he would have to act quickly—and use good judgment. Stotter did not want to inflict any more psychological harm on Stephan than the child already had endured.

Stotter telephoned his client after receiving the good news. "Claudine, I think you and your father better come out here now." He had waited to tell Claudine to fly over until he was certain that she could be reunited with her son. "We're going to get Stephan," the lawyer announced. He was enjoying to the fullest one of the most rewarding moments of his career.

Claudine could hardly believe the words, and her voice caught in her throat. "Thank you," she simply said. "I'll be arriving on the next plane to San Francisco."

Her father joined her on the flight. They tried to hold on to their emotions, neither of them yet willing to say that the nightmare was almost over.

While father and daughter were in transit, Stotter and Chamberlin began orchestrating the reunion of Claudine Michaux and her son. It was not easy. "I've called the sheriff's department and been given one hour's worth of runaround," Chamberlin wrote his boss in a summary memo on January 18. "I finally got through to the Civil Division at 4:35 this afternoon to reach a recording that the office closes at 4:30 P.M. I've also been forewarned that it might be the [city] police [rather than the county sheriff's office] who should be dealing with this." Chamberlin noted that he had not called the court to arrange a hearing because he wasn't sure when and where Stephan would be picked up.

A sense of urgency pervaded all of the planning. The lawyers and detectives would have to move quickly. Paul's attorney, Robert Moran, had warned them that his client could be "preparing to disappear again."

Although Stotter had been in touch with the uncooperative Moran over the months and years that Stephan was missing, he certainly was not about to give away the fact that they were closing in and would pick up Stephan any day. Providing notice to Paul's lawyer would serve only to alarm Paul. Stotter decided instead to ask the local court to order the school principal to release Stephan to his mother. With the warrants issued in August 1977—four and a half years earlier—he also contacted the sheriff's offices in nearby counties so that they, too, could spring into action if necessary and prepare to arrest Paul. While Hafner had argued against this, Stotter could see no other way to guarantee success.

At 1:00 P.M. Friday, January 22, 1982, Claudine, her father, detective Ian Withers, one of his assistants, and Rick Chamberlin met at the courthouse.

"Stephan isn't going to be in school today," the investigator told the others. "We've found out that he has a dental appointment and he's been excused for the entire day." Claudine was surprised.

"Don't worry," Chamberlin told her. "I have the order directing the headmaster to release Stephan to us just in case he shows up. And I have the warrant for the sheriff in the next county over so he can pick up Stephan at home if that's where we find him."

That sheriff would prove less than cooperative, however. Despite the warrant, his office flatly refused to help Claudine and bucked the call instead to the city police department, explaining that Paul's home was in their territory.

In frustration, Chamberlin called the police department's headquarters. Luckily that office agreed to send a car to meet Claudine, her father, and Chamberlin a couple of blocks from Stephan and Paul's home. The police said that yes, they would execute the warrant.

In the meantime, Withers and his assistant headed over to the office of the company where Paul worked. The sheriff's office there, proving far more cooperative than the one in the neighboring county, rendezvoused with Withers, but they could not find Paul. Either he had heard that they were coming and left by a back door or, as Chamberlin believed, he was hiding out somewhere in the company plant. Whichever ploy Paul used, the sheriffs left empty-handed.

Back in the home neighborhood, Claudine and Chamberlin ran into their own snags. After six city police officers in six separate cars met them near Paul's yellow-and-white single-story home, the officers proceeded to argue for forty-five minutes about exactly whose responsibility it was to execute the warrant. Evidently they refused to step in as they had promised because the warrant's wording indicated that it was directed to the county sheriff rather than to the city police.

"Look," said Chamberlin, who was doing his best to stay calm while fearing that Claudine was on the verge of panic. She and her father were sitting in the backseat of Chamberlin's car. "The sheriff's department refused to help and told us to ask you," he argued with the police. "And you said you would execute the warrant." The young attorney was not going to back down. Not this close, anyway.

Finally, after seemingly interminable squabbling, one of the police officers picked up his car radio and called the county sheriff himself. "He's agreed to help because they're the agency named on the warrant," the officer explained after he hung up and stepped back into the street. Before long, six more cars from the sheriff's office pulled up, with one officer in each, joining the six police cars already on the scene. Stephan would not be the only one surprised by their visit. Surely the whole neighborhood—a peaceful, hilly neighborhood of young middle-class families—was beginning to wonder what was going on.

Although Chamberlin was surprised by the police officers' and deputy sheriffs' concern about responsibility and procedure, law enforcement personnel typically do adhere to their boundaries of authority. In an era when even police and sheriffs offices find themselves the subjects of lawsuits, they are particularly careful to stay within the limits of their authority unless legally justified to exceed them.

The almost ludicrous display of manpower, with the parade of police and sheriff's cars, was not that extraordinary, either. "They needed to totally control the area," Chamberlin would explain later when describing the scene. "They wanted to have so much firepower there that no one would ever cross them. It's a basic tenet of police procedure."

The firepower turned out to be unnecessary. The band of police knocked on the door of Paul's house, and when it opened they stepped inside. A few minutes later the small cadre of officers stepped back into the sunlight with Stephan in their midst, and when he saw his mother with the detectives, he immediately raced into her arms. Any doubts Claudine had harbored about her son's continuing love melted away. She had had good reason to worry, however. Stephan essentially had been in captivity for four and one half years, and by now he could have been convinced by Paul that his mother was an unloving parent who did not care about his welfare or his whereabouts. Sociological studies of kidnapped children show that their reactions upon discovery may not be rational or logical.

But Stephan, who by then was fifteen years old, was overwhelmed with relief. "I've been waiting for you to come," he cried. "I knew you would come." Claudine did not question, nor would she ever ask, why the docile Stephan had never tried, or could not try, to reach her. She was only happy to have him back. It seemed as if in their joy, mother and son could not stop hugging each other. They were shepherded to the backseat of one of the sheriff's cars, where they continued their long-awaited reunion.

Years later Chamberlin would vividly recall in detail the "very touching" meeting and the flow of unbridled affection and warmth he had witnessed that day. But in the meantime, the attorney began a new debate with the sheriff's deputies and the police officers who had responded to the call for help. Now that they had Stephan in their custody, what should they do with him? The officers said they wanted to take him to the juvenile detention home until a judge could decide his fate.

"He's been missing from his mother for more than four years and you're going to take him to jail for the weekend?" asked Chamberlin in disbelief. He was stunned. "This is astounding to me."

"Well, that's what we have to do unless somebody tells us otherwise," replied one of the officers.

"Well, try and get somebody to tell you otherwise," the attorney snapped back.

Chamberlin headed across the street to a neighbor's house to use the telephone, and after introducing himself and explaining what was happening, he called the family law court. Unfortunately, it was three o'clock on a Friday afternoon. Just about everyone had gone home—everyone except a family law commissioner, a court officer appointed by a judge to help hear the cases.

Chamberlin quickly explained the situation to the commissioner. "Can I bring this kid into your court with all of these law enforcement people," he asked, "and get an order from you that he be turned over to his mother for the weekend pending our return to court in another county?" Claudine would have to appear in a different county to reclaim custody of Stephan because the original warrant Stotter had requested for Paul's and Stephan's apprehension had been issued from a court there and because the Bolling custody case had been heard there back when Paul had tried to keep the boys during their 1975 summer visit.

When Chamberlin explained that the commissioner had agreed to his request, the sheriff's deputies were dubious about the arrangement, but one of them, the deputy manning the car in which Claudine and Stephan sat, realized quite clearly that the juvenile detention home, or "Juvie," was not a good place for a teenager like Stephan. He obviously had been through a lot, the deputy decided, and deserved some peaceful time with his mother. "OK, we'll go see the judge," he agreed. The whole gang of officers took off, a law enforcement entourage moving up Highway 101 toward the courthouse.

In a brief proceeding held almost at court closing time, the commissioner agreed that Stephan could stay with his mother over the weekend until the case could be heard the following week. But in return for that time together, he asked Claudine to turn over her passport, as well as Stephan's and her father's, to the court to guarantee that they would not leave the country.

"That's fine, but the passports are in San Francisco," explained Chamberlin. "We have to run up there to get them, and how are we going to do this logistically? It's Friday afternoon and your clerk is not going to be happy about sticking around here until six o'clock while we get in the traffic, run to San Francisco, and run back."

"Let's call the father's lawyer," said the commissioner, "and see what he says." He called Bob Moran in his office and put him on a speakerphone so that the others could hear.

"Bob, we have the kid," said Chamberlin. "We don't want him to go to Juvie over the weekend; we want him to stay with his mom. Will you agree, will you stipulate that Stephan can spend the weekend with her and we'll all appear in court on Monday." If Moran agreed, Claudine would not need to fetch the passports. Chamberlin did not believe that Paul's lawyer could possibly refuse.

"No, I want him to go to Juvie," replied the hard-nosed Moran.

"I beg your pardon?" inquired the shocked commissioner. "I've seen this boy. He's *not* a candidate for Juvie."

"Well, I still think he should go. I don't think his mother can be trusted with him."

Chamberlin broke in. "We're going to deposit the passports and we'll deposit the return trip tickets as well," he offered, at this point planning to race back to San Francisco. "This is absolutely ridiculous."

The commissioner agreed, and the group moved back into the courtroom where they began talking again about how they would get the passports to the courthouse. At that point the sheriff's deputy who had driven the car in which Claudine and Stephan sat came to their rescue. After observing them through the entire ordeal, he wanted to help.

"I'll tell you what," he began. "I live nearby. I will agree that the mother and boy can go to my house and spend as much time as necessary with me and my family there while Mr. Chamberlin runs up to San Francisco to get the passports and bring them back. I will take the passports into custody and deliver them to the courthouse clerk on Monday morning for the hearing. And when I get the passports later this afternoon, I will release the boy to his mother and everybody can go back to San Francisco for the weekend."

Everyone, including the commissioner, was impressed with the deputy's compassion. He was the hero of the day, working overtime to keep Stephan out of the juvenile detention home and allow him the weekend to become reacquainted with his mother.

The next day, Saturday, January 23, the sheriff's department apprehended Paul after an all-points alert and a high-speed chase on Highway 101. They arrested him and jailed him for the weekend to await a hearing.

The proceeding Claudine had been waiting for actually was held four days later, on Tuesday, January 26. The court was alive with activity, almost like a movie set. One of the private detectives working on Claudine's case had issued a press release, so local television and newspaper reporters had positioned themselves in the elevator lobby outside the presiding judge's chambers. The normal cast of lawyers and clients were milling around as well, perhaps hanging on a little longer to try to figure out why the press was there. Paul was being held, under arrest, in another part of the building.

Arriving in the central hallway outside the courtroom door, Claudine, her father, and Stephan tried to sit quietly on a bench. They, too, were waiting for the judge, a man they had never seen before, to determine Stephan's destiny. Claudine was in a perpetual state of teariness. She had told Stotter that it was important to find out what Stephan wanted to do, and she had worried that he might feel differently about returning to Spain after so much time away. Because she had tried not to press her son about his feelings over the weekend, she continued to be anxious about his final decision.

Stotter knew that the court might decide to reevaluate Stephan's custody for the same reason, recognizing that he had been separated from his mother for so many years that his circumstances had changed drastically. The judge could decide, despite Stephan's kidnapping, that after so much time in the United States he would be better off simply remaining with his father.

As the hearing was about to begin, Judge William Fernandez allowed the press to enter, telling the reporters that they could sit in his jury box. Others, drawn by curiosity, took their seats among the courtroom's benches.

When they had the judge's undivided attention, Stotter and Chamberlin began to argue their case on Claudine's behalf. They explained that in their view the policies and provisions of the Hague Convention, which by that time had been approved in principle by the United States but not yet enacted into law, should prevail in the Bolling case. Stotter said that the representative nations of the world had modeled the treaty on the concept of the Uniform Child Custody Jurisdiction Act and that the experts of the United States—and he was one of them—had signed their names to the document because they had felt that it was the proper way to deal with international child snatching. As a result, the senior attorney argued, Stephan should be returned to his mother and the jurisdiction of the Swiss court that had first awarded her custody.

All the same, the judge responded, he wanted to know how Stephan felt. Judge Fernandez had heard scores of child-snatching cases during his years on the bench, and although most had involved divorced parents living within the state, several had touched on custody disputes reaching such distant lands as the Far East, the Middle East, South Africa, and Europe. Even when the law did not require the child's immediate return to his or her original home, as was the case with Stephan Bolling, Fernandez's natural inclination was to send him back to the jurisdiction that had had the most contact with the child. This, he thought, was generally the community in which the child would be most comfortable. But the judge also took into consideration any other competing factors presented to him. And this included the child's point of view.

Before the Bolling hearing had started, Judge Fernandez had asked the director of Family Court Services to interview Stephan. Once the court had convened, Warren Weiss formally reported his findings to the judge, the lawyers, the family, and everyone else who had eagerly followed the proceeding that day.

"I spent about thirty or forty minutes this morning talking with Stephan," Weiss began after being sworn in, "and essentially allowed him to free-associate with regard to what his feelings are and have been as nearly as he can remember since he left his mother's care in Barcelona in 1977. And Stephan indicated to me that he has from that time until he recently saw his mother—"

"Excuse me," interrupted Paul's lawyer, Robert Moran.

"Be still, sir," shot back Judge Fernandez.

"My client is not here," insisted Moran.

"This is not a criminal proceeding," Fernandez abruptly replied, referring to the judicial rule that a criminal defendant must be allowed to confront witnesses testifying against him. "Go ahead," he nodded to Weiss. The judge felt no sympathy for Paul's plight.

"Stephan has missed his mother and brother and maternal grandparents, with whom he described a very close relationship," Weiss testified. "He described his relationship with his father prior to the time of the removal from the home in Barcelona as having been not close—in fact, somewhat anxiety producing in terms of his perception that his father was a very domineering force."

Claudine shot a glance at Stotter. She had told him that the boy was overwhelmed by his father.

"Nevertheless," continued Weiss, "Stephan adjusted reasonably well to his situation, which included a stepmother and a stepsister, with whom he described the relationship of strong rivalry and discomfort.

"He was very surprised to see his mother when she showed up a week or so ago and tearfully described to me his desire to return to her care." Claudine felt a sigh pass through her body.

"He also indicated to me," continued Weiss, "much to his credit I think in terms of his emotional strength, that he would like a continuing relationship with his father, but hesitated when I asked him whether or not he would choose to come to the United States again this summer, perhaps after school is out. He indicated that he would like more time to spend in terms of adjustment in the family home in Barcelona, if that's where he's allowed to return, and would like after that time perhaps—after this summer when he would hope that his father would choose to visit him in Barcelona—to then occasionally come to the United States to be with his father."

"Your Honor," insisted Moran, standing up, "may I interpose an objection?"

Judge Fernandez looked weary. "What's that?" he asked.

"My client is not before me. Even though this is not a criminal action, the least he should get is the chance to hear why he's not going to see his son for the rest of his life."

"I think that's an overly dramatic statement," replied the judge. "You heard that the young man said he'd like to see his father again in the summertime." Judge Fernandez knew how painful custody cases were, but he accepted the pain as part of the process. "You can't divide the kid in half," he would often say, "so one parent is going to see the child a lot less."

"Excuse me," said Moran. "Shouldn't his father at least be present to hear what this man's findings are?" Moran reminded the judge that Paul was being held elsewhere in the courthouse.

"Sure," replied Judge Fernandez, not wanting to argue the point anymore. "We'll bring him out, and the court reporter will read it to him exactly. Mr. Bailiff, would you ask the gentleman to be brought up?"

Before Paul could even step inside the courtroom, however, Fernandez had announced that Stephan should be returned to his mother. Although Moran had wanted the judge to rehear the custody issue, Fernandez insisted that he had no authority to do so. He could only enforce the order requiring the sheriff's office to bring in Stephan and Paul. Then the judge could decide whether Stephan should be returned to his mother under the preexisting custody order. He could not, the judge told Moran, change the custody or the visitation.

"The young man was here," concluded Judge Fernandez. "We simply say the order of this court that was previously entered by Judge Brenner [in 1975, when Paul tried to keep his sons in California] is to be carried out in full force and effect. The order says that the boy is to go with the mother.

"I think you heard some very good reasons from Mr. Weiss [the court's director of family services]," Judge Fernandez reminded Paul's lawyer. "I think we have a situation where you have closed your mind to what's best for this child.

"That's what this court is supposed to do—think of the best interests of the child and not of the best interests of one side or the other. I think what we've done is best."

Stotter was relieved that Stephan had still wanted, after all those years away, to live with his mother in Spain, thus cementing the case for his return. If the boy had testified that he was willing to stay, Judge Fernandez might have felt compelled to rule differently. Of course, no one will ever know for certain what would have happened if Stephan had reacted differently to the pretrial interview.

Yet, Stotter still could not understand why the boy had not tried to reach his mother, why he had never picked up the telephone to call her. He would never get a satisfying explanation. He could only surmise that Stephan, a passive child by nature, was simply too reticent to break away from his very strong-willed father.

Paul was brought into the courtroom wearing the county's regulation orange prison suit and handcuffs. He also had been in leg chains, but these were removed before he entered the room. "Have a seat, sir," said the judge. "You're Mr. Bolling, as I understand it." A sullen, angry Paul only nodded.

Fernandez summarized for Stephan's father what Weiss already had told the court. Paul simply stared ahead silently, convinced in his own mind that Stephan would have much preferred to stay with him. He was particularly angry that the law enforcement officers and the courts had given him no opportunity to tell his son good-bye.

But by the time the judge had finished his explanation and by the time he had told Paul that he was free to leave since Stephan was now back in his mother's care, Claudine, her father, and Stephan had quietly thanked Stotter and left. They were on their way to the airport and their return flight to Spain.

Claudine never pressed criminal charges against Paul for stealing Stephan away, but she did file a civil suit to recover her legal fees and expenses. Stotter served Paul with notice of the suit before he left the courthouse. By then the American lawyer's bill alone totaled more than $10,000. Claudine's Swiss attorney had billed her for $12,500 and her Spanish lawyer almost $7,000. Harold Lipset, only one of the many investigators she had hired, charged more than $14,000 for his services. In all, Claudine's investigative fees were more than $76,000, and her father had paid for everything, all of the lawyers and all of the detectives. A hearing on Claudine's fee request was set for April 15.

Stotter wanted to question Martha Bolling and Dennis Bolling to help him with the civil suit, and he asked the court to grant them immunity from criminal prosecution by the state so that they might be compelled to respond. He and Claudine also decided to drop their suit charging the two Bollings with conspiring to kidnap Stephan. They never were able to determine whether the Bollings had assisted Paul after he had taken Stephan, and they worried that the family would countersue Claudine for bringing a claim she could not support.

Eventually Stotter would decide that dropping the suit had been a mistake, based on an experience with a television talk show and its aftermath. In 1980, Stotter had appeared with Phil Donahue on the "Today" show for a segment on child stealing. Donahue had brought into the studio the mother of a child who had been kidnapped and an unrelated father who actually had kidnapped his child—and was still hiding from the law; here he was disguised with a wig. Both parents and Stotter appeared on the air, and they discussed their personal kidnapping experiences before the national television audience. During the show, a company secretary baby-sat off-camera for the man's little boy. The ex-wife of the disguised father, who just happened to be watching the show, later sued Donahue's production company for not reporting her child's whereabouts, claiming that baby-sitting the child assisted the criminal behavior of the father. After a 1983 jury trial, in which Stotter testified, the Donahue TV production company was ordered to pay the mother $5.9 million dollars in damages. The verdict, which the Donahue company announced it would appeal, convinced Stotter that he might have been able to win his conspiracy case against Paul's mother and brother after all.

Paul hired a new lawyer, Richard Such of Palo Alto, to fight the civil suit. In March 1982, about a month before the hearing was scheduled, Such asked that the suit be dismissed because the court lacked jurisdiction. Paul and Claudine's original divorce case had been heard in Switzerland, so subsequent proceedings also had to be filed there, the attorney argued. After a series of hearings on this motion to dismiss, the court finally denied it one year later, in March 1983. As a result of this extra legal maneuvering, which Stotter clearly viewed to be a stalling tactic, he tacked another $22,000 onto the amount he and Claudine demanded from Paul.

The hearing on the fee issue was set again, this time for May 11, 1983, but Paul's lawyers managed to have it postponed three more times. On February 1, 1984, more than two years after Stotter had filed his reimbursement request and just days before the fee hearing was to go forward, Paul filed for bankruptcy. Claudine never would receive a penny from her ex-husband. Stotter ended up writing off the remainder of his bill.

Today Stephan and Jean Paul Bolling are young men living on their own in an apartment they share in Switzerland. Despite their tumultuous history and long separation, they are as close as brothers can be. Both have visited Paul in California and both continue to lobby him for some sort of reconciliation with their mother. Children of divorce, regardless of their age and their experiences, never stop hoping that their parents will get along. It seems unlikely that Paul and Claudine will ever make up.

Paul continues to live in California with Marie. He married her in the early 1980s, when they moved west from Texas, shortly before Stephan was recovered. Paul and his brother Dennis manage a hotel in California that their mother had owned and left to them in her will when she died in 1988.

While he continues to feel justified for the child snatching, Paul blames Claudine's father for the years of running and hiding. "If it had just been my ex-wife, this never would have escalated to this level," he asserts. Rather, says Paul, his former father-in-law's money, "vindictiveness," knowledge of the law (Claudine's father had passed the bar in Switzerland), and prominence in high governmental circles enabled Claudine to pursue Stephan until she finally succeeded in reclaiming him. In effect Paul is saying that if Claudine had been left on her own, the kidnapping would have been entirely successful. Paul also complained that he still is recovering from the "bad effects" of declaring bankruptcy, citing both a bad credit rating and the emotional burden of his financial status. He guesses that the warrants for his arrest in Europe might still be pending.

Bob Moran, Paul's earlier attorney, had even bigger problems after the kidnapping case than did Paul. While his former client was still fighting Claudine's fee award suit with the help of Richard Such, Moran was indicted by a federal grand jury in Seattle and later convicted of conspiring to defraud the IRS by laundering millions of dollars of drug money. Moran was sentenced to eighteen months in prison and fined ten thousand dollars. He resigned from the state bar while disciplinary charges were pending.

Claudine, who had returned to Geneva for several years after she was reunited with Stephan, says today that the years reincorporating him into her life with Jean Paul were stressful, for the younger brother had grown accustomed to his mother's undivided attention. "We had a hard time," says Claudine. "There was a harmony problem among the three of us because Stephan needed so much affection and Jean Paul had to start sharing me."

And because Stephan had developed a memory block about his life in Spain in response to his father's kidnapping him, Claudine had to reintroduce him to his past. Even when she took him from their Geneva home back to the Barcelona school from which he had been abducted, Stephan had not, at first, been able to remember it. Slowly, with time, the memories did come back.

Eventually, after both sons were grown and her parents had died, Claudine moved back to Spain for good.

Since the Bolling case, additional steps have been taken to fight parental kidnapping. While all of the states have adopted the Uniform Child Custody Jurisdiction Act, many also have begun actively to penalize parents who have kidnapped their children. A Houston, Texas, jury, for example, awarded $53 million to a woman whose former husband and in-laws had abducted her two young sons and taken them to a remote town in northern Scotland. More than half of the 1985 award, $27 million, was in punitive damages for the intentional infliction of mental anguish. Today legislation in at least forty-five states makes child abduction a felony subject to severe criminal sanctions.

And on October 9, 1986, the Senate ratified the Hague Convention on International Child Abduction. President Ronald Reagan, who transmitted the treaty to the Senate for ratification, noted that

> the Convention would represent an important addition to the state and federal laws currently in effect in the United States that are designed to combat parental kidnapping. In short, by establishing a legal right and streamlined procedures for the prompt return of internationally abducted children, the Convention should remove many of the uncertainties and the legal difficulties that now confront parents in international child abduction cases.

New federal legislation enforcing the convention went into effect on July 1, 1988. Stotter appeared several times before Senate committees to testify in support of the law, named the International Child Abduction Remedies Act.

Still, the number of international child snatchings today remains high, and the missing youngsters' faces appear regularly on television and in advertisements, even on milk cartons. Fifteen times more international kidnapping cases were reported in the five-year period from 1980 to 1985 than in the same period ten years earlier. While the numbers have fallen slightly in recent years, close to three hundred international child snatchings were counted in 1989 by the State Department's Office of Citizens Consular Services.

While the problem persists, resources dedicated to fighting it are building, including the Washington, D.C., Office of Citizens Consular Services and the National Center for Missing and Exploited Children in neighboring Arlington, Virginia. However, only fourteen countries to date have signed the Hague Convention, and if a parent absconds with a child to a country that is not a signatory, the parent left behind has no definitive recourse for justice. Nonetheless, some trial courts in the countries that have not yet signed informally accept the convention's goals and policies as both rational and persuasive.

While legislative efforts and parental assistance programs expand worldwide, parents facing family separation and divorce also should take steps to protect themselves and their children from potential kidnapping. The National Center for Missing and Exploited Children provides suggestions on how to do this. For example, the center recommends that the custodial parent emphasize to the child how much he or she is loved, no matter what anyone else says. The center also tells parents to teach their children how to telephone either them or a close friend.

Custodial parents should notify schools and day-care centers about custody decrees and visitation arrangements so that they will not be caught off guard and turn over a child to the wrong parent at the wrong time. Parents should also discreetly obtain information about former spouses, such as his or her social security number, passport number, driver's license number, car registration number, checking and savings account numbers, and other information that may help law enforcement authorities locate an abducting parent.

Finally, all parents should keep a complete written description of their children, including hair and eye color, height, weight, date of birth, and specific physical attributes. And they should keep on hand recent color photographs of each child (taken every six months). Under the Missing Children Act, passed in October 1982, parents can enter complete descriptions of missing children into the FBI's National Crime Information Center computer even if the abducting parent has not been charged with a crime.

Resources for assistance in cases of parental kidnapping are available as they never have been in the past. But like Claudine Michaux Bolling, the parents most likely to find their children are those who help themselves and persist in doing so.

6

TRACING ASSETS:
SEPARATING MARITAL FROM
NONMARITAL PROPERTY

Irene Frances Nations v. Danny Jack Nations

> *Divorce is worse than death. Death is part of the
> cycle of life; we expect it. But with divorce, you have
> guilt, blame, and second guessing, and the other
> person is still around to create all kinds of trouble.*

—ATTORNEY LOUISE RAGGIO

DALLAS

With the advent of no-fault divorce nationwide, couples no longer have to place blame for marital failure, publicly proclaiming tales of infidelity, mental cruelty, or desertion. A more practical topic now dominates divorce proceedings—the division of marital wealth. Yet the battle here can be just as painful, demoralizing, and debilitating as public faultfinding, and in most cases the more money a couple has, the more they fight over how to divide it.

Marital property consists of material possessions or dollars that the couple, together or as individuals, acquired *after* they were married. Separate property, by contrast, is that which is brought into the marriage by each spouse and kept distinct from all marital property. Any inheritance after marriage also belongs to the individual who receives the bequest, making it separate property, too.

Community property states divide marital assets in half in a divorce whereas equitable distribution states try to divide them fairly, basing their determination of what is equitable on a variety of factors, including the length of the marriage, the spouses' economic and noneconomic contributions to the marriage, individual need, and potential earning power. There are nine community property states: Arizona, California, Idaho, Louisiana, Nevada, New Mexico, Texas, Washington, and Wisconsin. All of the rest are equitable distribution states.

But before a couple or the courts can consider any distribution of assets in a particular divorce case, they first must identify the marital property involved. Then a court also must determine the value of that marital property in order to distribute it between the two spouses. The disputes that follow, fights over who wants what and how much it's worth, stymie many couples early in the divorce process. In some cases spouses even try to hide assets from one another.

René Nations had to battle her husband Danny just to get back her separate, individual property. When she finally summoned the courage to leave their seven-year marriage, Danny argued that all of their holdings belonged to them jointly, including René's substantial inheritance from her parents and grandparents. The Nations had placed all of their stocks and properties, including those from Rene's inheritance, in both names, so Danny said that under the community property rules of Texas, where they lived, he was entitled to half of everything. René countered that Danny had wrongfully convinced her to open a joint brokerage account with her inheritance so that he could quit his job as a management consultant and spend his time investing her money. Though he did make a profit with some of the investments, René's net worth was less at the time of the divorce than it would have been had Danny left her inheritance alone, simply letting the investments grow.

In contrast to Danny, René claimed that the bulk of the couple's assets were hers alone, since their joint holdings stemmed largely from her inheritance. Separating nonmarital from marital property in cases like this is complicated when joint and separate accounts and investments have been intermingled over time.

The story told here shows how a team of lawyers and their determined client, Irene Frances Nations, were able to work through a maze of financial records. Her lawyers' mission was to identify her original inheritance monies as the source of the Nations' wealth and to assert a claim for the assets René felt were rightfully hers. The technique they used is called "tracing."

One day in March 1988, when René Nations realized that her husband Danny would be leaving shortly to get a haircut, she made a telephone call that changed her life. Seconds after he pulled out of the driveway she rang the Dallas law firm of Raggio & Raggio and made an appointment for the following week at lunchtime. Then she started to plan her cover.

She called a college classmate with whom she recently had renewed a friendship, one of the few friends she thought she had left after years of devoting her time and attention only to Danny. "Will you say you're having lunch with me—even though I'm *not* going to have lunch with you?" René asked her friend. She explained her plan for visiting a divorce lawyer. The friend, recognizing how possessive Danny was of René, that he knew her every move, agreed to help. When the day came on March 29, 1988, René arrived for the appointment on schedule.

During an initial visit, attorneys usually talk with new clients to make sure they really want to take the drastic step of divorce, but after forty-year-old René, a slender, neatly groomed woman, sat down in the Raggios' offices, she quickly let them know that she had no doubts about what she was doing. Though she had been uncertain and equivocal about the marriage throughout her seven years with Danny, finally—at last—she was filled with conviction. That very day she signed a retainer agreement and paid the lawyers five thousand dollars.

Doing so required tremendous courage, years of talking herself into a step that eventually would save her from a lifetime of misery. When the appointment was over René gathered her courage again, this time for the final trip home to her forty-eight-year-old husband. In the meantime, the mother-and-son lawyer team of Louise and Thomas Raggio prepared to file for her divorce.

By the next day, the papers were complete. The case was in motion. René's journey toward freedom had begun.

René Nations grew up the child of a traditional, conservative Dallas couple, in a small house in which her parents had lived her entire life. Her father was a salesman with a steel manufacturing company and her mother, a housewife. René never felt that she wanted for much, but then she did not ask for much, either. One of her mother's friends regularly handed down her daughter's dresses. As a teen, René never had a car like many of her friends did, but was perfectly content to take the bus to school.

This simplistic home life was complicated by the fact that René's parents, Sydney and Dorothy Elizabeth Wright, were alcoholics. "I didn't get to be a kid," she says today, explaining her responsibilities caring for her parents when they were "under the weather," which was often. Neither parent was abusive—they withdrew in their alcoholism rather than lashing out—so René generally was left to fend for herself. Her mother also suffered from depression, and at the end, after a series of strokes, she needed full-time care. When René's older brother left for college, she assumed the role of family caretaker, a job that lasted throughout her high school years, her college years, and until her parents died. While she understandably might have resented her predicament, René never considered that her life should be different.

Throughout this simple but often constrained existence, she also was oblivious to the fact that her family had more money than their lifestyle portrayed. In her house, no one talked about money or even seemed concerned about it. And certainly no one explained to her that one day she would be a wealthy woman. Her grandfather, Dan Greenwell, executive vice president and treasurer of *The Dallas Times Herald* and a former farm boy who had risen to prominence in Dallas and the state newspaper industry, had arranged in his will to leave trust funds for René, her older brother, and his other grandchildren, stocks and cash to be theirs when each turned twenty-one. When Grandfather Greenwell died in 1958 of a heart attack at age sixty-one while giving some visitors a tour of the *Times Herald,* the flag atop the building was lowered to half staff in his honor. René was eleven at that time.

"When I was twenty-one, I remember being taken down to the bank and signing some papers," René recalls today. "I should have asked some questions then, but I didn't." Six months later, in January 1969, she graduated from Texas Christian University in neighboring Fort Worth (she completed college in three and a half years), and within days began teaching elementary school. The following weekend she married a young man she had met through her church. "It was one of those things twenty-one year olds do," says René. She never gave a thought to her inheritance, which was predominantly in *Times Herald* stock; she had put the certificates away in the lockbox at her bank. Instead of selling any of the stock, René and her husband, who worked in real estate development, lived conservatively on their paychecks. She concentrated on her teaching, which she dearly loved, and earned a graduate degree as a reading specialist. When her son Michael was born on June 5, 1975, she quit her job to become a full-time mother. The carefully modulated, middle-class life she and her young family lived suited René.

She had no idea that trouble was brewing. Fifteen months after Michael was born, that happy, simple world fell apart. "We're like good friends and good roommates," her husband suddenly announced one day, "but there aren't any sparks and skyrockets. I think there should be more to a marriage." So he left, cold. René was dazed more than she was angry or hurt, and she kept hoping that her husband would come back. He didn't, however, and the financial support he sent was minimal. Because it was too late into the year to get a teaching job, she took on clerical work.

Life went from bad to worse. René's mother died in 1978 and her grandmother and father passed away in 1980. René, whose self-identity had always revolved around her family and her teaching, suddenly was alone, with only her son Michael.

Unlike many who might have been in her predicament, she could not even find solace in the monetary windfall from her family's deaths. Her legacy was significant. From the combined estates, she had inherited about $1.5 million. Because the Times Mirror Company had purchased *The Dallas Times Herald* in 1970, the vast bulk of René's holdings were converted to Times Mirror stock. But riches meant nothing to her. Whenever more stock certificates arrived in the mail, she simply put them in her lockbox at the bank and forgot about them.

During her years as a single mother, René went back to elementary school teaching and continued her activities in the Baptist church. It was there, in a Sunday school class, that she got to know Danny Jack Nations, a strong-willed, confident man who clearly was able to help her and care for her. A take-charge kind of person, Danny was a consultant to corporations and businesses who traveled around the country conducting management development seminars, in particular teaching managers how to deal with unions. Danny had been with his company, Industrial Relations International, for almost five years and held the impressive title of vice president. Before that he had worked as a training director with two other companies.

A companionable man, Danny entertained René with interesting tales from his work and travels, and she fell head over heels in love. On October 16, 1980, only five weeks after her father's death, she and Danny married. René was his third wife. "Sid would be glad to know that I'm here to take care of you," forty-one-year-old Danny said, referring to René's father. And René, who was then thirty-three, wanted that care. Like many children of alcoholics, she had taken on far more family responsibility than normal, giving more nurturing than she ever received. Now it was *her* time to be nurtured and loved. Of course, Danny soon realized that taking care of René was also an opportunity for him: She was a wealthy woman.

During the first months of their marriage, René realized that the wonderfully comforting, self-assured person she had wed actually was most interested in managing her life. Danny was a domineering man who apparently needed to be in control of his surroundings—including René. First she quit her teaching job, at his insistence, so that she could accompany him on his business trips. Well, René reasoned, I have a new life and a new job traveling with Danny. At the same time, they decided, she could finish settling her father's estate and sell her parents' house.

That done, Danny convinced her to put her own house on the market. "We need more room," he told René. She was understandably anxious about a move; the mortgage payment on the modest two-bedroom home was only $188 a month. But she went ahead and sold it, and with the proceeds from the sales of both houses they bought a new, bigger house, this one for close to $300,000.

Then about two months later, in March 1981, Danny quit his consulting job. It was just five months after their wedding. "I want to spend more time with you than on the road," he told René. "And you can use me to help you manage all your affairs." Just as important, Danny was sick of traveling. He hated flying, hated hotels, and hated being on the road week after week. Years later René would learn that her husband actually had a phobia about flying; her financial resources offered an escape hatch from his fear. All of a sudden he was around the house constantly, and looking to her for entertainment. When they were not talking about René's inheritance and potential investments, they shopped, worked out at a health club they had joined, and, as René would put it, "wandered the streets" while her son was at school or home alone. They lived off her stock dividends and other inheritance income.

"Let's get all your stock certificates and put them with a brokerage firm in a joint account so I can help manage your money more easily," Danny announced one day in late summer 1981. "I've had lots of experience in the business world, much more than you, and I'm used to making decisions. Why should we just leave the certificates in a lockbox when we can probably do better spreading the money around?" Although Danny's "business experience" was limited, René naively agreed to his plan to diversify her holdings. Danny began to consider René's stock, and the various investments they made, as *theirs* rather than *hers*. He would claim later that he had gone to great lengths to make sure René wanted to do what he had suggested; she would remember simply feeling overwhelmed by his pressure to open the joint brokerage account. "It was almost as if Danny said, If you love me and want to make it work, do this," René would recall years later. Innocent though she was, she knew at the time that something was not right. She just couldn't articulate her feelings.

The couple turned to Kenneth Bingham, a Merrill Lynch stockbroker recommended by an accountant who had helped René when she was single. When they met with Bingham, Danny again insisted that his name be on the brokerage account with René's, ostensibly for the con-

venience of helping to manage the investments they would make. Bingham politely tried to ascertain if René truly knew what she was doing
by shifting her inheritance into a joint account with Danny, but despite
the broker's good intentions, any possible warning signs went unheeded
and, most likely, unrecognized. Seated next to her domineering husband in the midst of the large Merrill Lynch offices, René simply was
incapable of asserting her own will or even of figuring out what she
wanted to do with her inheritance. She signed some of her stock certificates over to the brokerage firm and, in an initial sale, cashed in
17,356 shares of Times Mirror for $854,900. Danny had plans for the
proceeds.

He had hit on the idea of investing in commercial real estate. In the
fall of 1981 he and René went to see one of his old fraternity brothers
who was a commercial real estate broker. Through him they bought a
shopping center called White Rock, using money from the sale of the
Times Mirror stock as the down payment. They would use both Times
Mirror proceeds and additional money they borrowed to remodel and
maintain the shopping center. Danny insisted that the shopping center
purchase be in both of their names.

He then turned to another college crony to help him spend more of
René's money. Danny pushed aside Ken Bingham to make way for his
friend Billy Bob Harris, who was with A. G. Edwards. Then, when
Harris got into some problems from insider trading charges, his partner
Jimmy Jack Beal took over the Nations' brokerage account.

Along with the shopping center and other investments that followed,
Danny developed a taste for the finer things in life. He began buying
boats, condos, jewelry, and expensive clothes. In the boat category
alone he purchased a fifty-two-foot yacht, a twenty-one-foot Chris
Craft, and a Ranger bass boat. He also bought a Harley Davidson mo-
torcycle.

As fancy and luxurious as it had become, for René, life with Danny
was growing unbearable. Theirs was a doormat relationship, with
Danny assuming the dominant role and the emotionally needy René
taking the recessive. Instead of fighting back and asserting herself in
the face of her husband's demands for her money and her time, she
was intimidated and became increasingly subservient and passive.
Danny yelled at her and she sometimes yelled back, but because she
hated conflict, she always gave in. She felt trapped, knowing that he
wanted her with him at the very moment he called and that he objected to her going out alone with friends.

He even complained that René spent too much time with Michael,
so mother and son would sneak hugs and kisses when Danny wasn't
nearby. Perhaps because he had been unsuccessful in trying to get cus-

tody of his children from an earlier marriage, some of Danny's resentment spilled over to Michael. "If I can't have my own children, why do I want to raise someone else's?" he would ask René. He insisted that Michael visit his biological father as often as possible. When the boy was home, Danny took over disciplining him, although he and René fought over how he handled the job.

About three years into the marriage, René did find a brief respite. Danny finally admitted he had a problem and that it was the reason why he had quit his job. After having had a panic attack during a trip to Colorado, he told René, he had suffered from phobias and anxiety attacks while traveling. "I never could understand why you acted the way you did," René said when she finally understood the source of his quirks. She had wondered why her husband exhibited various types of bizarre behavior, always demanding that she be with him when he traveled, insisting on an aisle seat whenever he was in an airplane, and refusing to travel in anyone else's car. "You just have to be in control and able to escape from a situation if you don't like it," she said as she began to comprehend the needs that drove Danny. It helped to know the truth, and René sensed that her days were becoming calmer.

But it wouldn't last. Within months, life returned to an endurance test, with René trying to withstand Danny's self-indulgent behavior and attempts to rule her every move. In October 1983 he talked her into moving a second time, to Dallas's exclusive Highland Park, near Southern Methodist University. Their house there, measuring almost five thousand square feet, cost $575,000.

In the fall of 1987 Danny decided he wanted to live during the winter in a condominium he and René owned in Crested Butte, Colorado. There was, however, a catch. "It's no place for a boy," he told René, referring to twelve-year-old Michael.

She was confused about what to do. I've got to decide if the problem is Michael and this triangle relationship we have, René said to herself, or whether I just can't live with this man. After talking over the situation with Michael and his father, she sent her son to live with him.

"Mom," said Michael as they confronted the decision, "I don't want to leave you, but I think it would be better because then Danny would have more time to be with you." René was saddened to realize that her son felt so unwanted. She hated to have him leave.

After the first week at the Colorado ski resort, she knew for certain that she had made a mistake. Danny seemed as critical, irritable, and verbally abusive as ever. Psychologically, René hunkered down and proceeded to wait out the season; in her mind she was preparing to make a change. The only relief during their stay came when she and Danny flew Michael and Danny's children in for skiing over Christmas vacation and then again in early spring.

"Let's go home," René suggested shortly after the children's second visit. Her tolerance for life with Danny had ended. All she could think about was making a beeline back to Dallas and finding a divorce lawyer.

"Well, all right," Danny replied, surprising her. "If you don't want to ski any more, we won't." They headed home.

Like many women, René found it hard to leave her husband, no matter how miserable the marriage. Historically women have been dependent, if not for financial support then for an emotional reliance on men. It took René a long time—years of self-doubt and suffering—to take her big step. "It was like [living on] an up-and-down roller coaster," she says, recalling her emotional state back then, "and I was ready to get off. I just realized I had more self-worth."

René knew about sixty-eight-year-old Louise Raggio from an earlier incident during her marriage to Danny. About a year before, Danny had asked René to demand more child support from Michael's father.

"I don't know why. We already have more money than we need. We have more money than he has," she told him. Nonetheless, she did try to comply with Danny's wishes, and the real estate lawyer who had been working for them recommended the Raggios. After an initial meeting, and after the Raggios had telephoned an attorney representing Michael's father, they advised René that seeking an increase from her first husband would be difficult. He had fewer financial resources than she had, and a court order for an increase in support would be highly unlikely. René dropped her request, but she kept the Raggios in mind.

Lawyers all over Texas recommend Louise Raggio to help with domestic problems. A legend in her time, she is known to be the best female lawyer in Dallas and is in the top tier of Texas family law practitioners. Raggio was the first female assistant district attorney in Dallas, the first female prosecutor in a Dallas County criminal court, the first woman to serve as a director of the State Bar of Texas, and the first woman trustee of the Texas Bar Foundation. "I have been the token female for thirty-five years," she says, "but I'm not really token. Having me around is more like having a pet rattlesnake." She is very proud of all the trouble she has made on behalf of women, and of the changes she has wrought in Texas.

In truth, Raggio has gotten far more with honey than with venom.

Whatever her struggle, she has approached each task with a smile, seeking to keep good long-term relations with her colleagues in the law profession. Perhaps the greatest accomplishment in her career was spearheading a much-needed revision of the state's marital property laws. When she first entered practice, Texas was still the wild West, where cowboys (both real and urban) owned cattle, real estate—and their women. Before 1965 a married woman in Texas could not borrow money without her husband's signature; she could not sell her own property without his permission; and if she had property before marrying, her husband controlled all income from that property after the wedding. Raggio, whose diminutive frame belies her confidence and savvy, helped change all of these property rules and more, eventually revising the state's marriage and divorce laws, too. By 1979 she had rewritten the entire Texas family law code and convinced the legislature to bring the Lone Star State into the modern age.

When René kept her appointment to begin a divorce proceeding that fateful day in March 1988, she met with Louise Raggio and her son Tom and explained to them her plight.

René described how her life changed soon after she and Danny married.

"I married this person who realized I had the money that I didn't realize I had. Then his life-style just took off." She filled the Raggios in on all of the details.

Danny was the boss, especially in their financial affairs. Actually, she told the Raggios, when it came to managing their investments, she did as much as Danny, but he claimed all of the credit. "He would say, 'All you want to do is sit at home in the office,' but he never would do the paperwork," René explained. "If we ran out of money, he'd say, 'Find it.' It was like he wanted people to think he had a job, but that was just his cover—that he was an investor."

René also told her lawyers that Danny had made her change her will. The one she had written while she was single bequeathed all of her possessions to her son, but in her new will she left half of everything to Danny. "I didn't really want to do that," she explained, "but it's hard for me to tell you how afraid I was to speak up against him. So in 1986 I got really depressed."

"What did you do?" Louise Raggio asked her.

"Danny kept saying it was my problem, it was my fault, so I went to a psychologist. Even though I knew there was more to it than that, I was willing to try anything. I was always upset; my stomach hurt and I was getting worried about my health. So I went."

"Did it help? asked Tom Raggio.

"I only went for two or three sessions, because Danny wasn't at all supportive. He didn't want me to go back. Finally, in the summer of '87 I got him to go with me to a different psychologist."

Both Raggios looked at her, waiting.

René continued: "He went to maybe two sessions, and the psychologist asked me, 'Well, can you ever just get up in the morning and have a cup of coffee in your bathrobe and just hang around the house?' and I'd say no. Then she said, 'Can you ever just go shopping for the day and be back later?' and I'd say no. Well, Danny was hearing this and he said, 'I'm not going back if you two are just going to knock me.'"

By then, René told her lawyers, she finally had begun to understand, with the psychologist's help, that *she* was not the one with the problem. She had rights that she could stand up for. It was the turning point. "I decided there's got to be more to life than this," she explained, as if all of a sudden a bell had gone off. The winter in Colorado had set off even more bells.

Louise Raggio listened carefully to René's predicament. Although Raggio often tries to underplay a client's chance of success—the vagaries of the court system generally keep her optimism in check—she was supportive and encouraging with René. Here was a client who would need all the emotional buttressing the lawyers could provide.

Raggio told René that she would try to have someone come to her house the next day at 4:00 P.M. to serve the necessary papers on Danny. She selected a private process server rather than leaving the task to a court functionary, because the former could guarantee that the job would be handled quickly, whereas the court staff was overloaded with divorce suits.

In the morning Danny and René went out to play golf, and they were both back at the house by afternoon.

"Let's go out," Danny suggested. There was an errand he wanted to run.

René caught her breath. "No," she answered as calmly as she could. "A friend is going to drop off a book for me and I want to be here."

She felt nervous and strange, as if she were acting in a play. The suspense was made even worse by the knowledge that the process server might not even appear. And she was very worried about Danny's reaction once the papers were served on him; understandably, he would be really, really angry, she thought.

Louise Raggio had told her that the man she had selected was experienced in the job and would stay until she packed her bags and was ready to leave the house. That way Danny could not turn on her after the process server had left.

When the doorbell rang, René thought she was going to jump out of her skin. Danny answered the door.

"No, no . . . it can't be," Danny said when the process server handed him the petition for divorce. "You must be wrong. René . . ." He turned toward her.

"No, you can't talk to her," the man at the door announced firmly.

Then the man gave Danny a second document, a temporary re-straining order preventing him from engaging in a long litany of behav-iors, including hiding or changing his and René's records and property, making withdrawals from their bank accounts, entering their safe-de-posit boxes, withdrawing or borrowing all or any part of the cash sur-render value of René's life insurance policies, changing any of their insurance policies, opening René's mail, or communicating with René in person, by telephone, or in writing.

While Danny continued reading, René went to get the suitcase she had packed and hidden away. Arriving back at the front door, the man stepped aside for her and she quickly slipped through. He escorted her to her car and waited while she drove off. Danny stood back also, watching René, not angry as she had anticipated fearfully, but speech-less with shock.

For a short while René moved in with the friend who had covered for her during her initial meeting with the Raggios. But within weeks her lawyers had convinced the court to force Danny out of the house and to award it to René instead. After all, they explained, she, not Danny, was the one who paid the mortgage and all of the household bills. Danny rented an apartment. He begged for a reconciliation on several occasions.

Once it became clear that René would not change her mind, Danny entered the legal arena ready to draw blood. His entire strategy would be based on claiming that *everything* he and René owned at the time of her petition was theirs as a couple, to be divided equally between them, as proscribed by Texas's community property law. René had agreed to share the money, Danny would say, and as her investment manager, he had *earned* his half.

René faced a long road ahead trying to prove that the source of their current assets was her inheritance. She and Danny had combined her inheritance and the profits from their investments in a variety of subse-quent investments and purchases. The court battle would require that she search her memory and her records for supporting documentation and dive headlong into the world of high finance. She gulped at the thought, having no investment background and no role models; her parents, after all, had cared as little about business and investing as she did. "I'm just a little elementary schoolteacher," she told the Raggios plaintively.

To help her straighten out the financial record for the case, the Raggios turned to the technique of "tracing," which follows monies backward in time from year to prior year, from account to account, until the exact origin becomes clear. They were experienced in the technique, relying on another of Louise's sons, Kenneth, the family computer whiz, who uses a special software program for organizing and cataloging clients' financial data. For René, Ken and his computer would be a critical resource.

"If you have a granary with wheat in it," Louise Raggio explained to René, "and the granary is community property—you and your husband own it together—and then you pour a bushel of your own, separate-property wheat into it, you can never get it back. The two kinds of wheat are hopelessly commingled."

The moral to Raggio's story? Keep separate property distinct from marital property if you ever again want to guarantee independent ownership. A spouse still may be able to claim that an asset constitutes separate property if the asset's own character has been preserved and can be identified independently. But once that property becomes hopelessly mixed in, or commingled, as in the wheat example, original ownership no longer can be proven. For example, pieces of jewelry, furniture, and other material possessions obviously maintain their distinct, separate identity, as can independent investments, so long as they are not combined with financial assets earned after the marriage. But a spouse who contributes separate savings toward the purchase of a house, for example, would have a difficult time claiming a portion of that house as belonging independently to him or to her. The same would be true if a spouse sells his or her own piece of property to purchase a new asset in the names of both partners.

Fortunately, with the tracing technique, all may not be lost, even if some commingling has occurred. That is, if a lawyer and client can trace a current asset back to its original source, the current asset still may be claimed as individual, separate property. The tracing must be complete, however, without any steps missing along the way. For example, a couple may have bought during their marriage a piece of land now worth $1 million. But if one of the spouses can show that the land was purchased with the proceeds from the sale of stock, and the stock was purchased with funds from a separately kept bank account, and the bank account was opened with the money received in the sale of a different piece of individually owned land, and that piece of land was owned by one of the spouses *before the marriage,* then that spouse can claim the million-dollar piece of land at the end of the transaction chain.

"You must be able to document all of this," warns Louise Raggio when explaining the details of the tracing technique to her clients. "If you have *one link* gone in the chain [one missing piece of written proof], you don't have a chain anymore. You only have two pieces."

Courts in different states look at tracing in different ways, and their standards vary for the following assets back to separate property. Generally, however, they begin by labeling all property acquired by either spouse during a marriage as marital property, unless one of the spouses can prove otherwise. That is, the burden of proof is on the spouse who wants to claim certain assets as his or hers alone rather than as assets to be shared.

This can be done by proving that the property was acquired as a gift or as a bequest in a will, in exchange for property owned before the marriage, or in exchange for property received as a gift or bequest. The last two claims require the use of tracing to prove ownership.

The degree to which the trace must be convincing to a court varies among states. Some require "clear and convincing evidence," while others require only "a showing" of evidence. That is, some states require that the evidence be more specific than do other states, pointing to exact pieces of property as a trace proceeds backward in time.

To guarantee that René got back what she had brought into her marriage—and what she had received during the marriage through her inheritance—the Raggios had to meet a high standard. Under Texas law they would have to provide clear and convincing evidence of René's claims. The Texas courts had firmly stated in an earlier case that a spouse must produce "factually sufficient evidence" that property was separate rather than marital. Louise, Tom, and Ken Raggio would use their combined skills in ferreting out Danny's investment maneuverings, scrutinizing his and René's records, and re-creating a paper trail revealing the movement of millions of dollars.

"I want to introduce you to my son Ken," said Louise Raggio after telling René about the use of tracing. "He is the businessperson in our firm—he works with computers and he's going to help you get all this financial information organized."

Ken and his brother Tom are partners in Louise's nine-lawyer firm. So is a third son, Grier, Jr., who practices primarily in New York. The

youngest of the three Raggio children, Ken had been born when his
mother was in law school and as a baby had ridden in her bicycle basket
when she peddled to the law library to study. It seemed particularly
appropriate that he should ultimately join her and the rest of his family
in their law firm. Ken, who would later follow in his mother's footsteps
as chairman of the ABA's Family Law Section, fondly calls her
"Wheezer" when they are alone. But in front of clients he uses "Louise"
to downplay the close family tie. (The more traditional Tom always
refers to her as "Mother.") Whatever name they're using, it is clear
that Louise, Ken, and Tom hold one another in the highest regard.
After chatting for a few minutes with René, Ken suggested a meeting
to start work on his new task.

He would work most closely, however, with René's new accountant,
Ken Travis, who had been recommended by her earlier accountant
when he moved to Houston. Travis helped Ken Raggio identify the
necessary financial data for the computer program that would set up
René's case and trace the Nations' money back through the years of
their marriage.

Ken Raggio describes the program, which he calls an "outliner" or
"information manager," as "the tool of choice for organizing—and
thinking about—projects or tasks." Says Ken, "An outliner is to ideas
and information what a word processor is to documents. It allows you
to organize your thoughts, to focus attention on a particular 'level' of
the project at hand, and to quickly move to another area."

Looking at his computer screen Ken Raggio could see on his outliner
all of the work required for the Nations' case:

Nations v. Nations

- —To Do
- —Legal Issues
- —Fact Issues
- —Research/Briefs/Cases
- —Pleadings
- —Discovery & Production
- —Expert Witnesses
- —Depositions
- —Property
- —*Trace*
- —Proposed Division

Under the heading *"Trace"* Raggio would accumulate in his computer a listing of all of the assets in René's case, beginning with her
inheritance. He could scan his screen for a broad overview and then

quickly switch to other screens showing more detail about each asset described at different levels of the initial outline. The first screen of the trace looked like this:

—*Trace*
+ Inherited Property
+ Times Mirror Stock
+ Times Mirror Stock [Sale and Diversification]
+ A. G. Edwards Account
+ American Bank in Sherman, Texas
+ American Bank in Denison, Texas
+ Merrill Lynch Account
+ Sun Energy Stock
+ Municipal Bonds
+ Single Premium Insurance Policy
+ Mutual Fund Investment

Under each of these categories Raggio and Ken Travis, the accountant, inserted pages of data, piecing together chronologically dates of subsequent investments, purchases, and sales, with exact dollar amounts. By the end of the process they had worked up to the Nations' current assets, re-creating a paper trail that revealed the intricacies of René's financial past. If the lawyer and accountant reviewed the data in reverse, they could trace ownership of the Nations' so-called marital assets back to René's inheritance.

Even more important were the supporting spreadsheets and flowcharts listing dates and descriptions of every financial transaction made during the Nations' marriage. The flowcharts were key for the trial. "We can blow up the flowcharts for the judge so he can just look at them at any time and know exactly where we're at and where we're going," Ken Raggio explained to the accountant as he prepared the tracing presentation for court. "At any point along the way we can say, 'We're right here, the boat was purchased right here,' or, 'The mortgage was paid right here.' It makes a very complicated thing simple."

Page 180 shows what one simple flowchart looked like, with dollar amounts deleted. Each marking E1–E8 refers to a spreadsheet that shows individual transactions that took place in each account and distinguishes between original investments and interest earned.

Throughout their planning for the trial, Louise, Tom, and Ken talked regularly to discuss strategy. Early on they identified several legal problems. First, if a spouse puts money into a joint account, the courts

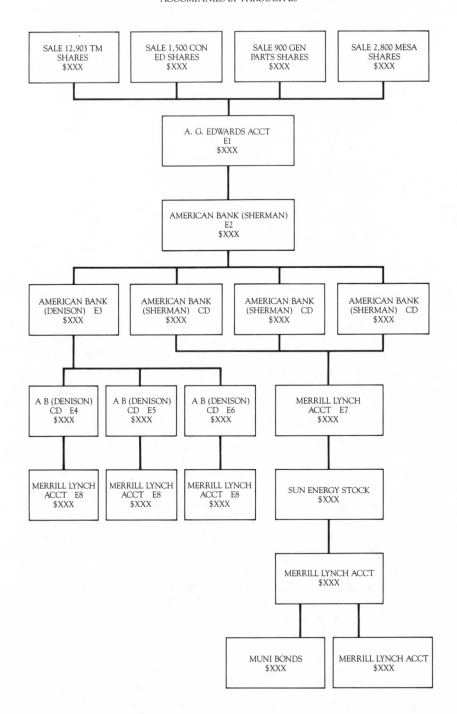

presume that it was intended as a gift. Danny would argue strongly in support of this conclusion. René would counter that she had thought that he wanted the account in both names only to make it easier for him to help her manage *her* money.

Second, if nonmarital assets are commingled with marital assets before being spent to acquire new property, that new property is by definition considered to be marital. Specifically, dividends and interest income received during a marriage, even if they derive from separately owned property, may be considered marital property. That is, the money earned belongs to both spouses. By allowing this earned money to be commingled or accumulated with the original individual investment, the entire fund takes on the mantle of marital property. In his spreadsheets Ken Raggio had to distinguish interest income from investments purchased with René's inheritance money.

Third, René and Danny had diversified her inheritance savings, often investing both the original, separate funds jointly with marital funds in a new purchase or investment. Fourth, when Danny and René placed money down on an investment, such as real estate, and then financed the remaining amount, they cosigned the promissory notes. Because they had taken on the debt jointly, relying on "community credit," as it is called, the profit on the investment was considered community property. Danny claimed that those profits were considerable.

But perhaps the overriding challenge of the case was the burden the court placed on René to prove that any of the funds and property were in fact her own. She would have to trace both hard assets and monetary accounts back to her separate inheritance.

The Raggios wanted the court not only to return René's separate property to her but also to require Danny to reimburse her for any funds of her own that she had spent on their joint investment projects. Some courts have ruled that a spouse should be reimbursed for contributing separate property to marital assets, even when these amounts cannot be identified and separated out from the marital property at the time of a divorce.

"René told me that she's the one the contractors contacted whenever they needed anything," Tom told Louise. "She kept the files, did the paperwork, and handled the day-to-day money, selling more of her stock whenever she needed to meet their payments."

Unfortunately, while selling those stocks and making those payments, René had no understanding of the larger financial picture in which she and Danny were operating, and she had no idea whether they were making money overall. For example, after they sold White Rock, Danny announced that they made about a million dollars on the investment. René wondered if that could be so. During the three years they owned the shopping center she spent a lot of her separate money for remodeling and upkeep costs. "Look, is this really all profit?" she inquired of her husband. Even she had not been able to believe that he had counted in all of her ongoing costs.

It was only toward the end of the marriage that their accountant had told her that they were spending more money overall than they were making.

Tom Raggio handled much of the day-to-day detail work on René's case because his father, Grier Raggio, died of a long-term heart ailment shortly after René retained the firm. Although Louise and Grier had founded the firm together, he had essentially retired from law practice years earlier. After Grier's death, Louise did lighten her load for several months, but she continued to work almost every day and she regularly conferred with her sons about their cases.

While working with René, Tom became particularly incensed over Danny's treatment of her during their marriage. "A husband who assumes the role of managing spouse has a fiduciary duty to keep his wife's property separate," he reminded his mother one day as they discussed René's divorce. Danny had not done that, but instead had commingled the separate and marital funds and, as a result, completely muddied up René's separate property ownership.

"The man was able to intimidate her into doing what he wanted," Tom explained, adding that he thought it would be important to offer testimony about how Danny was able to bulldoze René psychologically. In doing so the Raggios hoped to get the sympathy of the judge hearing the case, but just as important, they also wanted René's testimony to overturn any presumption that she intentionally had made a gift to Danny of her family's wealth.

Louise and Tom were perhaps most concerned about René's emotional and mental well-being. "I'm not sure whether she can withstand the pressure," Louise told her sons in one of their strategy conferences. "When this is all over, we don't want to say, The surgery was a great success, but the client died. I'm worried René could snap." Thus, in addition to her role as the firm's top legal strategist, Louise Raggio took on the additional job of mothering her client, a habit of hers. Often she gives a traumatized spouse a hug in the morning before the client heads to court. She fixed one man a tuna fish sandwich to take with him to court every day. Her goal: to keep the client functioning and confident.

* * *

René relied on all of the Raggios for emotional support. As she prepared to confront Danny about their separate views on the divorce, she relaxed at home, writing a lengthy letter to Tom Raggio on a legal pad. "Dear Tom," she began in her large, even script.

> After I left you Wednesday, I went to my exercise class, came home for a candlelight dinner and curled up with our notes. I need to put some things down in writing to see if I have it straight. So, bear with me, please.
>
> Overall, I really do feel much more calm about it all. I'm glad you kept encouraging me to gather all the financial data that I did. I should have kept up with [it] since I turned 21, but better late than not at all. I certainly have a better picture of my position.
>
> I wrote out to myself questions regarding time, place, atmosphere, etc. [she was referring to a cataloging of the events surrounding her past financial transactions with Danny]. I have avoided him (or tried to) for a month. Surprisingly, last night, I finally felt control over my life and its future outcome.

René talked about her first planned encounter with Danny since her abrupt departure from the house. "For a first meeting," she wrote, "I decided to keep it casual. I think your office would be too intimidating and he would become extremely defensive. I [am] going to see if he will meet me at a public restaurant so that either one of us has the option to walk out if need be."

But before seeing Danny, René had some questions for her lawyers. "Should I ask him first what he thinks he deserves, his intentions, does he think he deserves 50 percent, etc.?" she inquired, adding that "that may end the conversation right there." Or, she asked, should she tell Danny she was worth less at the time of the divorce than she had been when they married?

René was just beginning to grasp the legal underpinnings of her divorce suit and financial claims. "Would you explain to me again the right of reimbursement?" she asked in the letter, adding that Danny "would have to agree that it was my money that acted as collateral, down payment and carry for our commercial real estate deal." She was confused about their capital gains from the sale of the shopping center and the combination of this cash with proceeds from the sale of more Times Mirror stock.

René's letter concluded,

When I look back on all of this, I realize I paid for all of our homes, boats, condos, clothes, jewelry, etc. and that his taste was expensive. He only wanted the best. Of course, I like and appreciate the material things I have. But, if I never had a fur coat or Rolex watch, it would be no big deal.

I really feel that one meeting with Danny by myself is all it will take for him to see that I am not going to be pushed around. And I will not settle for just half community property. . . . I am *finally* going to make my own decisions. However, I do want you to lay out my options from best to worst with resulting outcomes.

. . . My meeting with Danny could be very short or long, drawn out. However, I am not staying if he mentally harasses me and tries to coerce me. . . .

An upbeat postscript followed: "I actually slept most of the night Wednesday. We must be getting somewhere for me to finally relax!"

But René would not be able to relax completetly. When she finally did talk with Danny, he made it clear that he was going to fight for half of everything they owned, whether or not she claimed it was hers. Her new confidence notwithstanding, he expected to win.

By June, Louise, Tom, and Ken Raggio were ready to take Danny's deposition. Tom was to be in charge that day. He, Danny, Danny's lawyer Reyburn Anderson, and René gathered with a court reporter in Raggio's offices.

After asking Danny about his work as a management consultant, the job he had quit shortly after marrying René, Tom Raggio inquired about earlier jobs.

"What was your employment prior to Industrial Relations International?" he asked.

"I was with Trailways Bus Companies as a national training director," Danny replied.

"You were the national training director?"

"Uh-huh."

"Mr. Nations, then how long were you employed with Trailways?" Raggio inquired.

"About a year," said Danny.

"Okay. Prior to that employment, how were you employed?"

"I was with the American Cyanamid Chemical Company in New Orleans, Louisiana," Danny answered.

"What was your position there?"

"Southern regional training director."

"How long were you employed?" Raggio asked once again.

"Approximately a year."

"Prior to that how were you employed?"

"Oh, gosh . . ." stumbled Danny. "Let's see . . . WKM Valve Division of ACF Industries."

"What capacity?"

"Divisional training director."

"And how long did you work for them?"

"About five years."

"All right," Raggio said with finality. "That takes us back far enough." Having made his point, he moved on to other topics.

In response to more questions, Danny tried to say that all of the business decisions in his marriage had been made jointly. But he could not resist taking credit for his own self-perceived abilities.

"Is it a fair statement that you would consider yourself," asked Raggio, "and I'm not asking you to pat yourself on the back, but that you were more sophisticated so far as stock purchases and real estate transactions than René?"

"Not more sophisticated, not more knowledgeable," said Danny, "just that I was used to making decisions I think more so than René was. And sometimes I'd take the lead in initiating the process." It was becoming clear in Danny's own testimony who had been the driving force behind René's financial decisions. Of course, Raggio knew that she had in effect been a rubber stamp to whatever her husband wanted to do.

"Were you making the investment decisions?" he asked Danny, referring to 1981, shortly after Danny had quit his job.

"Well, yeah, we were jointly making decisions about changing our investments," he answered. "At that point probably 99 percent of the portfolio was in one stock. Every advisor we would talk to said that wasn't smart and that some changes needed to be made . . . . they advised us to diversify ourselves into some other areas. So we had a lot of conversations about how to do that best and sought a lot of advice."

Danny's deposition ended within a few hours. A judge had ruled that the Raggios could not ask any questions about the property Danny and René held until after Danny and his lawyer had had enough time to study the various records René would turn over to them as part of their discovery. Raggio adjourned the session with the understanding that he would be allowed to continue later, when Danny and Anderson were ready for his second stage of questioning.

* * *

That time came almost two months later, on July 26, 1988. The Raggios had made René's financial records—seven boxes in all—available to Danny and his lawyer for a two-week period earlier that month. This time both Tom and Ken Raggio were present at the continuation of the deposition; they had conferred carefully with their mother in advance.

Danny agreed immediately that the stocks and cash the Raggios and René's accountant had listed in one of their exhibits had in fact come to René through her inheritance, with the one exception of about three hundred shares of Times Mirror stock, which Danny said he could not identify. Thus, they all concurred that the original source of the Nations' wealth was René's stocks and family holdings, which had been hers at the time of the marriage.

Then Tom Raggio again asked Danny more about his job when he married René and about his own financial circumstances at the time.

"What was your salary?" he inquired.

"Ending salary with benefits and profit sharing was approximately $40,000 a year," said Danny.

"Mr. Nations, did you own any real estate at the time of your marriage to René?" asked Raggio.

"No."

"Did you have any stocks or bonds?"

"No."

"What assets did you bring into the marriage?" asked Raggio.

"Other than some cash, I don't remember," replied Danny. Then he admitted what Tom Raggio already knew: "Nothing else," he said.

"Is it safe to say then it would have been personal property, I think you had a station wagon, an older station wagon?" Raggio kept probing.

"Yes," said Danny.

"And personal property. And then what amount of cash—are we talking about a couple thousand dollars or are we talking—"

"Yes," Danny interrupted.

"A couple thousand dollars," Raggio reiterated slowly. "And what debts did you bring in?"

"None that I can remember."

"Would it be a fair statement then that you had personal property, bank accounts, assets of approximately $10,000?"

"Yes," Danny agreed.

It was a piddling amount compared to the $1.5 million René had brought into their union. But Danny made it clear that René had considered him an equal partner in handling her money.

"Mr. Nations, is it your position that your wife intended to make a gift of the monies that were put into a joint account?"

"Yes," said Danny.

"Mr. Nations," continued Raggio, "did you ever tell René that you didn't want her to keep her property separate?"

"I had told René that if I were going to give up my job—I had responsibility to my children, my children's future and to my own future and that if I was going to help her run our family business, that it had to be a joint effort and it had to be a joint responsibility and a joint ownership, and that's the gist of our conversation," said Danny. "I can't quote to you exactly eight years ago how that conversation went, but that's the essence of it."

"So in fact," Raggio queried, "you told René that the ownership of these assets had to be joint?"

"I didn't tell René anything. We discussed this jointly."

"And Mr. Nations, is this still, is this your position today, that all of the assets are in fact joint, jointly owned by you and Mrs. Nations?"

"Yes," said Danny firmly. But he would produce no witness or documents to prove that that was what René truly had wanted.

Tom Raggio went with René to her deposition, in Anderson's office, on August 2, 1988; lawyers prefer to take depositions on their own turf, perhaps because they believe that it gives them a "home-court advantage." The goal, in any case, is to make the other side feel as uncomfortable as possible. Tom did not like the way Anderson treated René, but then, he admitted, he had not been particularly kind to Danny during his deposition.

Anderson, a family law specialist in practice by himself, began slowly, asking simple questions and painstakingly explaining them whenever the business terms seemed too complicated for René's understanding. But instead of being helpful, Anderson appeared condescending, even disdainful. His ultimate goal was to get René to admit, even inadvertently, that she had known exactly what she was doing with her money. Anderson contended that Rene willingly had agreed to let Danny share equally in all of her wealth, that she supported Danny's decisions fully, and that he had done well by her.

"Do you understand what the word diversify means?" Danny's lawyer asked at one point during the day.

"I could not give you a definition probably," answered René.

"In the context that I'm using it, let me give you an example," Anderson began to explain. "The example being that you have a choice of putting, say, a million dollars in one asset, say Times Mirror stock, or you have a choice of putting a million dollars in ten assets, say $100,000 in General Motors stock and $100,000 in GE stock and $100,000 in General Dynamics stock and $100,000 in Texas Instruments stock and $100,000 in General Foods stock, so that you spread your risk among ten $100,000 investments instead of putting all your risks in one one-million-dollar investment. That would be a diversification of an investment portfolio. Do you understand that concept?"

"I think so, somewhat," René answered.

Anderson wasn't so sure. "What I'm saying," he said, "is that you always have a choice as to whether to put all your eggs in one basket or to put the same number of eggs in several baskets so that you spread the risk. That's really what diversification is about. You see what I mean?"

"Yes," said René. She had been very nervous before the deposition—it was her first—but she found that by speaking calmly, Anderson didn't bother her as much as she had anticipated. She was determined to stay calm despite the hostile environment surrounding her.

"If you had ten eggs and put them all in one basket and you drop the basket, you might break all ten eggs, right?" he continued, wanting to make sure he had made his point.

"Yes."

"If you took those ten eggs and you put them in ten separate baskets, you might drop one or two of the baskets, but the chances are you wouldn't drop all ten of them. So it's a way of spreading the risk of your investment dollars or your investment portfolio. Do you understand it now?"

"Yes." Anderson's persistence would not unnerve René. This was just a deposition; the trial was still ahead.

"Understanding that," continued Danny's lawyer, hoping to drive his point home, "do you believe that that's a good idea, to spread your risk, to diversify your assets?"

"Are you asking me specifically about the transaction we did or just my general—"

"I'm asking you about your philosophy now," broke in Anderson.

"I have been told that from probably brokers, you know, suggesting that advice over the [recent] years." The point was that René had not known about diversification before Danny got hold of her funds.

"Actually, would it be accurate to say that every expert that you and Danny ever talked to shared that philosophy with you, that it was a good idea to diversify and thereby spread the risk? Would that be accurate?" Anderson pushed on.

"I'm just responding," she began. "I don't know. When Danny and their brokers and we'd all be discussing it, probably."

"What I'm saying is, isn't it true that every broker that you went to suggested that it was good business practice to diversify?" Anderson clearly wanted to make the point that Danny's plan had been sound.

"I don't know," René said.

"Do you ever remember one taking the position that it *wasn't* good business to diversify?"

"I don't remember specific brokers' discussions," René stated firmly. "Usually if it was on the phone, Danny handled it. In meetings, I sat. I was the passive listener and I don't remember. Like I said, business was not my forte."

But Anderson did not believe her. "Well, the truth of the matter is, René, you understand exactly what I've been talking about today, haven't you?" he demanded later during the deposition.

"I don't know what you're trying to ask," she replied frostily.

"Well, what I'm saying is, you are not nearly as dumb about these things we've been talking about as you've been trying to act, are you?"

"That's your impression," she said.

In fact, René was not trying to play dumb; rather, she was trying, although perhaps not very successfully, to differentiate between what her knowledge had been in 1981 when Danny had convinced her to open the joint brokerage account and what it was currently, at the time of her divorce proceeding. If René had been savvy enough about investments early in her marriage to know the significance of adding Danny's name to her account, then why would she have been so content to leave all of her stock certificates in a safe-deposit box? Why hadn't she considered on her own that she should be diversifying her inheritance monies? And why had she let Danny run over her time and time again? By 1983 all of the accounts containing proceeds from the sale of René's Times Mirror stock were in both her name and Danny's.

"Did you ever," asked Anderson, "in talking about the money in those accounts to other people, refer to that money as 'our money,' meaning 'his and yours'?"

"At the beginning of our marriage," said René, "Danny made a very specific, definite statement to me that he did not like me to say 'I' and 'my,' like he didn't want me to refer to 'my house' or 'my money,' and by that time, I had been programmed to say 'we' and 'ours.'"

"Well, is the answer to my question then yes?" demanded Anderson.

"Yes, by then I would say 'we,' 'ours,' you know."

"Our money, our houses, our cars, our yachts. Is that what you mean?"

"Cars, we probably designated like 'his car' and 'my car.'"

"But it would be 'our yacht' and 'our condo' and 'our home'?" Anderson persisted.

"Yes," said René.

"Okay. Well, would it be accurate then to say that you *never* referred to them as 'my car'—not 'my car,' 'my yacht,' 'my condo,' or 'my home'?"

"Yeah, that's correct," René acknowledged grudgingly. After all, Danny had insisted on it. Anderson had just ignored her explanation.

"All right," he said contentedly and sat down.

The deposition was over.

"How do you feel?" Tom inquired after he and René had left Anderson's office. Despite her composure inside, she looked shaken.

"Like I've been beaten with a rubber hose," she answered.

On August 3, Tom Raggio filed an amended petition for divorce to allege Danny's breach of fiduciary responsibility, or violation of trust, in handling René's funds. This second pleading was far more detailed, a necessary precursor to presenting evidence in court supporting the new allegation. Even in the legalese in which it was written the words were scathing: "Respondent [Danny] acted with conscious disregard or an evil intent to harm Petitioner [René]," Raggio wrote. Danny had, Raggio alleged, "wrongfully converted," René's separate property to joint ownership. "Respondent's conversion of the property was intentional, willful, wanton, and without justification or excuse and done with gross indifference to the rights of Petitioner," Raggio continued. The longer he worked on René's case, the more angry he became.

As the trial drew closer, Anderson decided to hire another lawyer to help him out. After learning through discovery the extent of the Raggios' preparation for René's case and getting a handle on their tracing activities, Danny's lawyer began to fear that he would need to bring a bigger hired gun to court. Regan Martin boasted a reputation as a scorch-the-earth litigator, a man quick on the uptake and ruthless during cross-examination. Anderson and Martin would appear together on Danny's behalf.

René had been considering settlement through the summer, but by the time fall came, she did not want to hear of it anymore. She was so mad thinking that Danny was going to get any money from her, when he had come into the marriage with only about ten thousand dollars, and considering what she had had to put up with emotionally.

"We might be able to settle still," Tom Raggio said to her one day, hoping to keep the possibility open. Like many of the best divorce lawyers, the Raggios believe that an acceptable settlement is far preferable to trying a case. A good settlement is a sure thing; a courtroom trial is rife with chance.

But René was fighting mad and would not hear of it. "I'm ready to go to court," she told Tom defiantly. "I want my story to be told."

The trial began on September 29, 1988, less than a year after that fateful day when René had first told the Raggios that she wanted a divorce. The case had progressed rapidly because René—who suddenly had become assertive once she took the initial action of seeking a divorce—had pushed her lawyers to end the entire proceeding quickly. "I've got to get moving with this," she had told them time and time again. And the Raggios had responded; they were so efficient about filing the various papers and completing discovery, René would say later, that her time in court came quickly enough.

Going into the trial, Danny had softened his fifty-fifty proposal and replaced it with one that would give him 40 percent of all of the assets he and René owned. Under Danny's calculations and proposed division, his total would be worth $1,022,412, and René's $1,547,470. René refused even to consider it.

She took the stand first. Accountant Lynn Warren and stockbroker Ken Bingham followed her after lunch, and then René went back on the stand for the rest of the day. Regan Martin was even harder on René with his questioning than Anderson had been during her deposition two months earlier. Again René tried desperately to remain calm and controlled.

Surprisingly, the very next morning, before the trial could reconvene, Danny and his lawyers offered to settle the case. But René still was not interested, even though the Raggios were trying to talk her into it. She wanted Danny to have to take the stand as well; she wanted her lawyers to give him the third degree, too.

"What's the deal?" René asked her attorneys; she was crying as they paced together up and down the hall and talked over the offer. "You're switching over on me," she pleaded. She was so geared up that she could not stop the fight, even when the time had come to do so. René did not want to admit that she would have to give up anything to Danny to get the case over.

"Your attorney fees are only going to go up if we continue," Tom Raggio told her gently but directly, "and we guarantee you that the judge will give Danny *something* anyway. So if you can settle in a way that's comfortable for you, you'll be better off in the long run." Tom felt that Danny's offer was favorable to René. "We've bludgeoned him into your position," Tom informed her.

Louise Raggio especially wanted René to settle. She was very concerned as to whether René could withstand more days of Martin's blistering cross-examination. He's just here to put fear and trembling in René's heart, to make her crumble, Louise Raggio worried. She feared that the cost of pushing harder for a bigger victory could outweigh the benefit. It was a timely and shrewd analysis, one that all lawyers owe their clients at every turn in the litigation process.

So with her lawyers' urging, René finally agreed to settle with Danny. The Raggios drafted and made final the divorce decree itself, as well as all of the closing documents, within a four-day period, a remarkable feat given that the process frequently takes thirty to forty-five days. They worked rapidly because they felt the deal they had made for René was a good one and they did not want to give Danny time to change his mind. The divorce decree became effective as a court order on October 3, 1988, only months after René had first contacted the Raggios about a divorce and mere days after she and Danny had agreed on a settlement.

The decree gave René the vast bulk of the furnishings, furniture, jewelry, and personal effects in their homes, their Dallas house, two investment lots in Grayson County, Texas, their 1986 560 SEL Mercedes, all stocks and bonds held in either her name or Danny's name or both, the yacht, the Chris Craft, their A. G. Edwards account, a bank account, and "any and all other property, whether real or personal or mixed and whether tangible or intangible, in the possession of or registered in the name of Petitioner [René] or Respondent [Danny], or either of them, or both of them, unless express provision is made herein to the contrary." René's share of the settlement, says Tom Raggio, totaled about $1.8 million.

Danny's share was worth about $500,000, less than half of what he had wanted and approximately $100,000 less than the Raggios' proposed settlement offered two days earlier. He would get the country club membership, the Ranger bass boat, about $130,000 in cash, the 1987 BMW and the 1987 Nissan, the Colorado condominium, his Harley Davidson and trailer, some oil interests property, one of their bank accounts, and all of the personal property already in his possession at his rented apartment.

Both René and Danny would have to pay their own mortgages and other property-related expenses and attorneys fees. Most important, perhaps, Danny was to remove his name from all of René's stocks and investment accounts.

"They realized that with the tracing we were too well prepared," observes Louise Raggio today. For Louise, every legal victory is a glowing personal victory, and with each—including the case of René Nations—she seems as thrilled as if she has just completed her first day in court.

Today René, who has reverted back to her maiden name, René Wright, is philosophical about her past mistakes and naiveté. Most important, she finally has begun to like herself. "I realize I have more self-worth," she says, reflecting back on her days as René Nations.

Surprisingly, she also has a sense of humor about her past. "If I ever get married again," she told Merrill Lynch broker Ken Bingham one day after her divorce, "you grab me by my collar and get my attention more than you did in 1981!" She wishes that those who had warned her had been much stronger in talking about the possible consequences of her actions. Now, of course, René knows enough to invoke such warnings on her own.

She lives conservatively once again, tutoring part time, volunteering at a local elementary school, and overseeing her own investments. Now on her own, she maintains a strict budget. "People tease me when I say I can't afford something," she says. But if a purchase is not within the budget she has set, René refuses to make it.

Louise Raggio advises her about estate planning, and she introduced René to the Dallas Women's Foundation, which together with Southern Methodist University offers a series of detailed personal investment seminars for women. After taking that series René enrolled in other investment courses and some women's investment programs. Most recently she joined a new organization of women called Managing Inheritance, whose goals are to offer emotional, technical, and social support to women who have inherited wealth and to educate women about philanthropic concerns. Above all this group says it wants "to empower women to take responsibility for their finances."

René Wright provides them and others with an example of a woman who learned her lesson the hard way. Today she says she realizes that Danny "never really *managed*" her inheritance as she knows it should have been managed. "He would never really talk with the brokers to work out a financial plan," she observes. "And he never sat down and *discussed* asset allocation." He spent her money, rather, on a piecemeal or shotgun basis, without any careful, well-articulated, long-range considerations for the future.

With her newfound knowledge about financial management, René finally is following in the footsteps of her Grandfather Greenwell, like herself, a simple person with solid common sense but one who always understood money. After all, he had risen from his first newspaper job in the *Times Herald's* classified department to his last job, where he directed the newspaper's entire accounting system, from bookkeeping to payroll. He would be proud of his granddaughter today.

René's son Michael stayed on at his father's house during the divorce, at René's request. His father had remarried and René was glad that her son could have a stable home during her own period of personal upheaval. But in 1990 Michael, then a high school student, moved back in with his mother to the smaller house she had purchased after the sale of her last marital home. When René asked Michael how he felt about her divorcing Danny, he simply replied, "Mom, I'm OK, I'm just fine," and she accepted his reassurance.

As for Danny, despite René's years of unhappiness with him and the trauma of her divorce, she only speaks matter-of-factly about their marriage. Even as she explains Danny's behavior and handling of her money, she portrays no emotional rancor. Although she never sees him now and has no knowledge of his life-style or work, René says that Danny started changing the day they divorced. The angry, hostile husband René had known disappeared, leaving a more gentle person behind. About ten months after settling the divorce case, Danny married again, for the fourth time, and then moved to a new home in Dallas. He also apologized to René.

Though Danny did owe René an apology, the Raggios would be more likely to dwell on the difference they made in René's life. They had what they call "a good result" in the case: René could lead a much better life *after* her divorce was over. "One of the things that makes this law practice bearable," says Louise Raggio of her many cases and clients, "is years later, seeing a happy, productive person." A spry seventy-two years old today, Raggio continues to work full tilt, both for her clients and for the statewide and national organizations in which she is active.

RELOCATION:
WHEN THE CUSTODIAL
PARENT MOVES AWAY

Robert Jordan v. Linda Jordan

*Judges are human beings, even though they are
supposed to be impartial.*

—ATTORNEY BEVERLY GRONER
BETHESDA, MARYLAND

Imagine a reasonable, even friendly, divorce. The couple divides property, agrees on custody, arranges support, and plans visitation with their
children. Everything goes well for a few years.

Then enter the villain: relocation. The custodial parent decides to
move away—out of the city, the state, or even the country—leaving
the noncustodial parent behind, alone. Tempers flare, harsh words follow, turmoil sets in.

Because mothers are awarded custody more often than fathers, mothers commonly take the children with them if they move following a
divorce. The greater the distance between the mother's new address
and her former home, the more difficult the logistics of visitation for
fathers who stay behind. Previous visitation schedules become awkward, expensive, even impossible.

For some parents there is irony in this situation. Too few fathers pay
the child support required of them—only about one half of divorced
mothers receive support due, says the U.S. Census Bureau—and far too
few fathers visit their children regularly. Yet a father who does fulfill
his obligations may find that, nonetheless, he has little control over

where his children live. Regardless of his support and visitation record, a male parent's feelings and needs may not even be considered when his ex-wife wants to move. He will be asked to continue the payments in full, even while seeing far less of his children. Understandably, many caring fathers balk at such an arrangement.

This conflict is not a simple one. In an age when women increasingly pursue careers of their own—and increasingly are expected to provide their own support after divorce—they may have little choice about moving if an employer directs them to do so. Or they may decide on their own to move in pursuit of career advancement opportunities. Still other mothers move because their fiancé or new husband works elsewhere, is required by his employer to move to a new location, or is seeking to advance his career. These women can hardly be expected to stay behind.

"Without question, the issue of a custodial parent's relocation is a relatively common occurrence in which family law attorneys are regularly involved," says *Family Advocate*. In fact, that magazine devoted its entire Winter 1989 issue to relocation. "No issue in family law is more volatile than relocation," proclaimed editor in chief Arnold Rutkin. "It causes actions and reactions that have long-term ramifications for the family."

While some states, such as Minnesota and New York, have adopted rules and guidelines for determining when a move by the custodial parent is acceptable, the majority of states have no such criteria. As a result, uncertainty is the only common variable. Ex-spouses, their lawyers, and the courts are left to resolve relocation disputes on a case-by-case basis. Sometimes a judge may ask the children about their wishes, but all too often younger children are afraid to speak out or cannot articulate their feelings. As in other custody disputes, these children can become victims in a tug-of-war between parents who hope their offspring will choose one parent over the other.

The case of Bob and Linda Jordan exemplifies the conflict divorced families face when the custodial parent relocates. While Linda was living in Potomac, Maryland, Bob visited his sons Chris and Garrett twice a month, either in Maryland or at his home in Darien, Connecticut. Bob was actively involved in his children's lives, and he cherished his time with them.

But then one day in the summer of 1979 Linda announced that she was moving to South Africa to marry the man she loved—an American who was convinced that job opportunities for him were much better halfway around the world. The Jordans' older son, twelve-year-old Chris, asked to stay behind in Connecticut with his father, and Linda agreed. But Linda was determined to take seven-year-old Garrett with her to South Africa.

Bob Jordan objected vehemently. He did not want his sons separated, nor did he want the younger boy uprooted from his country of birth. Not only would Garrett be a nineteen-hour plane ride away, but he would grow up in an environment that was politically unacceptable to Bob. For all of these reasons, Bob decided to fight Linda's decision with every resource he could muster, psychologically, financially, and legally.

It would be a long battle for Bob Jordan and for his lawyer, noted Maryland attorney Beverly Groner. They faced a judge who would decide the relocation dispute based on his own views, despite reasoned arguments to the contrary. It was a time when Groner would witness, to her dismay, the unpredictable subjectivity and limitations of the legal system in the resolution of custody cases.

Fatigue overcame Beverly Anne Groner as the garage elevator lifted her toward her Bethesda, Maryland, law office. There she would check her messages and scan the next day's schedule. She had spent a long day in court, and the fifty-seven-year-old attorney looked forward to a quiet dinner with her husband Sam. As the automatic door slid open she stepped onto the familiar carpet of the office building hallway.

She was surprised to see a very tall man standing by the bank of elevators, where he seemed to be waiting for someone.

"I'm sure that you're Beverly Groner," said the man, smiling and walking toward her. He was handsome, Groner observed, and attractively dressed in a business suit.

"That is true," she answered warily.

"I'm Bob Jordan," he said, extending his hand, waiting for her response.

Groner had the feeling she was going to be late for dinner.

Robert Jordan had telephoned long-distance from Connecticut early that morning in the summer of 1979. The thirty-eight-year-old marketing consultant wanted to know if Groner would represent him in a dispute with his ex-wife over their two sons. Bob lived in Darien, Connecticut, while his ex-wife Linda, who had custody of the boys, continued to live in Potomac, Maryland, the affluent Washington, D.C., suburb where she and Bob had lived when they were married. Bob had learned recently that Linda was going to move to South Africa and wanted to take the boys with her. He felt that he must stop her from moving, and if he could not do that, then he wanted the boys to live with him. Because a Maryland court had granted the Jordans' divorce, any subsequent argument over their sons' custody would have to be adjudicated in that state's court system as well. So Bob needed a lawyer, a top-notch member of the Maryland bar.

Whenever he had a problem Bob Jordan did his homework carefully. This time, when he asked around, he found out that Beverly Groner, a vivacious and colorful woman, was considered the top domestic relations lawyer in the state. She chaired the Governor's Commission on Domestic Relations Laws, which was spearheading major legislative changes, and was a leader in family law activities for local and national bar associations. But Groner's services were not easily obtained. She never accepted a client with whom she had not spoken, and she did not talk to everyone who came looking for help. There were just too many needy people. Moreover, because Groner was in the top echelon of the domestic relations bar, her fees were among the highest around.

When Bob called that morning, Groner was leaving for a hearing. "Call back late today or tomorrow," she told him. "We can talk about your case, but I must tell you now that I already have a number of custody suits pending." She limited her case load because she knew that custody fights could accelerate without warning. If too many heated up at once, the crises and emergencies might be overwhelming.

"Mrs. Groner," said Bob when he saw her that evening, "I flew down here today even though you didn't expect me so I could convince you to take my case. I feel you must represent me."

"Well, let's go into my office and talk about it," she replied. "Let me hear what you have to say."

Her keys and bracelets jangled as she unlocked the reception room door. A brass sign on the front said PLEASE KNOCK TO ENTER. Groner maintained two entrances to her suite so that clients could wait in different areas without seeing one another. She wanted to protect their privacy, to make them feel more comfortable, particularly her many clients who had high profiles in the Washington, D.C., area.

"We had a rather straightforward divorce," Bob began when the lawyer was seated behind her large desk, a photograph of her three grown children nearby. The July sun, still shining at that late hour, glimmered through the windows. Despite her fatigue, Groner listened carefully. "I won't bore you with the reasons our marriage failed," continued Bob, "but suffice it to say that Linda got custody of both Christopher and Garrett, who were nine and four.

"The divorce was final in April of last year, 1978," he added. "I visit my children on a regular basis—the decree says that I can see them two weekends a month, on holidays, and in the summer—either in Darien or in Potomac. I've been married to my new wife, Marianne, since last October, about nine months. She's in marketing, too. In fact, she has an M.B.A. from Harvard."

Marianne, who was much younger than Linda, was a professional with career plans of her own, while Linda was content as housewife and mother. The sharp contrast between them was not lost on Bob. He was like many men today who, after marriages to traditional home-makers, opt for younger, career-oriented second wives.

"The problem," he continued, "is that Linda has told me she is going to marry a man named Bill Cahill. Bill Cahill is a civil engineer, an American who lives and works in South Africa, and Linda says she's taking the boys there to live. But Chris—he's twelve now—says he wants to stay with me in Connecticut, and I think Linda may be con-vinced to leave him. I don't think she likes children as much when they're older as when they're babies, and she's been having a hard time with Chris. But Garrett is another story. He's just seven years old, and Linda thinks he's hers.

"Mrs. Groner, I don't want either of my children living in South Africa," said Bob, his voice starting to crack with emotion and fatigue. "It's a horrible place," he explained. "It's physically dangerous and it's morally bankrupt. And I'll never get to see them; South Africa is eight thousand miles away. Can't you please help me?"

Groner had a full case load at the time; about one third of her clients were lawyers themselves, and many others were politicians. But she was intrigued by Bob Jordan and his story. She liked him immediately and thought it unfair that his sons should be snatched away. It again proved to her the fragility of noncustodial parents' relationships with their chil-dren. Groner guessed that she would have at least a fifty-fifty chance of winning Bob's case, but like many lawyers, she refused to make a firm prediction. The courts were too unpredictable.

"I'll think about it," she said after talking with Bob for almost two hours. "But first I must meet your wife, Marianne. I must be convinced that she is willing to go through this lawsuit with you. It will be very hard on both of you." Groner had seen custody fights destroy second marriages. Today Bob might wish he had paid closer attention to the warning in his lawyer's request.

Bob Jordan smiled. "Of course," he replied, rising from his seat. "We can be here together early next week." He knew that he had found his lawyer.

Groner had long been familiar with personal tragedy and divorce. Raised by a divorced mother and married herself for the first time at eighteen, she never finished college but was granted admission none-theless—some fourteen years and three children later—to law school. Groner had always wanted to be a lawyer, and sensing that her marriage

would not last, she doggedly pursued her degree and graduated in 1959
from American University's Washington College of Law. The following
year she divorced her husband.

She applied for work with a lawyer named Samuel Groner, a sole
practitioner. They married in 1962. The couple first had a general practice, but after ten years Beverly began specializing in family law. Sam,
who was in a serious automobile accident in which his fifteen-year-old
son from his first marriage was killed, and who later suffered from an
unsuccessful back operation, accepted a job as trial counsel with the
navy and then as a U.S. Labor Department administrative law judge.
Beverly Groner maintained on her own the firm of Groner & Groner,
and her practice flourished. A success long before women made inroads
into the law, she scoffed at the notion of clients choosing an attorney
because she is a woman: "You ought to get the very best lawyer you
can—man or woman."

Bob Jordan was convinced that he did have the best. When he went
to bed that night after meeting Groner, he was excited and happy. He
kept thinking about his fair-headed, blue-eyed sons, how much he
loved them, and how much fun he had when he was with them, playing soccer, watching movies together, visiting the entertainment parks,
everything kids liked to do on special outings. He was going to write
the State Department and the United Nations to ask for help. Surely,
he thought, there must be some U.S. policy or international regulation
to help him prevent the children from moving to South Africa.

"You should know," Groner told Bob and Marianne when they met
together in her office, "that you should not enter custody litigation, or
any litigation, unless you are prepared for the possiblity—even if it isn't
strong—of a loss. You have to confront that potential and accept it
before you proceed."

The attorney continued, her hands folded on the desk and her voice
firm and direct. "You must also know that a custody suit is misery. It
pervades your whole life. They're going to ask you personal, probing
questions, some of which will have implications that are not compli-
mentary to you. Some of them will be unfair and misstatements of what
you know to be the truth. It isn't fun. And it's expensive; there are
costs incurred, and you'll be spending money that you'd rather be
spending on family vacations or fixing the house. There is no way anyone is going to be able to tell you what it will ultimately cost. And
there is no way anyone can tell you that you'll win."

Groner was not about to mince words; she was doing her new clients
a favor by preparing them for what lay ahead. She looked Bob and
Marianne in the eyes and waited.

Bob looked over at Marianne. "I think it would be good for the children to be with us," she told the attorney sincerely. "I understand exactly how Bob feels. And we all get along very well together."

"I must stop them," said Bob. "And I think we'll win." His determination had set in.

A few days before the new school year began, Linda agreed to send Chris to live with Bob in Darien. The boy had vehemently rejected moving to South Africa and repeatedly insisted that he be with his father. A large, husky adolescent, Chris had been having trouble in school, too, and he hoped that his father would give him more help with his homework. His mother did not seem as willing. In fact, she might have been relieved to see Bob take over Chris's upbringing.

"I'm going to pay for your plane ticket to Connecticut with money from your savings account," she told Chris while helping him gather possessions from his bedroom on the second floor of the large colonial home in Potomac. "I spent a lot of money on your school clothes because I thought you would be staying with me. And now I don't have much left. So you're going to have to pay for this yourself." Like many ex-wives, Linda was determined not to let Bob get the best of her financially.

Bob was jittery when he drove to meet Chris at the airport. "I'm so proud of him," he whispered to Marianne as he spotted the boy disembarking with the other passengers.

"Hi, Dad," said Chris, grinning. He was balancing in his arms a large cardboard carton in which Linda had piled his belongings.

"That's just like her not even to give him a suitcase," Bob muttered under his breath. He threw his arm around Chris. "Welcome home, son," he said.

A week later Groner petitioned the Montgomery County Circuit Court for a change in the Jordan boys' custody. Chris was already living with Bob, she wrote. As for Garrett, a move to South Africa would seriously harm him, particularly his relationship with his older brother, with whom he was close. After the trauma of the divorce, the Jordan boys needed predictability, stability, and continuity in their lives, Groner argued, and that would be best provided by living with their father and stepmother in Connecticut rather than by moving with their mother to South Africa.

Most important, Groner asked the court to issue immediately a temporary injunction prohibiting Linda Jordan from moving away with either Chris or Garrett until a judge had reached a final decision in their case. Within a few days, Circuit Court Judge Stanley Frosh met that request, granting the temporary injunction. At the same time he ratified Bob's custody of the older boy.

Linda panicked when she learned that Bob wanted Garrett as well as Chris. Garrett was her baby, a child with natural charm who won over everyone he met. She couldn't possibly marry Bill Cahill if it meant losing her little boy. Shaken, she scheduled an appointment with Jeffrey Greenblatt, a young attorney with an aggressive courtroom style. Greenblatt was generally unemotional about his clients; he likened his job to that of a surgeon who remained personally uninvolved with patients. But Greenblatt experienced an usual reaction when he listened to Linda. He saw before him a pretty, fair-complexioned, thirty-eight-year-old woman whose simple, gentle manner made her appear not only naive but also helplessly innocent. Insecurity cloaked her words as she struggled to articulate her feelings. Greenblatt learned that Linda's only profession had been as a typing teacher before her children were born; she was neither ambitious nor worldly. He guessed that she had always given in to Bob Jordan in the past and probably lacked the wherewithal to fight any threats to her future happiness.

But this time would be different. Greenblatt liked Linda, but even more, he felt sorry for her. She needed a white knight. The lawyer decided he would come to her rescue, and despite his professed callousness, he enjoyed the role. Many lawyers do.

Linda might have needed a white knight in court, but in her personal dealings with Bob she fended for herself quite well. Though their relationship up until then had been coolly cordial, she reacted to Bob's lawsuit like a cornered animal, striking out to protect herself. As in many custody battles, fear led to pettiness.

"Bob," said Linda when he called Garrett to plan an upcoming weekend visit, "I can't drive Garrett to the airport on Friday. I guess he can't go to Connecticut to see you."

Bob was shocked. "What do you mean?" he asked in disbelief. "You can't or you won't?"

"My car isn't working well. And besides, there's lots of construction around the airport. Driving him there and parking and taking him in will just be too hard for me."

Bob tried to think fast. "Well, is it OK if I ask Marianne's father to pick him up and drive him to the airport?" He was trying to hold his anger in check.

"No. I don't know Marianne's father," replied Linda curtly. "I've never met him—he's a complete stranger—so I'm not going to give Garrett to him."

"But Garrett likes Marianne's father," Bob insisted. "*He* knows him."

"I'm sorry," said Linda. "It's just not going to work out this time."

Bob's head was spinning when he hung up the phone. I'm not going to let her do this to me, he said to himself. He dialed Linda's number again. "Tell Garrett I'm flying down on Friday and *I'll* pick him up." He slammed down the phone. It was going to be a tough weekend. When he arrived at National Airport he would have to rent a car to drive out to Potomac to get Garrett and then drive back to the airport for their flight north. And the whole ordeal would have to be repeated again on Sunday when he took Garrett back to Maryland. Bob wasn't sure who had won this one.

"Have you called off your engagement?" Beverly Groner asked Linda Jordan during her deposition that October. They were seated around a table in Groner's office; Jeff Greenblatt, Bob, and a court reporter were present as well.

"No," replied Linda tersely.

"Have you called off the impending ceremony?"

"Yes."

"Why is that?"

"Because of Garrett," said Linda impatiently, "and there is a chance I will have to make a decision between Garrett and my future husband, and if so"—she paused for emphasis—"I would choose Garrett because he is more important to me."

Groner was unimpressed. "Do you think Garrett needs the influence of a father?" she asked Linda.

"Yes."

"Do you think he needs the influence of his father?"

"No."

"Why?" asked Groner.

"Because I don't believe his father is the best person in his life. I don't believe his father is that good a father." For one thing, she said, Bob traveled too much.

Groner probed for other reasons.

"He also drinks quite a bit," Linda added.

"What is the source of your knowledge?"

"I went out with him in August in the evening for dinner and he had a number of drinks."

"Do you think that was a normal circumstance," asked Groner, her eyebrows raised, "having dinner with a divorced spouse?"

Greenblatt bristled. "I am going to object," he called out. "What difference does it make?"

"Well," Groner retorted, "she says he drinks a lot because he drank when he was with her one night for dinner."

"Well, you may not be satisfied with that response—"

"I would like her to elaborate on it," interrupted Groner.

"I am not going to allow her to elaborate," Greenblatt countered.

But Linda, anxious to prove her point, continued anyway. "He has been to our house for dinner also," she said, "and he has had a number of drinks. He would say 'Do you mind if I help myself to a Scotch?'"

"Do you think that's wrong?" Sarcasm hung from Groner's words.

"Well, the amount of liquor that he consumes is quite a lot."

"Have you seen him intoxicated?"

"No. I have seen him emotionally disturbed."

"Are you qualified to make that diagnosis?" shot back Groner.

"I have seen him cry," replied Linda smugly.

"Do you think crying is a bad thing?"

"Crying per se, no. But maybe being brought on by drinking too much."

Groner was getting disgusted. "You are not a very demonstrative person, are you?" It was more an announcement than a question.

Linda would never offer any evidence that Bob had a drinking or emotional problem.

Despite the lawyer's sharp questioning, Linda remained cool, even when asked about South Africa. "Did you in going through South Africa get any idea as to why the South Africans seem to be leaving the country in droves—the white South Africans?" asked Groner.

"No," Linda replied matter-of-factly.

"Do you know that white South Africans are leaving in droves?"

"It is my understanding from Realtors that the South Africans are coming back in droves."

"From Realtors?" Groner looked dubious.

"Yes."

"Do you know the reason why they left?"

Linda shrugged. "They weren't happy. I don't know."

"Did you walk through or visit or drive through Soweto?" Groner continued. She had carefully researched the squalid and strife-ridden communities in which black South Africans lived.

"No, we did not."

"Did you go through Homelands?"

"No."

"You have been there," said the lawyer, looking directly at Linda, "so what would your response be to someone who said that South Africa is racist?"

"That I just didn't see any racism there."

Groner's face formed a mask of incredulity.

Groner also deposed Bill Cahill the following January—he was in the United States visiting Linda—but his deposition provided little new information. Cahill, forty-six years old, Irish Catholic, and a New Englander by birth, simply refused to answer any questions relating to his relationship with Linda. "On the advice of my attorney, I respectfully decline to answer the question on the grounds that I may tend to incriminate myself," he repeated time and time again. Cahill's lawyer, William J. Chen of Rockville, looked on approvingly.

Groner understood why he was being so coy. "Do you know whether there has been any prosecution in the State of Maryland for . . . fornication in the last 25 years?" she finally demanded of Chen after Cahill had recited his response so many times that the deposition had grown maddenly dull.

"I have certain information on that matter," responded Chen vaguely.

"I can suggest to you that those prosecutions have been nonexistent," Groner told him. Still, neither Chen nor Cahill would budge.

Jeff Greenblatt deposed both Bob and Marianne to help prepare Linda's defense, grilling Bob in particular about his financial records and the way in which he calculated his monthly expenses. Money was important; Bob was sending Linda one hundred dollars a week in alimony as well as making all of the payments on the Potomac house, and Greenblatt would demand that he also pay Linda's legal bill—Greenblatt's fee—for the new courthouse battle.

Some lawyers fight each other in court and then share a friendly drink afterward. But Greenblatt and Groner clearly disliked each other, both professionally and personally.

"I am sick and tired of your suggesting answers to him," Linda's lawyer shouted at his legal opponent during Bob Jordan's deposition.

"I am suggesting he should be completing his answers," Groner responded indignantly.

"If I have to," retorted Greenblatt, "I will suspend the taking of this deposition and I will take it into the duty judge tomorrow morning for some suggestion from him that you not continue to suggest answers. This is getting ridiculous."

"I am applying the same standard to depositions taken by you." Groner tried to stay calm, but it was difficult. Greenblatt wanted to change the rules.

"Fine," he snapped back at her.

While the lawyers barked at each other, while the months of discovery wore on, relations between Bob and Linda grew more strained. "You're going to lose," Bob told his ex-wife during one of their brief telephone conversations in the spring of 1980. "You're going to lose," he said when he saw her the next month during one of his visitations with Garrett. It sounded mean spirited, but Bob increasingly felt in control. Perhaps Linda, too, would realize that the court suit was working against her. Chris had been performing well in his school in Darien. Groner was working hard on the case, and Bob could not believe that a judge would rule against him. He wished that Linda would just give in on Garrett, too.

Throughout the turmoil of the custody suit, Bob sought advice and counseling from his minister, Walter Taylor of St. Luke's Episcopal Church in Darien. Bob and Marianne had grown close to Taylor since he'd married them. They attended services at St. Luke's because Bob could not continue in the Roman Catholic church after his divorce, and the couple eventually joined the Episcopal church. Bob was particularly excited that Chris, now that he was living with them, also had decided to join—despite the Catholic upbringing he had received with Linda. Neither father nor son worried that Linda might react negatively, an oversight that would turn out to be a fatal mistake.

"Do you think it would be possible for me—through my position with the church—to approach Linda's priest at the Catholic church in Potomac?" Taylor inquired one day when he and Bob were seated in the rector's office. "Perhaps the two of us could help work out some agreement, an understanding, between the two of you." Taylor knew Bob's son Garrett because Bob had brought him to the church when the boy visited in Darien.

"That would be very kind," Bob replied with surprise. Although he had confided in his rector about the relocation and custody battle, he had never expected Taylor, who was only a few years Bob's senior, to take an active role in the dispute. "We would certainly appreciate any help you can give us," Bob added. "But you know, of course, that any reconciliation could in no way permit Garrett to live in South Africa—for any time at all."

Bob respected Taylor tremendously. He was a popular priest with a large number of highly educated, demanding parishioners. "He might work something out," Bob later told Marianne. It was a naive thought, given Linda's feelings about her sons' religion. She was indeed unhappy that Bob had introduced them to another church.

Bob also sought assistance from Dr. Neil Schiff, a clinical psychologist in Washington, D.C., whom Beverly Groner had recommended. In fact, the attorney had insisted that Bob and Marianne meet with Dr. Schiff so that he could evaluate the family and offer his professional opinion on what would be best for the boys. Groner had told Bob that she would accept his case only if a mental health expert thought that Bob's attempt to block Linda's move and gain custody would be in Chris's and Garrett's best interests. She was anxious to do only what was best for the children. So Bob and Marianne had talked with Dr. Schiff the previous summer. Because he was supportive they had scheduled several more sessions.

In June 1980 Bob, Marianne, Chris, and Garrett visited the psychologist's office for their last meeting before the trial. Dr. Schiff arranged five chairs in a semicircle and stood quietly after greeting the Jordans, waiting for them to be seated. He wanted to observe who sat next to whom, indications of the family members' bonding and relationships.

As he had anticipated, Bob and Marianne chose adjoining seats. Chris sat down opposite them. But Garrett, rather than finding a chair, simply climbed onto his father's lap. Bob put his arms around the child and they stayed together for the session's first half hour. Dr. Schiff, seated in one of the two remaining chairs, noticed that the concerned look he first saw in Garrett's eyes faded as the boy grew more relaxed in his father's arms.

But eventually Garrett grew fidgety and squirmed to the floor. The small group's conversation continued as Dr. Schiff observed the child to see what he would do. This time Garrett chose Chris's lap, and he stayed there for another half hour, enjoying the closeness with his big brother, whom he had seen only intermittently since Chris's move to their father's house. Finally Garrett wandered over to the one remaining empty chair in the semicircle and sat down.

"Garrett," began Dr. Schiff after the child had been seated for several minutes, "if you had a money tree, which means you'd have as much money as you wanted so cost would not concern you at all, who would you live with? And how often would you see your other parent?" The psychologist spoke in a calm, soft voice.

Garrett chewed his lip, not saying anything at all. "I'd live with Dad and visit Mom," he finally replied.

"Even if she is in South Africa?" inquired Dr. Schiff, trying to make sure that Garrett had understood what he was saying.

"Yes," replied the boy. "I'd visit her twice a week."

Bill Cahill, Linda's fiancé, asked Bob to meet him for dinner when both men would be in Washington. Bob Jordan actually liked Bill—he was a recovering alcoholic who was divorced himself, with children, and he related well to Bob's own sons. Bob was curious to see if they could resolve the South Africa dispute together. In some ways he felt sorry for Bill, recognizing that the man was anxious to make a new life for himself—a life with Linda—but that the court suit was preventing this. Despite having such sympathetic feelings, Bob still firmly believed that any resolution of the case could not involve his younger son moving to South Africa.

Bob also knew that Bill had moved to South Africa voluntarily, leaving his own three children behind in the United States with their mother, so he was not sure that Linda's fiancé could identify with Bob's own need to see both of his sons regularly.

Their dinner started out pleasantly.

"If we can settle this," began Cahill, whose short, stocky physique contrasted with Bob's towering frame, "Linda will give you her share from selling the house—and I'll pay her legal fees as well." It was clear that they were willing to do what they could to avoid a trial.

"That's quite an offer," responded Bob, "but the real issue is the welfare of my son. The money part just isn't important."

"But Garrett will be fine," insisted Cahill earnestly. "We have servants, the house is wonderful, the neighborhood is beautiful, the schools are great. He'll love it—I can guarantee you that. And we hope you'll visit—and Garrett can visit you."

Cahill leaned across the table. "The South Africa you see on the television is just an invention of the media. That has nothing to do with what life will be like for Garrett. We'll have a pool; he'll have his own horse. He will be very protected."

The more Cahill talked, the more Bob realized that Linda's fiancé simply ignored apartheid and the South African value system. He did not even acknowledge the moral controversy.

"Bill, I do not approve of South Africa," Bob emphasized as they ate their meal. Bob understood that Linda would always be a good mother, he explained, but he did not want his son growing up away from his brother, in a society with values that he abhorred. "And you know," Bob continued for emphasis, "Chris and I can't lose Garrett. You and Linda are trying to take him half a world away from us."

"But it's not forever. It's probably only going to be for three years . . . ten years at the outside."

Bob felt sick.

"Listen, Bob," Cahill continued. "The job is great. The pay and fringes are great. I just can't turn away from this assignment. Surely you, a professional man yourself, can understand that."

"Surely you can understand," Bob replied as calmly as he could, "that I love my son and I need to see him regularly—not once in awhile. And he needs to see me and Chris, too. What you and Linda want to do is inhumane, taking a child like that to South Africa. I just can't allow it."

The two men found no common ground between them. After the dinner they shook hands and left the restaurant.

Like Bill Cahill's unsuccessful effort to end the battle, Dr. Taylor's outreach through Linda's priest also failed. Linda resisted the Episcopal minister's attempts to intervene, saying she wanted to defer instead to the judge. On June 30, 1980, one year after Bob had flown down to Maryland to ask Beverly Groner for help, the trial began in an old courthouse in the heart of Rockville, the county seat for Montgomery County. Groner was pleased that Judge Frosh, who had signed the temporary injunction prohibiting Linda from leaving, was assigned to the case; surely this was a good sign that he understood Bob's point of view. Groner also knew that in an earlier case the judge had decided in favor of a custodial parent who was moving to Malaysia with her two sons. That decision had been overturned on appeal, so perhaps this time the judge would be on guard to prevent being overturned again. Judges typically do not like to be overruled.

Because Bob and Linda had agreed already that Chris would stay in Connecticut, the court fight would focus on Garrett alone. Bob and Marianne Jordan, Linda Jordan, Bill Cahill, Beverly Groner, and Jeff Greenblatt all concentrated on the seven-year-old boy.

In one respect Garrett was a fortunate child. According to a University of Pennsylvania study of divorced families, more than 50 percent of the children who do not live with their fathers had never been in the father's home, and 42 percent had not seen their fathers at all during the previous year. Here Garrett's father was fighting to be with him all the time.

At the time of the Jordan trial, the few rules that defined the conditions under which a custodial parent could relocate and move children were confusing, if not contradictory. Since then, some state courts around the country have tried to clarify the issue, but standards vary.

States like Minnesota defer to the custodial parent unless the other
parent can prove that the move would be detrimental to the child. At
the other extreme, states such as New York absolutely bar a child from
moving unless the custodial parent shows compelling reasons for the
change. Still other states—like Illinois, Nebraska, South Dakota, and
Michigan—take the middle ground, saying that a child can move with
a custodial parent if the parent has legitimate reasons for moving and
the move is in the child's best interests.

    Groner realized that Bob's case was breaking new ground in Maryland
law. As she chose her arguments on his behalf she tried to determine
what sounded most convincing, since Maryland had no clear rules on
relocation. Rather than asking that the move be forbidden the lawyer
simply decided to ask for a change in Garrett's custody based on Linda's
plan. To win she would have to prove that because of the anticipated
move, Garrett's circumstances had changed since Linda was first
awarded custody, and that he would be better off living with Bob in
Connecticut rather than in South Africa with his mother.
    As the plaintiff's attorney, Groner called her witnesses first.
    "Your Honor, the plaintiffs call Dr. Neil Schiff," she announced
after making her opening statement. In custody cases lawyers typically
call mental health experts to testify on a client's behalf.
    "What impression did you get as to Garrett's state of adjustment to
his family situation?" Groner asked the psychologist after he took the
stand. She was inquiring about an early meeting.
    "I concluded that he was a happy, well-adjusted child who perceived
himself to be involved in a difficult family situation," responded Schiff,
a scholarly looking and reflective man.
    "Did you ask him if he had a preference as to where he lived?"
    "Yes, I did."
    "Before we come to that," Groner said, preventing an immediate
response, "did you discuss both parents or only one parent or neither
parent?"
    "I discussed both parents with Garrett."
    "What was his attitude toward his respective parents?"
    "He seemed very fond of both of them."
    "Did he demonstrate any fear of either?" Groner wanted to prevent
Greenblatt from suggesting that it had been a one-sided interview, that
Garrett had been under pressure to respond in Bob's favor.
    "May I refer to my notes on this?" asked the psychologist, hesitating.
He interviewed scores of families in his practice, and wanted to be
certain that his recollection was correct.

"Of course," answered Groner.

Schiff thumbed through some papers on his lap. "No, he did not," the psychologist replied.

"Did you have an opportunity to observe Garrett physically with his father?"

"Yes, I did."

"And what, if anything, did you observe about the relationship?"

"That he appeared to be very affectionately involved with his father. . . . It seemed mutual and spontaneous."

"Did Garrett express to you a point of view at that time as to what his preference was as to where he would live?" Groner asked.

"Well, the first thing he said was that he would rather live with his father because he did not wish to go to South Africa. And then I asked him what would his preference be if he were not to live in South Africa, and he said his preference would be to remain here." Like many children, Garrett enjoyed the status quo.

The lawyer's questions turned to a subsequent meeting. "What did Garrett tell you on that day about his preference as to where he wanted to live?" she inquired.

"On December 26, 1979," replied Dr. Schiff, "he said categorically that he wanted to live with his father no matter how sad his mother was. He hesitated when I asked him if he would still want to live with his father if he knew his mother would be mad. He told me that he missed [his brother] Chris.

"He said he got along well with his mother except when he brought up the issue about living up with his father and when she got mad, and he seemed very definite about living with his father."

Groner was pleased with this response.

"Dr. Schiff," she concluded after he had testified for almost an hour and a half, "is there one word that, in your opinion, could express the consequence to Garrett if he were required to move with his mother to South Africa?"

"I think that would be a devastating experience for him," responded the psychologist.

Groner sat down.

When Judge Frosh adjourned for lunch he asked Dr. Schiff if he could return the next morning for Jeff Greenblatt's cross-examination. The judge wanted time to talk with Chris and Garrett alone, he said, and he knew that the boys were waiting in the hallway. He would invite them into his chambers. Both Bob and Linda were apprehensive about the private hearing; they each left, with their lawyers, to get some lunch.

•   •   •

After several hours Judge Frosh, a small, dapper man in his early sixties, walked back into the courtroom, seated himself authoritatively behind the bench, and announced that he would tell them what he had learned from the children. While Greenblatt had urged the judge to report on the meeting, Bob and Groner were upset. They thought that the judge had promised both Chris and Garrett full confidentiality. Frosh ignored their objections.

"I asked Chris whether he talked to his brother frequently and he told me he did," related the judge. Judge Frosh had asked Chris how often he, Bob, and Marianne had told Garrett that they wanted him to move to Connecticut. "Chris said that every time anybody talks with the boy, Garrett is told that they would like to have him come up to Connecticut," relayed the judge.

"I asked him if he thought that was not a bit of pressure on his kid brother who was at that point only seven to have three people to whom he is very closely attached constantly asking him about whether he would like to come to Connecticut. And I asked him if he thought that it wouldn't be a good idea to cease pressuring his young brother and let the boy alone for a while." The judge looked pointedly at Bob and Marianne.

"He said that he thought that was probably a good idea. That was something we discussed in some depth."

Judge Frosh explained that he had talked to Chris about spending more time alone with Linda, perhaps visiting her when Garrett was visiting Bob. But Chris also said he wanted more time with his brother. "He expressed, again, a very deep affection for his father, deep affection for his mother," the judge stated, looking down on everyone seated before him. "And, I told him that in my view, I felt that he was old enough to understand that however his parents might be fighting with each other in court, they were fighting over their love for him and his brother.

"I said I didn't think that he ought to allow that in any way to affect his love and affection for both his mother and his father—and that the time would come when he became eighteen, nineteen, twenty, and he would begin to have some insight into what caused them to drift apart and he would recognize that they both loved him during his childhood.

Judge Frosh paused. "I said he should be sure that he maintained the best possible relationship with both his father and his mother because it was on this kind of relationship that his future lies and his relationship with his own wife and his own children." Everyone else in the room was silent. "I can tell you," the judge added, looking at Linda and then at Bob, "that the older boy is a well-adjusted, beautiful young man and, obviously, has a very high intelligence quotient." He paused again before turning to the subject of Garrett.

"The young boy is a very charming seven-year-old, full of playfulness and full of life. But he is very equivocal about where he would prefer staying. He tells me he wouldn't mind living in Connecticut; he wouldn't mind living in Bethesda. He tells me that he enjoys Connecticut a great deal because when he is up there, he is always on the go to a baseball game, to a picnic, and to whatever—that there's always something being done for him.

"But he has no problems, he said to me, with living with his mother. He likes it very much, and he would not be drawn into any kind of a firm choice between his mother's home and his father's home."

"Was any reference made to South Africa?" Groner asked.

"I didn't press him with it," said Judge Frosh. "He didn't mention anything himself."

Bob considered the judge's interview worthless. "He takes Garrett's ambivalence as proof that Chris and I—and everyone else—lied about his preference for Connecticut," Bob complained to his lawyer. "He's taking it as permission to ignore the rest of us. He doesn't understand that Garrett is only avoiding a public choice."

Although the judge might have seen Bob Jordan as an overbearing father, neither Groner nor Bob thought that his discussions with Garrett were inappropriate. Yet many parents involved in a custody battle become so consumed with their own choice of what is best for their children that they become too anxious for the children to agree with that choice. In seeking this goal, these parents can overlook both the negative impression they may create on others and any harmful impact their lobbying may have on the children.

When Groner resumed her case, she devoted the rest of the afternoon to three witnesses—two men who worked in the same consulting firm with Bob and the guidance counselor at Chris's school. Bob's colleagues testified that their company, Marketing Corporation of America, accommodated parents' needs by adjusting travel schedules and work assignments; the counselor talked about the school environment in Darien.

That evening Bob and Marianne took Chris and Garrett out to dinner and to stay the night at their hotel. Judge Frosh had told them they could do so. All four were tired, but they did their best to take the day in stride.

*   *   *

By the next morning, Greenblatt was hungry to cross-examine Dr. Schiff.

"Now," he began purposefully, "you testified that on each occasion that you saw Garrett, you asked him where it was that he wished to live. Correct?"

"That is correct," replied the psychologist.

"And, you also testified that he didn't demonstrate any fear or any stress on the occasions that you saw him. Is that correct?"

"That is correct."

"Okay. Now, is it possible, Doctor, that you missed any of the signs, any stress or pressure from his father? Is there that possibility?"

"It's possible."

"Okay." said Greenblatt. He was just getting warmed up. "And, is it possible that there were pressure and stresses outside of your presence which you were unaware of?"

"That's within the realm of possibility."

"You are aware, are you not, Doctor, that studies reveal that in situations such as this, the parent with whom the child appears at a testing situation or interview situation is influenced by the fact that he's brought by a specific parent? You're aware of those studies, are you not?"

"No, I'm not." Schiff remained expressionless.

"You concur," continued Greenblatt, "do you not, that if indeed Mr. Jordan made every visit for Garrett a holiday, this might in some way influence Garrett's decision as to where he wanted to live?"

"Did you say 'might'?" asked Dr. Schiff.

"Yes."

"It's within the realm of possibility," he admitted.

Groner called her next witness that afternoon, hoping to get to a key issue in her case, an important argument in Bob's favor. Until then, little reference had been made to Garrett's potential life-style in South Africa, and she wanted the judge to know how undesirable it would be, emphasizing one of Bob's major reasons for objecting to the move. Groner called Lorna Hahn of the Association of Third World Affairs.

"Dr. Hahn, what is your occupation?" Groner began.

"I'm a political analyst for foreign affairs specializing in Africa," she responded, proceeding to list her credentials.

While Hahn's curriculum vitae was extensive, it was not good enough for Judge Frosh, and he was critical of Groner for her choice of witness. "How does her personal experience," he demanded, "translate itself into an ability to tell this court where Mrs. Jordan may be living, what that community is, the availability of schooling, the availability of friends, the availability of medical care, the availability of all of the other amenities of life?

"Can she testify," continued the judge, "on the location where you are anticipating, perhaps, that Mrs. Jordan will go—and be able to express for me an expert opinion on what the environment of this child is going to be when he steps into that peculiar situation—so that I can use this testimony as a basis for my decision?"

Judge Frosh clearly did not think Hahn could do what he was suggesting. "I am *not* interested in the pervasiveness of anything in South Africa in its total," he told Groner. The political system there simply did not interest him, for he cared only about the microcosm of Garrett's future home life. It was a perspective with which Groner, and Bob Jordan, disagreed vehemently.

Although Dr. Hahn spoke of South Africa's system of apartheid, its systematic violation of civil rights, and the tense political climate throughout the country, her words were to no avail. "Let's assume that you have her testify on the record that there is discrimination," Judge Frosh demanded of Groner. "Now, how do you translate that from the glittering generality, again, down to what is going to happen to this child and how it's going to affect him when he is there, assuming he is?"

Judge Frosh says today that he was troubled by the Jordan case. During his career—he is now retired—he presided over many different kinds of trials, and he feels that domestic disputes are among the most difficult. He saw too many husbands and wives try to hurt each other. Such acrimony upsets him, says the judge, because it prevents couples from finding a middle ground where they can resolve their disputes. Instead they fight with every psychological and legal weapon they can find.

Judge Frosh recalls that he was impatient in the Jordan case, just as he was in other domestic relations cases. But in this instance he also felt sorry for Linda. She was not a young woman, and she might not have another opportunity to marry. How could he possibly tell her to reject Bill Cahill and wait for a more suitable man to propose? Should it work against Linda that Cahill lived in South Africa? What had she done to have her future happiness denied?

It was hardly surprising that Frosh responded to Linda on a personal level: Domestic relations law is not cut and dried, and judges are only human. Judge Frosh wanted to be fair to Linda, he explains today, because he believed that in Maryland divorced women generally suffer far more than do their husbands, particularly economically. Bill Cahill was a successful professional who would change Linda's life for the better.

On the third day of the trial Groner called Linda Jordan to the stand. As she raised her right hand and placed her left on a Bible to take her oath, she was fortified by lessons from Greenblatt on how to testify. The lawyer had spent hours with her, pumping her up, preparing her to show what kind of mother she was.

"*Tell* the judge what you do with Garrett," Greenblatt had pleaded with her during their practice sessions.

"Oh, stuff," she would say with a shrug.

"What does that mean," Greenblatt would beg, pacing the room. "When you go home today, make a list of all the things you and Garrett do together. Write down everything you do between now and the next time we meet. And write down Garrett's reactions. This is *very important.*" Greenblatt knew that the heart of his case was in proving Linda's motherly attributes.

Now, as she seated herself in the witness chair, Linda prepared to prove that she was a good mother. She wanted to keep her son, but she also wanted to please her attorney, whom she always addressed as "Mr. Greenblatt."

But Beverly Groner focused instead on Linda Jordan's relationship with Bill Cahill and on Bob's visitation with the children, and she gave Linda little opportunity to shine.

When it was Bob's turn to testify, Groner repeated the advice she had given him. She worried about the way Bob would appear before the judge—and rightfully so. "Please, you have a very warm way about you. Let your own personality shine through when you are on the witness stand. Don't be efficient and competent; be human and warm and conversational in your testimony. And please," she added, "turn from time to time to the judge, because the judge sees you only in profile when you're sitting in the witness box. If you're never looking at him, he doesn't get the impact of you as a person." She patted her client's arm.

Once on the stand, Bob began to talk about his shock and dismay over Linda's plans to move.

"When you picked up the boys in the summer of '79," said Groner, "Linda told you about South Africa and you said that you were stunned. What action, if any, did you take to find out anything about South Africa?"

"When I recovered from my numbness, I became immensely concerned. We, in the short run, continued with our . . . continued with our plans for the day. Christopher was at the University of Maryland basketball game. Marianne and I went there and spent the day with him and we returned to Connecticut.

"I began to investigate all I could find out about South Africa. I read everything that was available in the ordinary popular press and what I happened to be seeing on television at the time and, in addition, I went to the library and went through the Reader's Guide and saw the various articles and publications that had been written on South Africa and obtained copies of those articles."

Bob continued, trying to turn and look at the judge. "I felt very threatened. I had a great relationship with these boys. I had worked very hard to maintain and build that relationship. It did not seem possible to me that that kind of relationship would be possible if they went to South Africa." Bob wanted to emphasize the vast geographic separation he and his sons would have to endure in such a move. "And," he added, "I felt very frightened for them after my reading."

Despite the intensity of his testimony, Bob failed to follow Groner's advice about his posture and demeanor. He seemed stiff and uncomfortable, and as time wore on, Groner grew increasingly disappointed.

"Try to look at the judge when you testify," she told him again during a break. Over the years she had learned how clients make the best impressions on a judge.

"I can't," replied Bob. He was six feet five inches and barely fit in the witness box. "The space is so cramped, I can't even turn around to look at him. I have to sit with my feet sideways."

"Well, do the best you can," she replied.

Groner worried that Judge Frosh did not like Bob and even wondered if he was put off by her client's commanding size and polished, executive manner. When he testified, Bob Jordan appeared confident and capable in the way he held himself and spoke—perhaps too capable for his own good. Linda Jordan, on the other hand, seemed needy, and Groner worried that the judge would want to help her.

The lawyers had predicted that the trial would require three days at most, but after day three, Groner was not close to completing her presentation. And Jeff Greenblatt had not even started. The judge adjourned until two weeks later, scheduling another two days of testimony on July 15 and 16. Like many of the court cases clogging the country's judicial system, this case was running longer than anticipated. But Groner was determined not to leave out any argument on her client's behalf.

By the middle of that second July day, the fifth day of trial, Groner finally exhausted her witness list. She was not prepared, however, for what happened next. As she waited for Greenblatt to begin his case, anticipation hung in the air; Groner could not understand why both Greenblatt and Linda, and even the courthouse staff, appeared tense. Was she imagining the charge in the atmosphere?

When the courtroom door swung open, she almost gasped. Bill Cahill paraded in to take the stand as Greenblatt's first witness. Groner had had no idea that he would be testifying, that he had arrived that morning on a private jet from Johannesburg. As Cahill walked up the courtroom aisle he seemed to radiate the mystique of a foreign visitor. Linda, dressed in a khaki dress and red hat, proudly watched him take the stand.

During his earlier deposition Cahill had responded awkwardly to Groner's questions. But now, guided by Greenblatt, Linda's fiancé spoke confidently about the life they planned to lead. He described the environment in Bryanston, South Africa, just outside of Johannesburg, where he and Linda were planning to live.

"Would you describe for the court, please, what the house is like starting from the property on which it's located?" Greenblatt asked his star witness.

"The property," Cahill began, "is a three-acre piece that has a fronting on Mount Street and a fronting on Bryanston Drive. It has a swimming pool and a tennis court and it is a home with three bedrooms, a study, a den, a living room, a breakfast room, a dining room, a sun porch, and a two-car garage."

"Can you compare Bryanston with any other American community with which you are familiar?" Greenblatt continued.

"It very much reminds me of Potomac."

"What comparison is there between Bryanston and Potomac in terms of its distance from a major city, or are there any comparisons?"

"Its distance from the major cities, its makeup, its educational system, its recreational facilities, its medical facilities. The complete social political makeup," answered Cahill concerning this last assertion.

Groner was shocked by Cahill's comparison of the two communities. "Mr. Cahill," she asked on cross-examination, "the law that applies to Bryanston is, is it not, the same law that applies to the Republic itself of South Africa?"

"I am going to object." Greenblatt stood up. "He is not an expert."

"We have information," responded Groner, "as to what the law in South Africa is, and there's been some suggestion . . ."

"What the law is as to what?" asked Judge Frosh.

"As to human rights, civil rights. And, I wanted this witness to tell me whether a different law applies to people who live in an affluent suburb of South Africa than it applies to the other citizens of the Republic of South Africa," Groner explained.

"Mrs. Groner," Judge Frosh said candidly, taking off his glasses and setting them on the bench, "you know, there is a portion of the case that interests me because you can't fill it [that is, she couldn't prove that living in South Africa would be *directly* detrimental to Garrett], and it's the only relevant testimony that I would want." The judge was giving Bob's lawyer an extremely hard time.

"In order for you to show me that there is a change in circumstances so traumatic that this child would not have to leave," continued Judge Frosh. "I would want to know how many children there are in the Darien public schools who are blacks. I would want to know how many black families visit at the home of Mr. and Mrs. Jordan in Darien on a day-to-day, month-to-month, year-to-year basis. I would want to know every demographic fact of Darien, Connecticut, and Potomac, Maryland, and Bryanston, South Africa, in order to make a conclusion.

"This is an eight-year-old child, and he isn't from day-to-day dealing in this community on the same level that this gentleman, Mr. Cahill, is. To say that just because he is going to a country that has mores and laws that are different than those that he enjoyed during his early childhood, doesn't, per se, mean that this is a change in circumstance that is detrimental to his best interest."

Groner was losing heart, for Frosh seemed unconcerned about Garrett's long-term welfare in a country with a government like that of South Africa. He again adjourned the trial, this time until October 8. It would be another long wait.

The strain on young Garrett was enormous and hard to justify even if both parents loved him so much that neither could bear to give him up. Bob continued his visitations, as scheduled, hoping to cement further his ties with his son and solidify any preference the boy might have for his Connecticut home. Even Chris got involved, writing and calling Garrett incessantly, asking that he come to Connecticut permanently, telling his younger brother how wonderful their life would be. Both Bob and Chris were so committed to Garrett's remaining with them that they failed to see the stress they were causing. Because Beverly Groner was working closely with Bob, not with the entire family, she remained focused on the legal challenge in the case and on her own responsibilities in court.

Just before the trial was to reconvene, Bob flew down to Potomac and took Garrett to his soccer game and to King's Dominion, an amusement park. They went to church, bowled, ate out, and played games together.

But after Bob returned Garrett home to Maryland on Sunday evening, he fell apart. "Mom," cried the blue-eyed, towheaded child. His fair skin was flushed pink with anxiety and he crawled erratically around his bed as if to escape his bad feelings. "Terrible things are going to happen in court," he wailed. "Terrible things are going to happen in court. Dad said to say in court that brothers need brothers and I need Chris. He will be very upset if I don't say these things. I feel like I'm being torn apart," Garrett sobbed, knowing how strongly both his mother and father felt about the impending move. "I feel like somebody is yanking my arms and legs off me."

The image is a familiar one to many children of custody disputes whose parents don't understand the impact of such a legal battle.

When the trial reconvened in October, Greenblatt first called a psychologist named Mary Donahue. Even Groner had to admit that Dr. Donahue made an effective expert witness for Linda. So many trials depend on which expert witness makes the best impression on the judge or jury.

"I first met Linda Jordan on January 29, 1980," explained Dr. Donahue after Greenblatt put her on the stand. "Mrs. Jordan came to me and told me that she would like my opinion as to what would be in the best interest of her son, Garrett, regarding this present custody situation.

"She also gave me at that time, I believe, the reports of Dr. Schiff on both Garrett and Christopher. I was struck by Mrs. Jordan because she presented her concerns as what would be in the best interest of Garrett, and said that she would go along essentially with my evaluation in assessing the situation."

Dr. Donahue had seen Linda five times and Garrett six, but she also had accidentally observed the mother and son together outside of her office, unbeknownst to them, once in church, and once in a parking lot. "They were outside crossing the parking lot," recalled Dr. Donahue, "and Mrs. Jordan was holding Garrett's hand, who in turn was holding the hands of two other boys. It was very obvious that this was a warm and happy experience for them all."

"What's the significance to you, in your professional opinion, of those two observations as opposed to an observation in a clinical setting?" Greenblatt asked his witness.

"Well, they were natural," the psychologist replied. "I mean, I felt that I was seeing them function with each other without regard to some outside person for whom either one felt they had to respond in a particular way."

Then Greenblatt asked Dr. Donahue what Garrett had said about the lawsuit.

"He said that he just wanted it to be over with, to know where he was going to live and with whom, and I inferred from that that he wanted to pick up his life with some sense of security." Nor did Garrett indicate any strong need to live with Chris, Dr. Donahue added. "He actually said, 'I don't care if I'm with Chris. I just want this to be over so I know where I'm going to be.'

"I think Garrett feels that it's very important to his dad that he be with his dad," she added, "and Garrett wants to receive approval from his mother *and* father. I tried to get into that area with him, but he was very uncomfortable about it, and he could only respond with 'I don't know.' . . .

"My feeling," concluded Dr. Donahue, "is that he clearly wants the affection and love of all parties—and is very anxious that he may not receive it from the noncustodial parent."

"Doctor," asked Greenblatt, "based on a reasonable psychological certainty, do you have an opinion based upon the information that you have obtained in this particular case whether or not it would be in Garrett's best interest to transfer custody at this time?"

Judge Frosh listened carefully. He clearly was impressed with the defense expert.

"Yes," she replied.

"What is that opinion?"

"I believe that Garrett should remain in the custody of his mother."

"Why?" asked Greenblatt. He wanted the judge to hear her explanation.

"I feel there is a good relationship with his mother," stated the psychologist. "I feel that although he is not able to verbalize it for the reasons stated, he would articulate where he wanted to live if he felt he would not receive rejection.

"Developmentally this is an important time for a youngster to be with his mother, and I see no reason to change that situation."

That afternoon Greenblatt called several of Linda's neighbors, asking them to testify that Linda was a good mother. The next day Linda herself took the stand, and her lawyer kept her there for hours, asking about her life with Garrett—everything they had discussed in preparation for the trial—and some of the problems that had occurred since Bob filed the lawsuit. Through her answers Linda repeatedly criticized Bob for trying to cut her out of her sons' lives. He, of course, thought she was trying to do the same to him.

The trial was drawing to a close. On the last day, Groner called as a rebuttal witness a South African legal expert. Despite his warnings that Garrett would be subjected to the country's harsh legal and political realities, Judge Frosh still appeared unmoved.

Finally Groner decided to put thirteen-year-old Chris on the stand. She knew it was a risky move, one lawyers generally shun because of the stressful position in which it puts the child.

"I know we've been trying to avoid this," she told Bob, "but Judge Frosh has said he won't accept some of our evidence unless he hears it directly from Chris." At least that was what Groner thought the judge had wanted; later he would deny any such suggestion.

"Chris understands that he is only to tell the truth, not to take sides," Bob replied. Linda was upset when Groner called the boy to testify and later would say it was a cruel thing to do.

The lawyer purposefully kept her questioning brief, asking Chris how often his father had visited in Potomac and inquiring about friends there, church attendance, and early visits to Darien.

"Did either you [or Garrett] have any conversation with your mom [while you were in Connecticut] to tell her where you wanted to live?" Groner asked Chris.

"Yes, every time we talked on the phone, she would ask if we wanted to stay up in Connecticut," he replied. "We would tell her that we did." But at that point in their past, even though the boy had announced his preference, Linda had not yet agreed to Chris's move to his father's home.

"And then you returned to Maryland, didn't you?" Groner gently inquired.

"Yes."

"And what conversation if any did you and Garrett have with your mother when you returned to Potomac?"

"We asked her if we could go home with our father."

"What did she say?"

"She said 'no,' she had custody of us and we could not go back."

When Chris stepped down, Bob was so impressed with his demeanor that he told Groner that his son had been the best witness of all.

Judge Frosh, however, did not agree.

The room was silent as the judge began to read his opinion. Groner suspected that he would not look favorably on her case. He had made Bob's task, and hers, particularly difficult throughout the trial.

"The Court believes," the judge announced, "that the bottom line in this case must be that the plaintiff has not borne the burden of proof, and that there will not—and cannot—be at this juncture a change in custody so far as Garrett is concerned.

"Let me go into the details of why," he continued.

Judge Frosh explained that the only reason he had placed Chris in Bob's custody rather than in Linda's was that the older boy had expressly asked to be with his father. "Were it not for the preference that Christopher expressed," said the judge, "I would expressly find that Mrs. Jordan is a fit and proper person to have the custody of Christopher as well."

But *why* would he not change Garrett's custody? wondered Groner as she listened.

"First," he said, as if to answer her thought, "the testimony of the experts in this case, both from the standpoint of the plaintiff and from the standpoint of the defendant, indicate that Garrett is a well-adjusted and thriving young man." Judge Frosh saw no reason why Garrett would suffer by staying with his mother, even if she were to move to South Africa. For the judge, South Africa was not an issue, no matter what Groner argued. It did not matter that Linda was moving—or where or how far she was moving—as long as Garrett was with her. Clearly Judge Frosh favored the boy's mother.

"But there are some factors that compel me to remark for the record," he added, "that even in a case of original custody, I would not award the custody of Garrett to his father—and all the more reason why I would not change that custody at this point." Bob was shocked by the harshness of the words.

Judge Frosh said that Bob should not have changed Chris's religion, a step that the judge thought could alienate the boy from his mother. The judge said he interpreted the change in churches as a clear violation of the Jordans' separation agreement, in which they had agreed to foster the respect and love of the children for each other. "I can think of nothing that would go further to estrange a child from his parent and make him feel ill at ease with his parent than to change the religion of that child so that, if he is visiting his mother and wants to attend church services or worship with her, he is no longer comfortable in the faith in which he was originally reared," said Frosh, who was not Roman Catholic but Jewish and perhaps religious himself. Frosh said he thought Bob would have changed Garrett's religion, too.

He spoke equally disdainfully of a letter that Bob had claimed Garrett sent his mother indicating a preference for Connecticut. "It's obvious to the court that this letter was not the handiwork of Garrett," said Judge Frosh. "It was at the very least the handiwork of Chris, and it was the inspiration of the father. I believe that this, too, was a violation of the separation agreement and an attempt to drive a wedge between this child and his mother." Frosh was angered by the letter rather than convinced of Garrett's desire to move.

Finally, Judge Frosh objected to Bob's having put Chris on the stand to testify on his father's behalf. He considered it a further sign of forced alienation from Linda. In another court this might have been a successful strategy, but before Judge Frosh, it failed.

Groner had been unable to convince Judge Frosh that moving Garrett to South Africa would be harmful to the boy or that he needed to be with his brother Chris. Garrett's ongoing relationship with his mother was clearly more important to the judge. In fact, Frosh was so one-sided in his view of the case that he did not even worry about Bob's opinions. "I do not believe," he concluded, "that the cases in the state of Maryland or anywhere else in this blessed union dictate that simply because a judge or one of the parents disapproves of the locale to which a custodial parent is about to go that that in and of itself is a reason for depriving that parent of custody. Mrs. Jordan's custody is not limited to her remaining in the United States," he ruled. "She may follow the dictates of her own happiness and marry if she so chooses, and she has custody of Garrett Jordan pending further order of this court."

Bob could visit Garrett in South Africa, Judge Frosh noted, or fly him to the United States during school vacations. He ordered Bob to pay Linda's legal bill—twenty thousand dollars—to be taken from his share from the sale of the Potomac, Maryland, house.

Linda and her lawyer were elated with the ruling. Bob was shocked; despite all of the warning signs that Frosh was leaning in Linda's direction, he had remained convinced that the court would rule in his favor. "It was gut-wrenchingly painful," he would later say in recalling the decision. "It was almost as if it was a death sentence." He cried in the courtroom and sobbed convulsively in private. Groner, who had grown more pessimistic as the trial wore on, was drained, disappointed, and distraught.

She appealed, but the intermediate court of appeals in Annapolis upheld Judge Frosh. He "did not abuse his discretion in denying the change of custody request even though the younger son was going to move with his mother to South Africa," the appeals court said in early 1982. Nor did Frosh err in demanding that Bob pay Linda's twenty-thousand-dollar legal bill, the court added, but asked nonetheless that the lower court reconsider whether she should be required to pay some of those fees. Ultimately Groner and Greenblatt negotiated Bob's share down to fifteen thousand dollars.

Linda Jordan and Bill Cahill finally married, and in August 1982 they and Garrett left for South Africa, three years after Bob had sued to stop the move.

While Groner had represented numerous clients during her legal career, few cases upset her as much as Bob Jordan's. She had grown close to Bob during their ordeal together; he had gotten to know Groner's husband Sam and her children. In fact, the entire Groner family had followed the case, although in the end only Sam remained optimistic. "I just don't think this is going to stick," he announced after the failed appeal. "I don't think this is the end of it in any way, shape, or form."

But Beverly had lost all hope. Why did she lose? Because Judge Frosh disliked Bob? Because he felt sorry for Linda? Was Bob trying to take Garrett out of Linda's life? Wasn't it Linda who was trying to take Garrett out of Bob's? They were both Garrett's parents. Groner clearly had seen that.

She called the lawyer in Connecticut who had recommended that Bob hire her, a friend whom Groner had known for a long time through her bar association activities.

"I'm so sorry," she said to him in describing the case, its evolution, and final outcome.

"You haven't learned to lose a case," the other lawyer replied consolingly. "You have to learn how to lose."

Intellectually Groner knew that not even the best lawyer wins every case. The vagaries of the court system are too great. "But it's so wrong," she lamented. "This is not the case to lose."

Groner still believed in Bob's case, even in the end. In fact, she never sent him a final bill.

The following summer, in 1983, Garrett visited Bob in Darien. Despite his unhappiness over leaving his father, he returned that fall to South Africa. In the summer of 1984 he again traveled to Darien while his mother visited her parents, who lived in Watertown, Connecticut, about one hundred miles away. At the end of this stay, Garrett joined Linda in Watertown, where she proceeded to pack for their long flight home.

This time Garrett, who was by then twelve years old, decided he could not leave his father—he simply would not go—so Linda telephoned Bob. "This has been going on for two years," she announced. "It's clear Garrett does not want to go back. He wants to stay here. Why don't you pick him up." So the court's ruling had not ended the fight for Linda; the ongoing turmoil and family conflict finally forced her to relent. Bob met Linda in a parking lot on her way to the airport. There Garrett joined his father and Linda went on her way back to South Africa. For both parents the exchange of their son was surely a heart-wrenching and emotional experience.

Thus, the Jordan case was like many other custody cases decided by judges: The fight is seldom over at the end of a trial. At the very least, hard feelings continue for some time. At worst, the losing parent continues to work for his or her own cause, prolonging the personal battle and the anxiety and discomfort for everyone involved. Whether Bob continued to lobby Garrett to return to Connecticut is unknown. He denies having done so, but Linda may have a different impression of what happened.

Any sustained battling could have been eliminated if Bob and Linda had recognized initially each other's parenting needs and considered what was best for their children. Linda might have asked Cahill to shorten his stay in South Africa and later find a job in the United States. Or she might have agreed to return Garrett as soon as he reached a certain age, allowing him to spend his school vacations in Connecticut until then.

In today's mobile society, all states should have guidelines to help courts deal with relocation disputes, including an indication of when a move is permissible. These guidelines should consider both the reasons and distances involved and the potential impact of a move on the children. They should encourage new visitation schedules, perhaps providing larger blocks of time for a parent left behind. They should require some relocating parents to arrange transportation.

Of course, relocation guidelines should prevent custodial parents from moving away for improper reasons, for example, simply to start their lives over or to get away from the ex-spouse. But to suggest that relocation should be permanently, consistently prohibited is extreme. One ex-spouse should not be held hostage by the other. A middle ground, considering in each case both parents' and the child's needs, is the best approach. As with many issues involving divorce, the legal system should encourage compromise and accommodation on both sides. The wisest couples will work out their own solutions, avoiding new battles that bode additional discomfort and unhappiness for their children. Divorced parents have an obligation to be flexible with regard to each other's schedules and to work together for the benefit of their children, who must maintain strong ties with both mother and father. Clearly neither Linda nor Bob understood this need.

*   *   *

Over the next several years, Bob Jordan continued to pay Groner according to his own calculations of his debt. In all, his total bill, including psychologist and expert witness costs, ran close to $100,000. The amount apparently never bothered him because he considered it well spent. Ultimately he had won his victory.

But the custody suit cost Bob in another way, too. The grinding litigation destroyed his second marriage. While Marianne had always been supportive of Bob and had tried to befriend his sons, she never had the same investment in the custody battle that he did. Undoubtedly, the case robbed her of time and attention that Bob otherwise would have devoted to her. Although they would stay together for several more years, in what Bob would call a "marriage of convenience," their love was the casualty in the battle for Garrett. They divorced in 1987.

Bill Cahill's job in South Africa did turn out to be permanent. Linda continued to live there with him until he died in September 1989 from recurring medical problems, including diabetes. The following summer she returned to the United States in time to see Garrett graduate from high school and to attend Chris's wedding.

8

STEPPARENTS IN DIVORCE: FIGHTING FOR THEIR RIGHTS

Patricia Stockwell v. Dan Stockwell

> *This phenomenon about who we were—the intact*
> *nuclear family during the first seven decades of this*
> *century—and what we have become in the last two*
> *decades—the "blended family"—is a subject of*
> *everyday life which now faces virtually every*
> *American.*

—ATTORNEY PAUL BUSER

CHICAGO

FROM *FAMILY LAW QUARTERLY*

The hateful image of the "wicked old stepmother" in Cinderella's tale has faded in modern times with the increasing number of stepparent families. But because stepparenting continues to be one of the family's most difficult and ambiguous roles, even kind, gracious stepmothers and stepfathers may be undervalued and underappreciated. Appearing suddenly in their stepchildren's lives, they can be made to feel like extra adults around the house, often ignored, their authority questioned. Emotional bonding with stepchildren is tenuous, particularly if the children are preadolescents or teenagers when the remarriage takes place.

It is understandable, then, that when a stepparent divorces, as happens in two out of three remarriages involving children, relationships with stepchildren can come apart, too. The former spouse and the children are no longer legally bound, and emotional remnants of the stepparent-stepchild tie may disappear as well. Few people, after all, talk about their former stepmothers or their former stepchildren. Unless the stepparents and stepchildren have grown close during the marriage, they may never see each other again.

However, some stepparents and stepchildren do want to continue their relationships following a divorce. If the stepchildren are adults by that time, they and the divorced stepparent can decide their own future. But if the stepchildren are young, the biological parent may forbid or discourage future communication with the former stepparent. This can be upsetting for both parties.

While the parent generally should allow visitation unless future contact with the stepparent would be harmful for the child, not all state judicial systems support this view. The trend is one of change, however, and some courts are becoming more receptive to stepparent requests, ordering biological parents to provide former stepparents with visitation rights.

An even thornier problem arises when a divorced stepparent wants full custody of a stepchild. Can the stepparent argue in court that a child would be better off living with him or her than with a biological parent? Should a court consider the best interests of the child, taking into account both the parent's and the stepparent's requests?

These were the questions that faced an Idaho judge when Dan and Patricia Stockwell divorced and fought for custody of their two young daughters, Amber and Danielle. Amber was not Dan's natural child. She had been conceived before Dan and Patricia met and fell in love and was born shortly before Dan and Patricia married. The girl never knew she had another father. The younger child, Danielle, was born two years after the marriage. While the judge admitted that both girls would be better off living with Dan, he said he had to give custody of Amber to Patricia because she was her biological parent. Dan, who had never adopted Amber, was only her stepfather. Under Idaho law he had no basis for custody.

"But Dan is more than a stepfather. He is the only father Amber has ever known," argued Paul Buser, Dan's lawyer in the case. Still, the judge said, his hands were tied.

What follows is the story of Dan Stockwell and Paul Buser* and their fight to prove that stepparents have rights, too.

"Patricia has left with the children. We have no idea where they've gone," Jean Stockwell told Boise, Idaho, lawyer Paul Buser after frantically dialing his number. "They're just gone."

Jean and her husband Bob, a successful electrical contractor, were

---

*Paul Buser practiced law in Boise, Idaho, for seventeen years. He recently moved to Chicago, where he joined the firm of Cantwell & Cantwell.

grandparents of a large, closely knit Mormon family in the small town of Nampa, Idaho, twenty miles west of Boise. The Stockwells had first turned to Paul Buser in 1975 with a work-related liability case, and Buser later wrote their wills. Now, in 1986, they needed help again, this time for a family crisis.

Their former daughter-in-law had just left town with their grand-daughters. No one, including the girls' father, Dan Stockwell, knew they had even been planning to leave. (Later, their mother, Patricia, would say she had left a letter with a forwarding address.)

"We'll pay Dan's legal fees," an angry Jean Stockwell announced on behalf of her son. "She can't take those girls away from him." Dan had held a series of blue-collar jobs and Jean knew that her son could not afford a lawyer. She had no idea how substantial his legal bill would be.

Buser had learned about the Stockwells' son Dan and his wife Patricia through his earlier work for the family, and he knew that the young couple's life had been complicated from the beginning.

Dan and Patricia met in California in early 1976 when he was twenty-two and she was twenty-nine, the divorced mother of two young teenagers and six months pregnant by another man. Dan and Patricia soon began living together, and he was with her at the hospital when the baby was born on April 4, 1976. They married two months later, on June 4. Although Dan never legally adopted the baby girl, named Amber, her birth certificate was changed later to show Dan's name as the father. From the beginning Patricia told Amber that Dan was her dad, and the child loved them both.

The new family moved to Boise, where Patricia, a strong, outgoing woman, and Dan, who was more mild-mannered, worked on local assembly lines. Two years later, on March 13, 1978, they had a daughter together, whom they named Danielle. Although Patty was not a Mormon, they embraced Bob and Jean Stockwell's extensive family network, including Dan's five siblings. Dan's sisters and mother baby-sat Amber and Danielle while Patricia and Dan worked and, later, while Patricia attended welding school. Over the years, the growing clan of Stockwell grandchildren played together regularly, and the family photograph collection, memories of happy holidays, birthdays, and years sliding by, grew steadily, too.

But the good times would not last.

Patricia and Dan separated in 1983; by then their entire household had fallen apart. A court would note later that "each due to drug involvement, legal difficulties or chronic unemployment, found their lives unstable and inconsistent with child rearing." Patricia and Dan agreed that Dan's parents should take care of Amber, then nine, and Danielle, seven, while they resolved their problems, although Patricia later would say she was *not* using drugs at the time. Given the family circumstances, however, it was a sound decision. At Patricia and Dan's request, the local court appointed Bob and Jean the girls' guardians. Buser was the senior Stockwells' lawyer at the guardianship hearing.

One of the attractions in the grandparents' guardianship, the court then observed, was that Bob and Jean traveled internationally through Bob's work and the girls could benefit from that opportunity, too. The four of them soon moved to Colombia, South America, where Bob had been retained for a large construction job. They returned to the United States some eighteen months later. While waiting for Bob's next contract they settled in Colfax, Washington, where Jean worked in one of four video stores owned by the Stockwell family.

By this time Patricia was on her feet again, and she sued Dan for divorce. The marriage officially ended on June 7, 1985, in a decree that made no mention of the girls' guardianship. Presumably the court still considered Amber and Danielle to be under their grandparents' care, and Patricia never raised the issue of their custody. Later she would say she wanted it handled separately.

Shortly after the divorce, Patricia and Dan each remarried. Patricia wed Rick Porter, who at age twenty-four was even younger than Dan and thirteen years Patricia's junior. They lived in Nampa, Idaho, where Patricia worked as a welder and Rick as a machine operator.

Dan, thirty-one, and his new wife Rhonda, twenty-six, lived in Tualatin, Oregon, a small town near Portland where Dan had moved after he and Patricia separated. Rhonda, a down-to-earth, unpretentious woman, helped in her family's liquor store. Dan, who was working in a gas station when they first met, moved to a new job as an iron worker. Together they lived with Rhonda's eight-year-old daughter Amy.

But while Dan and Patricia settled into their new marriages, the matter of their daughters' long-term care still hovered overhead. Dan was content for Amber and Danielle to continue living with his parents, but Patricia clearly viewed the guardianship as a temporary measure. She claimed that she never had given the senior Stockwells permanent custody of her children. The time had come, she decided, to get the girls back. With Rick at her side pushing her on, she began to assert herself.

Patricia soon became convinced that the Stockwells had ganged up against her. "I want Amber and Danielle," she informed Jean in a phone call to Colfax, Washington. The conversation was tense and filled with apprehension on both sides. Patricia claimed that the senior Stockwells didn't want her to see the girls, but Jean would later recall welcoming Patricia for a visit. "Patty, come out here and see them," Jean says she told Patricia. "We'll book a hotel room for you." Jean loved both granddaughters as if they were her own children, and she didn't want to give them up. But if she was going to lose Amber and Danielle, she wanted her son to have them. Then she could still have some control over the girls' activities. Jean would be a major force—both financial and psychological—behind Dan's quest for custody.

"You don't want me to have anything to do with those girls," Patricia shot back. "You're trying to take them away from me—you were only supposed to have them for a little while!" Patricia finally did go to Colfax, visiting with Amber and Danielle and trying to ignore her former in-laws. Bob and Jean, in turn, hovered nearby to guarantee that Patricia did not take the girls back to Nampa. Her fury only grew.

On July 18 she petitioned the court to terminate Bob and Jean's guardianship and award custody of Amber and Danielle to their mother. Although Dan had hoped that his parents would keep the girls, he also filed for custody himself should his parents' guardianship be ended.

Bob and Jean Stockwell considered asking Paul Buser to represent Dan at that point, but Buser had represented the elder Stockwells already during the guardianship hearing; appearing for their son Dan in a subsequent custody proceeding where the senior Stockwells' guardianship would be ended could raise conflict-of-interest charges. More important, Buser asked for a large retainer to handle Dan's case because he thought it would be particularly difficult. So instead the Stockwells decided to hire a Nampa lawyer named Edwin Schiller. Patricia retained Terry Michaelson, also of Nampa.

The hearing was held in neighboring Caldwell, Idaho, the judicial seat for Canyon County, where Nampa was located, on October 21, 1985. Magistrate Stephen Drescher (in Idaho, magistrates are the judges who handle misdemeanors, smaller civil cases, and family law matters) presided. It appeared to be a simple custody proceeding until Judge Drescher learned that Amber was not Dan's natural daughter.

"Mrs. Porter, it's your testimony that Amber's father is actually Fernando Mendez, is that correct?" asked Schiller when questioning her on the stand.

"Yes, sir," responded Patricia.

"Were you and Mr. Mendez married?"

"No, sir."

"And you testified that Amber's name was changed on her birth certificate to Stockwell?"

"Yes, sir."

"How was that done?"

"They petitioned a birth certificate," began Patricia tentatively. "I'm not really sure because LaFonda Merrick [Dan's sister] handled all of that. I didn't—I don't know what happened with all that."

"Was there an adoption, or . . ." Schiller probed.

"I don't believe so. There—see, on the birth certificate it said 'father unknown.' They had his name put in there," responded Patricia, describing the Stockwell family's early attempt to erase Amber's bastardy.

"And isn't it correct that you signed on the birth certificate as Patricia Mendez?" continued Schiller.

"Yes, sir."

"But that wasn't your legal name?"

"No, sir."

"Where was Amber born?" asked Schiller.

"In Oakland, California."

"And so this birth certificate was changed in California?"

"It was changed here in Idaho," answered Patty. "They sent for it in Sacramento. As I've been telling you, LaFonda handled this, not me."

Dan's lawyer paused. "Now," he continued, "concerning this divorce action. Originally you filed your own divorce complaint, did you not?"

"Yes, sir," she responded again.

"And isn't it true in that complaint that you list both Amber and Danielle as born since the marriage between you and Robert D. [Dan] Stockwell?"

"Yes, sir."

"Why did you do that?"

"Because he's the only father that she knows."

"She does not know, is it not correct, that Dan's not her father?" Schiller asked.

"No, she doesn't."

Judge Drescher was shocked. "Let's not spill the beans here during this litigation then," he announced. "Don't tell Amber," he warned both Patricia and Dan, "once you've embarked on this course of leading Amber to believe that Dan's her father. She's ten years old now; don't upset that relationship. It's of longstanding. It would just be pernicious to the interest of the children."

It was ironic that during the custody fight Danielle wanted to stay with Patricia—and Amber specifically requested to live with her "father." But at the conclusion of the October 21, 1985, hearing Judge Drescher gave custody of both girls to their mother, noting that she had been primarily responsible for the care of the children during her marriage to Dan and also had been the family's primary breadwinner. The decision seemed logical.

The judge awarded Dan visitation rights with both girls, even though Amber was not his biological child, because of the strong emotional tie she had with him and with Danielle, who would be visiting Dan at the same time. The judge did not order Dan to pay child support for Amber; he would pay sixty-five dollars a month for Danielle alone. "There is no legal basis [in Idaho] for imposition of support obligation with respect to Amber," noted the magistrate.

Bob and Jean were to be allowed visitation so that the entire family unit could continue as originally described, as if Amber were Dan's natural daughter, because the judge thought it would be best for both children. Patricia, however, did not agree and would later, foolishly, decide that she, not Judge Drescher, knew what was best for Amber and Danielle.

"May I talk to the girls?" Jean asked Patricia when she called shortly after the hearing. She missed her granddaughters—they had been together for so long that she felt their absence keenly.

Patricia refused to speak directly to Jean, by then her confirmed enemy, but she did summon her daughters to the phone. After several more attempts to reach Amber and Danielle, Jean realized that the hostility her calls provoked in Patricia upset both girls so much that she decided, with great sadness, to phone less frequently. Perhaps that would reduce some of the turmoil in their lives, she hoped. Patricia and Rick's relationship with Dan's sisters also became strained, and Amber and Danielle saw far less of their aunts, their cousins, and the rest of the Stockwell family.

While Patricia was trying to pull away from the remnants of her earlier marriage, Dan decided he wanted to spend more time with Amber and Danielle. In December he moved from Oregon back to Nampa, and his wife Rhonda and her daughter joined him the following month. The judge had said that Dan could visit Amber and Danielle on the third weekend of each month, during spring break and other holidays, and from June 15 until August 15 each summer. Now that he was in town, where he worked in one of the family video stores and later for a local pizza parlor and a construction firm, he planned to see his daughters even more frequently. Dan's wife, too, enjoyed having her stepchildren around as companions for her own child, Amy, who was a year younger than Amber and a year older than Danielle.

Patricia, however, refused any part of this plan—and Dan's renewed presence displeased her second husband. Often the new husband or wife in a subsequent marriage plays a key role in disputes regarding children from the previous marriage. The new spouse anxiously guards his or her spouse's right to have access to the children, serving as a far stronger advocate of visitation or custody than the actual parent. Such circumstances can be hard on the new spouse, who takes on the cause of the stepchildren as an investment in the new marriage. In Patricia's case, her husband, Rick Porter, actually wanted to be Amber and Danielle's father. He became almost obsessed in his campaign to do so.

In February, Rick and Patricia purposely—and cruelly—told Amber that Dan was not her father. It was time, they said, for the child to learn her true identity. Later Patricia would claim that Amber was happy to hear the truth, but it is more likely that she was shocked and distressed.

Patricia and Rick also denied Dan any more than the minimal court-ordered visitation; in March they turned him away from the door, saying they had misunderstood the visit date and had already planned a birthday party for Danielle and her friends. During the girls' spring break Patricia and Dan fought over the amount of time each would have with Amber and Danielle. "I'll see you in court!" Dan shouted in frustration as he was forced to leave without the children.

"I can't stand the way he plays that 'poor Daddy' routine," Patricia told Rick angrily and she shut the door. "I wish he would just get out of my life."

"Let's move," she suggested suddenly. It was a radical idea, something new for them both. Idaho was their home and they each had jobs they liked. But the thought of a fresh start sent Patricia's mind racing ahead. At last, she decided, all of the Stockwells would be out of her life.

She called her family in California to see if they knew of any job opportunities there, but they could offer no encouragement.

"Let's call your family in Connecticut," Patricia suggested to Rick.

"All right," he responded. "I'll call my folks—they'll put us up until we get settled. And my uncle can probably help us get jobs at Pratt & Whitney." Patricia grew even more enthusiastic when Rick's uncle said she could work there as a welder.

Three days later she and Rick told Amber and Danielle that they were moving East to a new state, new family, new school, and new friends. "You're gonna love it," Patricia reassured her wide-eyed daughters. But Amber would later testify that she believed they were moving because their mother did not want them to see Dan.

At daybreak on March 30, 1986, Rick, Patricia, and the girls loaded up their pickup truck and new five-foot trailer and pulled away from Nampa, defying Dan, the entire Stockwell family, and Judge Drescher. All they left behind were a few empty boxes and an old suitcase.

When Jean called Buser to help find Amber and Danielle, he had narrowed his general practice to a domestic relations specialty, so her new request fit right in. Buser had earned a strong reputation in the eighteen-lawyer Boise firm of Givens, McDevitt, Pursley, Webb & Buser, both for his legislative activity and for his precedent-setting cases across the state.

"I can take the case, Jean," the thirty-eight-year-old attorney calmly advised his client after learning that she wanted to renew the custody fight, "but it isn't going to be easy. Dan and Patricia's backgrounds are not the best." Proving *either* parent to be a good role model for the girls would be very difficult.

"An awful lot of preparation will have to go into this," he warned, "and it will be very difficult for a court to go through and separate the wheat from the chaff. We'll have to highlight Dan's strengths and minimize his weaknesses without appearing insensitive to the needs of the children." Buser knew that the court could decide that neither parent was fit and turn the girls over to the state health and welfare agency.

"We have to put everything that has happened in a historical context for the judge," he continued thoughtfully, referring to Dan's past, "and explain what Dan did, why he did it, how he got there, and how he got out of it. We have to show that he is a changed man."

An even larger challenge, said Buser, would be proving that Dan should have custody of Amber when he was not her biological father. The Idaho courts had never dealt directly with the subject of stepparents' rights; existing case law addressed it only tangentially. Buser would have to develop a legal argument on Dan's behalf with no substantial precedent to back it up.

Out of every five American children living in married couple families, one is a stepchild. The growth of this new phenomenon has been rapid. According to the U.S. Census Bureau, nearly seven million children lived in stepfamilies in 1985, an increase of almost 12 percent since 1980. Some demographers predict that one third of the children born in the 1980s will, at some point, live with a stepparent.

Yet when divorce hits these homes, often the stepfather's or stepmother's relationship with the children is virtually ignored. Most states presume that they must award custody to a child's natural parents unless both are found to be unsuitable. "A lot of stepparents have no idea of what their rights are," says Buser. "And a lot of natural parents don't consider the feelings and sense of alienation and anxiety that their children suffer when they don't see a stepparent anymore."

The current upheaval of the American family through divorce and dislocation has led to more stepparent and other "third-party" custody claims. Increasingly stepparents, grandparents, and other relatives argue that their care would be in the best interests of the child. Usually in these cases the stepparents or relatives have served as surrogate parents to the child, as Dan Stockwell did for Amber, or, under a more modern term, as "psychological parents," those who have assumed the status and obligations of a parent without formal adoption. Alaska's supreme court has perhaps defined "psychological parent" most eloquently as

> one who, on a day-to-day basis, through interaction, companionship, interplay, and mutuality, fulfills the child's psychological need for an adult. This adult becomes an essential focus of the child's life, for he is not only the source of the fulfillment of the child's physical needs, but also the source of his emotional and psychological needs. . . . The wanted child is one who is loved, valued, appreciated, and viewed as an essential person by the adult who cares for him. It is this relationship, the psychological parent–wanted child relationship, which over and above all others is worthy of protection by the legal system.

Nationwide, stepparents have begun to educate themselves and to band together in support groups. A Lincoln, Nebraska–based stepparents' association organized in 1980 lists more than fifty chapters. Such heightened self-awareness among stepparents has forced more enlightened thinking by state legislators and judges. According to Buser, "all fifty states now have statutes or case law on the books regarding custody, visitation, or support relating to stepparents, grandparents, or stepchildren." The American Bar Association drafted a model stepparent act to guide further legislative efforts; it addresses stepparent custody and visitation and, in some cases, child support. Final passage of this model law should encourage greater and more uniform recognition of stepparental rights and obligations following divorce.

With efforts like these, stepparents have been gaining ground steadily. Dan Stockwell would help usher in the new era.

*   *   *

When Patricia left Idaho with Amber and Danielle she claimed she was doing what was best for her children. Although Mormons are known to be supportive, protective families, Patricia felt that the Stockwells were intrusive and that Dan and Rhonda were suffocating her and the girls and preventing them from developing their own independence. Even though Rick was young, Patricia believed that he could be a much better father than Dan, and she wanted a chance to start over with him.

She had asked Michaelson, the Nampa attorney who represented her in the custody hearing, if she could keep Dan and his family away from the children, but he had said that the court's visitation order barred her from moving. So Patricia sought out a new lawyer, a former judge named Roger Williams, who told her that in his opinion, nothing in the order prevented her from moving away. Patricia and Rick headed for Southington, Connecticut, where Rick's parents lived.

There they settled into a one-hundred-and-eight-year-old home that had once belonged to Rick's grandmother and had been converted into a two-family dwelling. The Porters took the first floor. Rick's mother, who taught at the local elementary school, helped Patricia enroll Amber and Danielle there.

As promised, both Patricia and Rick found jobs through Rick's uncle at Pratt & Whitney, Patricia as a welder and Rick as a laser technician. Rick's other relatives were friendly and supportive, too. He and Patricia were happy in their new surroundings, and they tried to put the Stockwells and the past behind them.

But the past would not leave them alone. While Patricia's desire to start over was not unusual, the Idaho legal system would not let her do so. Dan was her former husband, the father of one of her children and the stepfather of the other, and an Idaho judge had awarded him visitation rights. Without a change in the court's order, Patricia's life would be intertwined with Dan's as long as the girls were young. If she had recognized this, she could have made the best of the situation and reformed her life with Rick while Dan enjoyed his visitations. Or she could have petitioned the court for permission to move. But by moving away and trying to change her lot surreptitiously, Patricia worsened her situation. Her move violated the court's visitation order, Dan's lawyer would argue, and she should lose all rights to her children, forever.

To do his job, Buser knew he would have to move quickly. Within a day of Jean's phone call he filed papers with the court asking that Patricia be ordered to return to Idaho.

He also sent out more than one hundred letters to lawyers and judges he knew around the country who might have information on stepparents' legal rights. Buser outlined the facts of the Stockwell case and asked for any relevant precedent from other states. The tactic was common among leading domestic relations lawyers. They develop information-sharing networks to help them stay in the forefront of their practices. Although each state follows its own domestic relations laws and rulings, sometimes judges are swayed in cases lacking local precedent by the opinions of courts that have handled similar matters in other jurisdictions.

Within days Buser began receiving legal briefs from all over the country. Sifting through them, he selected the cases that might be most helpful to his client, amassing more material more quickly than he ever could have found with a simple search in the local law libraries. Additional library material supplemented what he was able to gather through his networking.

Before the Stockwell case concluded, Buser had filed six separate briefs on Dan's behalf. In them he outlined the facts in the case; reviewed the history of third-party custody suits in Idaho; discussed the concept of psychological parenthood; highlighted favorable testimony from various hearings throughout the case; and reviewed current sociological research on child custody disputes.

In the meantime, Dan, dazed with disbelief and devastated that his girls were gone, desperately looked for clues to their whereabouts. Like many fathers who care about their children but are stymied in their parental relationship by an angry ex-wife, Dan had to devote countless hours, money, and effort simply to see Amber and Danielle. He had not been an involved parent in the past, but his attitude had turned 180 degrees, and he desperately sought to make up for lost time.

He began his search at the girls' school, East Side Elementary. "I'm wondering if you know where the Stockwell girls have moved," he asked the principal.

But the principal did not know Dan. "I'm sorry, but I must have identification as proof that you're their father," he replied. "It's a regulation we have to follow." Schools today are wary of invasion of privacy and potential child snatchings.

The principal finally told Dan that the records had been sent to a school in Connecticut. Dan remembered that Rick had family there.

He called the post office to see if Patricia had left a forwarding address and a U-Haul dealer to find out if she had rented a truck or trailer. Dan's sister LaFonda joined the search, calling Patricia's employer and the local power company to ask if she had left a new address. No one could help.

Weeks passed by and Dan heard nothing from his missing children. He received no correspondence or communication, not even a phone call. Later Patricia would say that she had left a letter at LaFonda's house saying where they were moving and that Dan could have found her through the girls' new school. But Dan never got such a letter and he was never able to track down the school.

Almost two months later, on May 23, 1986, Judge Drescher responded to Buser's request for action. He ordered the missing Patricia to appear before his court to prove why she should not be held in contempt and should not lose custody of her children. The hearing date was set for June 10 at 9:00 A.M. According to the courthouse records, Terry Michaelson was still Patricia's attorney, so he was notified on her behalf. Buser requested either a completely new custody trial or a modification of the original custody award, and Judge Drescher said he would consider the latter.

Unfortunately, Terry Michaelson had no idea that Patricia had left, much less how to find her to explain what was happening. When he appeared alone at the courthouse on June 10 he immediately told Judge Drescher that he wanted to withdraw from the case because he was not able to contact his client.

The judge rejected the motion to withdraw. "I appreciate the circumstance in which Mr. Michaelson finds himself," he said. But he believed that Patricia, despite fleeing from the state, had a right to representation. "The relief requested by the defendant [Dan] profoundly touches upon the plaintiff's rights and interests," Judge Drescher explained. "Moreover, I think to permit Mr. Michaelson's withdrawal at this time would be to suggest in some slight way that the Court has diminished its jurisdiction over this dispute." Turning to Buser, he asked him to call his first witness. Dan Stockwell took the stand.

It was important to Buser that Dan not appear hostile toward Patricia. He had spent a great deal of time with his client, now almost an oversolicitous father, to get him to understand how to act in court. He did not have to be apologetic, Buser explained, as much as he had to show that he had turned over a new leaf in his own life—and that he was *not* going to respond to the situation as Patricia was responding. Dan would want to show a concern that the girls maintain their relationship with both parents and a willingness to work with Patricia toward that end. Buser believed that his client actually felt this way, but he wanted to work with him to convey the right attitude when in court. The lawyer had to help Dan counteract his tension, his anxiety, and his anger about Patricia's move and superimpose over these feelings a more conciliatory posture.

For his part, Michaelson—forced by the judge to play an adversary role on Patricia's behalf—tried to undermine Dan's sincerity and to emphasize his limited involvement in the children's lives up until that time.

"Both the girls were in the custody of your parents for nearly two years, weren't they?" Michaelson asked him.

"Yes, sir," replied Dan, who in the 1980s still projected a casual, 1960s lumberjack appearance. His full mop of brown hair curled over his collar, and despite his husky build, he conveyed a gentle demeanor.

"And during that period of time the children were down in South America, correct?"

"Yes, sir."

"And obviously those children were not living with you or in your custody during that period of time, were they?"

"No, sir."

Michaelson pointed out that Patricia had been granted custody following the senior Stockwells' guardianship and that Dan was allowed only visitation. "Isn't it true then," he asked, "that with respect to Amber, who's neither your natural child nor your adoptive child, as well as Dani, neither of the girls have had contact with you other than just weekend visitation since December of 1983 [just before Bob and Jean were awarded guardianship]?"

"Telephone conversations," Dan replied. "Letters have been written. We sent tapes back and forth. We wrote on a regular basis."

"But, in terms of actual physical contact and living with you, or spending time with you, your contact with the two girls has been limited to weekend visitation since 1983, correct?"

"Correct, sir," admitted Dan, forced to acknowledge his past.

Judge Drescher, however, was more disturbed by Patricia's recent behavior than by Dan's lack of personal contact with Amber and Danielle. He felt that Patricia's leaving was inexcusable. "It strikes me," said the judge at the conclusion of the testimony, "that it would have been so easy for Mrs. Stockwell to conform her conduct to the Court's [original custody] order to keep her residency here, to provide for visitation with the defendant, to provide for visitation with the grandparents, and to just keep her dark secret to herself that Amber was not [Dan's] daughter.

"It probably would not have been perfect," he added, "but Amber and her extended family at least would have been accommodated. Amber and Danielle could have grown up with something approaching a normal family setting subsequent to the divorce. It would have been so easy." Judge Drescher's frustration and annoyance were apparent.

"However," he continued, "somewhere somebody injected this evil and sinister notion into Mrs. Stockwell's mind that she need not conform her conduct to the orders of this court and that she need not safeguard the best interest of these children by following the custodial and visitation prescription which we outlined in the fall of 1985.

"She's taken it upon herself to abscond with these children, effectively terminating the defendant's parental rights, keeping her whereabouts a secret," he added harshly, his ire still building. "Such conduct is so pernicious to the parent-child relationship that in my view it constitutes a substantial, material, and permanent change of circumstances to warrant change of custody regarding Danielle from the plaintiff to the defendant.

"There will be no provision made for [Patricia's] visitation" with Danielle, the judge said, noting that he wanted to see Patricia during a subsequent proceeding before even considering a visitation schedule.

Judge Drescher would have liked to change Amber's custody to Dan as well, he said, but that was not possible because Dan was not the child's father. He did, however, reaffirm Dan's visitation with Amber, to begin that summer within five days, on June 15.

The Stockwells had won their courthouse victory, but it was an empty victory as long as Dan's girls were still missing. Armed with Judge Drescher's new orders, they continued the search—and they vowed to fight all the harder to win Amber as well.

Buser contacted a Connecticut lawyer, who hired a private detective. Finally, in early August, Dan received the good news: The detective had found the girls. The local sheriff went to Patricia and Rick's house and took the children away from them while Dan and his mother flew out to Connecticut. Once there, they were allowed to have Amber and Danielle overnight until a hearing the next day, August 9, 1986. Jean, who had accompanied Dan to help him with the girls, was anxious to see Amber and Danielle safely returned to Idaho.

The New Haven judge who heard the case followed the Uniform Child Custody Jurisdiction Act, which gives precedence to custody rulings in a child's home state regardless of where that child might currently live. In this case the judge would consider Idaho, not Connecticut, to be Amber and Danielle's home state.

The proceeding was tense. Patricia argued that the children should not be taken back, but the court wouldn't listen to her reasons. As required by the law, the Connecticut judge enforced Judge Drescher's order—the custody and visitation ruling from Idaho—and sent Amber and Danielle back to Nampa. Even though Judge Drescher had not awarded Dan custody of Amber, the Connecticut court returned her to Idaho along with Danielle because Dan's summer visitation would not end until August 15.

After hearing the judge's decision, Rick stormed out of the court-room. Patricia stayed behind momentarily, crying and hugging her daughters. The police escorted Dan, Jean, and the girls to a car so they could reach the airport without mishap.

Patricia was not one to give up. She immediately called her new Idaho lawyer, Roger Williams, who petitioned the court to win back both girls. Williams would argue that Judge Drescher's June 10 ruling had been unfair, even unconstitutional, because Patricia was not present to defend her rights as a mother. But Williams also warned Patricia that she would have an uphill battle because Judge Drescher had spoken so strongly against her. Changing the judge's mind, Williams said, would oblige Drescher to admit that he had made a mistake.

A new trial was set for fall but postponed until mid-January; Patricia and her husband would have to wait longer to argue their case. In the meantime, Judge Drescher extended Dan's temporary custody of Amber, and Rhonda Stockwell suddenly found herself the mother of not one girl but three. The turmoil from the recent custody battle made her parenting challenge difficult. Danielle fretted that she could not keep up at school and complained about fighting at home with Rhonda. Amber suffered from recurring stomachaches and nervous vomiting. And Rhonda's own child Amy had trouble understanding that the Stockwell girls needed extra attention; they, in turn, thought Amy was spoiled and favored by her mother. Because Dan was working long days, Rhonda became the primary caretaker of all three children. For solace she joined the Mormon church, enrolled the girls in Sunday school, and, with Dan, sought counseling from church leaders.

Early on the first day of the trial, January 13, 1987, Buser and his associate Patrick Miller stopped for breakfast at Tom Sweeney's Dutch Oven, a country café on the road between Boise and Caldwell, where the courthouse was located. Miller had begun helping Buser with the Stockwell case a few weeks before the trial because Buser's own work load had grown so large.

"I think we should call the witnesses in this order," began Buser as the white-haired, balding proprietor brought plates of eggs, hash browns, and toast to their table. The attorneys talked over their strategy and reviewed possible questions for cross-examination. Buser was a little tense and excited but well prepared, and he enjoyed the chance to review his game plan in a favorite local haunt. But the breakfast was quickly over, and he and Miller headed outside for their car and the courthouse.

Some Idaho lawyers like to wear their western boots to court and prop them on the judge's table when in chambers, but Buser tries to create a more dignified presence in the courtroom. There he adopts a behavioral style he describes as "disarming," one in which he avoids aggressive, flamboyant tactics or overly pushy advocacy. The soft-spoken Buser does not want to look as if he is leading the judge down a path, but instead tries for subtlety, calmly but steadfastly homing in on key issues that could help sway the court in his favor. He held to his philosophy that day as he argued against Patricia's renewed claim for Danielle and requested a permanent change in Amber's custody as well. His goal: to keep both girls together in Idaho with Dan.

He was encouraged by his first witness, child psychologist Dr. Charles Gamble. Buser had never before asked Gamble to serve as an expert, but the psychologist's stature in the community and his pretrial interviews suggested that he would be superb in court.

Gamble had evaluated both girls thoroughly and was well prepared to explain his findings. He began by describing Danielle as an engaging and relaxed child who had responded well to his evaluation. Yet he was disturbed by Danielle's responses to some of the questions.

"There are references to her being unhappy," Gamble explained in his testimony. "She directly reports being unhappy about not being with Mom, having the family separate, the conflicts over separation and disintegration of the family unit. She's very, very open about that; it was a pervasive thing.

"Along that same line," he continued, "she has very vivid images of parent conflict and the fears that result from that. She does report sleep disturbances, waking up periodically in the middle of the night, and she does report some basic insecurities that I would see at this age like fear of being alone, but they appear, in my opinion, to be a little bit more pronounced. It's not unusual for an eight-year-old to not want to be in the house when Mom and Dad are not there. But she directly expresses more of a skewed negativity and it's very unpleasant, very uncomfortable."

"Regardless of who's not there?" interrupted Buser, hoping to emphasize Danielle's ambivalence about choosing one parent over the other.

"She does show strong attachments to both natural parent figures," Gamble replied reassuringly, "references to both as being very positive commodities, very positive influences in her life." But "she does have, again, recurring thoughts of, pardon the expression, 'scene of the accident'; she really still in her mind goes over what has happened, and it's something I think she's having difficulty dealing with.''

Danielle, explained Gamble, wished that her parents would get back together. ''There is a continual theme of hope of reunion, getting things back on track, making things all better,'' the psychologist noted, ''and that's not unusual at all.'' Many children like Danielle hope that their parents will reunite, even years after a divorce.

Amber had been much more guarded during her evaluation, Gamble said. ''She was very uncomfortable with any kind of hint of conflict or any kind of hint where there might be a sense of partisanship,'' he told the judge. ''For example, I might say something like, 'The person I trust most . . .' and she would say 'Mom and Dad.' *The* person you trust most, *the* person— 'Mom *and* Dad.' And there would be lots of situations like that where she felt uncomfortable with trying to take a stand and make a strong statement one way or another.''

The psychologist concluded that ''affectively, this is a gal that looks like what I call 'a stuffer.' She stuffs feelings. She puts them away someplace, they don't exist. If they do, she minimizes them.'' He was worried about Amber, he said, because ''she's an emotional oxen, she's carrying a lot of baggage and she doesn't talk—she doesn't seem to feel comfortable talking freely about it. It's an emotional drain, so to speak, and by this age it's becoming stylistic. It's the way you do things. It's not necessarily a reaction to a situation, it's just the way you handle yourself: 'Everything's okay, leave me alone, everything will be all right.'''

Amber, said the psychologist, was putting all of her energies into school and her peer group so that she could avoid acknowledging the conflict in her personal life. She did not want to leave Nampa, East Side School, or her friends.

The contrast between the two girls was striking. When Dr. Gamble had asked Danielle what she would ask for if given three wishes, she said first she wanted some ponies, second was being with Mom, and the third was playing and not fighting.

Amber's first wish was quite different. ''Here's a striver,'' said Dr. Gamble. ''She—her one wish—I mean, she gets three wishes, here's a ten-year-old kid [saying] 'My one wish is to get all A's.' That's very unusual. 'You know [I said], be a little bit greedy, go for it, be hedonistic, if nothing else,' and 'No, I just want to get all A's.'

'''If you could change yourself, what would you be?''' Gamble had asked Amber, and she had replied, he said, '''I'd be a person that doesn't make mistakes.'''

Buser was pleased with Gamble's testimony. Dan and Patricia's divorce and continual fighting had indeed left their mark; as with many parents, they did not understand the long-term sadness and trauma that conflict creates for children. Buser felt that the fact that Danielle and Amber were troubled argued in favor of the status quo, encouraging stability and keeping both girls in Idaho with Dan.

The witness list was lengthy, requiring a full day for completion. After Gamble, Buser called to the stand a general building contractor and then an Allied Van Lines moving consultant; both were active in the Mormon church and, through their church roles, had counseled Dan. Danielle's schoolteacher also testified, as did Tom Ray, another contractor for whom Dan had worked. Ray was a Vietnam veteran and a friend of ten years; his family and Dan's socialized frequently, and the two men confided in each other.

"You said, Mr. Ray, that you and Dan have been through some hard times," Buser questioned his witness.

"Yes, sir."

"And part of that helped develop your relationship. What were those hard times?"

"Well, I'm a Viet Nam veteran. I was wounded and discharged . . . serious wounds to the point of almost killing me. I had very deep anxiety, depression, was abusing drugs in the earlier years, and with Dan's help and the help of several other people, Viet Nam Veterans' organizations, I have no more problem with drugs, I get along much better with my family. . . ."

Buser paused. "To your knowledge, does Dan have any skills in veteran counseling?"

"No, but just really good communication skills. Dan's a very easy person to talk to, and you can trust him."

Buser asked Ray about Dan's parenting skills. "Do you see him favoring any of the three girls that live in his household?" the lawyer asked.

"No, sir," Ray replied. "They all get equal treatment. Every one of them do. I've never seen him take one over the other. If he brings one something, he brings them all something. If the girls are at my house, he not only brings his children a piece of candy or a cookie, he brings my children a piece of candy or a cookie. I've never seen him play favorites."

The trial moved into a second day, and the time came for Roger Williams to present Patricia's side of the case. He put Rick Porter on the stand.

Rick's testimony sparked the courtroom like a dry log on a fire. He spoke at length, even babbling at times in a high-pitched fervor he could barely contain, about his perceptions of his influence on Amber and Danielle. He blustered with enthusiasm and self-congratulation regarding his new role as a parent.

"I'd read to them, you know," Rick testified, "lessons, and this and that. And they just . . . within weeks they were totally different, you know, they just started relaxing and really . . . I called Amber 'Rocky,' you know, because Amber had no drive at all, you know, she just had no drive at all. So, I used to call her 'Rocky,' and I actually explained how the Rocky film was, and I actually showed it to her.

"And I called Danielle 'Tiger,'" continued Rick, "cause for her to compete with Amber, because Amber is so much bigger and stronger, Danielle would have to get mad, like just go out and try extra hard. And the reason why I called Amber 'Rocky' all the time was to build confidence in her, you know, in both girls."

While Rick appraised himself in positive terms, his testimony crackled with negativism toward Dan. He insisted that Dan could not parent Amber and Danielle.

"What are you saying about right and wrong?" asked Buser while cross-examining Rick. "Are you saying that Dan Stockwell and Rhonda Stockwell can't teach these children right from wrong?"

"If his family is an example of how these girls would turn out," began Rick, "lying, manipulating—"

"Okay," interrupted Buser, who was standing near the witness stand and using no notes. "Would you answer the question," he insisted quietly but firmly.

"I don't know if I can," retorted a defiant Rick. He was agitated and confrontational.

"Are they not able to raise Amber and Danielle and teach them right from wrong?" repeated Dan's lawyer. "Not their family, I'm talking about these two people. It's either going to be you and Patricia, I suppose, unless the Court decides to split custody, or it's going to be Dan and Rhonda. Can they teach right from wrong?"

Dan, said Rick, did not even know right from wrong himself. "Dan was wrong for coming in and destroying a perfect home," Rick insisted, referring to Dan's return from Oregon and his asserting his visitation rights. "We were willing to let both girls go for the summer. Right? But he kept on playing games and he would not be a man and say 'Okay, I'm gonna stop playing games.' But instead he tried harder and harder to play games with these kids' minds. We were ruined. We had to protect these kids."

"In his affidavit," said Buser, "Dan said that you advised him, when he came back [to Nampa] from Oregon, and I quote, 'Rick said he would do everything in his power to make sure I did not have anything to do with the girls. He has purchased books on how to tell a child they were adopted.'"

"That's a lie. That's a lie," Rick countered angrily.

"Is it a lie that you were studying books [on how] to tell Amber that she was not the real daughter of Dan Stockwell?"

"I never had a book on how to tell a daughter that you're adopted."

"You're the one who told her?" demanded Buser. He knew the truth and was not about to let Rick wiggle out from under his thumb. "Or was it Patricia who told her?"

"When it was time to tell her, we both told her together," he replied.

"Why did you tell her?"

"To stop this man from using her. Because she is the weakest one of them all."

"When you took the children to Connecticut," continued Buser mercilessly, "you changed the girls' names to Porter, didn't you?" He and Rick were nose to nose and he was not going to back down.

"That's the only thing . . ."

"Would you answer the question?" insisted the lawyer.

"Yes, sir," Rick admitted. His testimony did Patricia's case far more harm than good.

Although Patricia Porter was just as angry as Rick, she proved to be a more effective witness than her husband. She was far more articulate and she aptly conveyed her concerns about Dan's financial stability and his relationship with the girls.

"Do you have any concerns about Mr. Stockwell's ability to support these children?" Williams asked his client.

"Yes, I do," Patricia responded, perched on the edge of the witness seat. "In fact, he has had job after job after job after job, no stability in a job, he couldn't stay in a job more than three or four months. He showed us that at Adventureland Video and Pizza Hut. These are the types of jobs that he's had. He has had a chance, Dan is not stupid. He has had plenty of opportunity to make a success out of himself and he has not done so yet.

"He's what, thirty, thirty-one years old, thirty-two years old," Patricia continued, gritting her teeth, her face red under the stress of the examination. "By now, he should have some sort of profession. I just cannot believe that this man will support himself and his family and my two daughters on a regular day-to-day basis, without Grandma's support." Dan's sporadic employment record was a theme Williams played upon time and time again. In contrast to Dan, he emphasized, Patricia had worked steadily as a welder, both in Idaho and in Connecticut.

Patricia also accused Dan's father of having sexually abused Danielle while the grandparents were in South America with the girls, and she testified that the reason she left Idaho was to protect her children.

"[Amber and Danielle] told you about their grandfather," said Williams in discussing the days preceding Patricia and Rick's radical departure, "and you reacted did you not?" Williams was trying to help Patricia give the Idaho court an explanation for her move East.

"Yes, sir," Patricia responded emphatically. "I was very upset. That night when Danielle told us that something was—that her grandfather had done something to her, she was . . ."

"Then the next day you talked to Amber—or Amber talked to you about it," suggested Williams.

"Yes, Amber came in and said she had to talk to us about it," Patricia replied.

Patricia had raised these same allegations before the trial, and Buser had argued to the court then that no abuse had ever taken place. But at the custody proceeding itself he chose not to put on a full defense when it became clear to him that the judge would not consider Patricia's charges. Grandfather Stockwell was out of the country, far away from the girls, and even more important, he was unavailable to defend himself during the trial. Buser was relieved that the court took this tack because, he says, the alleged sexual abuse by the girls' grandfather had nothing to do with the parents' quarrel over which of them should have custody. "The alleged abuse," Buser insisted, "was a red herring."

Abuse charges have become more common in custody cases today—they are a weapon, whether true or false, that has gained in popularity, and one guaranteed to get attention—but such allegations generally are leveled against the father himself. The Stockwell case was unusual in that Patricia and Rick continued to press their accusations against the children's grandfather, even asking the court to review a counselor's report that had been completed after Patricia called a rape crisis center and the counselor had interviewed Amber and Danielle. But at the same time, Buser presented the report of a doctor who had examined the girls and found no evidence of any sexual abuse.

When Judge Drescher finally issued his ruling a month later, on February 20, 1987, he reaffirmed Dan's custody of Danielle. "The most compelling consideration," he noted, "is the Court's abiding conviction that if Danielle is placed in the custody of the plaintiff, the defendant will never see her again." Drescher was so worried that Patricia would abscond with the child again that he ordered her to post a fifteen-thousand-dollar bond during visitation to guarantee Danielle's return.

He did not think that Patricia had a valid concern regarding the sexual abuse allegations and Danielle's future safety; the grandfather, he noted, had not even been in the United States when Patricia fled from Idaho. Yet, at the same time, even though he believed that Bob Stockwell was working steadily overseas on various jobs, Judge Drescher did order him to stay away from Danielle. The reasoning was unclear; perhaps the judge was exercising an abundance of caution or simply was placating Patricia, who was convinced that the grandfather was in the country. But the judge never determined whether the alleged abuse actually had taken place, focusing his decision solely on the need to decide whether Dan or Patricia would provide the best care for Amber and for Danielle.

Despite Drescher's renewed support for Dan's custody of Danielle, the judge remained unconvinced that he could legally grant him custody of Amber. "The Court does not believe that an adequate legal basis exists in Idaho to make a stepparent the custodian when the natural parent is ready, willing, and qualified to serve," he wrote in his opinion. "This may, however, be an appropriate matter for appellate review." It was clear that he would have liked to give custody of Amber to Dan, and he urged him to try to find a legal way to allow it.

The judge concluded by ordering Patricia to pay Dan one hundred dollars a month in child support for Danielle plus almost six thousand dollars more to cover Dan's expenses while pursuing her in Connecticut.

While Judge Drescher suspected that the case was not over, he had no idea when he issued his opinion how many more twists and turns it would take before reaching a conclusion.

Buser immediately requested, and the judge granted, a stay of his order—a temporary hold on its implementation—until Dan's appeal could be heard. The girls would continue to live with Dan, as they had been, until the appeal was decided.

Four months later, however, Judge Drescher reversed himself, lifting the stay, presumably because the appeal was taking so long. Amber would have to return to her mother in Connecticut. Buser quickly responded to this change of events by deciding to go over Drescher's head, requesting a new stay from the judge who was scheduled to hear the appeal, District Court Judge Jim Doolittle.

"Let's ask Doolittle for the stay," Buser announced to Patrick Miller, his associate. The young lawyer winced at the idea, hesitant to ask a district court judge to grant a request that already had been rejected by the lower court. But Buser insisted. "We've got to do it, Pat," he announced firmly. "We need to keep these kids in Idaho." Miller, who had been in practice about eighteen months, was upset by his boss's directive. He had grown up in the small town of Caldwell, Idaho, and Judge Doolittle was a contemporary of his father. Miller thought he would look foolish, like an impudent kid, asking the district judge for the stay, but he followed his orders and set to work drawing up the papers.

To his surprise, Judge Doolittle agreed to a new stay; Amber and Danielle would remain together in Idaho with Dan, at least for a little while longer. It was a strategic victory, for the longer the children in a custody dispute stay with a given parent, the better that parent's chance for success.

Patricia was beside herself and tried everything she could imagine to fight back.

In May the Idaho Department of Health and Welfare received a complaint that the living conditions in Dan and Rhonda's home were unsuitable for children. Randy Kath, a juvenile officer with the Nampa Police Department, stopped by to investigate. Dan was shocked to see him.

"May I help you?" he asked the officer who appeared at his door.

"I'm Officer Randy Kath, and I'm here to investigate a complaint from Health and Welfare about the living conditions you're providing your children," the police officer replied, showing Dan his badge. "May I come in?"

Dan could only shrug at first. "OK," he replied, still not fully comprehending what was happening.

Kath checked every room in the four-bedroom ranch-style home, noting in particular the number of beds and the amount of furniture. He looked carefully in the kitchen.

"What's this all about?" asked Dan.

"We've received a complaint," was all Kath could tell him. "But I don't see any problem here," he added, finishing his rounds of the house. "The complaint has no merit at all, so I'll recommend that it be closed. Sorry to bother you."

He shook Dan's hand and left. By then Dan had figured out what happened.

Later Patricia also contacted Boise television station KTVB to complain about her predicament. The station ran a story about the Stockwell case on its June 12 6:00 P.M. newscast. Buser accused the station of being onesided in its coverage, and KTVB later apologized.

Finally, on December 17, 1987, eleven months after the trial before Judge Drescher, District Court Judge Doolittle upheld the lower court's decision regarding both girls. Danielle was to stay with Dan and Amber was to return to Patricia. Buser immediately vowed a new appeal—this time to the Idaho Supreme Court.

Several days after Judge Doolittle's decision, Amber and Danielle spent the night with their grandmother, Jean Stockwell. Both girls were upset by the continued battling, and Jean could do little to relieve their distress. When she finished running errands with them the following day, she decided to take them to visit their Aunt LaFonda. But as they approached the house they spotted Patricia and her grown daughter from her first marriage, Catherine, sitting in a pickup truck down the street. Patricia followed Jean and the girls to LaFonda's.

"Amber, come now!" Patricia screamed after Jean instructed the child to run into LaFonda's house. Patricia had thought that Judge Doolittle had upheld the decision sending Amber back to her, and she had arrived to claim her daughter.

"No, we have a stay order," said LaFonda, stepping in front of Patricia, whose fists were clenched with frustration and rage at being denied her own child. LaFonda told her that Judge Doolittle had put a hold on his own opinion while Buser appealed to the Idaho Supreme Court, so for now, Dan would keep both girls.

Patricia did not believe her. Hearing Jean coming up the stairs behind her, she turned. "I want my daughter," Patricia screamed at her former mother-in-law and Dan's wife Rhonda, who was at the bottom of the steps. Rhonda, Jean, LaFonda, another Stockwell sister named Lisa, and their brother John Stockwell confronted Patricia directly and angrily. "Get off of our property," they demanded.

Inside the house, Danielle and Amber stood silently at a window. Tears streamed down their faces as they saw the two women they loved most, their mother and their grandmother, screaming at each other. It was a horrible scene for them to witness, but no one, unfortunately, acknowledged its impact. Such oversight is common when custody battles are as heated as the Stockwells'. The warring parties become so hateful and so focused on each other that they forget the children, the very reason they were fighting in the first place.

Amber was fearful for both her mother and grandmother and very confused about what she should do. The twelve year old also was angry, and she felt helpless because she had no control over her own life.

"Why can't I have some choices in my life and make some of the decisions?" she later would ask a psychologist. She wanted to live with Dan and Rhonda, she would tell him, but she also wanted very much to visit her mother. The real problem was Rick. He picked on Danielle.

Danielle, who was nine and a half, had special problems of her own. Saddled with a learning disability, she was having difficulty concentrating and focusing on her work in school. She, too, was upset about the custody fight and the scene at LaFonda's house, but she was less able to express her feelings. Later she would tell the psychologist, however, that she also wanted to stay with Dan and Rhonda, visit with her mother, and avoid contact with Rick.

While Amber and Danielle tried to cope with the trauma, Buser continued his fight to maintain what stability they had, keeping them with Dan while appealing to the state supreme court, the last court available to the Stockwell family.

Over the years the case had slowly but surely worked its way up the ladder of justice. Two lower courts had ruled against Buser with regard to Amber, but he had not given up. And he was winning his short-term goal—keeping the girls with Dan throughout the ordeal. Amber and Danielle would continue living with Dan, Rhonda, and Amy as they had since the Connecticut court returned them to Idaho, a good omen for their future there. They visited Patricia in the summer of 1988, but this time Dan did not require his ex-wife to post the fifteen-thousand-dollar bond set by Judge Drescher to guarantee the children's return. Patricia had told Dan that she had no more money, and he sent the girls anyway. At the end of the visit they returned to Idaho without mishap and on schedule.

It was not until the following summer, on June 5, 1989, that the Idaho Supreme Court finally issued its ruling on Amber's fate. Although Dan clearly had won custody of Danielle in the lower courts, so only Amber's custody was under appeal, both girls' future was in limbo because Dan had decided that he would never separate them. If he lost custody of Amber, he would in effect lose custody of both girls.

But this time the Stockwell family celebrated its greatest triumph of all. "The paramount consideration in any dispute involving the custody and care of a minor child is the child's best interest," ruled the supreme court.

"In custody disputes between a 'non-parent' (i.e., an individual who is neither a legal nor natural parent) and a natural parent, Idaho courts apply a presumption that a natural parent should have custody as opposed to other lineal or collateral relatives or interested parties," the opinion continued. That is, unless the nonparent can show that the natural parent has abandoned the child or is unfit—or that the child has been in the nonparent's care for an appreciable time—the natural parent should have custody.

In the latter situation, the court held, "the custody of the child will be awarded to that party if the best interests of the child so dictate." According to the supreme court, the two lower courts were wrong when they said that to consider giving Dan custody he had to prove that Patricia had forfeited her rights to custody by abandonment or was an unfit parent.

"In view of the longstanding, substantial custodial and parental relationship Dan has had with Amber," the court held, "the lower courts were clearly obligated under settled Idaho law to consider Amber's best interests in determining who should be entrusted with her custody." While the supreme court did not actually award custody of Amber to Dan, it did reverse the two lower courts' rulings and sent the case back to the magistrate level for reconsideration and a determination of custody that would be in Amber's "best interest."

The state's highest court had held that even though Dan was not Amber's natural parent, he was her psychological parent, and if Amber would be better off living with him, he could be named her custodial parent. The decision would provide critical support for other stepparents in future cases wanting to assert their own claims to custody.

Along with this precedent-setting ruling, the Idaho Supreme Court put another twist on the Stockwell case. Because the earlier proceedings had been so acrimonious, time-consuming, and costly, the justices did not want the case to go back to trial right away. They ordered Patricia and Dan to enter mediation to determine custody "under the auspices of the district court before a qualified mediator." If that did not work, the justices said, they could begin the litigation anew. The Stockwell case was the first of its kind in Idaho where a court ordered mediation when it had not been an issue in the appeal or even under discussion.

In April 1989, two months before the Idaho Supreme Court issued its ruling, Dan and Rhonda moved to Otis, Oregon, the part of the country Rhonda called home. Dan gave up his position as a car lot manager to live in a trailer home and, with luck, find a new job. He eventually began work as a U-Haul technician; Rhonda took a job in a kite factory.

But at the same time, Amber, then thirteen, and Danielle, eleven, began wanting more time with their mother. Dan realized that the girls were approaching adolescence and desired the role model their natural mother offered. "I love my mother, but I don't even know her," Amber told Dan. The girls had lived with Dan for almost three years and, as he had always believed, they needed to be close with both of their parents. This belief was Dan's strength as a parent, but it was also the source of his continuing battle with Patricia. Every time he wanted to give her a chance to fulfill her parental role, she seized the opportunity to renew the legal battle. It was as if Dan could not resist trying to work out the situation and Patricia could not resist spoiling it.

Dan was upset by the girls' change of heart in asking to live in Connecticut, so he turned to the school psychologist for reassurance. "As long as both parents make a valiant effort, don't fight in front of the children, and try to make the kids feel very comfortable, it can work out," the psychologist advised him. So he decided to send Amber and Danielle to Connecticut for a year. Rhonda agreed. She had cared for the girls, genuinely loved them, and been fully supportive—Rhonda had been the one who most closely monitored the court battle—but the trauma had taken a toll on her as well. More time alone together, she decided, would be good for her and Dan and for her own daughter, Amy.

Dan's mother and lawyer strongly argued against the move; they wanted him to continue fighting for full custody of Amber as well as Danielle. But Dan thought Patricia was more conciliatory and willing to work out a final resolution with him. She did not have the money to continue the litigation, she had said. "I want to do what's best for Amber and Danielle," she had told Dan. He believed her and chose to disregard his mother's advice and his lawyer's warning. On June 17, less than two weeks after the supreme court's decision giving Dan the right to fight for custody of Amber, he and Rhonda sent both girls to their mother's home in Naugatuck, Connecticut. It was time for their summer visit and Dan said they could stay for the entire school year.

He knew he was taking a risk because the court system had not yet issued a final ruling on actual custody—the supreme court had ordered mediation, which had not even begun. And Judge Drescher had warned Dan that once Patricia had the girls, he might never see them again. If mediation failed and the case went to trial while the girls were living with Patricia in Connecticut, a court might be inclined to leave them there rather than move them once again.

By this time, Paul Buser had left Dan's case in the hands of his associate, Pat Miller. Buser and his wife had divorced in May 1989 and he had decided to leave Idaho. After seventeen years practicing law in

Boise, he moved to Chicago, joining an old-line matrimonial practice in a firm called Cantwell & Cantwell. "I wanted to take on a larger challenge professionally," explained Buser of his jump from a small pond to a big one. The lure of the big city, with its steady diet of challenging cases and a larger cohort of dedicated family law practitioners, had been beckoning for some time. "The most difficult part," Buser said after the move, "was leaving my children—and leaving my law firm."

Buser had left, but Dan would be forever in awe of him, succumbing to what he admits is hero worship. "It was like a dog grabbing onto a stake, and someone trying to take that stake away from the dog," says Dan when describing his former lawyer's handling of the case. "He was tireless." To this day Dan still refers to him as "Mr. Buser" and feels nervous in his presence.

"I could sit all day long and tell you nice things about him and not begin to scratch the surface," Dan continues emotionally, "not because we were ultimately victorious in the case—that has something to do with it—but when you look into his eyes when you're talking about something, he doesn't talk [just] from his head. He talks from his heart. He believes in what he's doing."

Mellowed after the years-long court battle, still living in the trailer with Rhonda and Amy, Dan says he does not blame Patricia and continues to feel affection for her. "I like Patty," he says earnestly, with Rhonda sitting at his side. "We had two beautiful children together. No matter how destructive our marriage was, two wonderful, beautiful things came out of it. I don't think she acted much different than a lot of women do," he says with conviction. "How would you react if your babies were taken from you? I cannot blame her one hundred percent."

In December 1989 Dan wrote to Patricia suggesting a joint custody arrangement for Amber, with both girls alternating years living in Dan's and Patricia's homes and neither parent paying any child support. Dan also wanted his mother to have guaranteed visitation for one week a year and for Patricia to continue paying back her court-ordered financial debt, a debt owed to Jean because she had paid Dan's bills. He believed the proposal was as fair as possible to everyone involved.

Patricia surprised Dan. Despite her recent conversation and more congenial mood, she refused the offer and took up arms once again. When the court-ordered mediation process failed, Patricia and Rick hired a new attorney in Connecticut and reasserted her claim to custody. "My battle is not with Dan," proclaimed Patricia as she renewed the fight. "Dan is a sacrificial lamb so his mother can get custody of the kids. That's the whole game. He loves the girls but he cannot afford to support them. His mother wants them." Patricia did not recognize that Dan's ability to support the children was not a critical factor in awarding custody; after all, a court had ordered her to pay child support.

In the end, Patricia lost the long, grueling battle once and for all. After the new trial in Idaho in March 1990, the court gave Dan custody of his stepdaughter Amber. Judge Drescher had awarded him custody of Danielle already, and the new judge in the case (Judge Drescher had gone into private practice by then) did not want to split up the two girls. He also blamed Patricia for the turmoil in the children's lives: "The defendant [Dan] presents an image of a person that desires to put an end to the litigation between these parties and promote peace between the parties, allow substantial contact with the plaintiff and stabilize the lives of Amber and Danielle Stockwell," ruled the judge. "The plaintiff presents an image of a person that will stop at nothing to get her own way, is constantly on an evidence gathering function with the lives of the two children and will not give stability and continuity to the life of Amber."

The court said that Amber and Danielle were to spend summers with their mother and that Patricia must pay $492 a month for child support, a figure based on her annual income of almost $26,000.

Pat Miller was jubilant over the final victory but uncertain as to whether Patricia would cooperate in implementing the court's order. In fact, just days after the final opinion was issued, she said she was trying to work out a different arrangement. Dan, she said, was thinking of letting the girls continue with her during the school year and live with him during the summer. "Dan and I are going to try to work this out between ourselves," Patricia announced. "We're all tired of the fighting."

A few weeks later, however, she and Rick were angrier than ever and up in arms one more time, claiming that they were going to wage a new war through the media. Contrary to what Patricia has said, it appears that the fighting never will end, at least not until Amber and Danielle are grown and on their own.

The real winner in this case was Paul Buser. He had done his job—and a superb job at that. The Stockwell case set a new precedent with regard to stepparents' rights in Idaho, and Buser received national attention for his supreme court victory. In the years since the case was filed, legislatures around the country began addressing the issue of stepparents' custody, visitation, and support. The new laws they have been enacting are indicative of a trend that is sweeping the country. At the same time, in other states such as Idaho, where no state law exists, the local courts are nonetheless confronting an increasing number of stepparent cases.

The Stockwell decision in Idaho and the philosophy it embraces are not, however, without their critics: "By this gigantic step," wrote R. Michael Redman, a magistrate in Idaho's Fifth District, "stepparents are placed on equal footing with parents when they have established a substantial relationship with the child. Some would say their position is superior, because unlike parents they can choose to wash their hands of the children and walk away without further obligation."

The stepparent debate undoubtedly will continue as legislatures and courts continue to grapple with the problem, but the Stockwells and the Porters have little interest in any case but their own. These two families remain among the casualties, the debris along the road to victory for stepparents' rights. It was clear from the beginning that Dan was ambivalent about having custody of his daughters and sought them only because his parents' guardianship was going to be ended and his mother did not want Patricia to have custody. His employment record was unstable and his income erratic, and he might have felt ill prepared to raise three teenage girls (including his stepdaughter Amy). Dan did love his children, but he probably would have been happy with a full visitation schedule if Patricia only had cooperated. But it was her ill-advised move East, combined with Jean Stockwell's pressure to keep Amber and Danielle in the family, that forced Dan into court. Of course, Rick's fervor only added grease to the flames of this messy family fire.

While both couples—Patricia and Rick and Dan and Rhonda—focused a major portion of their lives on the custody suit, it remains to be seen whether doing so strengthened or weakened their own marital relationships in the long run. It certainly consumed them for some time.

For their part, Jean and Bob Stockwell had little to show personally for all of the money they spent on Buser's legal fees. Patricia hated the senior Stockwells and refused to let Amber and Danielle engage in normal family communications with her grandparents. And when Dan moved to Oregon, Bob and Jean were no longer close enough to maintain the kind of casual, close relationship they had envisioned with their granddaughters.

Of course, the biggest victims in the case were Amber and Danielle. The greatest irony in this story lies in the Idaho Supreme Court's instructions to give custody of Amber either to Dan or Patricia based, above all, on what would be best for her. Quite the opposite took place. Her best interests took a backseat to stubbornness, anger, and egotism.

9

VIOLENCE IN DIVORCE: PROTECTING THE INNOCENT

Kathleen O'Guin and William O'Guin v. Joseph Pikul

The law is not adequate to deal with crazy situations.

—ATTORNEY RAOUL FELDER
NEW YORK

Typically, ending a marriage through divorce is an emotionally ugly affair, but all too often it becomes a physical battlefield, too. Animosity and hatred surge into violence, leading to serious injuries and sometimes to death.

Abuse within the family is a readily acknowledged phenomenon, one that is distinct from the matter of divorce. The Senate Committee on the Judiciary reports that at least two million, and as many as six million, women are battered by their husbands each year. More than one million women annually seek medical assistance for the resulting injuries. In fact, according to one study, almost one in three husbands is guilty at some time of physical violence against a spouse. Almost all victims of domestic violence are women and children, and they come from all strata of society.

When a woman tries to extricate herself and her children from an abusive home by seeking divorce, or when she fears that a divorce may turn violent, how can she protect herself? Perhaps more important, how can she protect her children? If she is in danger, is it correct to assume that her children also are at risk?

New York divorce attorney Raoul Felder found himself face-to-face with this question after Diane Whitmore Pikul came to his office for help. When she first contacted Felder in the summer of 1986, Diane told him that she was terrified of her husband Joseph, a wealthy securities analyst prone to unpredictable fits of jealousy and temper. She was afraid that during one of his rages he could seriously hurt her. The problem was that Diane was so frightened of her husband that she was afraid to tell him she was leaving, and without her decision to move ahead and seek a divorce, Felder was powerless to guarantee her safety.

As the months passed, Diane continued to call and meet with her attorney, trying to gather the courage to confront her husband. At the same time, Joe Pikul's behavior became even more bizarre and abusive. He screamed at Diane repeatedly and locked her out of rooms, ransacked her belongings, bugged her telephone, and took their two young children, blindfolded, to a $1,650-a-month Battery Park City, New York, apartment he secretly maintained, ordering them not to tell their mother. Then Diane discovered photographs and a videotape of her husband in orgasmic ecstasy while wearing women's underwear, and she became convinced that if she stayed with him any longer, he might hurt the children. Finally, on October 19, 1987, she told Felder that she was preparing to act.

The attorney had little time to help forty-four-year-old Diane reach a final decision, for one week later, on Wednesday, October 28, 1987, she was dead. Her body was found in a drainage ditch near New York's Governor Thomas E. Dewey Thruway, three miles south of the Newburgh exit and about fifty miles north of Manhattan. Two days later the police charged fifty-two-year-old Joseph Pikul with second-degree murder; at the time of his arrest he was wearing women's underwear beneath his clothing.

Out on bail, Pikul resumed living with his two young children, eight-year-old Claudia and four-year-old Blake. With the support of Diane's father and friends, her cousins, Kathleen and William O'Guin, decided to seek custody of the children to protect them from their father. Felder offered to represent the O'Guins free of charge. Diane was dead, but she had turned to him to help safeguard her children, and the lawyer decided that on her behalf, he would continue to fight for their security and well-being.

Felder thought that his case against Joe Pikul's right to parent was clear-cut. Although he had not yet been found guilty of Diane's murder, everyone involved, including the law enforcement authorities, was convinced that he had indeed committed the crime. But Felder soon would find out that the government viewed Pikul's custody rights differently, relying instead on the tradition-bound presumption that a child is always best served by living with a natural parent. During a lengthy court fight the judge continued to support the sanctity of the parent-child bond and to leave Diane's babies with the man who had murdered her. Felder's task seemed doubly difficult because, in his view, he and the judge were too often at odds; their mutual ill feelings added another layer of tension to the courtroom conflict.

The Pikul case, Felder believes, clearly highlights the inability, if not the unwillingness, of public officials to shelter families from violence in a marital relationship. "How do you protect the children?" asks the lawyer incredulously. The challenge would prove almost insurmountable.

In many respects Joseph and Diane Pikul led an ideal Manhattan life. A financial whiz, Joe had risen above his working-class background to build a reputation as a successful Wall Street securities analyst and vice president of Arnhold & S. Bleichroeder, a firm that underwrites foreign and domestic securities. Diane had graudated from Mount Holyoke as an English major and worked as an assistant to the publisher of Harper's magazine. After nine years of marriage they had two beautiful, cherubic children, an apartment in Greenwich Village, and a summer place on Long Island. Joe and Diane also shared a past—both had been married previously and both were recovering alcoholics. They had met through Alcoholics Anonymous.

Yet, in other ways this husband and wife seemed mismatched. Tall and brawny, the bearded Joe Pikul was a difficult and unpredictable man who flew into fiery fits of rage toward friend and stranger alike. One time he was arrested for pistol-whipping a limousine driver. Diane, on the other hand, was funny and fun-loving, an attractive but fragile, almost wispy, woman whose enjoyment of the good life, lighthearted bravado, and close bonding with women friends masked an underlying vulnerability. By temperament, Joe and Diane clearly were opposites. They fought more than they got along.

For more than a year Diane had been calling and meeting with New York attorney Raoul Felder to talk about divorcing Joe, but she was far too frightened of her husband to follow through with it, fearful of the reaction she would provoke in him should she leave. She was afraid, too, that if she left him, she would not have enough money. Diane had become a psychological prisoner in the marriage. Despite the multi-thousand-dollar retainer she had paid Felder, he could not take any legal action without her consent, and she just could not bring herself to give it. "My lawyer won't let me do anything," Diane lied when her women friends asked about any progress with her situation. Finally, when the domestic turbulence became so overwhelming, when she began believing that her children could suffer, she seriously considered taking legal action.

About a year after their first meeting, Felder thought he had almost convinced forty-four-year-old Diane to seek the divorce she so desperately needed.

"Let me help you," he begged her, upset by new stories about Joe's behavior that she shared with him. "I think you're unsafe in there."

"Give me a little time," responded Diane, still hesitating but coming closer to a final decision. Her hands folded and unfolded, twitching nervously in her lap. She looked up at the lawyer. "I'm getting worried about the children," she said.

Her long-time fear of taking action was beginning to give way. She was getting ready to confront her husband. He was going to have to accept that she and the children were leaving, and he would have to support them, too.

But Diane Pikul would never take that formal step toward safety by filing for a divorce. Before Felder could meet with her again, she was strangled and bludgeoned on the head.

Diane was last seen on Long Island late on the night of Friday, October 23, 1987. When she was absent from work the following Monday, officials at *Harper's* reported her missing. Her husband had choked and beaten her that preceding weekend, in the early hours of Saturday morning, and buried her body in the sand near their Long Island home. Then he dug it up again and stowed it in the back of his Buick station wagon. Later that same day he decided to leave his children Claudia and Blake with friends so that he could try again to dispose of Diane's body, still hidden in the back of his car. Telling the friends that he and Diane were having marital problems, he said he had to take care of some "personal business."

When he tried to rebury the corpse in his ex-wife's backyard in Norwell, Massachusestts, she refused to let him do so, so it remained in the car. Desperately searching for a new solution while on the way to retrieve his children from the friends' home, Pikul finally dumped Diane's body, wrapped in his 1984 Mazda's green car cover, in a culvert thirty feet from the thruway. Later, with the children back in hand, he went to a car wash and had the Buick thoroughly cleaned, inside and out. A highway maintenance crew found Diane's body, with sponges stuffed into every orifice, on Wednesday, October 28.

New York State charged Joseph Pikul with the murder of his wife. He was arrested on Thursday night, October 29, 1987. "She deserved it," he muttered while sitting in the backseat of the police cruiser, lambasting the dead Diane for having been a terrible mother and proclaiming his love for their children. After the police delivered Pikul to the Orange County Jail in Goshen, New York—Orange County was where Diane's body had been found—officials there discovered that he was wearing a bra and panties underneath his suit.

A sergeant told *The New York Times* that the Pikuls had had "marital problems" and that "the incident [had] occurred after a violent argument." No one will ever know whether Diane finally told her husband she was filing for divorce, but the events surrounding her death lead to the conclusion that she might have done so. Despite his earlier mumblings, Joe would deny later that he had committed the crime.

In fact, he tried to resume his life as if nothing had happened. Released on $350,000 bail, he asked to see his children, who had been staying with some of his relatives in the Washington, D.C., area. Upon the children's return north, Joe took Claudia and Blake to Monticello, New York, in the Catskill Mountains, where he registered at a motel under a fictitious name. One of the family's relatives, worried about the children's welfare, tipped off a social worker, who called the office of Manhattan District Attorney Robert Morgenthau. Staff there responded immediately. It was only days earlier that six-year-old Elizabeth Steinberg, adoptive daughter of Joel Steinberg and Hedda Nussbaum, had been found beaten and dying in their New York apartment, just two blocks from the Pikuls'. The horrendous nature of the Steinberg crime and its ensuing national publicity had heightened many people's sensitivity to domestic violence against children. The story of Joe Pikul set off more alarms.

Aware that Pikul had whisked his children into the countryside and registered them under a false name, the DA's office contacted the child protective services agency in Monticello, New York. But caseworkers there said they could not take action unless they had proof that Claudia and Blake had been neglected or abused or were in imminent danger. There was no evidence of this, the caseworkers said, only (only!) a charge that their father had killed their mother. Even an act as heinous and immoral as that provided no grounds for removing the children from the father's custody because his offspring had not witnessed the murder and had not been physically harmed.

In fact, Claudia and Blake appeared healthy and well cared for. They attended private schools, benefited from child care, and enjoyed all of the luxuries provided by a father who reportedly earned between $250,000 and $400,000 annually. They seemed to have a warm, loving relationship with their father. In fact, they actually adored him.

Still, District Attorney Morgenthau's office was so worried about potential harm to the youngsters that his staff finally talked the child protective services caseworkers and the state troopers into seizing the children from the hotel at 1:30 A.M. on Saturday, November 14, and placing them in temporary foster care. But on Monday a local judge, citing the lack of necessary evidence to deny Pikul custody, returned Claudia and Blake to his care. As the natural father, he was in control, and regardless of the murder charges against Pikul, the child welfare authorities were powerless to deprive him of his parental rights.

The dispute revolving around Pikul and his children presented an unusual situation. Most often people on trial for murder cannot afford bail, as Pikul could, so typically they remain in prison while awaiting a verdict. In such cases, obviously, they cannot seek physical custody of their children. But knowing that he could afford the $350,000 bail set for him, Pikul hired a lawyer even before he was released to help with the inevitable custody dispute. Paul Kurland, a general business litigator whom Pikul had contacted for advice on an investment gone sour, would join him in the fight to get back his children and to keep them under their father's care.

Having served as Diane's lawyer while she was living, Felder was, of course, concerned about her children after her death. He was shocked and outraged that Pikul's continuing custody should even be considered, much less granted, and he thought about suing for temporary custody himself, even if it only proved to be a stalling technique. On his own he began a campaign, talking to friends and relatives of Diane, legal authorities, and social workers—anyone who might help him save Claudia and Blake from what he knew would be certain disaster living with a man like Joe Pikul.

One late afternoon, when Felder was sitting alone in a chair in his office, ruminating with the lights off and autumn's dusk darkening the room, the phone rang. District Attorney Morgenthau was on the line. Felder picked up the receiver; earlier he and Morgenthau had been on opposing sides in a different case, and the hard feelings that ensued still remained.

"You know, I'm very concerned about this Pikul thing," Felder recalls Morgenthau saying. "We can't get Special Services [in New York City] to begin a custody proceeding. Do you have any suggestions?" Although the Manhattan DA technically had no jurisdiction in the Pikul criminal case because it would be heard in Orange County, he still was trying to follow up, to no avail, on the citizen complaints he was hearing about Joe Pikul's worth as a parent.

The DA's office soon would assert that New York City's Human Resources Administration and its Special Services for Children branch were mishandling the case, failing to investigate the complaints about Pikul's behavior and bring the matter into court. *The New York Times* reported, however, that "a spokeswoman for the Human Resources Administration said an investigation had revealed no evidence that Mr. Pikul was an abusive or neglectful parent, and that there had been no reason to seek court action." Special Services for Children, which apparently had been following the children ever since Diane's disappearance, said that Claudia and Blake were in no danger. Quite obviously, the government's system for protecting children from neglect and abuse, a system renowned for its layers of intricate and often ineffective bureaucracy, had not risen to the challenge of investigating a man like Joe Pikul. Perhaps the potential danger he presented was not easily discernible to caseworkers because he was wealthy, articulate, and outwardly presentable, far different from most of the suspected abusers whose names filled their overloaded case files.

Morgenthau's own anxiety reinforced Felder's convictions. When he realized how deeply the DA's office shared his concerns for the Pikul children, he began working all the harder to find a solution.

For a short while after the Monticello incident, Pikul sent Claudia and Blake back to his relatives during the week and visited with them on weekends, but about a month later the relatives announced that they no longer could keep the children and would be returning them to New York in late December. Joe happily prepared for their return. Among Felder, Diane's family, her friends, and the DA's office, concerns grew. Even officials at the Human Resources Administration, which had tried to monitor Pikul's weekend visits with the children, were increasingly alarmed.

Finally Diane's father, Don Whitmore, told Felder's office about a niece who had offered to help. Diane's first cousin, Kathleen O'Guin, and her husband William (Mike) O'Guin, were medical researchers who lived in Yonkers. They had known nothing of Diane's marital problems. They were aware only that Joe was a difficult man with a temper. When they called Whitmore immediately after learning of Diane's death, Kathy O'Guin offered their support. Even then she knew that her telephone condolences could lead to a major commitment and a sizeable change in her and her husband's lives.

Felder talked with Kathy. "Can you help?" he asked. "Can you take the children?"

She and Mike agreed to step in, formally seeking custody of Claudia and Blake. "It's a shock," she admitted to the attorney when the reality of her prospective responsibilities set in, "but we're ready."

The O'Guins were an ideal couple, still young, attractive, and middle class, without children of their own. Even though they had seen Claudia and Blake only twice—Kathy and Diane had visited each other infrequently during recent years—the O'Guins felt compelled to step forward to guarantee the children's safety. "I want to do this for Don," Kathy told her husband. "He's just lost his only child and now he's about to lose his grandchildren." She knew that Joe Pikul would cut off all communications with Diane's family and Don Whitmore would never see Claudia and Blake again. The children's grandfather would never be able to guarantee their well-being or even know what happened to them.

Felder put the retainer money Diane had paid him in a special escrow account as a fund for Claudia and Blake's legal support, monies that he would return to the O'Guins later. Little did he know then that he would devote hours of his time—time for which he never charged—to the Pikul children's legal plight. "My whole life revolved around this case for many months," he recounts.

On December 14 Felder petitioned the state supreme court—the court of general trial jurisdiction in New York—to award his new clients, the O'Guins, temporary custody of the Pikul children pending the outcome of their father's murder trial, which was set for the following July. If Pikul was found innocent, the lawsuit suggested, the children would be returned to him; if he was found guilty, the O'Guins would seek permanent custody. Felder submitted with his pleadings the sexually explicit photographs and videotape Diane had given him, showing Pikul posing and masturbating in women's lingerie.

Robert Wayburn, the associate general counsel at the Human Resources Administration, had taken over the Pikul case for the city by then, and he encouraged the idea of a family custody suit. From the beginning Wayburn felt that the city did not have an adequate case for taking the children away based on its own criteria—that is, the city could not prove that Pikul was guilty of abuse or neglect or that the children were in imminent danger—but he did think that the accusation of murder was enough for the O'Guins to request a custody hearing. Wayburn wanted to take part in that hearing as an amicus curiae, or interested party. Such a proceeding would focus on serving the best interests of the Pikul children rather than on charges of parental abuse and neglect. The problem was that in custody suits between a parent and a third party, the parent always receives judicial preference unless narrowly defined "extraordinary circumstances" have destroyed the parent-child relationship.

From a moral standpoint, however, the case should have been a simple matter of deciding the children's best interests—period. Given that their father was accused of murdering their mother, he should not have enjoyed preference in the debate over their welfare. By his act, the murder, he guaranteed that Claudia and Blake would have only one parent left, and he should not have benefited by asserting his parental primacy in such a situation. A relative of the murdered parent should have been allowed to step in and argue on equal footing that she or he could serve the best interests of the children.

In the face of the judicial deference shown Pikul, Felder pounded away at Pikul's unfitness as a parent, a parent unable to serve his children's best interests. He hurled every charge possible at his opponent—he had a history of violent and unpredictable behavior; he was a transvestite and sexual deviant; he was indicted for murdering his wife; and his children might, in fact, have witnessed the murder. The attorney would try his case on behalf of Diane and her children using every resource available—law and logic, reason and emotion, the legal forum of the courtroom and the public forum of the press.

For his part, Paul Kurland, Pikul's lawyer, confronted the new custody suit head-on. "He is their father, and they are in no danger with him," Kurland announced to reporters covering the story, publicly asserting his client's parental rights. "The criminal case has nothing to do with his relationship with his children." Kurland, who says he likes to represent the underdog in a trial, accused the city of a "collective guilt trip" over Lisa Steinberg's death.

All the while, Pikul continued to act as if nothing had happened, despite the murder charge and despite the O'Guins' lawsuit. While Pikul prepared for Claudia and Blake's return to New York, the Human Resources Administration attempted to negotiate a new arrangement with him and with Kurland that would allow caseworkers to visit the children alone and with their father. The agreement would have to be voluntary because no one had any concrete evidence of cause for concern about Claudia and Blake's safety.

No one, that is, except Felder. He *knew* what he was dealing with and he refused to accept the proposed monitoring as adequate. Dropping in for one hour a week, he said, was not enough. While Felder said he was willing to provide Pikul supervised access to the children, he adamantly insisted that the court not leave them alone with their father, day after day, night after night.

Most people would not think of Raoul Lionel Felder as one who would handle a case without charge. He is better known as the showbiz whiz of matrimonial law, famous for his big-money clients and divorces, a practice that draws headlines and fans.

Felder attracts controversy, too. Many other divorce lawyers criticize him for having an alleged love affair with the media. Uppercrust New York divorce practitioner Norman Sheresky accused Felder of preferring to settle, rarely taking a case all the way to trial. "[He] pretends to be a trial lawyer when he is not. He has no familiarity with how to try a case," Sheresky reportedly once said. Felder hit back with a $7 million libel suit. It was later dismissed when a judge ruled that the comment was merely Sheresky's opinion, protected by the First Amendment, but Sheresky has been mum ever since.

Still others have only praise for Felder. "Do you know why so many matrimonial lawyers hate him?" asks New Jersey practitioner Gary Skoloff, another divorce lawyer of national note. "Because he's so successful!"

Despite his high profile and supporters like Skoloff, Felder is in many ways an outsider, a loner in the crowded field of divorce law. Although he clearly fits into the category of the best divorce lawyers nationwide, he is seldom seen in the company of his colleagues; they find him too unconventional for their trade. Nor does he travel with the fast-paced corporate law firm crowd, the large, multispecialty practices that have begun to hustle for previously scorned divorce work, jockeying for big names and wealthy clients in a field too financially hot for anyone to ignore. In fact, Felder thumbs his nose at the large law firms moving onto his turf. While he does not come cheap himself at $450 an hour, he says that the high-priced corporate lawyers are downright inefficient. They practice divorce by committee, explains Felder, which leads to multiple billings.

While some lawyers may scorn Felder's methods and style, clients flock to him. A high-profile, no-holds-barred approach on behalf of his protégés and their cases pays off handsomely for them and for him. Women in particular love him; Myrna Felder, his wife of almost thirty years, whose law office is down the hall, explained to one reporter that Felder has a terrific manner. On his tally sheet he lists such clients as Nancy Capasso, wife of Bess Myerson's lover, wealthy sewer contractor Andy Capasso, and the wives of novelist Joseph Heller, astronomer Carl Sagan, director Martin Scorsese, producer David Susskind, and playwright Alan Jay Lerner. Actress Robin Givens fired Los Angeles's Marvin Mitchelson to hire Felder to handle her divorce from boxing champ Mike Tyson. "Raoul Felder tops Marvin Mitchelson as the No. 1 unhitcher," proclaimed *Time* magazine. The occasional male Felder has represented includes director Brian DePalma and the husband of TV journalist Linda Ellerbee. Producer David Merrick hired Felder to represent him after seeing the attorney on the opposing side in Merrick's previous divorce. "I'm the hot game in town," Felder immodestly told *Time* in 1989. And he's still hot. He has even had to employ a personal PR man to help with media inquiries.

Perhaps the only thing hotter than Felder is the man's zest and love for the toys of success, not only the traditional materialistic trappings of monied men but also an array of colorful novelties, knickknacks, and eclectic souvenirs that can keep any visitor perennially entertained. Consider Felder's nine-lawyer Madison Avenue office suite: large movie posters cover the reception area, outdone only by a blow-up magazine photograph of Felder himself standing in front of expansive office windows with the New York skyline in the background. Framed articles and press clippings, celebrity photos, and memorabilia fill the firm's conference room, covering every available inch of wall space. Felder's inner sanctum, the work space inhabited by the soft-spoken, fifty-seven-year-old bearded New Yorker, is as much museum as it is office. On display are a collection of paintings and drawings, an army of World War I and II airplane replicas, rows of exotic bedroom slippers, and assorted historical artifacts, including Nazi war memorabilia (so people won't forget, he says). Felder, who grew up in Williamsburg, the working-class, Jewish immigrant neighborhood of Brooklyn, also owns hundreds of suits, drives showpiece automobiles, and lives in two apartments, one next door to the Museum of Modern Art and the other on Fifth Avenue.

Recently Felder expanded his practice, affiliating with lawyers in California and New Jersey so that he can take on clients in those states, too. While divorce law may be a localized practice, one ruled by state laws, Raoul Felder has become a national phenomenon.

Generally speaking, a parent who is charged with a crime, or indicted, maintains custodial rights up until conviction. Even then, those rights typically are restored once the parent is released from prison. In an article written for *Ms* magazine about the Pikul case, one of Diane's friends describes this judicial posture as "an accidental and mutually unintended marriage of conservative and liberal. Add the right wing's pro-patriarchal family stand to the liberals' reverence for due process—civil liberties and defendants' rights—and you come up with the violent husband/father as wolf-in-sweet-grandmother's-clothing, knocking on the courthouse door."

Such law is consistent with historical judicial reverence for the primacy of familial authority. In the eighteenth and nineteenth centuries a man was allowed to beat his wife with a rod as large as his thumb, leading to the expression "rule of thumb." Only in the late nineteenth century was wife beating redefined by most states as an assault. Today all states outlaw family violence. Still, even today law enforcement and judicial authorities are more likely to discount an assault of one family member against another than they are an assault against a non–family member.

Similarly, the government historically overlooked child abuse in deference to family authority, but that attitude also has changed nationwide. In some states child protection agencies can even intervene with the mere threat of violence, and in New York a child may be taken from his or her home if the child is in "imminent danger." Every state, including New York, has a mandatory reporting law, and many, like New York, have a child abuse hot line.

With such heightened awareness about family violence, Felder believed that he had an iron-clad case against Joe Pikul. He filed the O'Guins' custody suit in New York County rather than in Orange County, where the criminal charges against Pikul were pending, because the children lived in Manhattan. The case was assigned to Justice Kristin Booth Glen.

The first courtroom session related to the case took place on December 18, 1987, only days after the suit had been filed. Judge Glen first addressed the very nature of the dispute and the way it should be handled.

Initially, to avoid endangering Pikul's chance for a fair criminal trial and to protect the children, she closed the proceeding. She listened to testimony from the assistant district attorney in Orange County who was handling the criminal prosecution; then she talked with both Claudia and Blake privately in her chambers. The judge also questioned attorney Robert Wayburn, representing the Human Resources Administration, and a representative from the Special Services for Children branch to learn about its investigations into the Pikul family's situation.

After determining that the city did not have enough evidence to file a neglect case against Pikul, Judge Glen made it clear that she would follow New York law in reaching her decision on the custody suit, basing her ruling on the best interests of the children. She said, furthermore, that she would *not* abandon the concept of parental primacy in considering their best interests. The O'Guins and Pikul would not be considered on equal footing, and to succeed the O'Guins would have to prove that the relationship between the father and his children had been destroyed. The judge also made it clear that she considered the custody suit to be distinct from the murder case, even if Pikul was assumed to be guilty.

Nothing Judge Glen learned from her interviews that day convinced her that Pikul should not keep his children, at least during the following weekend, while the custody suit was pending. She scheduled the custody hearing to begin the following Monday, December 21.

On that day, witnesses began to testify as Felder presented his case. First, one of Diane's friends, a staff worker from Alcoholics Anonymous, took the stand, followed by Kathy O'Guin. "He doesn't want to be abusive, he wants to be normal and he definitely wants to be a good father," Kathy O'Guin would tell a reporter later. "But he is rageful, and it's asking a lot for him to be super-perfect while he goes to trial."

Pikul also testified, withstanding a heavy grilling by Felder while attempting to prove that Kathy's concerns about his parenting were unfounded. Throughout he denied that he was guilty of any dangerous behavior toward anyone. "I'm a wonderful father," he asserted, detailing his plans for taking care of Claudia and Blake. But he was nervous and defensive, twitching and often rolling his eyes during his questioning. When Felder introduced the still photos Diane had given him showing a lingerie-clad Pikul in various stages of sexual activity, and then showed the video, which displayed the same in full animation, Pikul ignored the display, reading the *Wall Street Journal* instead.

As bizarre and grotesque as Felder's evidence was, Judge Glen refused to consider it relevant to the custody case. The children were not involved, or aware, she explained. When the court recessed for the Christmas holidays she again granted Pikul temporary custody.

On January 4, 1988, Joseph Pikul was indicted for murder. When the custody hearing picked up for a third time on January 6, about forty of Diane's friends, neighbors, and coworkers stood outside the snowy courthouse in bitterly cold weather, picketing in protest. PROTECT THE CHILDREN, WIFE KILLERS MAKE BAD DADS, their posters and signs proclaimed. They already had submitted petitions with almost two hundred signatures asking Special Services for Children to take Claudia and Blake from their father's custody, sending duplicate copies to city officials and the press. The same day the pickets appeared, Judge Glen finally opened the courtroom proceedings to the public and the press.

William O'Guin, who is called Mike, testified first. He explained that living with the man on trial for murdering their mother did not provide the children with an acceptable home environment. Then Felder and the city's attorney, Robert Wayburn, questioned Pikul again at length about his aberrant psychological and sexual behaviors as well as his parenting practices and plans. Pikul's lawyer, Paul Kurland, successfully objected to any testimony unrelated to parenting and to testimony that might affect the criminal trial.

Despite Felder's efforts inside the courtroom and despite public pressure outside, Judge Glen, who was, ironically, noted for her liberal and feminist views, continued to favor Pikul throughout the continued hearing. After the third day, she held that she still saw nothing unusual enough in his behavior as a parent to take the children away from their natural father, even during the hearing itself. "Whatever he did or didn't do to his wife, he is presumed innocent until proven guilty," the judge announced. "This court has not determined that he is dangerous to his children at this time." Pikul would be allowed to continue his temporary custody of Claudia and Blake with monitoring by the state's Special Services for Children until the court could reconvene several days later, in mid-January. Judge Glen also issued a temporary order of protection forbidding Pikul from using corporal punishment against the children.

"It took him nine years to murder his wife! He has very little to lose," Felder burst out in frustration. He warned Glen of "playing Russian roulette" with the Pikul children's lives. "He's a murderer. He's a degenerate!" the lawyer proclaimed.

The O'Guins were equally distraught about their inability to effect any immediate change. "The burden is on the one seeking to take custody away," Felder explained to them, "even if common sense tells us the burden should be the other way around." The only reason the judicial system generally works, Felder believes, is because common sense generally prevails. But in this case "common sense would tell you if you were a judge that somehow it doesn't sound right to give children to a degenerate murderer. Here the system failed and there was no other safeguard."

Felder's arguments for common sense had no weight with the court. Judge Glen was adamant about applying the law as it had been written and as it had been interpreted in earlier cases. But Felder's question was right on target. Why, he asked all involved, should the state have to prove neglect to remove the children in such a situation? Why should a third-part custody suit have to show that extraordinary circumstances, as narrowly defined by the court, had destroyed Pikul's parental relationship? If the state found probable cause to arrest him and put him in jail on suspicion of murder, was there not probable cause to rule that his children would not be best served by staying with him—at least until he was proven innocent of the murder charge? Felder believed that from a moral standpoint, if not within the judge's legal interpretation, his opinions were the correct ones.

After Judge Glen's preliminary ruling, Pikul announced that he would take his children back to his Greenwich Village apartment and their schools there. The hearings challenging his right to do so would continue, spread out over four months. Felder, the O'Guins, and the small cadre of Diane's friends working night and day on behalf of her children vowed to fight all the harder.

Undoubtedly Diane's friends must have wondered why she had not left her husband earlier; many had encouraged her to do so. Why don't more women everywhere, adults seemingly in control of their own fates, walk away from violent homes?

Diane's halting efforts to break free from the domestic pain and bondage that gripped her were consistent with the findings of leading sociologists in the field of violence in the family. Richard Gelles of the University of Rhode Island and Murray Straus of the University of New Hampshire write in their book *Intimate Violence* (Simon & Schuster, 1988) that "human beings are less fearful of violence and injury than the violation of social order." Thus, it could be reasoned that they remain with abusive mates, whether physically or mentally abusive, to safeguard the facade of family security and safety and the predictability of their lives. For them, the known, despite its destructive, dehumanizing qualities, is better than the unknown. Other reasons suggested for women remaining with abusive spouses include fear of provoking a violent reaction if they leave, lack of independent financial support, fatalist feelings about the future, shame of public exposure, low self-esteem, and guilt. What's more, many women continue to hope and pray that their men will change.

Through their research, Gelles and Straus found that women who do leave abusive husbands seem to have experienced more severe violence, while those who stay are less educated, have fewer job skills, and are more likely to be unemployed. Diane's later behavior supported both conclusions. Her husband had become increasingly threatening and unpredictable, propelling her toward the decision to leave, and she was well educated and employed. She probably would have been able to support herself, although she was concerned about being able to maintain her life-style. While Gelles and Straus also found that women with young children are more likely to stay in an abusive situation, Diane's concern about her safety, and the safety of Claudia and Blake, overcame any possible yearning to try to keep the household intact.

Some women may rationalize that they are staying in a marriage to protect their children's future, but in fact, spousal abuse is really a form of child abuse as well. "When you hit a kid's mother," says Felder, "you are hitting a kid, you're doing damage to that kid. You really can't separate the two." Even if a child does not witness the actual abuse, he continues, "these kids have to know it. They have to sense it in the response. The household is crazy by definition at that point." Further, some family experts argue that spousal abuse is likely to lead to child abuse. This view alone, says Felder, should affect the other parent's rights as a custodian of the children. But in fact it may not.

The issue of direct child abuse is a separate matter altogether. The problem here is that children have even less wherewithal to seek assistance than does a spouse. Furthermore, as occurred in the Steinberg case, child abuse often continues undetected because both parents are involved. In such a situation, the child is the epitome of a victim, both of a pathological family, when the family should be the child's refuge and source of security, and of the state government, too often characterized by bureaucracy, ineptitude, and overburdened social workers struggling with bulging case files.

Sexual abuse of children is even more difficult to detect and treat than outward battering because the damage, both physical and psychological, generally is hidden. Nonetheless, the problem has been receiving greater attention and scrutiny due to heightened awareness and media attention.

An increasing number of women allege sexual abuse of a child by the father to help guarantee sole custody awards during divorce or to limit or deny the father's visitation rights. Sometimes the accusations are justified; sometimes they are not. In one highly publicized case, Washington, D.C., plastic surgeon Elizabeth Morgan accused her former husband, oral surgeon Eric Foretich, of sexually molesting their daughter Hillary during his visitations with her. When Morgan lost her case, her parents fled the country with Hillary. Morgan went to jail for refusing to reveal the child's whereabouts.

In situations where a mother alleges sexual abuse by the father, the lawyer's first and often worst problem is trying to decide whether the client's charges have any validity. If the lawyer talks a client out of making such allegations—perhaps because the evidence is too flimsy—and the suspicions prove to be true, the attorney has done great harm in not protecting a child. And, of course, the client never forgives such a grievous error of judgment.

If charges of child abuse are false, public accusations from one spouse against the other destroy *any* possibility of the two parents ever working together on their child's behalf. Some lawyers will drop a case of alleged violence when they are unconvinced that a client is portraying what has happened accurately. There is a practical side to such a decision. If a judge believes that the allegations are not well founded, the accusing parent is automatically held in disfavor by the court.

The issue is so problematic for lawyers that continuing legal education programs now teach techniques for assessing the veracity of sexual abuse allegations.

*   *   *

Felder was concerned about the continued deterioration of his relationship with Judge Glen. During the ongoing custody hearing, he and the judge argued constantly. To lessen the strain, Felder tried to avoid going up to the bench to take part in the off-the-record discussions about issues or arguments. He did not want to antagonize Judge Glen. Instead the divorce expert chose to send up Stephen Biener, an attorney from his firm who was helping with the case. Nonetheless, while seeking to avoid unnecessary confrontation in this manner, outside the courtroom Raoul Felder continued to criticize Judge Glen's rulings in the case.

The sparring was no more evident than when the expert witnesses in the case began to testify. Perhaps the most vital testimony for determining Claudia and Blake's future came from the psychiatrists called to offer their opinions.

Dr. Michael Kalogerakis, a sixty-year-old clinical professor of psychiatry at the New York University School of Medicine, served as the court-appointed psychiatrist for the case. He testified first, and Felder objected to the doctor's qualifications as soon as he took the stand. Kalogerakis's practice, complained Felder, focused primarily on adolescents.

"Let me ask you this," announced Felder. "How many children eight years old [Claudia's age] are you presently seeing in your private practice?"

"None," replied the doctor.

"How many children five years old [Blake's age] are you presently seeing in your private practice?"

"None," the doctor said again.

But, Kalogerakis was assistant director of child and adolescent psychiatry at Bellevue Hospital as well as having spent four years as associate commissioner for children and youth for the State of New York. He was also an expert on violent behavior. Judge Glen, who had asked him earlier to help out with the case, ruled that he was qualified to testify.

While on the stand, Kalogerakis, who had interviewed the children at the request of the court, said that he thought Claudia and Blake should remain with their father, but under supervision. A person can be violent toward specific individuals, he explained, and that violence need not necessarily spill over to others.

Felder would not buy this logic. "Doctor, you speak of supervision, going to psychiatrists. One hour a week, two hours a week. How many hours a week?" Felder inquired during his cross-examination.

"I'm sorry?" asked Kalogerakis.

"You speak about having the children go to psychiatrists?" repeated Felder. . . . "And I think you said Mr. Pikul is going to a psychiatrist. I think that's what you said?"

"Yes."

"So let's say that would encompass six hours a week maybe, all these people going to psychiatrists?" asked Felder.

"Yes," agreed Kalogerakis.

"What happens the rest of the time?" Felder demanded. "What control is there the rest of the time though?"

"What would you propose, Mr. Felder?" the psychiatric expert asked him.

"Please, Doctor. *I'm* not the witness. I can propose very simply, but this is not my role here."

"I think," began Kalogerakis, "you are well aware of the fact that a line has to be drawn as to what adequate supervision is. I'm giving you [my] best judgment as to what would be adequate. It's a flexible judgment. I'm not nailing it down to one hour or two. I think that that can be determined on the basis of what unfolds."

"Let's say it's ten hours a week," Felder pushed the point. "Is there anything that would prevent something untoward . . . the rest of the six and a half days of the week?"

"I object!" called out Kurland, Pikul's attorney. "This isn't examination. It's argument."

"Sustained," said the judge.

Felder reworded his concern. "How do you know that six hours a week is going to afford adequate protection or adequate monitoring for what's going on here?"

"I don't, and nobody else does," admitted the psychiatrist.

"And you're ready to take a chance?"

"If we don't take chances, how will the world run?" replied Kalogerakis. "What is the alternative?"

"Who are you taking [chances] on, Doctor," demanded Felder angrily. "You are taking chances with a child eight and [a child] five?"

"You were taking a chance in removing the children from the custody of the father," responded Kalogerakis, referring to his opinion that Claudia and Blake would be better off psychologically with their own parent.

Felder would not give up. "Let's assume, *ad arguendo*, the Pikuls get these two kids—"

"You mean the O'Guins," said the judge, breaking in. Felder was apparently upset by Kalogerakis's responses, and he had misspoken.

"The O'Guins," he corrected himself. "Do you have any worry that the children will be physically harmed?"

"Absolutely none."

"If Mr. Pikul retained custody, do you have maybe [an] itty bitty worry that something could happen to the kids?"

"Yes, I think this is an open possibility."

"Open possibility," Felder repeated slowly. "No further questions."

When the judge herself questioned Kalogerakis directly, he remained steadfast in his original opinion. "As far as the children are concerned," he insisted, "their father is innocent of any of the criminal charges. . . . He is their daddy and they love him and he loves them.

"There is no way in the world," the doctor continued, "that any of us adults are going to be able to explain to those children that we are removing them from the custody of their father, who at the moment is not a convicted criminal, because we fear for their safety when they have expressed no fear whatsoever, and have, indeed, demonstrated a feeling of total safety."

But Felder's essential point was that in all probability the children's security was an illusion. Given Pikul's violent unpredictability, surely their lives were in danger.

A second expert, Dr. Arthur Green, a child psychiatrist at the Family Center of the Columbia Presbyterian Medical Center in Manhattan, also landed squarely in Pikul's corner. He supported Kalogerakis's view that Pikul should be allowed to retain custody of his children. Again the three attorneys arguing the case—Wayburn, Kurland, and Felder—took turns asking questions.

"Although this is a man who has exhibited questionable behavior in certain areas of his life," said Green when Felder cross-examined him, "both in personal areas, in his sexual behavior, and certain problems in the history and problems in the marriage, by and large his relationship with the children appeared to be good, and that, I think, would be the overriding importance."

Felder repeatedly pushed Green to consider Pikul's impulsive behavior record. "Nobody is supervising the kids weekends, evenings," he reminded the witness.

"Sure I have concerns," admitted Green, "but, again . . . the thrust of this man's psychopathology has not been toward the children, and it's theoretically possible that, yes, he could act impulsively towards the children in a similar way that he has acted impulsively toward others who have annoyed him or bothered him or put him down. It's possible, but not likely, since it had not occurred to any degree prior to this."

"He never murdered his wife prior to the murder either, right?" Felder said angrily.

Contrary to Kalogerakis and Green, Dr. Ava Siegler, a clinical professor of child psychology at New York University and an outspoken child advocate, testified that Claudia and Blake would be in danger in their father's care. After hearing about the case, Siegler volunteered to testify. Although she did not interview the children, as Kalogerakis had, Siegler said that in her general professional opinion, any rage that led to the murder of a spouse would be so uncontrollable that it easily could be transferred to other family members.

"When the wife, who has been the scapegoat for his violence and shielded the children from it, has been removed, the children—known to be provocateurs [by their very nature]—are next in line," she testified. Although Siegler indicated that Pikul should have liberal visitation rights, she urged that his visitation always be in the presence of someone else.

As with Kalogerakis, each of the three lawyers questioned Siegler, with Wayburn of the Human Resources Administration going first. In responding to his queries, Siegler differentiated between the impact of the murder charge on a child like Claudia and the impact on a child like Blake. "I believe the five-year-old would be aware on some level . . . but because of the limitations of the mind of a five-year-old, his understanding of [the murder charge] would be much more troublesome and confusing to him."

In contrast, a nine-year-old girl "would be immediately placed in a situation of great emotional turmoil," Siegler continued, talking about a hypothetical case with characteristics similar to the Pikuls'.

"In a case where there has been no previous abuse, in my clinical opinion, the emotional turmoil is [even] greater, because there has been no understanding or comprehension or rehearsal or adaptation to repeated incidents of violence," Siegler explained. "I think that it would be an overwhelming emotional stress for the child. I would expect that that child would begin to display symptoms, but post-traumatic stress disorder in children is often delayed. It can be delayed by as much as six months . . . and sometimes even much more than that. I would say she [the hypothetical nine year old] was definitely in a situation of emotional conflict and struggle.

"Children love us for all kinds of ways that we have. We can be loved if we're cruel. We can be loved if we beat them.

"I have seen children who begged to be returned to psychotic mothers, children who have no trouble loving a father that whips them or whips their mother.

"So for a child to say, 'I love my daddy,' or 'I want to stay with my daddy,' or 'I want to protect my daddy,' or 'I don't believe that my daddy did it,' is not something that we should take on face value. Children love and protect people who can be very dangerous to them. This is the nature of the emotional understanding of child abuse. It's a very difficult matter to understand that we love those that abuse us."

Judge Glen looked concerned, but for a different reason than Dr. Siegler might have expected. "Excuse me for a moment," she said. "In the hypothetical [case under discussion] there is no abuse, there is only the fact of the murder charge."

"That's why I am saying it will be much more of a shock to her with no prior history of abuse and no adaptation [should she learn of the charges against her father]," replied Siegler. The psychiatrist referred also to children's defense mechanisms: "Children operate on the premise [of] 'what I don't know can't hurt me,' and in trauma, and I believe this would constitute a trauma, a child of nine years old would, most likely, begin to heavily rely upon defensive denial in order to continue to exist in the state that she was in. She might even cling much more poignantly to the remaining parent."

Others took the stand as well over the course of the hearing to testify in the O'Guins' favor, including a friend of the Pikuls and a former detective and wiretap expert who had discovered that Pikul had bugged the Greenwich Village apartment in which he and Diane lived. A baby-sitter testified that she had run away from Pikul in fright after one of his outbursts, without even stopping to collect her pay. The same baby-sitter, however, said that she never had seen him hit Diane.

Pikul rebutted them all, steadfastly describing a warm, loving relationship between him and his children. He was supported by a neighbor named Mary Bain, who later would testify that she had been perfectly comfortable allowing her daughter to play with Claudia in the Pikuls' home while Joe was the only adult in charge.

Felder was upset throughout the course of the testimony because he felt he was fighting with the judge constantly, more so than in other trials. While Judge Glen was known to be a women's movement advocate, he thought that in this case she was backing herself into a corner. Perhaps the media's interest in the custody battle was making her feel pressured; reporters had started to run rampant with the story and *New York* magazine had run a cover piece on the trial.

While Felder says he was concerned about the judge's position in the case, Pikul's lawyer, Kurland, was most critical of Felder's aggressive behavior and outspoken statements. Kurland viewed Glen as the white knight in the courtroom, a hardworking, courageous arbiter of justice, an officer of the court trying to interpret the law as accurately and fairly as she could. But then, Glen was ruling in Kurland's favor.

All the while, as the two lawyers fought each other and Felder repeatedly questioned the judge, Pikul—the man whose custody was being challenged—sat in the courtroom seemingly unmoved either by the charges against him or his attackers' outrage. On his coat he wore a large plastic button with a picture of Diane and the children, a badge he proudly displayed to reporters and spectators when he walked in the hallways. He had reason to be proud: At the end of each day's hearing, Claudia and Blake went home with their father.

Nothing during the entire proceeding would change the judge's mind about Pikul, not the charges of erratic violent behavior, not Diane Pikul's murder, not his admitted pleasure in wearing women's clothing, not his allegedly aberrant sexual behavior. Two psychiatrists had testified that regardless of any behavior Pikul exhibited, and regardless of any charges against him, the children's best interests, from a mental health standpoint, would be served by allowing them to remain with their father. After seven days of hearings spread over four months, Judge Glen ruled on April 29, 1988, that Joe Pikul could retain custody of Claudia and Blake. There was, she said, no indication that he would be a danger to them, even if it turned out that he had murdered their mother. Under the current law, she said, she had no other choice. "Despite the heinousness of the crime with which he is charged, and despite isolated incidents of anger and even possible violence in his background, there is no evidence on this record that [Pikul] is physically dangerous to his children," the judge wrote in her opinion.

Nonetheless, to help prepare the children for the future should their father be convicted, she ordered that the O'Guins should visit Claudia and Blake to get to know them better and that they spend increasing amounts of time with them during the summer months. The children would be transferred to the O'Guins' care in September to enroll in a new school they would attend while their father was on trial for Diane's murder later in the fall. (The trial had been postponed from its earlier date.) Pikul would, however, still retain legal custody and would have liberal visitation rights. If he was acquitted, Claudia and Blake would return to him; if he was convicted they would continue living with the O'Guins.

But who knew what would happen to them in the meantime? "We'll appeal and appeal and appeal until rights prevail and these kids are protected," proclaimed Felder, arguing that this case was different from any other. Judge Glen, he said, could have decided differently in a situation as unprecedented as the Pikuls', where a man accused of murdering his wife is out on bail and taking care of their children. Many others also expressed their alarm.

Within the judicial system, the problem of protecting women and children from abuse in the home is one of the most perplexing challenges today, with no good solutions available. "The law is not adequate," says Felder. "It's inadequate to deal with crazy situations."

An order of protection, what Felder had hoped to get Diane, is the best measure available, and yet it can be too little, too late. Legally such an order is supposed to prevent a man from coming after his wife, but "it's after the fact," says Felder. The order is issued in response to an abusive situation that has already developed. "Even if a woman has an order of protection, she can call the police to come help her when need be, but often her husband won't let her near a phone. Then what good is the order to her?" Even if she reaches the phone, the order only makes it easier for the police to arrest her husband after he has hurt her; it cannot prevent the hurt in the first place.

"We live in a primitive society," adds Felder. "The best help is self-help, not in the sense of reparations or retributions [after the fact], but self-help in the sense of prevention." Felder describes self-help as escape—leaving the marriage altogether. How a woman chooses to protect herself while the divorce process is underway depends on the severity of her abuse.

When a wife decides that she can tolerate a violent situation no longer, says Felder, she must first assess the degree of abuse. "There's roughing up and there's roughing up," he comments, noting that a woman must determine if she can hold up during the lengthy divorce process. If she thinks she can, he says, she must keep a diary and document the abuse so that later, a court will believe her. But even if she worries about her welfare, she may have no choice but to wait it out. Most women have nowhere else to go. "Unless she's a really rich person," says Felder, "she's just going to hang in there."

Unfortunately, there are only two levels of prevention: prevention for the rich, and the very limited prevention for the poor. "If a woman has money, she can move into a suite in a hotel," Felder explains, "and that's what they should do. Then go to a lawyer and let justice grind its process while you're spending fortunes staying out of the home. Or," he adds, "hire a bodyguard." He does have some cases where clients have taken this route. (Felder notes that even in his practice, which is more genteel than most, one third of the cases involve some type of physical violence. He estimates that one half of all divorce cases are marked by domestic violence of some kind.)

If a woman is poor, however, there is nothing she can do, Felder continues, unless she is ready to go to a woman's shelter. Even then, there is a limit to how long she can stay. There simply are too many battered women and not enough shelters for them all.

Another alternative is to obtain a court order kicking the husband out of the house. The point is to get the husband away from his wife, because domestic violence usually is impulsive. "Why do you think it occurs most frequently in the bedroom and the kitchen?" asks Felder. "Sunday, in automobiles, a lot of stuff happens. On a lot of occasions they [husbands] push them out of the car, beat them up in the car, in front of the children. If you get him out of the house, that protects the wife from the violence." But, he emphasizes, getting a husband out is very difficult. "The roots of this lie deep in Anglo-Saxon law that says a man's home is his castle."

"The courts are surprisingly hostile to these kinds of cases, believe it or not," concludes the attorney. "They're treated almost as if they're an annoyance." Such a response may be due in part to the fact that the social welfare and judicial systems in this country are overburdened, with little time available to check out the veracity and seriousness of every reported domestic altercation. The lack of serious attention to individual cases also may reflect the fact that so many women are ambivalent about abusive mates and often change their minds after asking the police and the courts for help.

Even more, our overall tolerance for this kind of behavior is far too high. Says Felder, "We live in a very violent society. The threshold for violence is very high," particularly among families from certain cultural backgrounds. And our society supports hiding such incidents. Even when women go to an emergency room for treatment of an injury, their upbringing often has instilled in them an impulse to cover up domestic violence. Thus a woman hurts herself even more by losing an opportunity to document the danger should she decide to seek help later on.

However, once a woman is hurt by her spouse, the system does kick in. If she has a broken leg, for example, the police will arrest her husband for assault. "The law loves broken fingers," concludes Felder. "It's something to look at, it's proof. Most of these men, once they spend the night in jail with the drug addicts, they're able to control themselves [in the future]. It's miraculous." And then they go back home.

But someone who is consistently violent creates a long-term danger. "The key," says Felder, "is to get them out." That will protect a woman from any husband.

That is, unless he is a lunatic like Joseph Pikul.

* * *

Claudia and Blake continued to stay with their father during the spring and into the summer of 1988. Pikul quietly remarried on July 2, 1988, to Mary Bain, the plump but pretty neighbor who had testified on his behalf during the custody hearing. Mary had divorced her husband during the trial. She and Pikul moved to upstate New York, taking his children with them. Mary's daughter from her earlier marriage stayed with her ex-husband.

After the wedding, Pikul petitioned the court to ask that Claudia and Blake remain with Mary rather than the O'Guins during his trial, which was to take place several months later. Judge Glen called a hearing for September 14 to consider the new custody request.

When Mary Bain Pikul took the stand, Felder and the O'Guins knew they were looking at defeat. Testifying about the idyllic small-town life she and her new husband lived in Phoenica, New York, a small community in Ulster County, Mary had all but convinced Judge Glen that there would be no reason to take the children from their current home, regardless of their father being on trial for murder in Orange County. Even the city's lawyer, Robert Wayburn, had almost given up hope of removing the children from the Pikuls' custody. Kurland was savoring his anticipated victory.

Suddenly, as Mary sat in the witness chair, a telephone stationed on a table in the courtroom rang out. The call was for Wayburn. He took it in private from another extension in an anteroom, listened for a few minutes, and then hung up. After asking Judge Glen to step down and talk with him alone, he relayed to her the content of the message he had just received. The judge was shocked.

When Wayburn and Glen walked back inside the courtroom, it was alive with anticipation. Clearly everyone there knew that something had happened.

"Is it good?" Kathy O'Guin asked Wayburn as he took his seat beside her.

"Yes," he replied.

Kathy and Mike, the children's prospective guardians, brightened for the first time that day and squeezed each other's hands.

Having reseated herself, Judge Glen resumed the hearing. As Wayburn questioned Mary, he first reminded her that she was under oath. Then he asked her about an incident involving Joe Pikul and a knife.

Wayburn's office at the Human Resources Administration had received a tip from a report filed by the Ulster County Medical Center in upstate New York. The report said that a woman named Mary Eik had sought help there from a mental health counselor in late August, only weeks earlier. She was afraid of her husband because he had gone after her on repeated occasions, most recently with a hunting knife. Because she also told the counselor that the children were in the home during that episode, the counselor notified the New York State child abuse hot line. An investigation followed, with the findings rushed to Wayburn's office. It was one of his staff members who received them and then immediately telephoned the courthouse. Mary Eik had also admitted to the mental health counselor that her married name was Mary Pikul.

On the stand, Mary stunned the courtroom by confessing that the man she had been defending had slashed eight-inch tears in a dress she was wearing during a fight. The fight had ensued one evening when she returned from the grocery store later than expected. After greeting Mary, the children announced that their father was angry and then ran into their room, shutting the door.

Mary related how she had fled from her husband into the night, racing to a neighbor's house, where she hid in the shrubbery. Pikul chased after her, his flashlight's beam cutting across the darkness. The neighbors were not home, so she waited, but when the neighbors arrived, they did not want to get involved. So Mary spent the night with other friends further down the road. The next morning, Pikul would not let her back inside the house.

Incredibly, Mary tried to discount the incident, describing the knife Pikul used as "Claudia's Girl Scout knife." Listening to the new testimony, Judge Glen's mind must have been reeling.

First, in the earlier hearing, she had relied on Mary's testimony supporting Pikul as a father and on Mary's indication that she would leave her own daughter in his care. Learning that Mary had subsequently married him, an unusual development at the least, must have made the judge question her acceptance of Mary's opinion. After Mary testified about her wonderful life with Pikul in the New York countryside—only to admit later, when confronted with the truth, that she had run away from him while he chased her with a knife—Judge Glen clearly began to doubt the sagacity of her earlier decision. Finally, she began to question Pikul as a human being.

Unconvinced that the incident Mary described was a mere domestic tiff, the judge did an about-face and announced that she would, after all, put the Pikul children in the O'Guins' custody. Kathy and Mike could not believe their ears. Felder was ecstatic. "A knife is a knife," Judge Glen announced to the entire courtroom audience. The story had finally persuaded her that Joseph Pikul was indeed a dangerous man and that his relationship with his children was untenable.

Kurland, Pikul's lawyer, announced that he was quitting. His client looked chagrined but otherwise constrained. When Mary rushed over to hug her husband, he responded woodenly.

Judge Glen issued orders of protection for the children, the O'Guins, all of the lawyers in the case, and Mary Bain Pikul, who protested that she did not want protection. Under the orders, Pikul was forbidden to see his children. His only allowed contact with Claudia and Blake would be a monitored nightly phone call.

One final scene followed: contrary to Judge Glen's orders, Pikul raced upstate after the hearing to try to head off the O'Guins on their way to pick up the children, while Mary, who had volunteered to show them the way, drove very slowly. However, Wayburn had anticipated a problem with the custody transfer and alerted the police. They were able to head Pikul off and stay with the children until the O'Guins finally arrived.

Only a few days later, a neighbor who had cared for Claudia and Blake saw Pikul stopped in his driveway to change a flat tire, and he approached him to help. When Pikul opened his trunk to get out the spare, the neighbor saw something that startled him: lying inside among other belongings were a 12-gauge pump shotgun and an automatic handgun. Later he reported this to the police.

No longer could anyone deny what Felder had always known: it was not in Claudia and Blake's best interests to remain with their father. By the end of the case, Felder says, he had donated around $300,000 worth of free legal time and nonreimbursed expenses. He even gave Diane's original retainer to the O'Guins.

Joseph Pikul's trial for murder began in January 1989; he was represented by two criminal defense attorneys. Although he testified that he had strangled Diane in self-defense after she had attacked him with a knife, the jury did not believe him. They returned a guilty verdict on March 17, 1989.

While imprisoned and awaiting sentencing, Pikul died on June 3, 1989, of complications related to AIDS—cancer of the lymphatic system and pneumonia. Under a peculiarity of New York law, his conviction was erased from the books on August 22 because his appeal was still pending. Technically, Joseph Pikul was never convicted.

Felder had learned earlier, as did others investigating the case, that Joe Pikul had at various times said that he had AIDS. "There are many things you would lie about," reasoned Felder at the time. "You'd lie about your sex life, how much money you make, your education—but you'd never lie and say you had AIDS. That's *not* something you lie about." But Felder, who moved to have Joe tested earlier in the custody hearing, was unable to convince the judge even to consider the possibility. She denied his request, taking a firm legal position that the state could not force the AIDS test.

Perhaps one reason Joe Pikul killed Diane was that he knew he had AIDS. If he killed her, she could not live on after his death and keep the children to herself. If she were dead first, she could never get the best of him, even with his AIDS. And because Pikul had AIDS, perhaps he reasoned that he had nothing to lose in murdering her.

Then again, perhaps Joseph Pikul was simply an uncontrollably violent man.

Today Kurland says that if his client knew he had AIDS, then the only thing remaining in his life after Diane's death would have been spending time with his children. Given that, Kurland also says that Pikul would have allowed the children to live with the O'Guins if he had been permitted free, unsupervised access to them—perhaps one night a week and weekends. But, the lawyer continued, Felder had had no interest in a compromise. Felder had insisted that Pikul have only *supervised* access, with absolutely no time alone with his children. "If Felder, very early on, had offered visitation, fair and reasonable and unsupervised," says Kurland, "Joe indicated he would have gone along with that. But he had no choice right from the outset."

To this day Kurland stands by his defense of Joseph Pikul, and even though his client was convicted of murder, he continues to maintain that he was a good father. "Plus, two of the most prominent psychiatrists in New York said the same," Kurland is quick to point out. "If I make it my job to be the judge and jury, I can't function as a lawyer. My job is to be an advocate for a client." He goes so far as to compare his handling of the case as "a wonderful intellectual and professional challenge. I felt somewhat like Clarence Darrow representing the unpopular cause," he explains referring to the protesters outside the courthouse during the custody hearing. "That's what good lawyers have to do." A father with a daughter the same age as Claudia Pikul, Kurland adds that if he had had "a personal feeling" that Pikul was dangerous for his children, he would not have handled the case.

He praises the other two lawyers and the judge for doing a job "in the best way they knew" and emphasizes that he "*never, ever* made any implied or direct or overt criticisms of the O'Guins as people or of their willingness to come forward. The case was about the right of a parent to be with his children." He feels he had "a courteous relationship" with the O'Guins.

Kathy O'Guin, however, does not feel the same way. Rather, she speaks out angrily against Kurland, whom she regards with distaste. As for Judge Glen, "I thought she was nuts," says Kathy. "I could not believe she was buying their story, that she was looking for a way to leave the kids with him." Kathy is particularly upset that the hearing served only to postpone the inevitable: when she and Mike finally took custody of Claudia and Blake, the challenge of serving as parental replacements had become all the more difficult. Their father, says Kathy, had consistently tried to turn the children against them and everyone else in Diane's family. "The kids were bratty and spoiled when we got them, and Judge Glen allowed him all that time to do this," she says. "They were already undergoing everything a family undergoes during a divorce," Kathy continues. "Glen made sure it was worse than it had to be."

She further disagrees with Kurland's description of her position during the hearing, saying that she would have let Pikul visit if she and her husband had been given custody of the children earlier, but he never offered to approve that arrangement. "He wanted nobody in our family to have the children," she emphasizes.

Claudia and Blake's time of immediate adjustment is mostly over now. "The children will be as OK as anyone is after that," Kathy responds when asked about their progress. "It's our job to ensure that their lives are as OK as they can be."

In trying to reach that goal, the O'Guins have severed all ties with Mary Bain Pikul. Mary has since remarried, this time to a lawyer in a prominent New York law firm. Paul Kurland says that she still professes a strong love and affection for the Pikul children and points out that at one time she even expressed a desire to adopt them.

Robert Wayburn, who had been handling child abuse and neglect cases for the City of New York for ten years at the time of the Pikul hearing, decided after that case that he wanted to enter private practice. He accepted Felder's offer to join his firm, considering it a good entrée into the field. Wayburn stayed there for about eighteen months, until June 1990, and then moved on. He is now with the law firm of Joel Brandes in Garden City, New York.

In some respects the Pikul case is similar to that involving New York City attorney Joel Steinberg and his illegally adopted daughter Lisa, although Steinberg's live-in lover, children's book editor Hedda Nussbaum, never sought to break off their relationship. The Steinberg case evolved during the same time period but received far more national attention because a child was murdered. Joel Steinberg was found guilty of that murder and sentenced to twenty-five years in prison. The Pikul children were only potentially in danger, a significant distinction in the eyes of the law but one that makes little common sense. The sad truth is that millions of children, not just Lisa Steinberg and Claudia and Blake Pikul, live in violent homes. Thousands suffer and die from abuse every year.

Some people familiar with both families' stories have expressed indignation that only the children of wealthy, educated parents can inspire in public the kind of moral outrage that such violent behavior deserves. Children who live in squalor and deprivation continue to suffer and die unnoticed. The greater attention given one group over the other is discriminatory and hypocritical; but perhaps it will always be the recognition of abuse and violence in a familiar home milieu that leads citizens to protest and legislatures to act.

At the very least, out of such reaction comes change, or perhaps the potential for change, that can affect broader segments of society. Felder believes that the Pikul case "may prove to be a landmark case in both legal and judicial thinking on the question of spousal and child abuse." At a minimum, it stretched the limits of child custody law by forcing the courts to acknowledge that in some cases, such as Pikul's, the parent may not be a child's best caretaker, a conclusion that challenges the judicial system's general presumption that natural parents are the ones most able to serve their children's best interests.

At the same time that the Pikul custody dispute was underway, the New York legislature did consider a bill limiting custodial rights of parents if violence has been evident in the home. The legislation would place the burden of proof in these cases on the parent accused of violence—that is, *the parent would have to prove his or her parenting capabilities.* The bill was reported unanimously out of the State Assembly Committee on Children and Family on March 22, 1988. However, it never passed the full legislature, and according to those who worked on the bill, it is unlikely to pass in the near future. Some groups wanted to expand the bill to include additional factors for depriving a parent of custody, and their lobbying created an impasse with other groups that wanted to leave the proposed legislation as it was. And, ironically, feminists began to worry that the bill actually could work against abused women when they resort to violence as a means of self-defense in the home.

In the fall of 1990, both houses of the U.S. Congress passed a resolution recommending that custody not be given to a parent who abuses his or her spouse. The resolution states that doing so would be "detrimental to the child." While attorneys for battered spouses will be able to cite this resolution in custody disputes, it does not have the force of law.

But perhaps legislative change is still in the offing. The Pikul case made it clear, at least in one judicial forum, that violence toward a spouse may be reason enough to challenge a parent's custody. Until state legislatures and courts universally recognize that truth, a void in the law persists. It is a deep, dark void into which women and children will continue to fall.

10

DIVORCE AND THE ELDERLY: TRAUMA IN OLD AGE

Ruth Lebeson v. Harry Lebeson

> *Divorce is the most difficult experience a person goes through alive. I often think that neurosurgeons have it easier because their patients are anesthetized. I have to keep clients not only conscious, but functioning.*
>
> —ATTORNEY IRA LURVEY
> LOS ANGELES

Divorce is stressful at any age, as painful late in life as it is in early adulthood or mid-life. Older divorced women in particular are known to suffer because they must readjust to a completely different life-style often characterized by a decreased standard of living, greater personal responsibility, and limited social opportunities. Older women who have been out of the work force and who look for employment after divorce have an especially difficult time reestablishing themselves. Socially, getting divorced at a later age is much like being widowed, but with an added stigma. Senior divorcées may find they are neglected, even shunned, by former circles of friends.

Although less often acknowledged, divorce is hard on older men, too. Typically they rely on their wives to handle domestic tasks, maintain social and family ties, and provide companionship. For them, the absence of a spouse leaves a vacuum that is hard to fill.

In fact, for both women and men, the older the person and the longer the marriage, the more difficult the divorce process. Habits shift, routines crumble, needs go unmet, and a person's sense of identity may dissolve. In one sociological study, older recently divorced men and women had lower morale scores than their younger counterparts. They were less optimistic about the future.

It is no wonder. The divorced elderly have fewer years to readjust and form new lives, and they are less flexible—mentally, emotionally, and physically—in attempts to change and to start over. Their problems spill over to their families as well, to grown children and even grandchildren who, often in the face of divided loyalties, must guide, support, and nurture these divorcing family members through a traumatic time.

Although the *percentage* of couples divorcing within the entire population of people over age sixty-five is not growing, it is holding steady. This means that the actual *number* of elderly divorces is increasing because the number of people in the over-sixty-five age group is becoming larger every year. And in the long term even more couples may divorce late in life because they are maturing in an era of high divorce rates. The impact of divorce on elderly persons can be particularly devastating because of their limited opportunities for the future and the life-style complications that naturally arise with increasing age.

This was the case with retired business executive Harry Lebeson, whose story is told in this chapter. Harry was ninety years old when his seventy-eight-year-old wife Ruth left him. He had thought that they had a good life and were comfortably settled into old age. The jolt of Ruth's departure sent Harry reeling, and he was able to survive the blow only with the assistance of his daughters, his granddaughter, and his lawyer.

On December 2, 1985, seventy-eight-year-old Ruth Lebeson told her ninety-year-old husband Harry that she would be going to Los Angeles in a few days to tidy up some estate planning with her lawyer. Harry was not surprised by the announcement, nor did he worry about Ruth traveling the one hundred or so miles from their home in Rancho Mirage, California, near Palm Springs. Although Harry and Ruth had been married for thirty-six years, both were previously widowed, and Ruth was an independent woman who knew how to take care of her own affairs.

"The day maid will come in and take care of you, Harry," said Ruth, who was often out in the community lunching with friends or meeting with volunteer organizations to which she belonged. Harry had retired three decades earlier but was still active himself. He had played golf into his eighties. Only recently had his eyesight weakened so much that he was considered legally blind and was no longer allowed to drive.

Ruth left with a driver early on Friday, December 6, telling her husband that she would return the same evening. He contentedly kissed her good-bye and commenced a day of puttering around the house. It was a beautiful home, one the Lebesons had purchased several years earlier when they moved from Chicago to California for its year-round warm climate. The house, situated near the Tamarisk Country Club, which Ruth and Harry frequented, was a one-story contemporary structure graced by large windows and cathedral ceilings. There was a swimming pool in back. Harry relished the hours he passed in a large office in the rear of the house; a secretary came several days a week to help him with his affairs. Managing his investments consumed his interest and required considerable time. Harry's assets totaled more than $4.5 million.

When the phone rang later that day, Harry was surprised to hear Ruth's voice.

"Where are you, Honey?" he asked, feeling anxious about the call.

"Oh, Harry, I've developed such a sore throat that I've decided just to stay over for a few days," Ruth told him. "I'm at the Beverly Hillcrest Hotel. But don't worry. I'm sure I'll feel better soon."

Harry was disappointed but he understood. He and Ruth had both made a point of taking care of their health and she had been hospitalized recently for surgery. He certainly did not want to push her when she was not feeling well.

But Harry did grow concerned when Ruth called again on Monday and said she still did not feel well enough to come home. After worrying all night, he called her back the next morning.

"Why, Ruth, why don't you let me arrange for a driver to bring you home right now. You'll recover quicker here than in a Los Angeles hotel," he suggested. He was lonely and he missed having her in the house.

"Don't fret, Harry," she replied. "I'm feeling better now and I'll be home later today. Jim will drive me." Ruth often relied on her sons from her first marriage who lived in the Los Angeles area. Jim Levy was the older of the two.

It was not Jim who finally called Harry that evening, but Ruth's other son, forty-eight-year-old Richard Levy.

"Dad, I've been trying to get you," he announced. "Mom's OK, but Jim and I really think she ought to stay here one more day. I'll be driving her back tomorrow. We'll arrive around suppertime. We hope you'll be there waiting for us."

"Well, certainly," responded Harry. He did not like Richard. Their relationship had always been strained, and Harry was critical that his younger stepson lacked professional ambition. He was, in Harry's eyes, a ne'er-do-well, and the old man was uneasy that Richard had been the one to call. "Tell Ruth I'll see her then. Drive carefully," Harry added and hung up the phone.

Ruth's day trip had turned into several days and nights, and he was anxious for her return. Even though Ruth had her own friends and activities, they were seldom apart for long, and Harry depended on her. He asked the maid to prepare a special dinner that day, a minicelebration upon his wife's return. Richard and, perhaps, his wife Lois would be joining them.

The following day, Wednesday, December 11, Harry waited, like an excited child expecting an important guest. When the doorbell finally rang, he rose from his easy chair and eagerly crossed the living room, heading for the front hall to open the door himself.

But when he got there, it was not Ruth who faced him, her arms full of packages and a smile on her face, as he had so fully anticipated. Instead, a deputy sheriff, in full uniform, stood sternly in the doorway.

"Are you Harry Lebeson?" the deputy sheriff asked.

"Yes, I am," replied a shocked Harry, his voice low and shaking as he tried to fathom the meaning of the sheriff's presence. The young man handed Harry a legal document.

"What is this?" demanded Harry.

"I think you better read it, sir," responded the deputy sheriff.

He made his way back to his office and placed the document under the specially lighted magnifying machine he used for reading. Harry could hardly believe the words that appeared. "NOTICE!" the paper announced. "You have been sued. The court may decide against you without your being heard unless you respond within 30 days. Read the information below." Harry's eyes pushed ahead. "If you wish to seek the advice of an attorney in this matter, you should do so promptly so that your response or pleading, if any, may be filed on time." Harry slowly eased himself into his desk chair.

"The petitioner has filed a petition concerning your marriage," he read on. "If you fail to file a response within 30 days of the date that this summons is served on you, your default may be entered and the court may enter a judgment containing injunctive or other orders concerning division of property, spousal support. . . ." Harry felt his chest grow tight. "The garnishment of wages, taking of money or property, or other court authorized proceedings may also result."

It became clear so quickly. Ruth was leaving him. She wanted a divorce.

Attached to the divorce summons was another paper announcing a hearing to force Harry from his own home. Ruth was claiming that he threatened her, both physically and mentally, so she wanted the court to issue a "kick-out" order, in effect putting him, a ninety-year-old man, out on the street. Harry felt sick.

At the top of the documents he saw the name of Ruth's lawyer. It was one Harry had heard before, a celebrity lawyer, someone, he recalled, who had been in the newspapers frequently. It was the name *Marvin Mitchelson.*

A flamboyant Los Angeles divorce attorney, Mitchelson is perhaps most famous for coining the term *palimony,* which stands for "alimony for pals." He first used the expression in 1979 when representing Michelle Triola Marvin in her lawsuit for half of the assets of actor Lee Marvin, with whom she had lived for seven years. The court upheld the concept of palimony for live-in lovers, but Mitchelson won only in theory because eventually his client was deemed undeserving of financial support. While palimony suits have continued to attract press attention, they are rarely successful. Nevertheless, Mitchelson continued to build on the fame he had garnered from the Lee Marvin suit.

Ruth Lebeson would be one more new client who hoped that a heavy legal gun like Marvin Mitchelson would blow her husband Harry away.

While Harry was being served by the deputy sheriff, Ruth remained at the Beverly Hillcrest Hotel. Both Richard and Jim were with her that day. The sons were especially close to her because their father, an insurance man, had died in a plane crash while the boys were still young.

"What do you want to do now, Mom?" Jim asked.

"Well, I suppose I'll stay here a few more days," she replied, shuffling some papers that she had stacked on the table in her hotel suite. "I will stay with each of you for a few days if I need to, and I can also stay with my sister Peggy and her husband, and with friends." A distinguished-looking, still vigorous woman, Ruth had dressed herself in a fashionable outfit, as she always did, as if this day was no different from others.

"What I want the most," said Ruth, her face grim, "is to get back in that house and get rid of Harry. I love that house; I created it. And I will just feel so much better when I don't have to deal with him there anymore." The arthritis in Ruth's hands was hurting and she rubbed them absentmindedly.

"He doesn't give me any money and he never involves me in anything financial," she continued, as if to draw courage from her own words. "He lies to me. You know that, Richard." Her son nodded. "He even hides our accountant's and lawyer's papers from me. I'm sick and tired of being excluded. What happens with our money and our affairs is my business, too." Ruth's anger was still building. She was especially worried, even panicked, that Harry was changing his will, leaving all of the assets he had brought into their marriage to his two daughters, with nothing for Ruth.

"He lies to you, Mom," agreed Richard, supporting his mother's concerns. "You've been naive too long."

"It's been too hard on me dealing with his attitude," she continued, acknowledging her son, "and he won't understand how I feel when I try to talk about it. So now I've had it. I want to be rid of him. I want to be on my own."

Richard looked at his mother sympathetically. He wanted her to be rid of Harry, too, even though he had been Richard's stepfather for a long time. He claimed that Harry had been mean to his mother, belittling her and treating her as if she was beneath him, and he resented Harry's overt favoritism of his daughters.

Whether any of these accusations were true is unclear. It might have occurred to Richard that if Harry did leave the bulk of his wealth to his own children, there would be little left for their mother to pass on to him and his brother. Richard's wife Lois had helped find a solution to the dilemma by providing Marvin Mitchelson's name. After all, Lois worked as a legal secretary at a law firm, so she should know who best could rescue their mother and guarantee her financial security and long-term comfort.

Harry, of course, had no divorce counsel at the time because he had had no idea that he would be getting divorced. In fact, he had not even known that Ruth was unhappily married to him; he had promised to leave her their house, which was in Harry's name, when he died, and he always felt he had made the appropriate arrangements for Ruth in his will. In fact, Harry had showered gifts on her during their entire marriage. Why should she want to leave him now? Clearly he and Ruth were operating under different assumptions about their marital relationship and their feelings and responsibilities toward each other.

Harry called his estate planning lawyers in Chicago and asked them what to do about the divorce papers. They referred him to another estate planning firm in Palm Springs, thinking that that firm would at least know the local divorce bar. In addition Harry contacted his two daughters and also a granddaughter who was an attorney in Berkeley, California. The Palm Springs estate planning lawyers found a small general practice firm where the lawyers knew the local courts and judges and how they operated. Harry asked that firm, Schlesinger, Fitzgerald

& Johnson, to serve as part of a legal team on his behalf; they immediately began to fight Ruth's petition to kick Harry out of the house. At the same time, Harry's granddaughter began a personal search for the very best full-time family law practitioner she could find. After several days she referred her grandfather to Ira Lurvey, a fifty-year-old Los Angeles divorce attorney.

Lurvey had worked for almost twenty years as a trial lawyer with a large Los Angeles firm, but he had left in 1984 to form his own family law boutique, where he could be in full control of a small, select clientele. While large general practice firms have been adding a divorce specialty as the area becomes more sophisticated and lucrative, most of the star divorce attorneys around the country prefer the more personalized style that characterizes boutique law firms. They continue to work in small offices with a handful of young associates and few or no partners.

When Harry contacted Lurvey, his stature in the divorce bar had grown considerably and he held a number of posts in family law organizations in the state and nationally. Lurvey clearly relished the challenge of his divorce work, which catered to affluent West Coast couples. He liked to refer to it as "the antitrust of the eighties and nineties," in reference to the many complicated and sometimes esoteric financial manipulations such marital dissolutions entail.

Harry paid his new lawyer a ten-thousand-dollar retainer. He had noted at the bottom of Ruth's income and expense declaration form, which was attached to her petition for divorce, that she had paid Mitchelson's office twenty-five thousand dollars, two and a half times as much. "Is Mitchelson really that good?" Harry wondered. He did not know then that the price tag on some high-powered divorce lawyers would double, and even triple, within a few years after his own case.

Ruth's suit for divorce was a shock to Harry, but he was no stranger to life's jinks and jolts. A Russian émigré orphan who would always speak with an accent, he worked his way through Ohio State University to become a veterinarian and served in World War I as a vet to the cavalry. Following the war Harry married his first wife, Sarah, and resigned his commission to pursue his entrepreneurial bent, giving free reign to his keen interest in industrial development. In 1929 he founded a tool engineering firm named the Allied Screw Machine Company. He quickly recognized a shortage of skilled workers, so he also established one of the first vocational schools in the United States, the Allied Institute of Technology. Forty years later it would be acquired by the International Telephone and Telegraph Corporation.

While Harry experienced early professional success, he faced tragedy at home. Sarah suffered from severe headaches—she had been hospitalized for them even before marrying Harry—and in 1930 she became intensely ill and died. Harry hired a housekeeper to help raise his two daughters; eventually Leah became a clinical social worker and ombudsman for Stanford University and Shirley went into private practice as a psychologist in northern Virginia.

Harry met and married Ruth almost twenty years after Sarah's death. He was fifty-four years old then and a very successful business executive.

Having overcome such early hardships, he developed a confident and assured demeanor which he maintained even in later life when he could not see well and wore a hearing aid in each ear. His gracious manners gave him an aura of refinement in old age. But Harry also remained a hardened entrepreneur, one with a knack for turning a dollar to his advantage. Although his authoritative manner had commanded respect and helped him build a fortune in his prime, his strong personality and will at times worked to his detriment in later life. Ruth found that her husband could be unbearably domineering, and any relationship Harry initially developed with her sons deteriorated over the years of the marriage.

Even though Harry had sought out Ira Lurvey and asked him for legal help, Lurvey initially regarded Harry as a father figure, a wise and seasoned veteran in the affairs of the world. But before the case was over, Harry would become so devastated emotionally and so confused that the two of them would switch roles. The attorney would be the one to protect and bolster his client, who would break down and cry.

Before Lurvey became involved in the Lebeson case, Harry's Palm Springs lawyers managed to get any initial hearing postponed for several weeks. In the meantime, Harry could stay in his house undisturbed and Lurvey could get to work on the divorce. With Harry still at home, Ruth refused to go back, even to stake her claim. She said she was just too afraid to face him, that he was a dangerous man for her to be around. She had no justification, however, to make such a claim, one that appeared ludicrous on its face, and she never tried to prove it. Most likely she simply was intimidated by Harry's manner and, in particular, his rage.

Ruth did ask her son Richard to drive her north to the Palo Alto condominium that she and Harry owned, where they spent part of the year near Harry's daughter Leah. She took from the condominium her clothes, the paintings from the walls (Ruth was a painter herself and much of the art was her own), and some of the other household items she wanted. But this did not appease her for long. By the end of the month she could not bear staying away from the Rancho Mirage house. At the very least, she told herself, she needed to get some more clothes.

On December 30, Ruth, Richard, and one of Richard's friends, named Willy, drove to Rancho Mirage. Ruth still had her keys, and the three of them walked in unannounced. Harry was in the living room.

"Ruth!" he said, shocked at her sudden appearance. He had never seen Willy before. "Who are you?" Harry demanded.

"I hired him to drive me down. He's a friend of mine," responded Ruth coldly. "I've come to get some of my things."

She headed for her closet in the bedroom and began taking dresses off the rack. With half a dozen draped over her arm, she then went to Harry's office and grabbed a raincoat and a topcoat from the closet there.

"Those are my files," Ruth announced to Willy and Richard, pointing in the direction of some steel cabinets along a wall. "Take them."

Harry was stunned. Ruth was pointing to his files. "Where are you going?" he asked, panicking. Willy and Richard had pulled three entire drawers off their gliders and were carrying them out of the room. "Hey, those are my files!" Harry shouted after the two men.

"I'm going back to Los Angeles," replied Ruth. "And those are *my* files. This is *my* house. You've given it to me—you've put it in my name—and you know it!" She walked out.

Richard was already halfway down the driveway, walking hurriedly, his arms wrapped around one of the heavy drawers. Harry rushed after him and frantically grabbed Richard's shirt, trying to hold him back. "Call the sheriff! Get the police!" Harry screamed out to his secretary, who had been in the office when Ruth arrived. But Richard just kept walking. Willy already had placed the two other drawers in the trunk of the car. He turned back to help Ruth with her clothes.

A week later Ruth returned to the house. This time, she announced, she had come to stay and guard her ownership rights. She brought Richard, whom she had asked to move in with her to protect her from Harry. When they arrived, entering through the back door, Harry was asleep in a chair. They walked past him, greeted the maid, and carried their suitcases into the guest bedroom and the den. Richard, who also brought some tools, installed new locks on the doors to those two rooms. He and his mother then walked back into the office to confront Harry.

Harry woke with a start. "What are you doing here?" he said, looking at Richard.

"We're going to stay here. We have every right to, because this is my house," replied Ruth.

"No, you're not," countered Harry, struggling to his feet. "You can't do that, or I'll call my attorneys." Frantic, he dialed Lurvey's office.

"*What!*" exclaimed the attorney. "They really have their nerve, don't they? But stay calm, Harry. I'll call Mitchelson's office and get them out."

"I can't stand Richard, he's horrible," pleaded Harry. "He keeps calling me 'the old man,' and he actually relishes going against anything I say. I've *never* been able to get along with him." Harry was as distraught as he ever had been.

Lurvey dialed the number and leaned back, his full-bodied frame pressing against his chair. "This is Ira Lurvey," he announced, trying to restrain his own anger. "I'm calling about the Lebeson case. Get me Mitchelson."

"I'm sorry, sir," the secretary responded, "but he's in conference now. May I take your number and ask him to call you back?"

Lurvey bristled with annoyance. While he was a gentle man in private life, a family man with six children, he was more like a cantankerous and ill-tempered grizzly when confronting professional adversaries.

Mitchelson did not call Lurvey back, but William J. Glucksman, another attorney in his office, did. "Mr. Lurvey," said the voice, "this is Bill Glucksman. I'm going to be handling Mrs. Lebeson's divorce for Mr. Mitchelson." Mitchelson sometimes delegated cases to other lawyers working in his office, claiming that he simply could not handle every single one. Glucksman, thirty-five, had taken over a number of matters for Mitchelson before, so he was used to carrying the ball for the more senior and more famous lawyer. Regardless of how disappointed Ruth might have been that she had lost her heavy hitter, her divorce case was simply added to Glucksman's list. He, in turn, did not mind that Mitchelson got much of the credit, particularly for the high-profile divorces of local movie stars and celebrities, because he had convinced himself that the opportunity to work on such big-money, complicated, and visible cases developed only as a result of his affiliation with the infamous Mitchelson. If the junior lawyer had been a sole practitioner working on his own, his daily fodder surely would have been far more bland and uninteresting.

Glucksman was unsympathetic when Lurvey voiced his complaint about Ruth and Richard's treatment of Harry. They were totally within their rights, he said. In fact, Glucksman had suggested that Ruth move back in.

"But if you want them out," he advised Lurvey, "your client should consider giving Mrs. Lebeson something to live on, just for now. I'm thinking of something in the neighborhood of twenty thousand dollars." Ruth had told her lawyer that Harry had canceled her credit cards and that she had no funds to meet her expenses while the divorce was pending.

"I won't bargain like that, Bill," Lurvey responded angrily. "Get back to me with something better than that." He slammed the receiver down.

Lurvey decided to document in writing, as many lawyers do, his fierce objections to Ruth's behavior. "Dear Bill," he typed into the word processor by his desk. "In our telephone conversation this afternoon, I asked you please to remove Mrs. Lebeson and her son, Richard Levy, from the house to which she and Richard barged in this afternoon and after being absent since [the] filing of the dissolution."

Lurvey took a deep breath. He had once been a reporter for the wire service United Press International and he usually wrote easily. But after twenty years of law practice, sometimes the legal style of writing, or "legalese," could cloud his thinking. "I particularly was distressed," continued Lurvey, "to hear from you that Mrs. Lebeson had returned to the house with Levy on your instruction. Her return in this traumatic fashion with Levy, a sworn enemy of Mr. Lebeson, may cause Mr. Lebeson, age 90, heart failure or other medical emergency. The advice was unconscionable. Please consider that you, personally, will be held responsible."

Harry was a client whom Lurvey was going to handle carefully. While his mental acuity and physical activities belied his age, he was still ninety years old. Lurvey would be especially gentle in helping him come to grips with Ruth's leaving. Harry would have to reevaluate his feelings about his marriage and family and learn to live without Ruth, and that was not going to be easy.

"I don't see how Ruth can claim that she is afraid of me," Harry told Lurvey when the lawyer called back. "I cannot even remember raising my voice to her in my life, let alone giving her cause to fear me." He could not believe that he had been anything other than a wonderful, loving husband.

"What do you think she wants, Harry? Why has she done this?" Lurvey asked.

Harry was at a loss. He couldn't imagine that their petty disputes and the inevitable difficulties of old age were enough to drive Ruth away.

"But what about your stepsons, Harry?"

"To tell you the truth, I think Richard is worried—and rightfully so,

I might add—that when I die, he and Jim won't get anything in my will. So now Ruth is trying to help them by getting my money ahead of time, through a divorce, and guaranteeing that those two will profit."

In fact, Richard was worried that Harry would leave most of his estate to his daughters, with fewer assets for Ruth. Naturally, the two brothers would be penalized later, when they received a smaller inheritance from their mother than they might have otherwise.

Even though Harry did not understand Ruth's frustration about the management of their financial affairs, speculation about his stepson was plausible; Richard very well might have been fanning the fire of Ruth's discontent. Children from first marriages often complicate subsequent marital relationships with their own personal concerns, which are often financial, and parents themselves feel conflicting allegiances. Once the divorce process begins anew, adult stepchildren commonly add to the animosity in their zeal to protect individual inheritances.

"Ira," Harry told his attorney, his voice breaking with humiliation, "Ruth and Richard lock me out of the rooms wherever they go. Ruth won't let me answer the phone and she took the mail today before I could see it. They eat by themselves and I have to wait until they're finished to get anything for myself. This is just intolerable." He sounded as if he was about to cry.

The next morning, January 9, Lurvey called Glucksman. This time the secretary said that he was out. "Tell him," Lurvey said pointedly, "that tomorrow at one P.M. I will be in the Riverside County Superior Court in Indio requesting a restraining order to bar Levy from Mr. Lebeson's house." The Indio, California, branch of the county courthouse had jurisdiction over the city of Rancho Mirage. Before the case was over, Lurvey would travel there many times on Harry's behalf, as well as to his house, where they would meet and discuss the divorce proceedings. "And if I must," Lurvey also told Glucksman's secretary, "I'll have Mrs. Lebeson kicked out as well." He typed another letter to Ruth's lawyer, informing him in writing of exactly the same thing.

Lurvey prevailed in court and the judge ordered Richard Levy out of the house. Ruth decided to go with him. Both Lurvey and Glucksman were there to watch them leave.

But a few days later Ruth and Richard returned again, and before Harry even knew they were back, Ruth had slipped behind the wheel of their 1978 blue Chevrolet Caprice and driven off. The next day, she and Richard came back in the car so she could get some more of her clothes. Richard waited out front while his mother went inside the house.

Without looking for Harry, Ruth headed directly for the bedroom. As she sorted through the closet racks she heard some shouting out on the street and a car horn blaring loudly.

Dropping her clothing on the bed, she rushed to the front door. Once outside, she saw, to her utter surprise, that Harry was driving the car away, with both the trunk and the hood open. Richard was standing in the street looking helpless and disgusted. "He's stealing my car! He's robbing me!" Harry was screaming as he pressed on the car horn with the heel of one hand and held onto the steering wheel with the other.

"What happened?" Ruth asked her son as she rushed up to him.

"He came up to the car and got in and started hitting on me with his fists," Richard replied. "Then he told me to get out of the car because it was his car. So I got out. And he drove away."

"Well, we'd better stop him," said Ruth, looking more annoyed than concerned. "He has no license."

She headed toward the garage, where she kept her golf cart. She and Richard got in and they drove around the corner toward the Tamarisk Country Club.

As Ruth had suspected, the Chevy was parked in front of the club's entrance, the hood and trunk door still up in the air. "You take the cart back to the house, Richard," she commanded, "and I'll take the car. I'll pick you up there." Harry was nowhere to be seen.

Ruth kept the car. She felt it was hers; Harry was not supposed to drive. And Ruth wanted the car for her many civic activities as well as for those at the country club. Ruth planned to continue her involvement with the local art museum. She also had been president of the Women's Board of the Jewish Federation of Palm Springs and chairwoman of the local chapter of the American Heart Association, and she maintained her interests in both organizations. She needed the car and Harry did not.

While Ruth was making her repeated forays to the house, Lurvey was working furiously to expedite Harry's divorce. The Lebesons' living situation had become intolerable since both he and Ruth wanted the house and neither would agree simply to coexist there while a final resolution was pending. Because Harry and Ruth were elderly, their lawyers knew that the stress of the divorce was especially difficult for them. Perhaps the only issue Bill Glucksman and Ira Lurvey did agree on was their genuine desire to help the Lebesons resolve their case quickly so that each could begin to live their last years in peace.

The two attorneys scheduled depositions for two days in late January.

Harry, Ruth, and Richard Levy were to be deposed. The lawyers for both sides needed to gather facts and get ready for the first hearing in the case. It was set for February 7.

Lurvey took Ruth's deposition first. Her face set with determination, she fixed a piercing, steely look on Harry's lawyer. She looked hard and cold. Her answers were uttered stiffly. In response to many of the questions Ruth said she could not remember. Before the day was over she was so fatigued that Glucksman had to call the proceeding to a halt earlier than planned.

Lurvey had even less success when he tried to continue the deposition the following morning. Again, Ruth's memory failed her, and Lurvey grew combative with frustration.

Glucksman was hardly passive himself. A tall, lanky man who looked as if he should be shooting baskets rather than fighting legal battles, he wrapped his long legs around the rungs of a chair at the conference table where they sat and scribbled furiously on a legal pad. "Objection," he called out regularly as Lurvey tried to question Ruth. "Wait! Hold it!" Glucksman would warn his client, instructing her on many occasions not to answer. Lurvey was being argumentative, Glucksman would say, he was harassing Ruth, or his questions were vague and ambiguous. "I don't want her coached," countered Lurvey. The deposition sounded more like a cat-and-dog fight than a civilized legal proceeding.

"Mrs. Lebeson, do you presently have in your name any property?" Lurvey asked as he continued his questioning. "In your name. Are you aware of any property?"

"Yes, sir."

"What?"

"My home in Rancho Mirage."

"Other than that."

"The question is not clear to me," replied Ruth. "Are you talking real property or what property?"

"Anything in the world, Mrs. Lebeson," sighed Lurvey. "Do you have any property anywhere that you hold—"

"Anything?"

"Yes, ma'am. Other than the clothes that you claim and whatever jewelry you've recited to me that you physically presently possess." Lurvey wanted to point out that Ruth was not living the life of a pauper. Harry had lavished her with gifts throughout their marriage.

"My clothes," responded Ruth finally. "That includes my furs and my jewelry."

"That's it, is that right, Mrs. Lebeson?" replied Lurvey sarcastically. "That's the totality of it? Clothes, furs, jewelry and whatever claim you have to the Rancho Mirage house, right?" Lurvey was growing impatient because he knew that Ruth had more. "Can you recall any *additional* jewelry that you possess beyond what you've described?"

"In total, yes. I cannot describe it in detail," Ruth replied.

"In total, Mrs. Lebeson?" Lurvey asked. "I don't understand. Do you have a total value?"

"I mentioned I have—" Ruth shot a glance at Glucksman. "I don't have a total value," she said, changing her mind and turning back to Lurvey.

"Do you have a partial value?" he asked.

"I don't have a value that I can give you at this time."

"Or that you've ever had in your memory?"

"No, I don't have any total value to give you at this time," Ruth repeated.

"Is there some other time when you'll have it, Mrs. Lebeson?" Lurvey was growing scornful. "You keep emphasizing 'at this time.' Are you aware of a value someplace?"

"Objection," shouted Glucksman. "Argumentative. Instruct you not to answer," he said pointedly to Ruth, who glowered at Lurvey.

"I don't think it's necessary to sneer at me, Mrs. Lebeson," said Lurvey. He was experiencing an intense dislike for the woman.

"Perhaps she feels you're sneering at her," replied Glucksman jumping to his feet. "The tenor of the examination has not been particularly pleasant." Ruth's lawyer was worried about her health and the strain the deposition was placing on her.

"Mr. Glucksman," said Lurvey, obviously restraining his own anger, "you've got a lady here who's trying to throw a man out in the street. Take all his property, end a relationship by surprise after 36 years. And I'm simply trying to find the answers to the questions so we'll understand what the lady leaves with. That's all we're doing. And Mrs. Lebeson has been extremely combative through the testimony, and I really don't need that. I'd ask you to use your good offices, which I have great confidence in, to explain to your client that nothing is gained by taking me on as an open adversary."

"Wait a second," retorted Glucksman. "I would ask you, Mr. Lurvey, to maintain some degree of respect for a 78-year-old lady whom I think you've treated like a 30-year-old drug-addict child abuser in a custody case." Glucksman was livid. "I would hope that we can maintain a manner of examination with both of these elderly people. We both have clients who are elderly and not in the best of health."

"I couldn't agree with you more," replied Lurvey.

•   •   •

As senior citizens, Ruth and Harry Lebeson were part of a demographic trend. The sixty-five-plus age bracket has grown over the last
two decades at least twice as fast as the rest of the population. And
the numbers of elderly will more than double over the next forty
years—from 31.6 million in 1990 to 65.6 million in 2030. By that time
they will compose more than one-fifth of our nation's population.

If the annual rate of divorce in this age group continues to hold
relatively stable, as it has over the last twenty years (about two men per
thousand married and 1.5 women per thousand married), the absolute
numbers of older couples divorcing will rise with the projected population growth. (Presumably the sixty-five-plus age bracket includes more
divorcing men than women because some of these men are married to
women who are younger than sixty-five.)

As with Harry and Ruth, the divorced elderly face particularly severe
emotional trauma. The problems of marital dissolution are accompanied
by other changes simply related to getting older, such as lessening mo-
bility and worsening illness. Both Harry and Ruth had been sick and
needed extensive care. New support systems must replace the companionship and assistance that each spouse had provided the other. Furthermore, the elderly—and the problem grows as age increases—find it
difficult to change their role identities from that of "wife" or "husband"
to a "single" individual, and they are uncomfortable reaching out. Even
if older divorced people find that they can change, they have fewer
new alternatives from which to choose.

At the age of ninety Harry Lebeson was indeed an extreme example
of an elderly divorce. But like other older people who separate from
their spouses, he had to change his self-image and begin a new life as
a single person, all the while recognizing that his options for rebuilding
that life were severely limited. It was unlikely that Harry would ever
marry again, or strike out and make new friends, or move to a new
community, or even develop new hobbies.

As Harry's divorce lawyer, Ira Lurvey set only two goals for his client. First, he wanted to safeguard Harry's financial well-being. Second,
he wanted to help Harry regain his dignity and sense of self-worth so
that he could enjoy the remaining years of his life.

Richard Levy's deposition was even rougher than his mother's. It
seemed that he could not—or would not—answer most of the questions
Lurvey asked. He did indicate that he had been divorced three times
before marrying his current wife, Lois, but refused even to identify his

social security number or tell where he lived, except to say his home was in the Malibu area. He claimed that he could not recall the exact details of his employment over the last two years, but after a long string of questions Lurvey finally was able to ascertain that he drove a cab in 1983 and had been largely unemployed since then.

"Mr. Levy," Lurvey charged, "other than being a cab driver intermittently, being a process server for law firms occasionally, building a house for your wife and family which you have stopped doing as of December 5, 1985, have you had any other employment since the beginning of 1983 that you presently recall?"

"Objection!" shouted Glucksman. "Irrelevant, not likely to lead to the discovery of admissible evidence in this case. I'll instruct him not to answer."

Lurvey then asked Richard about meeting with Ruth's lawyers, about moving back into the Lebesons' house with his mother, and about the incident when Harry drove off with the car, but his obdurate manner persisted. Ruth's son would not provide the full answers that Lurvey sought. After several hours, Glucksman asked Lurvey to hurry up; he still had to take his turn deposing Harry and get home that night in time for a family commitment. But the two lawyers still had time to pepper the deposition transcript with snappish remarks. As with most depositions, there was no judge present to referee the fighting.

"Is your testimony," said Glucksman to Harry, "as we sit here, under oath—"

"Whoa, Mr. Glucksman," broke in Lurvey. "That opens up with a little bit of intimidation. Do you want to start your question fresh again without the intimidating—"

"I'm so thrilled," countered Glucksman sarcastically, "[that] you recognize intimidation, and have exercised it, and—tried to exercise it—unsuccessfully, I might add . . ."

"Mr. Glucksman." Lurvey was trying to sound patient. "You don't mean that, and I'll ignore it. Why don't you just ask a regular question, Mr. Glucksman, and we'll answer."

"If a court is to decide," continued Glucksman in addressing Harry, "that you stay in the house or Mrs. Lebeson stays in the house, can you tell me any reasons why Mrs. Lebeson should not be the one to stay in the house?"

"Okay," snapped Lurvey. "Objection, Mr. Glucksman. You're not asking the witness to prepare opening and closing arguments. That question is totally improper. Asks for speculation, asks for a legal conclusion on the part of a witness. The question is ambiguous."

"I refuse to answer that question," interjected Harry. He looked pleased with his pronouncement.

"Mr. Lebeson," Lurvey said to him patiently. "Please don't refuse to answer questions. If I object to their form or their appropriateness, that's my job. Your job is to simply give facts under oath, Mr. Lebeson.

"Please," Lurvey continued, "you've heard these other people behave in the fashion that the court will address, but I don't want you to behave that way, sir. So you answer the question after Mr. Glucksman asks a proper one.

"Will you," Lurvey asked Glucksman, "please reframe your question?"

"Mr. Lurvey," replied Glucksman, "that last comment of yours is a good point to end, because it's typical."

"Any time you want, sir," said Lurvey, suggesting that Glucksman get on with it and finish up. "It's 4:15."

"It's so typical," continued Glucksman, "of the manner in which you have disrespectfully treated these people."

"Sir," said Lurvey, appearing to restrain himself, "the facts in this case are there, and I'm embarrassed that—"

"I guess I'm embarrassed, too," snapped Glucksman, and then he and Ruth and Richard Levy marched out of the room.

Despite their vituperative exchanges, Lurvey and Glucksman found that their mutual desire to close the Lebeson divorce case quickly helped them begin settlement discussions within a few days after the depositions. Their clients' health was an important consideration. Both lawyers knew that the strain of a trial would be more difficult for the Lebesons than for a younger couple. And they knew that, generally, any couple is more likely to abide by an agreement that they reach themselves, as opposed to a resolution that is forced down their throats by a court.

So on February 7, 1986, the day set for the hearing to determine whether Harry would be forced from his home, the two lawyers sat down in a conference room at the Riverside County Superior Courthouse in Indio and finished crafting a complete settlement agreement.

Although Ruth originally had demanded the Rancho Mirage house and $14,760 a month in support payments, the drafted settlement said that Harry would keep the house and their Palo Alto condominium and give Ruth one-third of the rest of his estate, or $1.5 million. Because Ruth would be getting a lump sum payment she agreed that she would receive no additional monthly support. Maintenance and health insurance coverage are more important considerations in divorces of moderate-income couples with limited assets, especially when one spouse is less equipped to reenter the job market because of age or lack of skills.

Under the Lebesons' settlement, Ruth also would keep the jewelry and furs Harry had given her, and he would keep the car for use with a hired driver when he needed one. Ruth would keep all of the furniture, furnishings, art, and antiques she brought into the marriage, but she would return to Harry everything else she had taken from their homes.

Richard Levy agreed, as part of the deal, to stay away from Harry's house, and Ruth and Harry promised not to disturb each other as well. All in all it appeared to be a satisfactory resolution of their dispute. After all of their years together, the marriage finally would be over.

Once in the courtroom, Lurvey stood before Judge Fred Metheny. He read out loud the final settlement, word-for-word, from a handwritten draft so that Harry, whose failing eyesight kept him from seeing the paper easily, could indicate that he understood it.

Glucksman then put Ruth on the stand to gain her formal approval. He made it clear to her that the settlement took into consideration several conflicting factors. In California, for example, property gained during a marriage is split in half when a husband and wife divorce, and under that rule Ruth could have claimed half of all of the Lebesons' holdings. However, Harry maintained that a substantial portion of their estate was his own, separate property that he alone had brought into the marriage from his prior business earnings and investments, and if his claims had been substantiated during a trial, Ruth would have received half of very little. To complicate matters even further, the Lebesons had signed an earlier agreement providing that upon Harry's death, Ruth would receive the Rancho Mirage house, which had been purchased in Harry's name with his money. That agreement could have further influenced the judge if he had been forced to dictate a division of the Lebesons' assets following a full-blown trial. Ruth might have received the house, but then she might have received fewer dollars than she wanted.

While the two lawyers talked, Harry's daughters, Leah and Shirley, and Ruth's sons, Jim and Richard, sat silently behind their respective parents, lending their support and offering their tacit approval.

Metheny was very pleased. Like all judges, he was concerned about the inordinate number of cases burdening the court system, and every settlement helped lighten the load. He declared that Ruth and Harry's divorce would be effective on June 11, 1986, six months from the date Ruth filed. But before adjourning, Judge Metheny announced that he wanted to say something.

"It's my responsibility to advise both these clients," he began in a soft voice that contrasted sharply with his college football and ex-Marine physique. He then asked Harry and Ruth to respect and stay away from each other. "Be what you are," he said to them, "a lady and a gentleman." They looked straight ahead, neither acknowledging their recent behavior. "I think it's amazing," the judge continued, "that you've had a marriage this long and you are as young as you both look. You look younger than I do. I'm sorry it happened this way." But, he added, "that's your business and not mine." Judge Metheny found it hard to understand how such an attractive, dignified, and well-mannered elderly couple could have come to this end.

Finally, he thanked the lawyers. "I appreciate the way you handled it," he said, emphasizing the end result and ignoring any earlier fighting. "It makes me very proud of the law when it's done right." In all, he said, the case had turned out well.

At least it did up until that point. Within days the two sides started arguing again over the details of the settlement, asking for modifications to the wording, some picayune and some more substantive, changes to which the other side could not agree. Ruth felt that Harry and his lawyer were not acting in good faith in beginning the stock transfers necessary for executing the agreement, so she wanted to change the settlement to make it more detailed for her own personal safeguard. Harry, on the other hand, felt that Ruth should sign the agreement as approved by the court before he began to give her her share.

Soon Ruth began to question the settlement, wondering whether she had given up too much. She also felt that Harry was continuing to hide the necessary financial information from her—and even from Lurvey. So she took a copy of the settlement agreement to her original lawyer, Los Angeles attorney Barry Friedman, to ask his opinion. It was in Friedman's office that Ruth's daughter-in-law worked; he was the one who had recommended Mitchelson as a divorce attorney.

Initially Friedman had supported Ruth in seeking a divorce when she explained that she was worried about what would happen to her when Harry died. She said she was convinced that he secretly was arranging to leave all of his assets to his daughters; because almost all of his wealth belonged to him independently before he married Ruth, she would not be able to claim it as community property upon Harry's death. This would be true in any state, not only in California. In fact, Harry could, legally, dispose of his wealth in any way he pleased.

When Ruth contacted Friedman later to tell him about the settlement Glucksman had arranged, the first attorney became alarmed. He felt that the divorce plan had not worked as he had envisioned and that Ruth was going to be shortchanged. Friedman announced that he would become involved in the case again. He would contact Glucksman and monitor the settlement to make sure that it was executed in Ruth's favor. Harry, Friedman said, had to start paying up.

Friedman's sudden involvement in a case that Glucksman had been handling—and handling professionally at that—was an aggressive move on his part. Whether he convinced Ruth that Glucksman had not gotten a favorable settlement and had to be fired or whether Ruth decided on her own to have Friedman take over is still unclear. Regardless of who made the initial decision to bring him into the case, Friedman barged into the negotiations during the months that followed, becoming increasingly embroiled in discussions between Lurvey and Glucksman over the transfer of Harry's property and funds. Although Lurvey was caught off guard and even dumbfounded by the intrusions, Glucksman never objected. Perhaps he was simply more passive in nature, or perhaps he consciously decided not to engage in a head-on battle with Ruth's other lawyer.

Friedman repeatedly challenged both the terms of the settlement and the manner in which it was proceeding, questioning in particular any unfavorable tax ramifications that might fall to Ruth. He also claimed that he could not even get an inventory of the amounts of money held in Harry's various accounts. The haggling over details escalated.

As Friedman's involvement grew, a full-scale battle broke out, marked by an almost-daily barrage of letters and far surpassing the first fight in both name-calling and gamesmanship. Lurvey and Glucksman had tried to work together, but it soon became clear that Lurvey and Friedman would be forever like oil and water. They would argue around, over, and under each other, each constantly perplexed by the other's interpretation of the settlement agreement, each convinced that he was behaving appropriately.

On March 5, about one month after Harry and Ruth had agreed to the settlement, Glucksman wrote Lurvey a five-page letter detailing new corrections and additions he and Ruth felt should be included in the agreement. He requested, for example, that Harry promise to stay away from Richard, just as Richard had promised to stay away from Harry.

"Absolutely not," responded Lurvey in his return letter two days later.

The request is insulting to Mr. Lebeson, though I am sure you simply are conveying what you were requested by Mrs. Lebeson or one of her other present attorneys or advisors. . . .

The issue is moot in any event. It is inconceivable that Mr. Lebeson will find himself anywhere in the presence of Levy, a resident of Malibu; and Mr. Lebeson, 90, functionally blind, infirm, still devastated by what he considers to be the deception and economical deflowering he suffered by an unexpected divorce in which Levy admittedly was an active protagonist, certainly is in no position physically or mentally to seek out unemployed Malibu cab drivers. Please do not raise the matter again.

Lurvey also told Glucksman that he thought Harry was meeting the terms of the settlement as quickly as possible.

There has been no delay in any documentation or transfer. An intricate arrangement of publicly-traded stocks has to be divided in Chicago [where Harry's accountant worked], and that is as you know already in process. You are being kept fully advised. We want the matter completed as quickly as you do. I appreciate that all you are doing is responding to unreasonable demands posed to you; but they unnecessarily clutter the record and help no one.

Despite Lurvey's protestations, by late March Friedman's involvement had intensified to the point that he was totally overshadowing Glucksman. While Harry was following the settlement discussions closely, Lurvey wanted to shield his client from this new round of bickering. He wrote to Friedman in protest. "Dear Mr. Friedman," he began.

You apparently are totally out of control in this matter. I have in hand two separate letters from you dated March 21, one of them consisting of four pages, single spaced, the other, two pages, addressed to [Harry's accountant] Randy Shaw; separate two-page letters to me dated March 24 and 25, both sent by messenger on March 26, and one [mailed to my office and addressed] to my client, Mr. Lebeson, dated March 24. . . .

While Friedman was functioning as a zealous advocate on behalf of Ruth, his aggressiveness was getting on Lurvey's nerves. The paper flow was overwhelming.

Glucksman had faded further into the background with Ruth's consent until Friedman finally notified Lurvey that *he* would be the only lawyer representing Ruth Lebeson. She wanted it that way, he said, and further communication with Glucksman would be inappropriate. Yes, a disgruntled Glucksman acknowledged, he was no longer in charge or even consulted. In fact, Ruth finally had fired him. Friedman filed a notice with the court that he, not Glucksman, would continue as the counsel of record in Ruth's case. Both Ruth and Glucksman had signed the document.

In the meantime, Ruth and Harry each complained regularly to their respective lawyers about the other's behavior. Ruth, for example, had asked Harry to forward any mail and telephone messages that she received at the Rancho Mirage house.

"I can't understand it," she told Friedman during one of their many telephone consultations. "I always received a lot of mail—every day—and my friends called me all the time. Harry is keeping all this from me. He's trying to cut me off from everything I ever had. He'll stop at nothing." Ruth was frustrated that her husband seemed to be getting the best of her.

"I'll write Lurvey today," Friedman reassured her. "Don't worry. This kind of behavior is unconscionable."

When he hung up he dictated a letter and asked his secretary to send Ruth a copy.

For his part, Harry thought Ruth was keeping from him, among other things, important documents that he had stored in the file cabinets she had had Richard and his buddy take from the house. Harry could not find his citizenship papers or his passport. When Lurvey asked that Ruth return them, she suggested that Harry look in the bottom drawer of his file cabinet. But upon doing so, he found nothing.

Day after day and night after night, the Lebesons mentally catalogued their various possessions, their papers, their souvenirs, their mementos, trying to figure out if each had claimed everything they possibly could. This kind of pettiness is not atypical in a divorce, but it is demeaning nonetheless.

With Glucksman out of the picture, Lurvey and Friedman continued to fight out the Lebeson battle in the Indio courtroom before Judge Metheny, who grew disgusted with their inability to bring to final closure what had been a reasonable settlement. It was almost as if the two attorneys had become the adversaries in the dispute and their clients, Harry and Ruth, had receded into the shadows of the courtroom. Rather than taking the time to plow through all of the financial documents himself—and the judge questioned whether he would be capable of mastering their intricacies—he wanted the lawyers to work out the resolution.

"Gentlemen," said Judge Metheny during a June 20 hearing, "I know you're trying to do your best. You're doing everything you possibly can, almost shooting at one another with loaded guns, and we're not going to achieve anything if we go in that direction. I think that we're all tough. I know I can be tough if I have to be," he added. "The way this case ought to be handled is that you two gentlemen should work it out to the best of your ability."

But the attorneys continued their combat. Lurvey claimed that he did not understand why Friedman was holding up the execution of the settlement, when Lurvey was trying to do everything in his power to expedite it. But Friedman told Judge Metheny that Lurvey was in fact stonewalling, dragging his feet, and Ruth was afraid she would be cheated out of her due. When one side pointed to specific allegations of stalling or cheating, the other simply returned the accusation. Finally Judge Metheny suggested that an independent court-appointed CPA study the financial information provided by both Harry and Ruth and make a recommendation for resolving their disagreements.

"I've almost cried for you guys on this particular case," said the judge at a July 11 proceeding attended by the CPA. "It's just one of those cases that doesn't move up and forward. It bounces around. It's been bouncing around for quite awhile."

He even pleaded with the lawyers. "You gentlemen are here," he said. "I don't see any reason why you can't get together and work this out. Don't come in here and tell me 'he's not talking to me.' 'He won't do anything I ask him to do.' I'm simply suggesting that you gentlemen, you lawyers, are going to be polite to one another. If you don't play it straight, we'll have to play Texas rules. You know what Texas rules are don't you?"

"I think I do, sir," replied Lurvey. "I'd rather play by Indio rules," he added, indicating that he would prefer following the legal practices found in Indio, California, courtrooms. In truth, Lurvey was not sure what Metheny meant by "Texas rules."

"What an ass-kisser," Friedman would recall thinking. He didn't know what Metheny was talking about, either.

But he kept pushing. Friedman asked the judge to set a deadline for Harry to pay Ruth's share of the settlement, ignoring the fact that they could not reach a final agreement on exact terms.

"Look, I'll tell you how you're dealing with me," barked back Judge Metheny. "When I tell you to drop your gun, drop it." He clearly liked his gunslinger analogy.

"Got it. We'll do it," said Lurvey.

"You get it?" Judge Metheny asked Friedman. "Both of you guys?"

"Yes, sir," replied Friedman. "Would the court give me a deadline?"

"I'll tell you to drop your guns!" the judge practically shouted. "No more of this gun fighting between you guys!"

He ordered them to get to work with the CPA. "I've got a death penalty case to work on," the judge announced, indicating that there were more important matters on his calendar than disagreements over assets in a previously settled divorce. And he left the bench.

In mid-October the CPA delivered a preliminary report of his findings and recommendations to the lawyers and Judge Metheny, and the two sides again met in the judge's courtroom. After nine months of wrangling, Harry and Ruth agreed to divide Harry's stock as the CPA had suggested, with Harry giving Ruth an additional $56,490 to satisfy any arguments or controversies that still remained. By this time, Friedman acknowledged, Ruth's attorney's fees for the divorce were up in the $100,000 range. For his part, Harry had paid Lurvey in excess of $100,000, much of it, says the lawyer, consumed by responding to Ruth's attacks after the first attempted settlement. Friedman's advocacy clearly had resulted in higher legal bills on both sides. "I think the relationship between the people involved is probably a lot less aggressive than the attorneys that represent them," concluded Judge Metheny. Whether Ruth's attorney was justified in rejecting outright Glucksman's original settlement and continuing Ruth's litigation for so long is open to debate.

Actually, once the case finally finished and the lawyers backed off, Ruth and Harry began speaking again. Harry even invited Ruth back to the house for dinner, and she came.

"Dad, I wish you wouldn't see her," Harry's daughter Leah told him. Her stepmother had hurt her father in the harshest way imaginable. But when Harry would not listen, Leah and the family decided not to argue with their strong-willed patriarch, who still, unbelievably, wished that Ruth would come back to him.

Although Harry got the better end of the divorce financially, neither he nor Ruth won emotionally. That late in life they would have been better off trying to resolve their differences. Ruth should have spoken up about her estate planning concerns and Harry should have been more open about his financial activities. He had been married to Ruth for a long time, and some trust must have been built between them. Harry, knowing that he was elderly and would not live forever, should have allowed Ruth full access to his files.

For her part, Ruth might have reevaluated her own expectations. After all, Harry had earned almost his entire fortune before their marriage. He was justified in wanting to leave an inheritance for his daughters rather than passing everything on to Ruth, who would in turn pass it on to her own sons. If Harry had gotten along with his stepsons, perhaps he would have felt differently about them. But given Harry's and Ruth's individual and marital histories and their relationships with their respective children, his only obligation to her was to guarantee that she be comfortable and well cared for should he predecease her. He had shown clear signs of wanting to do this by arranging to deed the Rancho Mirage house to Ruth at the time of his death.

Despite Harry's eternal hopefulness following the divorce that he and Ruth could become friends again, he realized after several visits that the feeling she had once felt for him was forever dead. He finally decided that she would always care more about what he could give her than about being with him.

"I'm sorry, Ruth, but I don't want to see you again," he finally told her. "I now feel sorry for you, for the way you feel. It is all over between us."

On December 16, 1987, not long after he last saw Ruth, Harry Lebeson was sitting at his desk reading a large-print edition of the *The New York Times* with his special magnifying machine when a pain grabbed his chest so fiercely that he could not call out for help. He collapsed from a massive heart attack and died.

One of the provisions of Harry's will endowed a Stanford University chair in cancer research in honor of his son-in-law Henry S. Kaplan, a Stanford medical professor and Leah's husband, who had died while pioneering new techniques in the use of radiology for cancer therapy.

"I am proud of what I have accomplished in my life, but I can honestly say that nothing makes me quite as proud as being part of the Henry S. Kaplan–Harry Lebeson Professorship of Cancer Biology at Stanford University," Harry had announced a few months earlier during a Stanford ceremony honoring him.

Ira Lurvey also attended the ceremony, with a very special pride of his own. He felt that despite Ruth, despite the divorce, despite all of the humiliation Harry had suffered, his dignity and sense of self-worth had been restored.

Several months after Harry died, the State Bar of California received a confidential request to investigate Marvin Mitchelson's role in Ruth's case. On November 7, 1988, bar officials filed formal disciplinary charges against Mitchelson for allegedly unethical behavior. They said that he had charged Ruth too high a fee, had delegated the case to Glucksman after promising to handle it himself, and had refused to provide Ruth with an accounting of his fees or a refund of unearned fees. The bar also charged Mitchelson with ethics violations stemming from other cases he had accepted. In a subsequent interview Glucksman candidly acknowledged that clients who hire Mitchelson—and who pay his significant fee—may feel that Mitchelson should do the work himself.

Although state bar officials would not comment on the outcome of their investigations into any of the Mitchelson charges, they obviously decided that he had misrepresented to clients his personal involvement in their cases. *The (San Francisco) Recorder* reported in May 1990 that while some charges had been dropped (including the charge of excess fees) and others were still under investigation, Mitchelson had admitted to a number of ethical errors, including the following: "failing to supervise an attorney working under him; failing to communicate with a client; failing to promptly refund unearned fees to former clients; and failing to 'fully communicate to his client the extent to which he would delegate responsibility for her matters.'" The similarity with Ruth Lebeson's complaints against Mitchelson is so striking that one could assume that the admitted violations resulted directly from her case. Ruth's son Richard Levy even said later that Mitchelson had admitted to the charges related to his mother's divorce. At that time, however, a punishment was still undetermined; it would be based on a then-unscheduled hearing where both Mitchelson and the state bar could present their own evidence.

But by then Ruth Lebeson was no longer interested in the bar's activities, looking instead to put her divorce case behind her. Although she was a millionaire as a result of her settlement, she was not wealthy enough to maintain her social calendar and the contacts she had in Palm Springs when she was married to Harry, so she moved to Leisure World near Newport Beach, California. There Ruth developed a new circle of friends and continues to play golf and paint, according to her son Richard, to whom she refers all questions and defers many decisions. Richard and his wife Lois moved, too, but they settled farther away, in Sausalito, north of San Francisco, where they live on a boat. It is unclear whether they benefited directly from Ruth's divorce settlement. Without a doubt, however, Richard Levy was very glad to have Harry out of his mother's life, and out of his own as well.

One can only wonder if Ruth, alone in her old age, was truly happier, too.

11

HIRING A DIVORCE LAWYER

When Sally Paulson's husband of ten years left her, she started looking for a lawyer. She interviewed a large number—fifteen, to be exact—with a list of questions in hand. How many cases had they settled and how many had they taken to trial? How many women had they represented and how many men? Were they divorced themselves and, if so, were they the ones who had initiated their divorces? Paulson, who lives in Potomac, Maryland, also followed her gut instinct, considering the lawyers' personalities and whether she actually liked them. She ultimately hired an attorney who was low-key, kind, and gentle, a "Mr. Nice Guy" whom she hoped could work out a reasonable and satisfactory settlement.

Paulson was happy with her lawyer for about six months. He filed the appropriate papers and requested a seemingly fair division of her and her husband's assets. But before the case could be resolved, her husband decided to refinance their marital home and borrow some of the equity. The lawyer advised her to agree to the refinancing, despite the pending divorce suit.

"My lawyer was of the old-boy school," says Paulson. "He said, 'He's giving you all this'—that is, he's paying my bills—'so you should be happy.'"

But she remained skeptical about the refinancing, not wanting to put her share of the home equity at risk. The attorney repeatedly tried to soothe and reassure her, and she found his behavior condescending. One day "when he patted me on the head as I left," she recalls, "I knew I was in trouble." She fired the lawyer and turned to another whom she had interviewed earlier but rejected.

Originally she had not hired this lawyer because he was so aggressive she thought he "would start fires," Paulson explains today. But she realized that that was exactly the kind of lawyer her husband had chosen, so she needed one to match him. "Bombs were dropping all around me and I wasn't even in an air raid shelter," Paulson says.

But even with this second, harder-hitting attorney, she was not certain she had made the right choice. The new attorney told her the case had to be continued (postponed), yet she couldn't understand why. "It was dragging on and it was not to my advantage psychologically," she said. So she told the lawyer off.

"I got him moving real quick," Paulson notes with pride. "He called me back apologizing and said, 'I like you so much, I like you so much.' I said, 'that makes me want to throw up. I want results.'"

Lawyer stories abound. Many clients are unhappy with the service they receive, if not their ultimate results.

There are certain expectations for all lawyers, observes Joel Henning, an attorney himself and a Chicago-based consultant to law firms. "First, you expect good lawyers to return clients' phone calls on the same day. Second, you expect them to tell the truth, for example, whether they have or have not met with opposing counsel. And third, you expect them to prepare."

Henning told of one divorce where he was amazed to learn that none of the lawyers met all three expectations. The husband's lawyer was totally unorganized and didn't return calls, Henning relates. "But he never lied and he was prepared." The wife's first lawyer, he continues, had a great reputation but lied about the work he was doing; when he said something was done, it was not. Her second lawyer was earnest and sincere yet simply could not handle the more sophisticated business aspects of the case.

Divorce lawyers vary drastically not just in quality but also in style. Kenneth Kressel, author of *The Process of Divorce* (Basic Books, 1985), found in his research that the highly elite divorce specialists practicing in and around New York City fell into six different categories or philosophies of representation. He labeled them as follows:

The undertaker—a cynical and pessimistic lawyer who thinks the job is a thankless, messy business.

The mechanic—a pragmatic, technically oriented attorney who simply implements what clients say they want.

The mediator—an attorney who seeks a negotiated compromise while emphasizing cooperation with the other side.

The social worker—the lawyer concerned primarily with the client's long-term adjustment and general welfare.

The therapist—one who seeks to address the client's emotional turmoil prior to solving legal problems.

The moral agent—an attorney who imposes his or her own sense of what is fair on a client, rather than basing case strategy on the client's objectives.

Given such variations in quality and style, and given the public's limited knowledge about divorce representation, it is little wonder that clients often are disappointed. Too frequently they choose a lawyer whose approach poorly complements their own temperament and needs. Or they hire a lawyer who cannot handle the opposing attorney's tactics.

Making Money

Despite the diversity among divorce lawyers, these practitioners do have some traits in common. While they generally enjoy helping a client through a life crisis, their efforts are never totally altruistic. Lest anyone forget, divorce lawyers are in business to make money. The question that arises at the outset, then, should be, Is it worth the price? Or, more important, When people hire a divorce lawyer, do they even know what it will cost them? *Does it have to cost that much?* Today's family law experts charge anywhere from less than one hundred dollars an hour in a small town to more than three hundred dollars an hour in a major metropolitan area. The highly publicized services of New York matrimonial lawyer Raoul Felder cost $450 an hour. That means that his clock ticks at a rate of $7.50 a minute.

Divorce lawyers know they are expensive. They also recognize that clients are typically so upset, if not outright hysterical, that even those experienced in business and finance may have their sense of reason clouded by emotional turmoil. If the lawyers do not make sure that their clients understand up front how much legal representation costs, they may have trouble collecting their fees after the divorce.

"Since divorce proceedings are emotional and clients are not likely to have had previous experience with legal fees," Houston divorce attorney Donn C. Fullenweider advises colleagues in *Trial* magazine, "take care to ensure that clients understand fee arrangements. Fee-collection difficulties in these cases are often rooted in misunderstandings from the earliest meetings between clients and counsel."

Fullenweider urges all divorce lawyers to require that clients sign a written fee agreement, or contract, before taking on a case, and most successful divorce attorneys do follow this practice. But Fullenweider does not acknowledge that some clients may be so distraught that they sign without understanding what the contracts say. Others may feel suspicious and distrustful of lawyers whose first concern is to guarantee the feathering of their own nests. With this attitude, how can lawyers say they put their clients' welfare above all else?

Typical agreements, called "fee agreements" or "retainer agreements," dictate the ways in which the lawyer will bill and how the client must pay. The agreements can include information about hourly rates for the attorney and for any associates and paralegals who might also work on the case. They may indicate whether hourly rates will be higher for time spent in court. They also might describe the format and frequency of the lawyer's bills, that is, whether they are monthly, quarterly, or at some other interval.

Fee agreements also explain whether a lawyer charges a "retainer" in advance of the case. Exactly what this means depends on the attorney. Some view retainers as deposits, billing their hourly rates against them and asking for more money when they exceed the initial payment. They refund any part of the retainer that is not used.

Other lawyers bill against the retainer, but if any money is left over, they keep that, too. Still others—and the most successful are among them—require nonrefundable and noncreditable retainers called "acceptance fees." Hourly charges for work done are additional.

Some lawyers even charge a "result fee" at the end of a case, a bonus or "kicker" assessed on top of earlier fees if they think they did a particularly good job for a client. Information about result fees should be included in the written fee agreement.

Regardless of individual billing practices, for many divorce lawyers the initial retainer, or advance payment, is sacrosanct. "The fee, which often is substantial, should neither be payable in installments nor refundable," argues Long Island attorney Willard H. Da Silva in the magazine *Family Advocate.* "If the client cannot afford the retainer, he or she can borrow from parents or relatives, sell a piece of jewelry or securities, refinance a car, or obtain a personal bank loan."

Once a divorce is over and a client refuses final payment, the lawyer may follow in hot pursuit. One nationally recognized divorce practitioner tells of a colleague who foreclosed on a client's house when she could not pay his bill. This same lawyer has been known to run out of his office an independently organized collection agency—specifically to collect on his own accounts.

Supporting an Industry

A lawyer's professional fee is only the beginning. Expenses add up alongside the retainer and hourly billing charges. These can include court filing fees, photocopying, payments for expert witnesses, such as accountants and child psychologists, travel costs, and investigator and private detective fees. The tab can skyrocket if a client wants to track down his or her spouse's out-of-town lover, complete with hotel bills, or dispute the value of marital property.

The list of possible experts in a divorce case looks like a career counselor's guide to job opportunities: investigative accountants (to find out about hidden assets), business accountants (to verify the accuracy and authenticity of financial statements), and tax accountants (to analyze the tax consequences of proposed property settlements); real estate appraisers, business appraisers, and other appraisers (to determine the worth of such personal property as antiques, art, and jewelry); pension actuaries (to analyze the worth of pension plans); and, finally, psychologists and psychiatrists (for child custody disputes). Clients pay not only for the time these experts spend testifying in the courtroom but also for time it takes to prepare testimony plus travel expenses.

Lawyers are inclined to rely heavily on experts. They do not, for example, want clients coming back to them after a divorce claiming that the worth of a particular asset was far more than the value given to it during trial. In extreme instances such complaints can lead to charges of malpractice. Lawyers also prefer to see that judges are guided by the professional opinions of outside experts, particularly in child custody disputes. This is considered safer than having a judge make a final decision based on his or her own experiences and personal reactions to a husband, wife, or child.

When one spouse—often the wife—cannot pay the legal bill and expenses, her lawyer can ask the court to make her husband pay both lawyers and everyone else involved on both sides of the case. Some people have suggested that attorneys whose clients cannot afford legal services should charge a contingency fee, or a percentage of the property awarded to their client in the divorce, just as personal injury lawyers charge a percentage of the awards they win. But such arrangements are unethical. In 1987 a Chicago judge ruled that a divorce attorney unfairly charged his client a contingency fee. The attorney had taken 25 percent of the client's share in a company for which her husband had worked.

Battle, Fame, and Glory

Lawyers do enjoy their incomes, but they also love a good fight, perhaps none more so than the litigator. Divorce specialists are a type of litigator, and they, too, relish the opportunity to champion a client's cause. Of course, this is what the client wants and needs, but the degree of warring can, in some cases, become extreme. A good divorce lawyer will seek a settlement, or compromise that can acceptably meet the client's needs, and only then, if that fails, rush into battle with sword drawn. But those who relish a high-profile existence—or have strong ambitions for their future careers—are the ones most likely to escalate a lawsuit to guarantee themselves a prominent role in the courtroom.

From the client's point of view, aggressiveness can be good and bad. If a lawyer is a strong advocate, he or she *may* be doing a better job than would a more passive attorney. On the other hand, an aggressive approach usually consumes time and runs up the client's legal fees. This does not mean, however, that the converse is better. A lawyer who settles too easily definitely keeps the tab under control, but may forfeit potential gains that could have been won through additional negotiation or in trial.

"Beware of 'barracuda' lawyers who fan adversarial flames," warns San Francisco attorney Melvin Belli, a famous personal injury lawyer who also handles divorces and who has been divorced himself five times. "However," adds Belli in his book *Divorcing* (St. Martin's Press, 1988), "be just as aware of don't-make-waves lawyers who sacrifice your best interests by not fighting hard enough for them."

But how can inexperienced clients decide how much is enough? Understandably they may find it difficult to identify that ideal middle ground, especially if they have no baseline or earlier experience against which to compare a divorce lawyer's activity. Rather, they must research other people's divorce experiences, ask other lawyers for their ideas, and seek the advice of additional experts knowledgeable in the field. Deciding how to pursue a divorce suit is a risky decision. At the least it should be an informed risk.

Whatever a lawyer's strategy, the best in the profession pride themselves on their winning records, either in court or through favorable settlements. Happy clients provide a source of compliments to feed these attorneys' sizeable egos. Generally outgoing and self-confident, they bask in success and eagerly collect kudos, not only from clients but also from fellow lawyers, judges, and the general public. For some, the biggest boost for the ego is in representing exceptionally wealthy or famous clients. They draw on these clients' power and prestige to build an aura of success and mystique of their own. While some lawyers may refuse to divulge their clients' identities, others readily spew forth names of business tycoons, movie stars, sports figures, and politicians (and their spouses) who have sought their counsel.

Such self-promotion is self-fulfilling. Powerful clients do enhance the stature of a divorce lawyer, and seeing this, even more clients flock to the attorney's door. People who are getting a divorce often think that a famous lawyer's name alone is enough to scare a spouse into submission. Many believe, for example, that Marvin Mitchelson's backing means automatic victory; little do they realize that he may delegate a case to others working in his office. While it is Mitchelson's name that appears in the court file, whether it is worth the price—often tens of thousands of dollars—is uncertain.

Along with big-name clients, high-profile attorneys prefer cases involving high stakes and intellectually challenging issues rather than run-of-the-mill suits involving limited property and money. The latter, especially since the introduction of no-fault divorce, are routine and no longer particularly interesting. Instead, community property and equitable distribution laws have made large-asset divorces the hot ticket items. On the other hand, the best divorce lawyers are less inclined to accept custody cases, which are equally grueling but less challenging intellectually. These trials often turn on subjective, emotional arguments; the parties' behavior is heart-wrenching; and no one really wins, especially not the children.

Ethical Pitfalls

Like other professionals, divorce lawyers face certain recurring ethical challenges, and some do succumb to temptation. "The grievance committees that handle lawyer disciplinary complaints see a large number of cases arising out of divorce law practice," writes Arlington, Virginia, attorney Richard E. Crouch in an article, "Ethics Aspects of Family Law Practice," published in the national magazine *Trial*.

Consider as an example the case of Wisconsin attorney Leslie Webster, reported in *The National Law Journal* in August 1990. A client whom Webster had represented in some business and real estate matters announced that his wife wanted a divorce, but that he hoped for a reconciliation. The client then asked Webster if he knew whether his wife had been romantically involved with any men. Webster simply replied that infidelity would not affect a court's decision about custody of the couple's children.

The catch? Webster himself was having an affair with his client's wife. Worse yet, he agreed to act as a scrivener in preparing the legal papers the couple would need for a divorce, and he accepted a retainer from both partners as advance payment. When the husband, Webster's client, found out about the attorney's relationship with his wife, he fired him and got another lawyer.

After a lengthy disciplinary investigation, the Wisconsin Supreme Court ruled that Webster's behavior was "deceptive" and reprimanded him. Even then he continued to insist that he had done nothing wrong. His punishment was surprisingly light.

But not all lawyers cross over the line of unethical behavior so willingly. Sometimes they err through a lack of skill or sheer sloppiness. Those most likely to get in trouble are general practitioners who take on divorce clients as part of an overall, varied case load and who are not up-to-date in the domestic relations field. Divorce law is changing so quickly and becoming so complicated that simply keeping up is a challenge for legal generalists. When general practitioners are guilty of ignorance, incompetence, neglect, lack of communication, or bad advice, their clients are the ones who suffer, and their dissatisfaction can lead to charges of unethical behavior or malpractice.

Even lawyers specializing in divorce face sizeable challenges maintaining the quality of their representation. Those who are overbooked and overworked may be guilty of neglecting a case, missing a filing deadline, or not communicating with a client, all among the more common violations of the attorneys' ethics code.

Those lawyers who more knowingly engage in unethical behavior often choose one particularly controversial area: sex. Some—and the stories are legion—misuse the power of client relationships to make advances toward individuals they supposedly are helping. Such activity, particularly reprehensible because of the divorce client's vulnerability, violates the very essence of the lawyer's moral and professional obligations.

Lawyers themselves are aware of the ease with which they can fall into this sex trap. Lynn D. Feiger, a partner in the Denver law firm of Feiger & Hyman, addresses the problem in *Family Advocate.*

> The phenomenon known as "transference" in psychiatric literature results when the client inappropriately and usually unknowingly transfers or displaces feelings from a marital or close family relationship to the professional relationship. A woman client may find herself suddenly attracted to her male attorney, who would under other circumstances not be so irresistible.
>
> Often attorneys fail to recognize transference because of their own needs for high self-esteem and flattery. Failure to recognize transference can easily result in abuse of the attorney's role at the client's expense.
>
> Perhaps the single most frequent ethical abuse by attorneys in the context of emotionally troubled clients involves sexual overtures toward the client. The emotional difficulties of divorcing clients render them particularly vulnerable.

Lawrence Dubin reports in a 1988 *Georgetown Journal of Legal Ethics* that none of the state bars' ethical codes directly confronts the problem of lawyers having sex with clients. Dubin suggests that divorce lawyers be prohibited from pursuing sexual relations, even when the client initiates the activity.

> Most divorce lawyers will acknowledge that it is not uncommon for divorce lawyers to engage in sexual relations with their clients. In fact, a few divorce lawyers with whom I have discussed this article have candidly admitted to sexual relations with their clients. One can surmise that the frequency of this situation is greater than most lawyers would care to admit.

Since Dubin's article, one state bar—the State Bar of California—adopted an ethics rule restricting sexual relationships between lawyers and their clients. This new California rule prohibits attorneys from requiring or demanding that a client engage in a sexual relationship. It also prohibits lawyers from providing legal representation to a client who consents to a sexual relationship unless the attorney can prove that he or she nonetheless provided competent legal services. But controversy still abounds—some lawyers claim that the new rule is totally unnecessary, while others say it does not go far enough.

Records of disciplinary cases around the country document a variety of unsavory lawyerly acts, not just those involving sex with clients. Often, unethical practices occur in the guise of zealous representation. Writes Crouch in his *Trial* magazine article:

> Some [lawyers] have been known to abuse opposing counsel in the courtroom. Others have pursued a delinquent husband in a high-speed car chase, solicited sex from the client while offering to shortcut matters by having the husband murdered, and masqueraded as impartial mediators and then turned overbearingly partisan. The bar has disciplined attorneys for complicity in child-snatching and for attempting to extort separation-agreement concessions in exchange for access to an abducted child.

In fact, the American Bar Association's Center for Professional Responsibility reports that sanctions against attorneys occur most frequently in the areas of family law and personal injury practice. Yet during the last ten years, from 1980 through 1989, the center recorded sanctions against only 1,138 lawyers for unethical behavior in the handling of family law matters. Undoubtedly the total is scanty because the ABA's record keeping relies on voluntary submissions of data by the individual states' disciplinary bodies. The ABA total also omits lesser disciplinary sanctions that remain private, as opposed to those that are announced publicly.

The low number of reported sanctions may further reflect divorce clients' unwillingness to complain formally about lawyers' alleged wrongdoings, suggests Cassie Dalla Santa of the Center for Professional Responsibility. "If someone is emotionally distressed already, the person may not want to deal with" filing a formal complaint. "But," she adds, "they may tell their friends not to use that lawyer."

The American Academy of Matrimonial Lawyers, a prestigious twelve-hundred-member organization of the nation's top divorce practitioners, decided to respond to concerns about divorce lawyers' ethics—concerns both within the profession and outside—by drafting a new code of ethics specifically for their specialty. The divorce code is more specific than the bar's universally applied Code of Professional Responsibility and deals with such issues as children's rights during divorce and sexual relationships with clients and opposing attorneys.

Stephen Sessums, a Tampa attorney who chairs the academy's committee that drafted the code, gives an example: "Divorce lawyers have responsibilities to their clients, but they may also have competing responsibilities to their clients' children. Sometimes a client, usually a man, says, 'my wife is a good mother, and she's doing a good job with the kids, and I know they're important to her, but I want to demand custody of them because I'm going to use that as leverage on the financial issue.' This situation needs to be addressed," says Sessums. The new code advocates that the lawyer in this case counsel the client against such a manipulative tactic.

The academy is well aware that it has no enforcement authority because the new ethical code is not legally binding unless approved by the individual states. Nonetheless, the members hope "to raise standards," Sessums explains. "There clearly is a deep concern about litigation out of control and lawyers out of control." While a new divorce lawyers' code may not sway older attorneys whose ways are well established, the academy hopes that it will find a willing audience among the specialty's younger members.

Working the System

Divorce clients who naively believe that justice works should think again. The most successful lawyers are those who interpret "justice" to mean what it is they want for their clients and then find a way to achieve their goal. They know how to make the divorce system work for them, a skill even the most unsuccessful lawyers try to cultivate. They schmooze with the court personnel, with the judges, and with each other, following a you-scratch-my-back-I'll-scratch-yours philosophy. Because lawyers have to continue dealing with the judges, their colleagues in the bar, and the various courthouse staff after every case is over, they are reticent to alienate anyone who could make their professional lives difficult later on. Lawyers also are concerned about their public reputations, and one of the biggest sources of recommendations—or, the converse, bad-mouthing—is from colleagues in the divorce bar itself. "Indeed," says Kressel in *The Process of Divorce*, "the positive ties between the two lawyers may well be stronger than those between the lawyers and their respective clients." Some clients may wonder if this colleagial bonding compromises a lawyer's adversarial role.

And while clients may think their divorce attorney is a close friend, a sensitive, caring individual, the bar develops its own hard-nosed attitudes about those it helps. *Newsweek* once defined some popular buzzwords divorce lawyers use in back rooms. A "bag lady" is a "wife who

arrives with a shopping bag filled with her husband's financial records";
a "kamikaze spouse" is one "who snitches to the IRS about a mate's
unreported income or double set of books"; and a "shopper" is "a financially dependent spouse with no personal income" and needing
heavy alimony.

Lawyers are not so kind about judges, either, often regarding them
as intellectual inferiors. While they praise some of the people who sit
behind the bench, attorneys also belittle others before whom they appear. "The lights were on, but nobody was home," says one attorney,
questioning the IQ level of a judge assigned to an important case.
"He was a football player," says another lawyer of a different judge.
"We wonder how many times he played without his helmet on."
Of course, these lawyers would never want the judges to know how
they feel, and they face a particularly interesting dilemma in affect-
ing the appropriate public deference for judges whom they scorn in
private—an important consideration given that most domestic relations decisions are essentially within the discretion of the judge
hearing the case.

While judicial intellect varies, judges fall victim to other personal
fallibilities as well. Lawyers complain that some are too readily influenced by personal feelings and predilections, that they form their opinions in a case based on subjective criteria, such as whether they like
the husband or the wife and even whether they like the way they look.
One attorney remains convinced that a judge in an important case felt
intimidated by the husband and was drawn instead to his pretty spouse.
The wife won the case.

That does not mean, however, that male judges always rule in favor
of females. "Women who come across as being angry have a hard time
with judges," says Emily Brown of the Key Bridge Therapy and Mediation Center in Arlington, Virginia. "They come across as being
bitches." It hardly matters, she implies, that they may be justified in
their anger.

Because divorce decisions depend so heavily on the unpredictable
thoughts and reactions of the judge assigned to the case, a savvy lawyer
may sometimes opt to settle just to stay in control of the outcome.

The Problem with Clients

While some judges and lawyers may be inconsistent or inexpert, not
all clients are ideal, either, says Kressel. "Attorneys have at least a 50-
50 chance of finding themselves with clients suffering from severe bouts

of lowered self-esteem, impaired powers of concentration, and ambivalent feelings about reaching a settlement," he writes. "In other words, from the attorney's perspective the divorce client is anything but a prize."

To begin with, understandably, many clients enter the legal process reluctantly and suspiciously. For good attorneys it is a difficult marketplace in which to build trust and peddle their expertise. "Selling divorce services is like selling cancer operations," says Los Angeles attorney Stuart Walzer. "People need them. They just don't like the idea." Although some current self-help books advertise do-it-yourself divorces, most spouses seek professional advice. While initial wariness is common and appropriate, at some point they must believe they can trust and work with an attorney.

This trusting relationship, however, can be misconstrued, and it can develop into inappropriate dependence. For example, some clients expect their attorneys to be confessors or even to provide psychological counseling.

Still other clients never give their representatives a chance, regarding them as the enemy when they attempt to compromise with the other side. Then there are those who may agree on major points of dispute but become inappropriately sentimental or absolutely unglued over items of little importance.

Lawyers also have trouble with clients who are in such a hurry to conclude their divorces that they waive anything and everything to which they might have a claim. Others can be so clouded by guilt that they give away everything acquired during the marriage. "My lawyer tried to warn me," says Carlo LaPorta, a Maryland economist and policy analyst who left his wife and three children following an extramarital affair. "She said I was being very generous and I was. That cut two ways: it bought me some peace of mind but it also made my life very difficult."

LaPorta's lawyer and others know that such magnanimity can be detrimental to an individual's well-being and to any subsequent marriage. But clients are often the last to anticipate possible life changes and to plan for a divorce settlement that will permit flexibility in future decisions regarding remarriage, career changes, and relocation. "People must very carefully sit down and help figure out all the options," suggests University of Virginia family law professor Walter Wadlington. Yet, looking at the long term is not so easy. Divorce clients "are about as goal oriented as a very sick patient," he observes. When they don't listen and regret hasty decisions later on, they often blame the attorney for letting them do exactly what they insisted on in the first place.

"I feel sorry for divorce lawyers," says Joel Henning of Chicago. "They're trying to deal with legal, accounting, and tax matters when the people are falling apart. It must be extremely difficult under the best of circumstances."

Walter Wadlington agrees. "The most rational of people," he observes, "become not irrational, but close to it."

AUTHOR'S POSTSCRIPT

This book does not tell the whole story. Although I have described as thoroughly as possible the legal issues involved in divorce, I have not addressed the emotional crises behind this personal tragedy. After all of my travels, interviews, research, and analysis, I still do not know *why* couples divorce.

I was divorced myself in 1980. And while I can spout off a list of reasons behind my first marriage's failure, there is still a small part of my psyche that continues to ask why. The day of my second wedding, I heard my future mother-in-law ask my mother (they had met for the first time that morning), "Were you surprised when your daughter got divorced?" Obviously my mother-in-law still had not recovered from her son's (my husband's) divorce, although it had occurred four years earlier. I did not hear my mother's response to the question, but I know it must have been a straightforward yes. Even though divorce is common today, for many it is still a shock—and its causes remain a mystery.

I am opposed to divorce. After traveling to Los Angeles to conduct my first interview for this book with attorney Ira Lurvey, I asked him over our early breakfast if he did not feel a moral commitment to talk his clients out of getting a divorce. Lurvey responded with a question: "If you had come to me when you wanted a divorce from your first husband, and I had told you that you ought to reconsider and try to make the marriage work, what would you have done?"

My reply to Lurvey was simple and without hesitation: "I'd have gotten another lawyer." I was forced to agree with him that by the time a person takes the actual step of visiting a divorce lawyer, the emotional separation in a marriage already has occurred. I also had to admit that the only thing I oppose more than divorce is a forced, unhappy marriage. The suffering in these homes is far greater than the pain of divorce.

But, lest anyone think otherwise, that pain is extraordinary. The emotion in divorce brings days of agony and nights of heartache. I recently attended a school reunion where one man was so distraught and embarrassed about his recent divorce—he and his wife had several young children—that he left halfway through the reunion. Another man wouldn't even attend because he was so depressed following his divorce. One of the women at the reunion told me that her husband had left her to move in with one of her friends. Another woman said she had had to be hospitalized when she lost thirty-five pounds during her divorce.

Sadness, disappointment, pain, and anger are the handmaidens of divorce, and their presence makes it difficult to behave with dignity. I can remember leaving my desk and sobbing in a back room of my office shortly after the breakup of my marriage. I have seen other people so driven by anger and the need for revenge against a former mate that they seemed almost demoniac. Knowing that such responses are common, some may say that the very term *dignified divorce* is an oxymoron.

Nonetheless, the *goal* in divorce should be some level of self-control, decorum, and reasonableness. I think this can best be approached through self-education, that is, by learning from others about their divorces and by becoming informed about the legal system. This knowledge, and the confidence that stems from it, can help a person achieve a greater sense of personal responsibility and direction during the divorce process. Too often the sense of failure in a marriage can lead to feelings of helplessness about the outcome of a divorce. The second does not necessarily follow from the first. While researching this book, I learned how poorly equipped I was to take care of myself during my divorce and to make sure that I was treated fairly. I wish now that I had learned more about divorce as a legal process during that time. I wish I had sought a wider range of advice and guidance from others.

Even after divorce the opportunities to learn continue. Although ten years had passed since my divorce, I found in interviewing couples and lawyers for this book that some of my wounds were still raw. Although I did not intend for the book to serve as a personal mission of self-retrospection, I know now how much talking with others can help in understanding and accepting the past. Discussions about custody and visitation were especially enlightening for me.

The best cure for overcoming the pain of a divorce is, of course, time. I remember that when I was getting divorced, another woman who had been divorced earlier reminded me that the misery would not last forever. "You'll feel better," she said while attempting to console me. "I know you don't believe me, but you will."

Recently one of my neighbors telephoned to say that she and her husband were divorcing. I had to smile inwardly as I began to tell her, "You'll feel better. I know you don't believe me, but you will." Yet when a marriage is disintegrating and a previously certain future dissolving, it is very hard to wait for time's cure.

More immediate help is needed. Perhaps, then, this is where I have made a contribution in writing this book. By helping people understand what divorce entails legally and by showing them how they can learn from others' experiences, they may find an admittedly rough road just a little smoother.

CASE SOURCE MATERIALS

Chapter 1

Prenuptial Agreements: Planning on Divorce Before Marriage.

In Re the Marriage of: Petitioner: Shirley Ann Warnack, and Respondent: A. C. *Warnack,* Superior Court of the State of California for the County of Los Angeles, Case No. D 122516.

1. Antenuptial Property Settlement Agreement between Shirley Ann Vezie and A. C. Warnack, March 8, 1971.
2. Antenuptial Property Settlement Agreement between Shirley Ann Rake Vezie and A. C. Warnack, September 7, 1975.
3. Declaration by A. C. Warnack, August 31, 1984.
4. Walzer and Gabrielson general office memorandum, September 11, 1984.
5. Declaration by Stuart B. Walzer, October 4, 1984.
6. Office memorandum from Stuart Walzer to Jan Gabrielson, November 5, 1984.
7. Declaration by Shirley A. Warnack, January 16, 1985.

8. Deposition of A. C. Warnack, Los Angeles, California, Tuesday, April 9, and Wednesday, April 10, 1985.
9. Petitioner's Trial Brief, December 9, 1985.
10. Respondent's Trial Brief, December 12, 1985.
11. Reporter's Transcript of Proceedings, February 25, 26, 27, and 28, 1986, including Ruling of the Court Re Antenuptial Agreements.
12. Statement of Decision (prenuptial agreements), May 23, 1986.
13. Further Judgment on Reserved Issues (final property division), April 17, 1987.
14. Two undated greeting cards from Shirley A. Warnack to A. C. Warnack.
15. Eight-page typed biography for Shirley A. Warnack from the files of Walzer and Gabrielson.
16. Twenty-eight-page typed trial questions and answers for Shirley A. Warnack from the files of Walzer and Gabrielson.
17. Uniform Premarital Agreement Act.
18. Interview with Stuart B. Walzer.
19. Interview with Shirley A. Warnack.
20. Interview with Charles R. Anderson.
21. Interview with Betty Warnack.
Note: A. C. Warnack declined to be interviewed.

Chapter 2

Joint Custody: A Quest for Shared Parenting.

Ingrid M. Nicholas v. George Nicholas, Superior Court of New Jersey, Chancery Division: Bergen County, Docket No. M-9688-81, Calendar No. 81-3271.

1. Ingrid M. Helmke and George Nicholas Antenuptial Agreement, April 25, 1980.
2. Plaintiff's Complaint, December 7, 1981.
3. Affidavit of Ingrid M. Nicholas, December 7, 1981.
4. Order to Show Cause With Restraints, December 7, 1981.
5. Plaintiff's Petition, December 7, 1981.
6. Two trial preparation notebooks for George Nicholas.
7. Letter from Allwyn J. Levine, M.D., to Hon. Conrad W. Krafte, Juvenile & Domestic Relations Court, Hackensack, New Jersey, January 22, 1982.
8. Answer to Complaint, July 30, 1982.
9. Plaintiff's Notice of Motion, October 6, 1982.
10. Certification by Ingrid M. Nicholas, October 6, 1982.

11. Certification by Howard Danzig, October 21, 1982.
12. Defendant's Cross-Notice of Motion, October 26, 1982.
13. Certification by George Nicholas, October 26, 1982.
14. Certification by Ingrid M. Nicholas, November 10, 1982.
15. Certification by George Nicholas, November 22, 1982.
16. Letter from Hon. Berger M. Sween, Bergen County District Court, to Howard Danzig and Gary Skoloff, December 28, 1982.
17. Order, January 24, 1983.
18. Letter from Allwyn J. Levine, M.D., to Howard Danzig, March 30, 1983.
19. Letter from Allwyn J. Levine, M.D., to Howard Danzig, April 4, 1983.
20. Certification by Ingrid M. Nicholas, June 21, 1983.
21. Plaintiff Notice of Motion Returnable July 1, 1983, With Consent of Adversary, June 23, 1983.
22. Dual Final Judgment of Divorce, June 30, 1983.
23. Certification by George Nicholas, June 30, 1983.
24. Interview with Gary Skoloff.
25. Interview with George Nicholas.
26. Interview with Virginia Gray.
27. Interview with Ingrid Nicholas.

Chapter 3

Equitable Distribution: Who Owns What?

In Re: The Marriage of Paul Irving Dubin, Husband, and Felice Dubin, Wife, Circuit Court of the Eleventh Judicial Circuit in and for Dade County, Florida, General Jurisdiction Division, Case No. 89-27160 FC 28.

1. Wife's Petition for Dissolution of Marriage, June 19, 1989.
2. Husband's Answer and Counterpetition, July 12, 1989.
3. Wife's Response to Affirmative Defenses and Answer to Counterpetition, August 7, 1989.
4. Wife's Financial Affidavit for Temporary Relief, November 21, 1989.
5. Husband's Financial Affidavit, November 21, 1989.
6. Deposition of Paul Irving Dubin, January 17, 1990.
7. Deposition of Lawrence Mizrach, February 14, 1990.
8. Deposition of Janison Foreman, February 16, 1990.
9. Deposition of Felice Dubin, February 28, 1990.
10. Deposition of Clara Valdez, March 26, 1990.

11. Deposition of Jay E. Fishman, May 9, 1990.
12. Deposition of Leroy Koross, May 9, 1990.
13. Wife's Financial Affidavit for Final Hearing, May 11, 1990.
14. Wife's Statement of Assets and Liabilities, May 15, 1990.
15. Wife's Trial Memorandum, May 23, 1990.
16. Trial Transcript, May 23 and May 24, 1990.
17. Husband's Trial Memorandum, June 7, 1990.
18. Wife's Post-Trial Memorandum, June 6, 1990.
19. Wife's Response to Husband's Trial Memorandum, June 14, 1990.
20. Final Judgment Dissolving Marriage, August 23, 1990.
21. Reported opinion, 15 *Florida Law Weekly*, C43 (August 23, 1990)
22. Interview with Melvyn Frumkes.
23. Interview with Felice Dubin.
24. Interview with Richard Lapidus.
Note: Mr. Lapidus declined an interview for his client, Paul Dubin

Chapter 4

Fighting Over the Business: How Much Is It Worth?

In Re the Marriage of: Gayle L. Wilder, Petitioner, and Howard L. Wilder, Respondent, Circuit Court of Cook County, Illinois, County Department, Domestic Relations Division, No. 80 D 12362.

1. Deposition of Howard L. Wilder, December 17, 1980.
2. Trial Transcript, January 19, February 16–17, March 8–9, March 19, March 29–30, April 1, May 3, May 17, 1982.
3. Petitioner's Trial Memorandum, May 3, 1982.
4. Petition for Award of Attorney Fees, May 3, 1982.
5. Respondent's Reply Brief, May 10, 1982.
6. Supplemental Judgment of Dissolution of Marriage, June 17, 1982.
7. Notice of Appeal, July 15, 1982.
8. Petition for Rule to Show Cause, August 5, 1982.
9. Brief for Petitioner-Appellant March 25, 1983.
10. Brief for Respondent-Appellee, August 5, 1983.
11. Reply Brief for Petitioner-Appellant, September 23, 1983.
12. Decision of the Appellate Court of Illinois, First District, Fifth Division, April 6, 1984, 77 Ill.Dec.824, 461 N.E.2d 447 (Ill.App. 1 Dist. 1983).
13. "Suburb lawyer indicted in client fraud," *Chicago Tribune*, March 11, 1986.
14. "Ex-judge guilty in Greylord Fixes," *Chicago Tribune*, May 8, 1986.

15. "New charges of $500,000 client fraud lodged against lawyer," *Chicago Tribune*, May 13, 1986.
16. "Judge jails lawyer in $570,000 client fraud," *Chicago Tribune*, May 14, 1986.
17. "Lawyer plea-bargains in client rip-offs," *Chicago Tribune*, May 16, 1986.
18. "From loving father to looting attorney," *Chicago Tribune*, July 9, 1986.
19. "10 years for ex-judge," *Chicago Tribune*, July 31, 1986.
20. "Greylord indictments hit suburban court," *Chicago Tribune*, December 10, 1987.
21. Interview with Donald Schiller.
22. Interview with Howard Wilder.
23. Interview with Gayle Wilder.

Chapter 5

Child Snatching: Running From the Law. A Story of International Abduction.

1. Court documents and other sources unidentified to protect kidnapped child's request for pseudonymity.
2. Office memoranda from Rick Chamberlin to Larry Stotter, October 29, 1981; December 11, 1981; January 18, 1982; January 22, 1982.
3. Gloria DeHart, ed., "International Child Abductions. A Guide to Applying the 1988 Hague Convention, with Forms," American Bar Association, Chicago, 1989.
4. David Finkelhor, et al., "Missing, Abducted, Runaway, and Thrownaway Children in America," Department of Justice, Office of Juvenile Justice and Delinquency Prevention, Washington, D.C., May 1990.
5. "International Parental Child Abduction," Department of State, Bureau of Consular Affairs, Washington, D.C., April 1990.
6. "Parental Kidnapping. How to Prevent an Abduction and What to Do If Your Child Is Abducted," National Center for Missing & Exploited Children, Arlington, Va., August 1988.
7. "Selected State Legislation. A Guide for Effective State Laws to Protect Children," National Center for Missing & Exploited Children, Arlington, Va., February 1989.
8. Lawrence H. Stotter, "The Light at the End of the Tunnel: The Hague Convention on International Child Abduction Has Reached Capitol Hill," *Hastings International and Comparative Law Review* Volume 9 Number 2 (winter 1986): 285–328.

9. "S.F. lawyer target of grand jury drug probe," *San Francisco Examiner*, March 27, 1983.
10. "Wealthy S.F. attorney indicted after 5-year drug investigation," *San Francisco Examiner*, April 17, 1983.
11. "Suspension urged for money-laundering lawyer," *San Francisco Examiner*, April 14, 1985.
12. Interview with Lawrence Stotter.
13. Interview with Rick Chamberlin.
14. Interview with Judge William Fernandez.
15. Interview with Luc Hafner.
16. Interview with Harold Lipset.
17. Interview with Robert Moran.
18. Interview with Claudine Michaux Bolling (alias).
19. Interview with Paul Bolling (alias).

Chapter 6

Tracing Assets: Separating Marital From Nonmarital Property.

In the Matter of the Marriage of Irene Frances Nations and Danny Jack Nations, District Court of Dallas County, Texas, R-254th Judicial District, No. 88-4318.

1. Original Petition for Divorce, March 30, 1988.
2. Respondent's Original Answer, April 7, 1988.
3. First Amended Original Petition for Divorce, April 21, 1988.
4. Temporary Orders, April 21, 1988.
5. First Amended Respondent's First Request for Production and Inspection, May 23, 1988.
6. (Defendant's) Motion for Protective Order, May 23, 1988.
7. (Plaintiff's) Motion for Protective Order, May 24, 1988.
8. Deposition of Danny Nations, June 1 and July 26, 1988.
9. Deposition of Irene Frances Nations, August 2, 1988.
10. Inventory and Appraisement of Petitioner, August 3, 1988.
11. Inventory and Appraisement of Respondent, August 16, 1988.
12. Husband's Proposed Division, trial exhibit.
13. Decree of Divorce, October 3, 1988.
14. Undated letter from René Nations to Tom Raggio.
15. Interview with Louise Raggio.
16. Interview with René Wright (Nations).
17. Interview with Thomas Raggio.
18. Interview with Kenneth Raggio.
Note: Danny Jack Nations and Reyburn Anderson declined to be interviewed.

Chapter 7

Relocation: When the Custodial Parent Moves Away.

Robert F. Jordan v. Linda S. Jordan, Circuit Court for Montgomery County, Maryland, Equity No. 68588.

1. Separation and Property Settlement Agreement, November 17, 1977.
2. Petition for Custody of Minor Children and for Other Relief, September 11, 1979.
3. Injunction and Order, September 11, 1979.
4. Deposition of Linda S. Jordan, October 23, 1979.
5. Deposition of William F. Cahill, January 3, 1980.
6. Petition to Find Defendant in Contempt, February 22, 1980.
7. Defendant's Answers to Interrogatories, June 5, 1980.
8. Plaintiff's Answers to Interrogatories, June 13, 1980.
9. Deposition of Marianne Jordan, June 23, 1980.
10. Deposition of Robert F. Jordan, June 23, 1980.
11. Deposition of Walter H. Taylor, June 25, 1980.
12. Trial Transcript, June 30; July 1, 2, 15, 16; October 8–10.
13. Plaintiff's Trial Memorandum, July 15, 1980.
14. Revised Order of Court, November 28, 1980.
15. Appellant's Brief, Court of Special Appeals of Maryland, September 14, 1981.
16. Decision of the Court of Special Appeals of Maryland, Md.App., 439 A.2d 26, January 7, 1982.
17. Interview with Beverly Groner.
18. Interview with Robert Jordan.
19. Interview with Judge Stanley Frosh.
20. Interview with Jeffrey Greenblatt.
Note: Linda Jordan Cahill declined to be interviewed.

Chapter 8

Stepparents in Divorce: Fighting for Their Rights.

Patricia (Stockwell) Porter v. Robert D. Stockwell, District Court of the Third Judicial District of the State of Idaho, in and for the County of Canyon, Case Nos. L-38106, D-5674, and IM-2799.

1. Answers to Interrogatories to Natural Father, October 17, 1985.
2. Trial Transcript Taken in the Magistrate Courtroom, Caldwell Section, at Caldwell, Idaho, October 21, 1985.

3. Findings of Fact, Conclusions of Law and Order, March 14, 1986.
4. Affidavit of Robert D. Stockwell in Support of Motions for Change of Custody and Alternative Post-Trial Motions, May 22, 1986.
5. Letter to Idaho Governor John Evans from Mr. and Mrs. Richard Porter, August 13, 1986.
6. Defendant's Memorandum Re: Custody of Child to Stepfather, June 2, 1986.
7. Transcript of Motion to Withdraw Taken in the Magistrate Courtroom, Caldwell Section, at Caldwell, Idaho, June 10, 1986.
8. Order to Show Cause, June 10, 1986.
9. Findings of Fact, Conclusions of Law and Order for Change of Custody to Defendant, July 1, 1986.
10. Legal Brief in Support of Non-Parent Custody, August 22, 1986.
11. Deposition of Patricia C. Porter, January 9, 1987.
12. Deposition of Danielle Stockwell, January 9, 1987.
13. Deposition of Amber Stockwell, January 9, 1987.
14. Transcript of Custody Hearing, January 13–14, 1987.
15. Defendant's Post-Trial Brief, January 1987.
16. Memorandum Decision Pursuant to Rule 52(a), February 20, 1987.
17. Notice of Appeal by Defendant, February 25, 1987.
18. Notice of Cross Appeal by Plaintiff/Respondent, March 5, 1987.
19. Letter to Whom It May Concern from Richard and Patricia Porter, April 14, 1987.
20. Affidavit of Patricia A. Porter, May 28, 1987.
21. Affidavit of Randy Kath, June 2, 1987.
22. Affidavit of Rhonda Stockwell, June 11, 1987.
23. Motion for Stay, June 12, 1987.
24. Affidavit of Jeanne Hirmer, June 16, 1987.
25. Memorandum in Support of Motion for Stay of Magistrate Drescher's June 11, 1987, Order, June 17, 1987.
26. Letter from Paul Buser to Robert E. Krueger, General Manager, KTVB, Channel 7, Boise, Idaho, July 2, 1987.
27. Appellant's Brief, September 28, 1987.
28. Plaintiff's Appeal, September 28, 1987.
29. Respondent's Reply Brief, October 5, 1987.
30. Defendant's Cross-Respondent's Response to "Plaintiff's Appeal," October 20, 1987.
31. Appellant's Reply Brief, October 23, 1987.
32. Memorandum Decision and Order on Appeal, December 17, 1987.
33. Affidavit of M. Harrell Poarch, Danielle's and Amber's School Psychologist, December 22, 1987.

34. Affidavit of Paternal Grandmother in Support of Appellant's Motion for Stay Order Pending Appeal Re: Custody, December 22, 1987.
35. Affidavit of Zane P. Nelson, Ph.D., Psychologist, December 23, 1987.
36. Order Staying District Court Memorandum Decision and Trial Court Decision Pertaining to Amber Stockwell, December 23, 1987.
37. Appellant's Brief, May 10, 1988.
38. Decision of the Supreme Court of the State of Idaho, No. 17261, June 5, 1989.
39. Brief in Lieu of Closing Argument, March 27, 1990.
40. Findings of Fact, Conclusions of Law and Order, April 20, 1990.
41. Judgment, April 25, 1990.
42. School English essay by Amber Stockwell, June 11, 1990.
43. Interview with Paul Buser.
44. Interview with Patrick Miller.
45. Interview with Robert Dan Stockwell.
46. Interview with Rhonda Stockwell.
47. Interview with Jean Stockwell.
48. Interview with Roger Williams.
49. Interview with Terry Michaelson.
50. Interview with Edwin Schiller.
51. Interview with Stephen Drescher.
52. Interview with Patricia Porter.
53. Interview with Rick Porter.
54. Interview with Ellen Effron.
55. Interview with Arnold Rutkin.
56. Interview with Kathleen Hogan.

Chapter 9

Violence in Divorce: Protecting the Innocent.

Kathleen Norman O'Guin and William Michael O'Guin v. Joseph Pikul, Supreme Court of the State of New York, County of New York, Index. No. 30615/87.

1. "Securities Analyst Charged in Slaying of His Wife," *The New York Times,* October 31, 1987.

2. Trial transcript, December 18 and 21, 1987; January 6, 13–15, 23, and 28, 1988; September 14, 1988.

3. "Suspect in Wife's Slaying Faces Child Custody Suit," *The New York Times*, December 25, 1987.

4. "Man Accused in Death Retains Child Custody," *The New York Times*, January 7, 1988.

5. "Lawyer Says Judge in Wife-kill Case Is Playing 'Russian Roulette With Kids' Lives'," *New York Post*, January 7, 1988.

6. "Custody in Dispute After Murder," *The New York Times*, March 6, 1988.

7. "The Strange Case of Joseph Pikul," *New York*, March 14, 1988.

8. "Middle-class Murder," *Ms*, May 1988.

9. "Defendant Is Awarded Custody of 2 Children," *The New York Times*, May 2, 1988.

10. "Pikul Gets Custody," *The New York Times*, May 15, 1988.

11. "Cops Say Pikul's Stories Conflict," *Newsday*, May 18, 1988.

12. "Sins of the Father," *7 Days*, May 18, 1988.

13. "Two Faces of Joseph Pikul," *Daily News*, May 22, 1988.

14. "A Phone Call Ends Custody For a Father," *The New York Times*, September 18, 1988.

15. "The Good Father," *Woman's Day*, January 17, 1989.

16. "Jury Chosen for Trial of Murder Suspect," *The New York Times*, January 28, 1989.

17. "Testimony Opens in Murder Trial of Stock Analyst," *The New York Times*, February 1, 1989.

18. "Man Testifies Wife's Killing Was an Act of Self-Defense," *The New York Times*, March 1, 1989.

19. "Wall St. Analyst Guilty in Murder of Second Wife," *The New York Times*, March 17, 1989.

20. "Wife Killer Dies While He Waits for Prison Term," *The New York Times*, June 3, 1989.

21. "AIDS Led to Death of Pikul, Autopsy of Prisoner Shows," *The New York Times*, July 16, 1989.

22. "Conviction Is Vacated in Pikul Murder Case," *The New York Times*, December 6, 1989.

23. Richard T. Pienciak, *Deadly Masquerade. A True Story of High Living, Depravity, and Murder* (New York: E. P. Dutton, 1990).

24. Interview with Raoul Felder.

25. Interview with Paul Kurland.

26. Interview with Robert Wayburn.

27. Interview with Kathleen O'Guin.

Note: Mary Bain Pikul declined to be interviewed.

Chapter 10

Divorce and the Elderly: Trauma in Old Age.

Ruth O. Lebeson v. Harry Lebeson, Superior Court of the State of California, County of Riverside, No. Indio D 14800.

1. Petitioner's Petition for Legal Separation, with Income and Expense Declaration, December 11, 1985.
2. Declaration of Harry Lebeson, January 9, 1986.
3. Declaration of Ira Lurvey, January 9, 1986.
4. Letter from Ira Lurvey to William J. Glucksman, January 9, 1986.
5. Declaration of Ruth O. Lebeson in Opposition to Respondent's Ex Parte Application, January 10, 1986.
6. Respondent's Request for Dissolution of Marriage, January 27, 1986.
7. Deposition of Ruth O. Lebeson, January 30–31, 1986.
8. Deposition of Richard Levy, January 31, 1986.
9. Deposition of Harry Lebeson, January 31, 1986.
10. Reporter's Transcript of Oral Proceedings. Motion for Joinder and Order to Show Cause Re: Injunctive Order, February 7, 1986.
11. Draft Stipulation for Judgment, February 7, 1986.
12. Letters from William Glucksman to Ira Lurvey, March 3, 4, and 5, 1986.
13. Letters from Ira Lurvey to William Glucksman, February 21 and March 4, 5, and 7, 1986.
14. Letters from Barry Friedman to Ira Lurvey, March 7, 12, 17, 18, 19, and 21, 1986.
15. Letters from Ira Lurvey to Barry Friedman, March 12 and 19, 1986.
16. Notice of, and Association of, Attorney, March 26, 1986.
17. Declaration of Barry L. Friedman, March 27, 1986.
18. Order to Show Cause and Declaration for Contempt, March 31, 1986.
19. Responsive Declaration to Order to Show Cause or Notice of Motion, April 26, 1986.
20. Property Declaration and Agreement, May 23, 1986.
21. Declaration of Ira H. Lurvey to Further Advise the Court Re Status of Performance Under Judgment, June 13, 1986.
22. Reporter's Transcript of Oral Proceedings. Issuance of Bench Warrant Re: Further Stays; Motion Re: Satisfaction of Judgment; OSC Re: Contempt; OSC Re: Modification to Temporary Restraining Order; Motion Re: Entry of Judgment; Motion Re: Attorneys Fees and Implementation, June 20, 1986.

23. Declaration of Ira Lurvey Re Completion of Activities Recited on June 20, 1986, July 2, 1986.
24. Reporter's Transcript of Oral Proceedings. Order to Show Cause, July 11, 1986.
25. Reporter's Transcript of Oral Proceedings, October 17, 1986.
26. Reporter's Transcript of Oral Proceedings, October 24, 1986.
27. "Mitchelson Settles 7 Ethics Charges; State Bar Dropping Six Allegations," *The San Francisco Recorder,* May 2, 1990.
28. "Bar Leak Adds Intrigue to Mitchelson Case," *The San Francisco Recorder,* May 4, 1990.
29. Interview with Ira Lurvey.
30. Interview with Leah Kaplan.
31. Interview with Ann Kaplan.
32. Interview with William Glucksman.
33. Interview with Richard Levy.

Note: Ruth Lebeson and Barry Friedman declined to be interviewed.

SUPPORT GROUPS
AND RESOURCES

Academy of Family Mediators
Box 10501
Eugene, OR 97440
(503) 345–1205

For a list of private divorce mediators in your area.

American Association for Marriage and Family Therapy
1100 Seventeenth Street NW
The Tenth Floor
Washington, DC 20036
(800) 374–AMFT

For a consumer's guide to marriage and family therapy and a list of marriage and family therapists in your area.

American Association of Retired Persons
601 E Street NW
Washington, DC 20049
(202) 434–2277

For the pamphlet "Divorce After 50: Challenges and Choices."

American Children Held Hostage, Inc.
30 Stepney Lane
Brentwood, NY 11717
(516) 231–6240

A parental support group that disseminates information, helps implement new legislation, and participates in court proceedings.

DAW²N
Divorced and Widowed Women's Network
Suite 455 G
De Vargas Center
Santa Fe, NM 87501
(800) 488-3296

A national organization to help newly single women become financially and emotionally independent.

Joint Custody Association
10606 Wilkins Avenue
Los Angeles, CA 90024
(213) 475–5352

For information on joint custody legislation and statistics.

Men's Rights Association
Route 6
Forest Lake, MN 55025
(612) 464–7887

For advice and assistance in the divorce process, including attorney referrals.

Men's Rights, Inc.
Box 163180
Sacramento, CA 95816
(916) 484–7333

For information and guidance in divorce.

Mothers Without Custody
Box 27418
Houston, TX 77227–7418
(713) 840–1622 or (815) 455–2955

A network and outlet for sharing the experiences of mothers without physical custody of their children for any reason.

National Center for Missing and Exploited Children
2101 Wilson Boulevard
Suite 550
Arlington, VA 22201
(703) 235–3900 or 800–843–5678

Assists parents searching for missing children and law enforcement and other professionals handling missing children and sexual exploitation cases.

National Center on Women and Family Law
799 Broadway
Room 402
New York, NY 10003
(212) 674–8200

For information on divorce laws.

National Congress for Men and Children
2020 Pennsylvania Avenue NW
Suite 277
Washington, DC 20006
(202) FATHERS

An advocacy organization for fathers trying to obtain joint custody, visitation rights, or fair child support orders.

National Council for Children's Rights
220 Eye Street NE
Washington, DC 20002
(202) 547–6227

An advocacy group supporting joint custody, equitable child support, full visitation, and divorce and custody reform.

Older Women's League
730 Eleventh Street NW
Suite 300
Washington, DC 20001
(202) 783–6686

For information about late-life divorce and group health insurance continuation.

Parents Without Partners
8807 Colesville Road
Silver Spring, MD 20910
(301) 588–9354

A support group for single parents and children offering social, family, and educational activities.

Pension Rights Center
918 Sixteenth Street NW
Suite 704
Washington, DC 20006
(202) 296–3776

For information on pensions and divorce.

Stepfamily Association of America, Inc.
215 Centennial Mall South
Suite 212
Lincoln, NE 68508
(402) 477–STEP

Promotes personal and family support through information, education, and advocacy.

Stepfamily Foundation
333 West End Avenue
New York, NY 10023
(212) 877–3244

Provides counseling and information for stepfamilies; offers training for professionals who work with stepfamilies.

VOCAL National Network
825 Circle Drive North
Suite O
Colorado Springs, CO 80909
(800) 848–8778

An educational, support, and advocacy organization to assist those harmed by the child protection system, including those falsely accused of child abuse or neglect.

GLOSSARY

abandonment. *see* desertion.

abuse. The treatment of a family member causing physical, mental, or emotional harm.

adultery. Sexual intercourse by a married person with someone other than that person's spouse.

affidavit. A declaration made under oath and filed in writing with a court officer.

alimony. *see* maintenance.

antenuptial agreement. A written contract signed prior to marriage by an engaged man and woman to indicate the future disposition of property and support arrangements in case of divorce or death following the marriage.

appeal. A request for new consideration of a lawsuit by a higher court.

appellate judge. The judge who hears and rules on an appeal from a trial judge's decision in a case.

arbitration. A process for resolving a dispute using a third individual selected by the two opposing sides, who agree to abide by that person's decision.

assets. Tangible possessions, such as cash, investments, property, and personal belongings, as well as intangibles, such as accounts receivable and goodwill. Assets are divided into premarital (acquired before marriage) and marital (acquired after marriage).

bailiff. A court official who helps maintain order during a trial and who oversees the jury and any prisoners in the courtroom.

blended family. A family composed of a husband and wife and children from prior marriages.

cohabitation. Living together in a sexual relationship without being married.

commingling. The mixing together of marital and nonmarital funds.

common law. The body of law originating in England and developed through court decisions in the United States, as opposed to more formal laws dictated by statute.

community property. As defined by nine states only (Arizona, California, Idaho, Louisiana, Nevada, New Mexico, Texas, Washington, and Wisconsin), assets acquired after the marriage by either the husband, the wife, or both with income earned during the marriage. Community property belongs to the husband and wife equally.

complaint. *see* petition.

confidential relationship. That between two closely affiliated persons, such as parent and child or husband and wife, where the law requires total trust and integrity in all transactions between them; this is particularly true because one of the two persons has great influence over the other.

counsel; cocounsel. The attorney representing a party in a court action, such as a divorce suit; cocounsel is a second lawyer assisting with the case.

court clerk. The official who files pleadings and other documents, who keeps the court's records of proceedings, and who assists the judge during a hearing or trial.

court reporter. The official retained by either party in a lawsuit or by the court to record verbatim the on-the-record discussions and testimony during an official legal proceeding, such as a hearing, a deposition, or a trial. These transcripts provide the factual basis for an appeal.

court seal. The court-ordered act of removing legal documents from public access.

custody. The right to maintain guardianship of a minor, specifically as awarded by a court or as agreed to by the parents or others who have a significant relationship with the minor.

cross-examination. The questioning of a witness in a hearing or trial by the lawyer representing the opposing side; typically follows direct examination by the lawyer who first called the witness to testify.

cruelty. The act of causing harm, pain, and suffering, either physical or mental, to another person.

deposition. A declaration of facts while under oath as part of the discovery process preceding a scheduled trial.

desertion. The act of leaving a spouse or child without his or her permission, in some cases refusing all legal obligations to them; another term is "abandonment."

direct examination. The questioning of a witness in a hearing or trial by the lawyer who called the witness to testify.

discovery. The court-sanctioned process of gathering facts before a trial to enable the lawyers, experts, clients, and witnesses on both sides to prepare their cases.

divorce decree. The court order granting a divorce, in some states called a "decree of dissolution."

earned income. Income derived from a paid activity, either mental or physical, as opposed to passive income, which accumulates through investments.

equitable distribution. The "equitable" or fair division of marital assets by a court that takes into consideration some or all of the following: the spouses' ages, health, employment history, earning potential, sources of income, and allocation of debts; the length of the marriage; and the tax consequences of distribution.

exhibit. Correspondence, documentation, financial records, and other written information, as well as videotapes, audiotapes, charts, photographs, computer tapes, or any other materials that a lawyer formally presents to a court in support of a case.

expert. A person of recognized knowledge and expertise who can comment authoritatively on an issue in a trial and who often is asked to give an opinion with regard to the specific facts in the trial to help the court reach a decision.

fault. The cause for the breakup of a marriage and subsequent divorce, one indicating blame, as opposed to no-fault divorce.

fiduciary responsibility. The duty to push aside one's own interests in order to act in a way that most benefits another.

gift. Money or property given to an individual during a marriage by a spouse, relative, or any third party, which is considered the sole property of that individual.

goodwill. The monetary value attached to a business or professional practice in excess of hard assets, such as real estate, equipment and supplies, and accounts receivable; this value represents intangibles, such as reputation and the development of return business.

inheritance. Money or property acquired by an individual spouse during a marriage through a bequest in a will, which is considered the sole property of that individual.

joint custody. The sharing of child-rearing responsibilities by divorced spouses; it may be joint legal custody, requiring shared decision making, or joint physical custody, requiring an approximately equal sharing of the child's time spent in the parents' two homes.

judge's chambers. The judge's office where the lawyers on opposing sides of a case, and sometimes their clients, meet with the judge for nonpublic and sometimes off-the-record discussions.

legal separation. The court-sanctioned separation of living quarters by married spouses.

litigation. A lawsuit; also the process of formally presenting arguments by the opposing sides in a lawsuit before a judge, jury, or other court officer.

magistrate. An officer of a court who sits as the judge in minor legal proceedings.

maintenance. A more modern term for alimony, taking several forms: (1) long-term periodic payments by one ex-spouse to the other to meet expenses while maintaining the life-style of the former marriage; (2) a lump sum payment at the time of divorce, usually occurring in cases of wealthier couples; and (3) short-term periodic payments, called "rehabilitative" maintenance, to support the divorced spouse during a time of further education and job training.

marital assets. Money and property earned during the marriage by either spouse.

mediation. The process by which an objective third party tries to help the opposing parties in an argument or lawsuit decide how to resolve their own differences.

motion. A formal request for a ruling from a court, usually asking that a particular action be directed to take place.

neglect. The disregard of a dependent family member's needs for support and nurturing.

negotiation. The act of trying to reach a resolution to an argument or lawsuit through discussion between the two sides.

no-fault. A form of divorce now available in all states in which neither party is blamed or found guilty of ending the marriage.

oath. A vow of honesty, usually in a courtroom or legal offices during an official legal proceeding.

order of protection. A legal document issued by a judge prohibiting one person from harming another, most typically a spouse.

palimony. Court-ordered periodic monetary support (shortened from "alimony for pals") that one long-term cohabitant must provide the other after their relationship has ended.

party. A person or group filing a lawsuit or a person or group against whom a lawsuit is filed.

passive income. Income earned through investments already in place.

petition. A legal document filed with a court requesting court action; also called a "complaint."

pleading. A legal document filed with a court with facts and sometimes argument supporting a request for court action.

postnuptial agreement. A written contract signed after a marriage by a husband and wife to indicate the future disposition of property in case of divorce or the death of either spouse.

precedent. A court ruling that serves as an example for resolving future similar arguments or cases.

premarital assets. Money and property owned by either spouse prior to the marriage and maintained separately from marital assets.

prenuptial agreement. *see* antenuptial agreement.

rehabilitation. The education and training of a spouse after divorce to enable that person to find a job and become self-supporting.

relocation. The move of an ex-spouse and children following a divorce, typically to a location more distant from the children's other parent.

rent-a-judge. An individual approved by the courts in some states whom the parties to a dispute can hire privately to hear and rule on their case; using a rent-a-judge can lessen the time delay that occurs when waiting for a traditional judge to hear a case.

retainer. The payment a client gives a lawyer when the lawyer agrees to take on the client's case.

retainer agreement. The written contract between the client and the lawyer indicating the terms of the retainer, such as whether future work and expenses will be billed against that advance payment.

settlement agreement. An understanding approved by a court setting forth the terms of a divorce, particularly with regard to custody of children, division of assets, maintenance, and child support.

sole custody. The assignment of child-rearing responsibilities, both physical and legal, to one spouse.

stepchild. A child of one's wife or husband from a previous marriage.

stepparent. An unrelated person married to the biological or adoptive parent of a child.

testimony. Statements of fact and opinions offered by an individual while under oath during a legal proceeding.

tracing. The tracking of assets in a marriage from the present back to their original source.

transcript. The written recording of words spoken by the parties in a case, their lawyers, witnesses, and the judge during a legal proceeding; may also include exhibits that pertain to that proceeding.

trial. The legal proceeding before a judge and sometimes a jury allowing the two sides of a case to argue their respective views and to offer supporting witnesses and evidence before a final ruling is made.

trial judge. The court official presiding over such a legal proceeding.

trial memorandum. A written brief or pleading filed by a lawyer with a court, presenting the facts and arguments supporting one side of a case scheduled for trial.

valuation. The assignment of a monetary worth to a particular asset, usually by an expert knowledgeable about that kind of asset.

visitation. Times scheduled by a court for a noncustodial parent to spend with his or her children following the divorce; some prefer language referring to "custodial time" and "shared parenting" time.

witness. A person testifying in a legal proceeding under oath.

Index